Until The Last Oak Falls

Adrian Fisk

British direct action environmental protest photography 1995–1999

This book is dedicated to all environmental activists who have sacrificed their lives defending our precious and beautiful planet.

To my mother & brother for their belief in me.

ROAD ALERT!
PO BOX 55?
NEWBURY
RG14 5FB
01635 521770

24th February 1995

Dear Adrian,

Hello, I've added you to our action update list which will fax through to you about once a week, probably at really antisocial hours (sorry).

I've enclosed our last newsletter ~~which~~, if you can supply photos they ~~could~~ could be included in the next one.

I hope you can get some stuff into the Zion Train CD rom.

Cheers

Phil x

1996 in United Britain, Great Kingdom...

Conservative Party	
Labour Party	
...Democrats	

STREET PARTY!

Representation of the Peoples Act 1996

This ballot paper conforms to the standards laid down by the Electoral Reform Society and is registered under Subsection a), Paragraph iii) of the You Mark a Cross On a Piece of Paper Once Every Four Years Meanwhile We Make a Right Pig's Ear of Things and Get Rich Act 1996, Patent No. 37649801.

NEVER MIND THE BALLOTS...
RECLAIM THE STREETS!

'Don't be a cog in the machine - be a spanner in the works!'

TWO DAY FESTIVAL
OF RESISTANCE!

SATURDAY 12TH AND SUNDAY 13TH APRIL

Introduction

Jay Griffiths

It was a sweet time, and a damaging time. It was a chaotic, cidery and injurious time, tender and daft, devoted and serious and, in all weathers, effervescently playful.

******

The soundtrack to the road protests was fiddles, tin whistles and chainsaws. When Reclaim The Streets exploded onto Camden High Street, with a staged car-crash rapidly followed by people up tripods, it used rave music to protest loudly against the autogeddon of a car-centric world. The movement was a party-animal, as these photographs illustrate: the buzzy atmosphere of face-painting and detournement, firebreathers and the gigantic stilt-walking Marie Antoinette, under whose voluminous skirts the angle grinders were at work, digging up the M41 in London to plant trees. Under the playful exterior was a deadly serious work in progress: reclaiming public space from the de facto privatisation of private cars, with sofas in the fast lane.

At the road protest sites, there was sheer theatre in the bunting and banners in the treetops where one streamer read 'We'll Fight Them In The Beeches'. Down the tunnels, the mud was carved into gargoyles, and a symbol of Horus, God of the Underworld, to ward off evil, with bog rolls stacked beside an ornamental gas mask. Everyone, it seemed, had circus skills and revelled in costume — fluorescent face paint, a silver tiara, lime green ski pants, dreadlocks and feathers, donning pantomime costume to bust security guard cordons.

Something both novel and ancient arose from the earth in that time, as natural as a magic mushroom: paganism. Not paganism as toy or relic but the real thing. The Green Man was there, actual, angry and ready to fight for the Wild Woods, for oak and ash and thorn. The full moons – the wolf moon, harvest moon, or honey moon – were honoured, and Pagan festivals were held on site: the solstices, the equinoxes, Samhain and Beltane. At one Beltane or May Day, a pagan wedding took place, a handfasting.

Politics, meanwhile, was handfasted to spirituality, for the defence of Mother Earth. Living in trees, wet in the rain, frozen in snow, sunburned in summer, people tuned themselves to the birdsong, and named themselves according to the living world, names like Badger, Animal and Twig. The movement was not just *against* roads, it was *for* nature, the rights of animals, birds and insects.

There were hunt-sabs, squaddies and students, punks, shamans and artists. What united them was a love of the land. They loved their land but hated their state, defying it with all they had when the bulldozers came building roads through beauty.

Sometimes it was as if fairy-tales had sprung to life. There were hobbits, borrowers, trolls and wombles. Sometimes there was an undeniable shamanic atmosphere. It was sometimes Arthurian (King Arthur turned up several times at the protests) and there was something from the age of chivalry, something of the knight errant in quest of adventure.

If there was something so old going on, many protesters were themselves very young. The protests appealed to the values of childhood,

Images: Original artwork from campaign flyers and literature 1995–1999

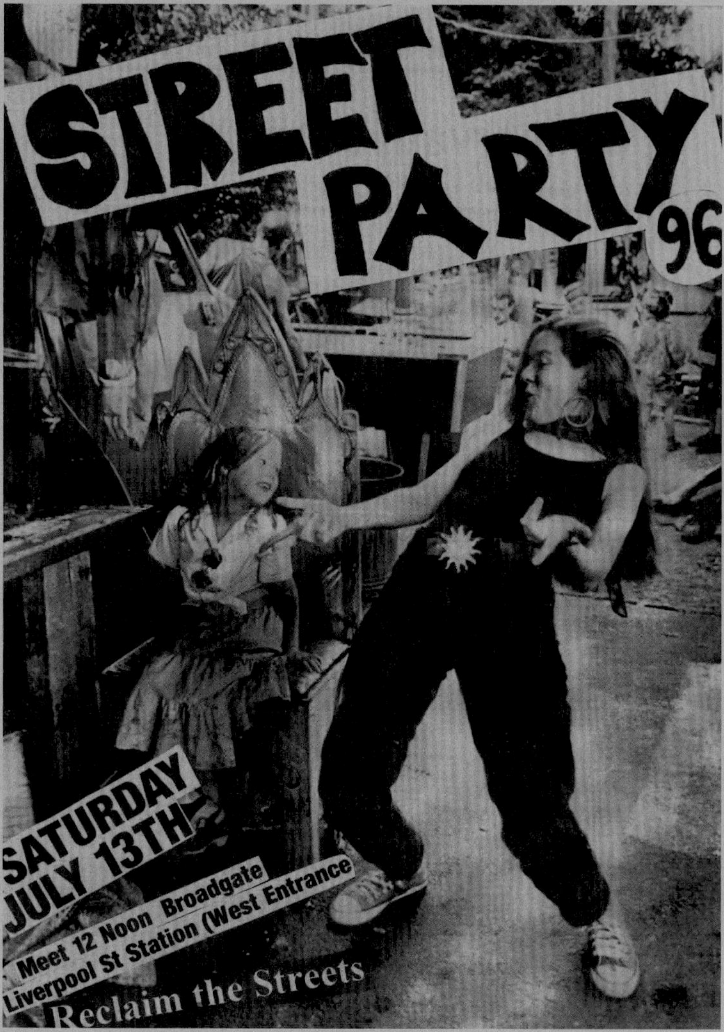

STREET PARTY 96

SATURDAY JULY 13TH

Meet 12 Noon Broadgate
Liverpool St Station (West Entrance

Reclaim the Streets

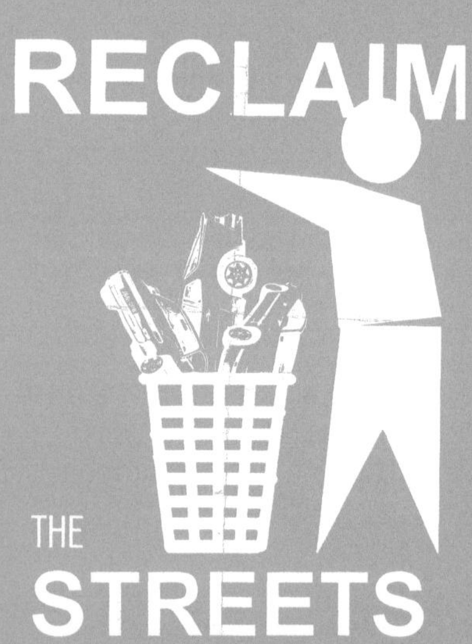

the justice of Robin Hood, and the importance of the voices of animals and trees. There is a clear parallel between the youthfulness of the road protests and many of today's protesters, Fridays for the Future, Greta Thunberg, and the young people in XR Youth. But there is a harrowing difference. The road protesters were protecting the lives of trees and animals while today's young people are seeking to protect their own lives as well.

Simply living in the protest camps demanded a heroic stamina, particularly in the winters (the temperatures reached ten degrees below freezing in Newbury.) People got frostbite. The darkness was deadly depressing. One protester, Balin, spent frozen days and nights up a tripod. A passerby compared him to Don Quixote, wasting his time tilting at proverbials. But the angle of tilt matters; the point where the angle is most acute between the line of heroism and the line of futility is exactly the point where symbols are created. And it is symbols which inspire people. These photographs are a poignant reflection of the passion and the pain, the mud and the magic of the time.

Protesters sometimes lay for hours under security guard coaches in freezing puddles, clamped with D-locks around their necks. Security guards could assault protesters with impunity. One protester, to save one tree, stood on one foot for seven hours on a branch too slender to take his second foot. One women spent eight hours up a tripod, and came down with threatened hypothermia. Vigilantes shot at protesters. When the bailiffs were violent, the police looked the other way, literally and metaphorically.

It was psychologically tough: most of the press were hostile, at the beginning. The Government introduced laws to outlaw them (the Criminal Justice Act) while Bray's detectives specialised in psychological intimidation. Many people burnt out, suffered PTSD and became emotionally exhausted. It was self-sacrificial, and many paid a heavy price. It tipped people into psychosis, breakdown and chronic illness.

Everyone was vulnerable, yet vulnerability could be a priceless asset. Digging tunnels underground meant that bailiffs were less likely to use heavy machinery because of the risk of a tunnel collapse. If tree protesters became like birds in the trees, Swampy, hair like pelt, morphed into a mole, occasionally coming up to the surface, blinking in the sunlight.

I was the person who first brought Swampy to the far brighter light of media attention, in a piece published in The Observer on 26 January 1997. That piece turned Swampy into media catnip. Everyone wanted him: the tenderness, tenacity, utterly appealing innocence and dogged devotion that he represented came to be the face of the road protests. Although it was not easy for him, people adored him and the protests – having lost woodland after woodland – won the ultimate success as public opinion swung behind them which led to the Tories dismantling their entire road building programme.

A generation later, and another tunnel. At Euston station, XR protesters tunnelled underground to oppose HS2: the protesters included Swampy and Son, symbolising the genealogy of the movement. XR bears a family resemblance to the road protests, in performance art, humour and music.

STREET PARTY II

Rave against the Machine!

SUNDAY, JULY 23rd

Meet 1.00pm, end of Battlebridge Road, behind Kings X
contact:

RECLAIM THE STREETS

0171 254 2290

There are threads of connections running through the protest movement of the last decades: the anti-capitalism of Stop the City and the Occupy movement and the early Climate Action, all feeding in to XR now, with its inherent critique of capitalism and its clarity over climate (in)justice. There are similar tactics: lie in front of bulldozers or cars, lock-on, glue-on, resist, defend and love.

And some things have changed. Arrest used to be a deterrent: now it is a goal. The earlier protests were at the mercy of the media while today XR creates its own media channels. XR is far more disciplined, more strategic, more serious and immeasurably more sober (at least on site.) Many more professionals are directly involved in XR, including doctors, lawyers and academics.

But the most significant difference between those eras is the scale of the problem itself. Today we collectively emit about 50 billion tonnes of CO_2 each year. This is more than 40% higher than emissions in 1990.[1] The stakes are infinitely higher now: it is not an issue of roads but of all fuel. Not just particular locations but everywhere. Not just woodlands but entire forests of the world. And nobody, in the road protest days, thought that it would ever be necessary to fight for the very idea of truth, as XR needed to make clear in its first demand: Tell The Truth.

If the scale of the problem has grown horrifically, so has the scale of the hostility to protest. The government of the 1990s brought in the Criminal Justice and Public Order Act, 1994, that contained key aspects intended to stop road protest, criminalising previously civil offences involving trespass. But as I write, amendments to the Police Bill are being set out in which people could be banned from protesting if they have previously committed a 'protest-related offence' or even if they had merely attended a protest 'likely to result in serious disruption' and banned from associating with particular people.

In the times of the road protests, social media hadn't been invented. Almost no-one had a mobile phone. No one had alternative facts or fake news. The protection of specific birds, animals and trees seems an innocent and antique desire compared to now, as we face millions of ash trees dying, and the unhallowed thing, the ending of entire species, while once-common birds become endangered (— swifts! swifts? *swifts* —) and the insect realm is destroyed.

At Newbury, an iconic event happened in the woods, as the chainsaws screamed and the trees fell. Two wild horses cantered out of the woods up to two police horses. The wild ones, disturbed and distressed, were sniffing and pawing, as if they were themselves protesting the situation, bewildered, beseeching and devastated. Life itself will fight for life, in any way it can.

Jay Griffiths is the author of *Anarchipelago* a short novel about the road protests; *Wild: An Elemental Journey* and *Why Rebel.*

[1] Source: Our World in Data

Stanworth Valley: M65
February – May 1995

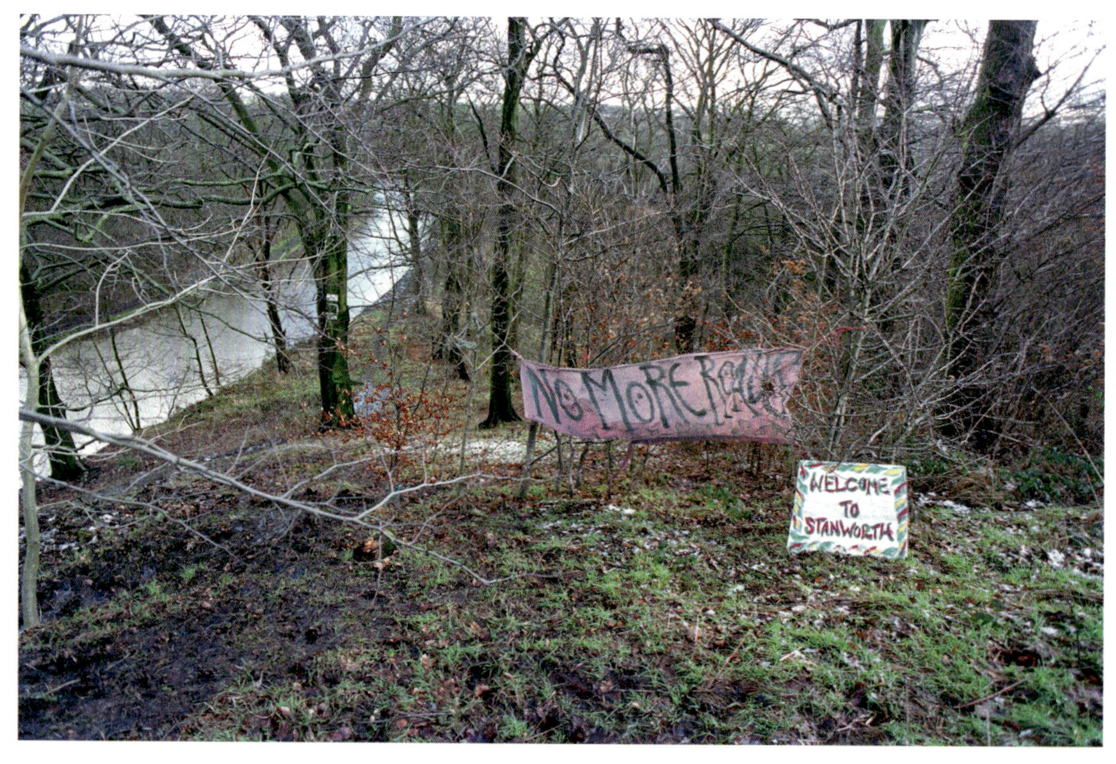

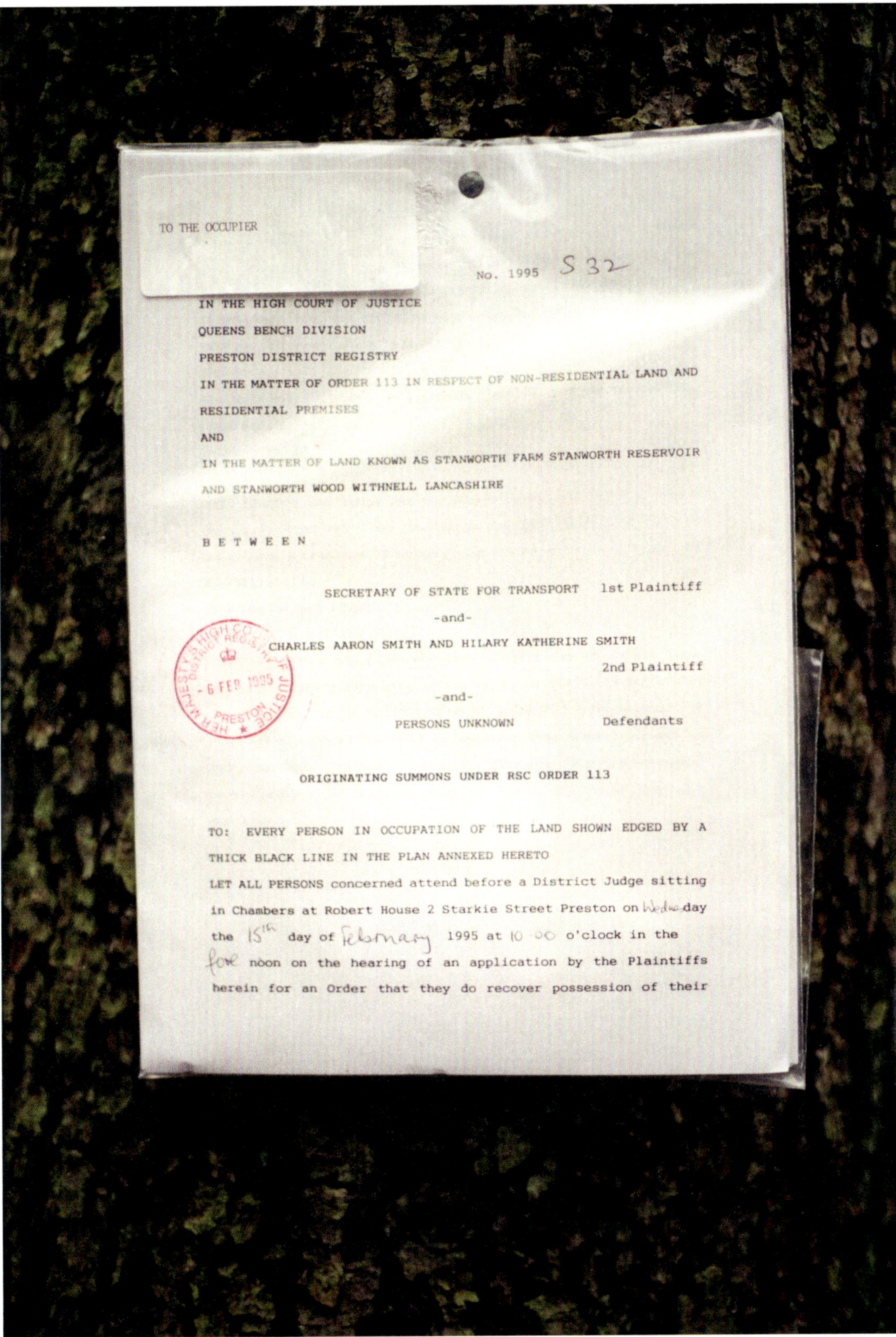
TO THE OCCUPIER

No. 1995 S 32

IN THE HIGH COURT OF JUSTICE

QUEENS BENCH DIVISION

PRESTON DISTRICT REGISTRY

IN THE MATTER OF ORDER 113 IN RESPECT OF NON-RESIDENTIAL LAND AND RESIDENTIAL PREMISES

AND

IN THE MATTER OF LAND KNOWN AS STANWORTH FARM STANWORTH RESERVOIR AND STANWORTH WOOD WITHNELL LANCASHIRE

B E T W E E N

SECRETARY OF STATE FOR TRANSPORT 1st Plaintiff

-and-

CHARLES AARON SMITH AND HILARY KATHERINE SMITH 2nd Plaintiff

-and-

PERSONS UNKNOWN Defendants

HER MAJESTY'S HIGH COURT OF JUSTICE DISTRICT REGISTRY - 6 FEB 1995 PRESTON

ORIGINATING SUMMONS UNDER RSC ORDER 113

TO: EVERY PERSON IN OCCUPATION OF THE LAND SHOWN EDGED BY A THICK BLACK LINE IN THE PLAN ANNEXED HERETO

LET ALL PERSONS concerned attend before a District Judge sitting in Chambers at Robert House 2 Starkie Street Preston on Wednesday the 15th day of February 1995 at 10.00 o'clock in the fore noon on the hearing of an application by the Plaintiffs herein for an Order that they do recover possession of their

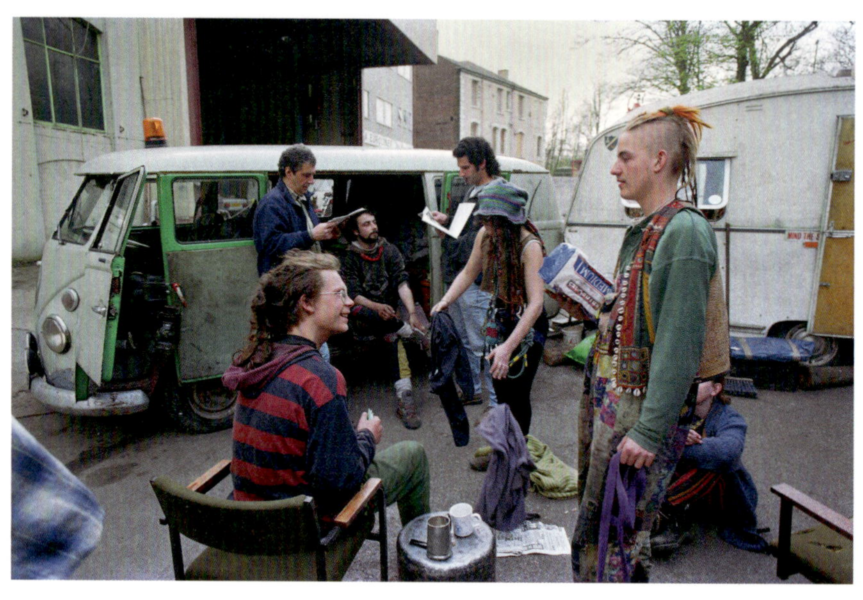

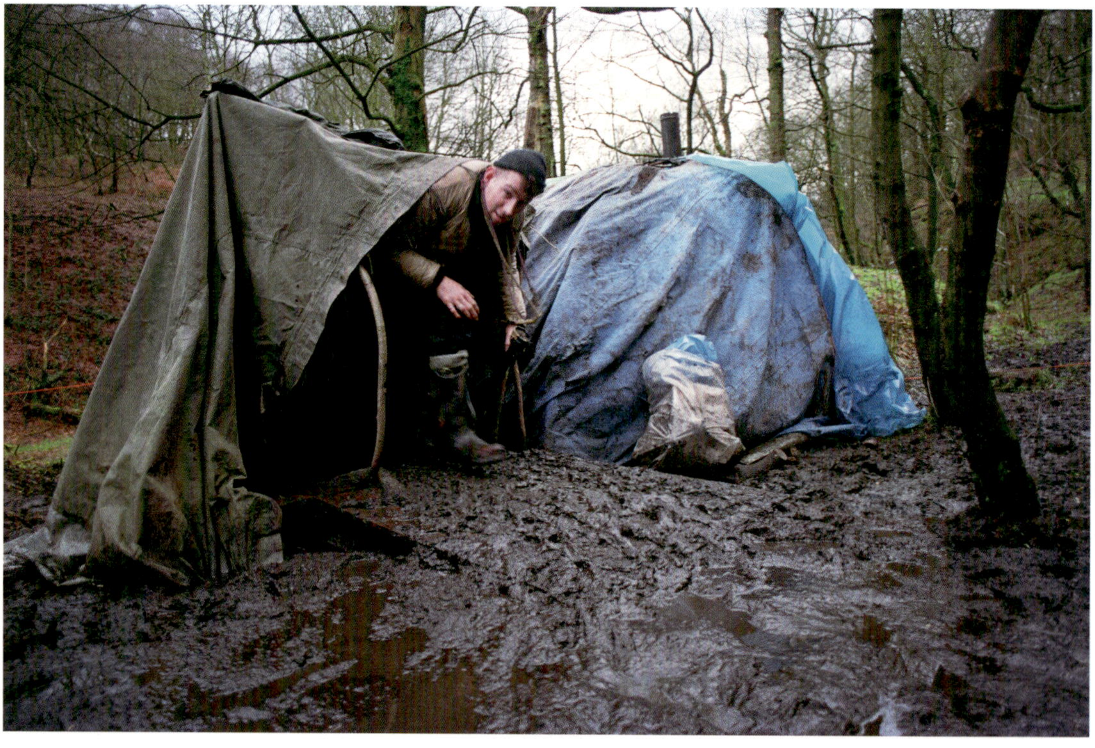

Stanworth Valley: M65

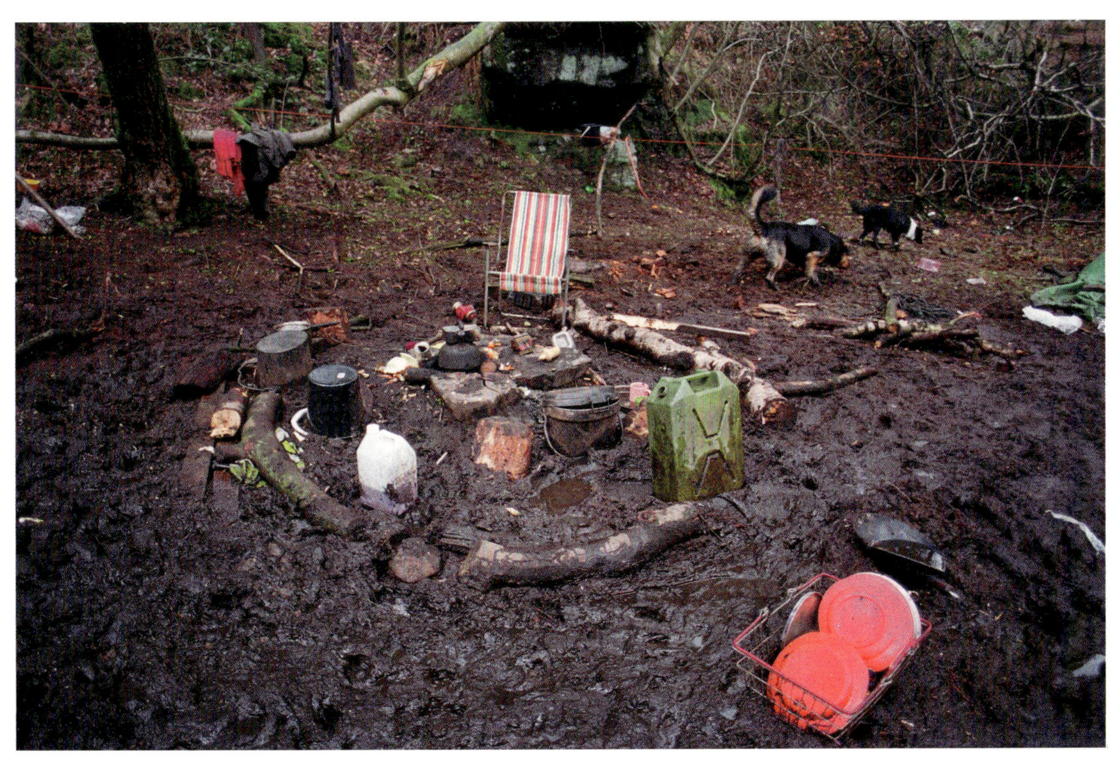

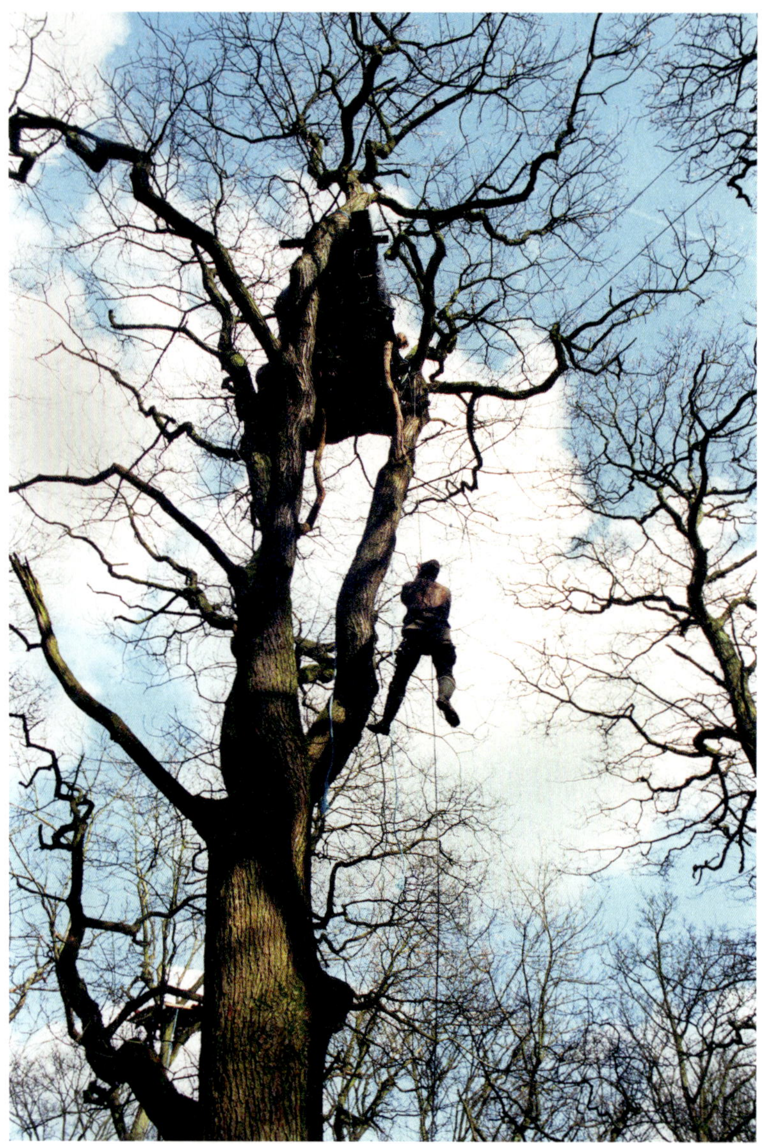

With the deftness of a medieval archer an arrow attached to a cord was fired over a high branch to allow a more substantial rope to be pulled to give access to the tree. Getting into a treehouse is never easy and involves an exhausting and laborious climbing technique called Prusiking. After 15 minutes pushing and pulling yourself up 60 foot of rope you finally clamber onto a platform holding a small simple Hobbit-like construction: cosy, secure and terrifyingly high off the ground. You'd pull the rope up behind you, much like a drawbridge, thus protecting the treehouse from unwanted visitors.

Stanworth Valley: M65

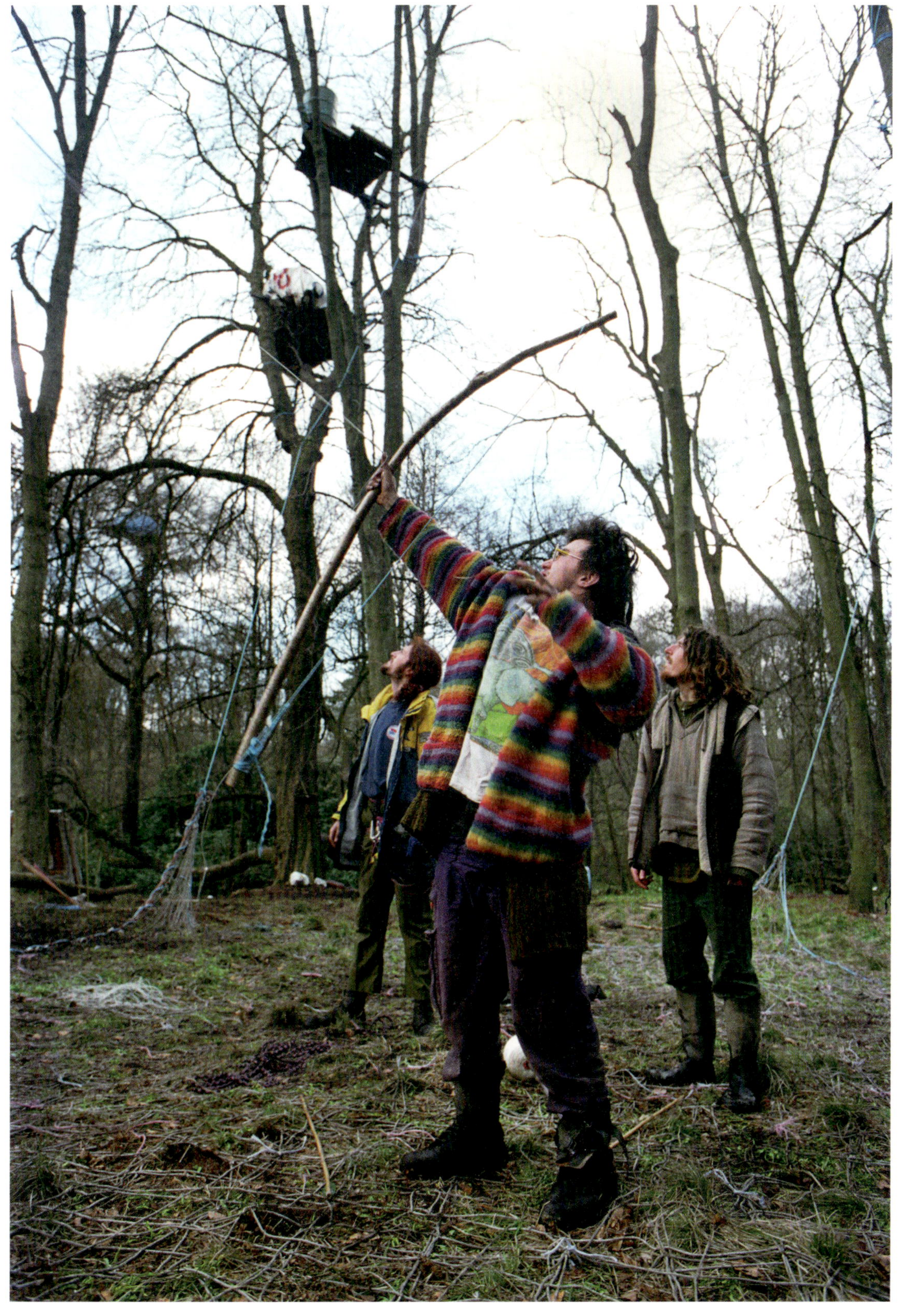

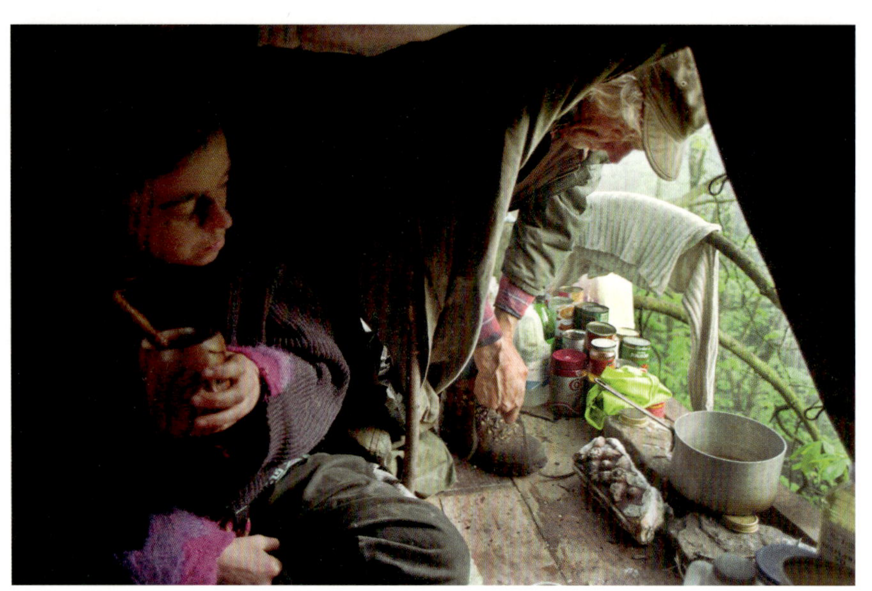

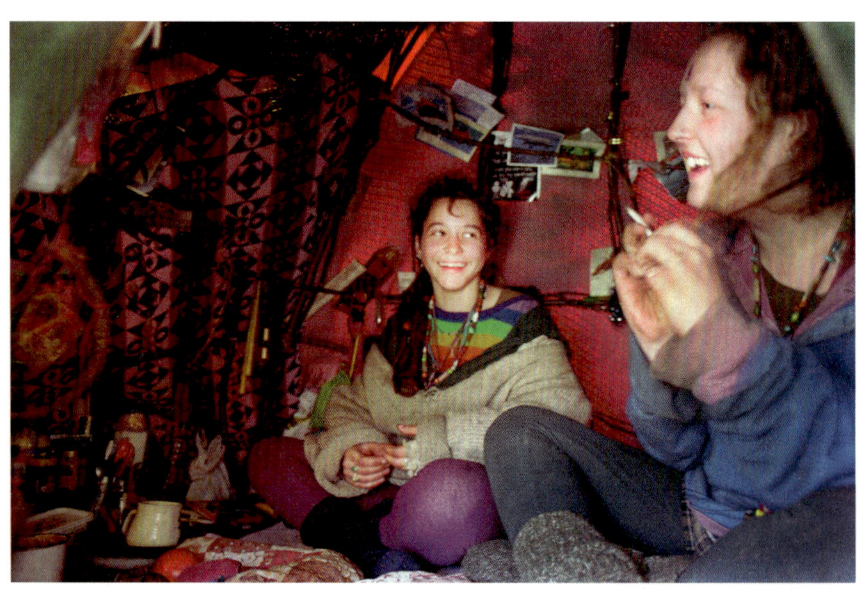

Stanworth Valley: M65

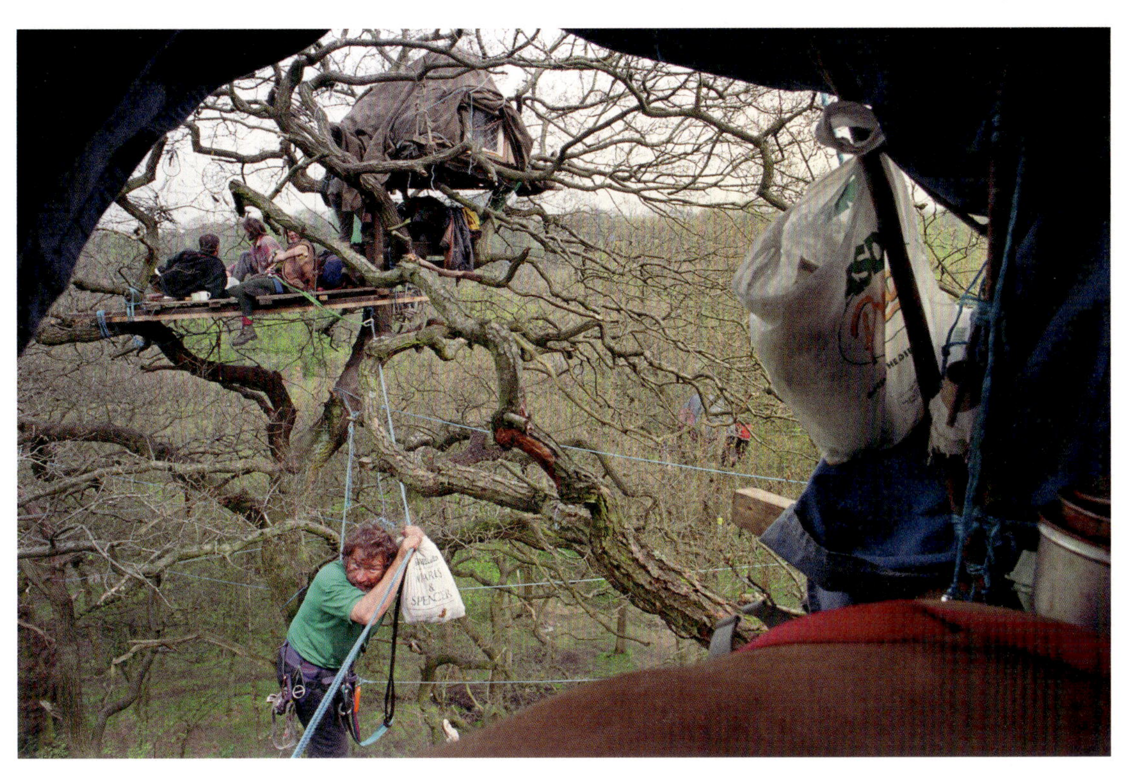
MARKS
&
SPENCER

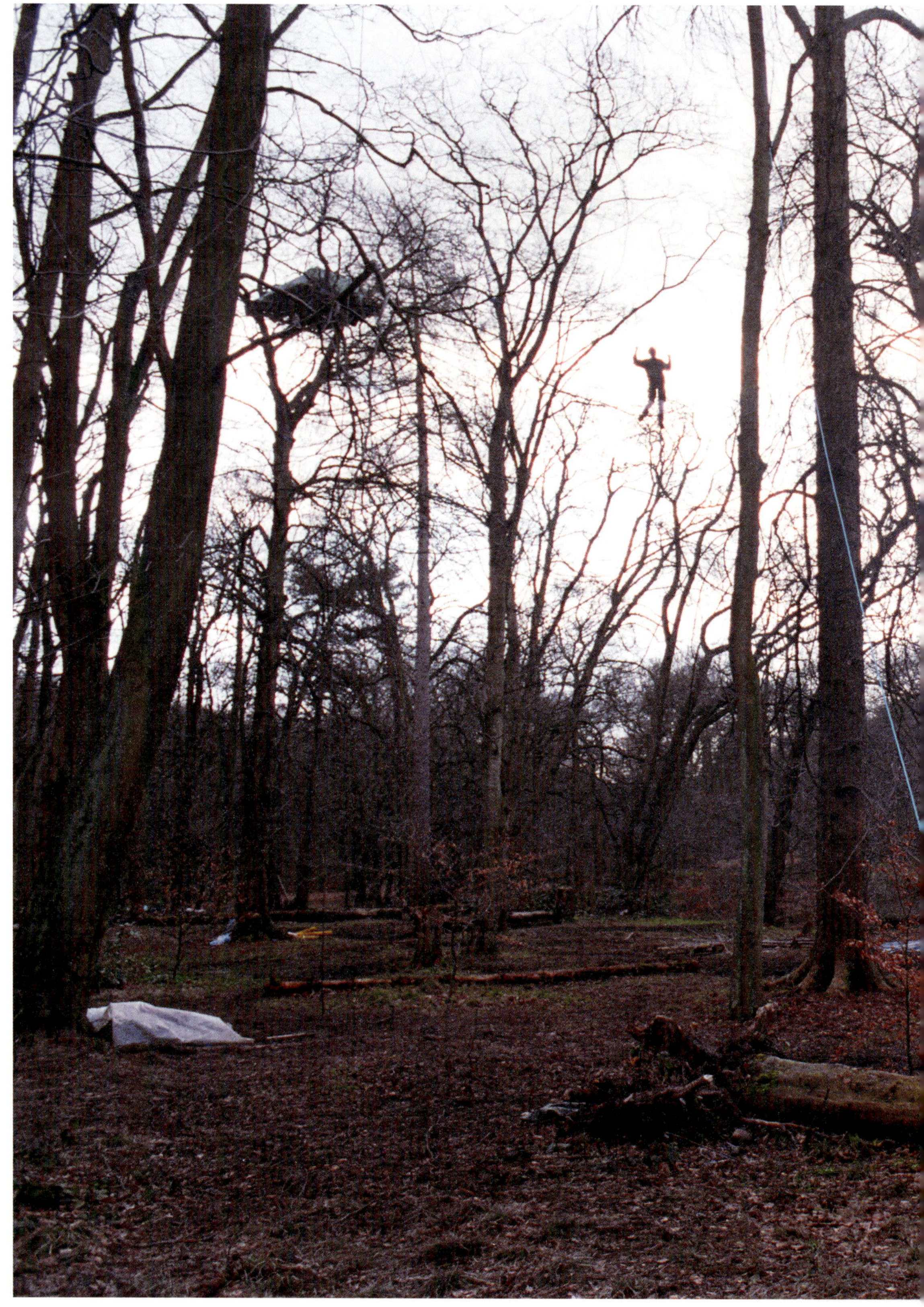

Stanworth Valley: M65

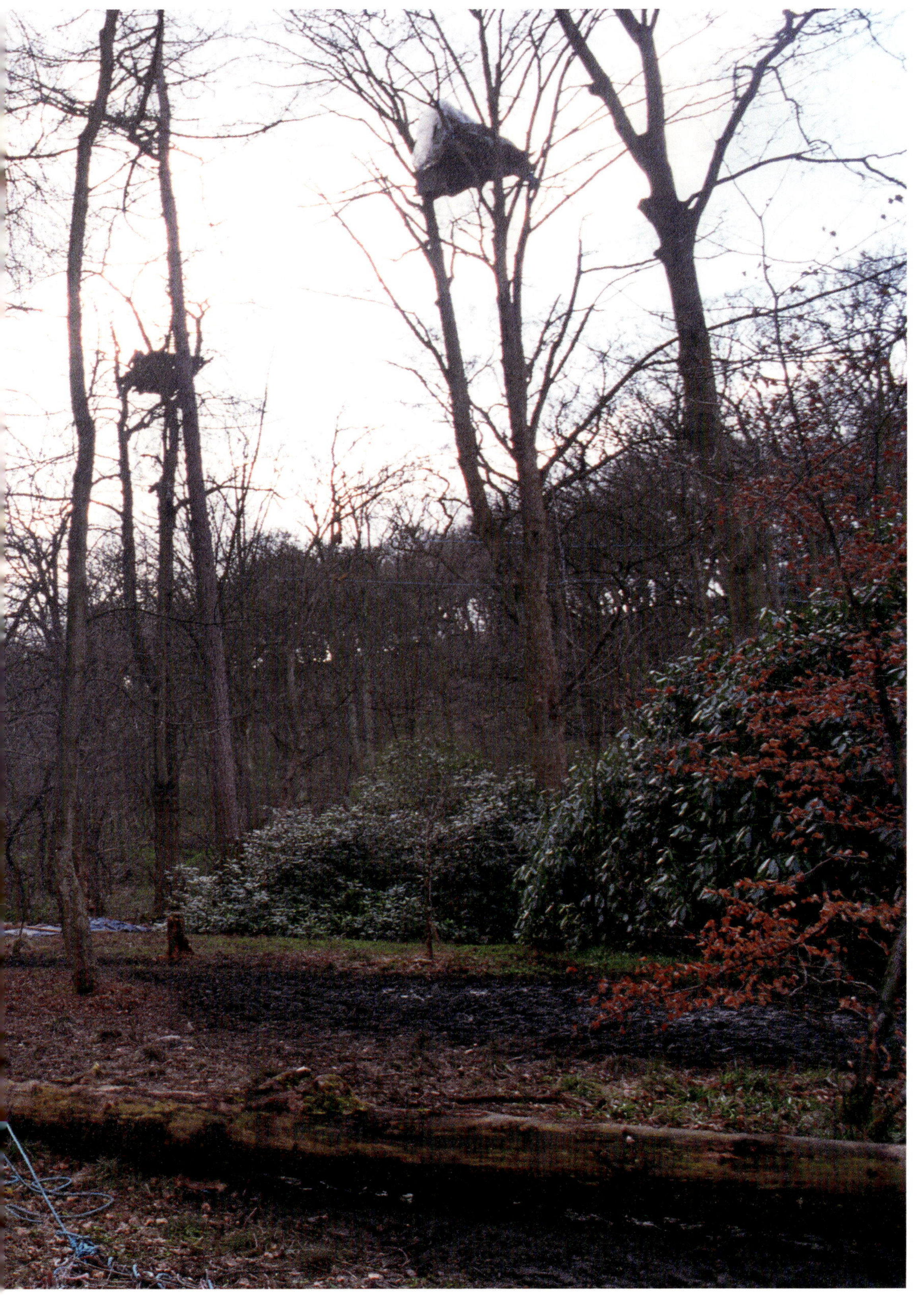

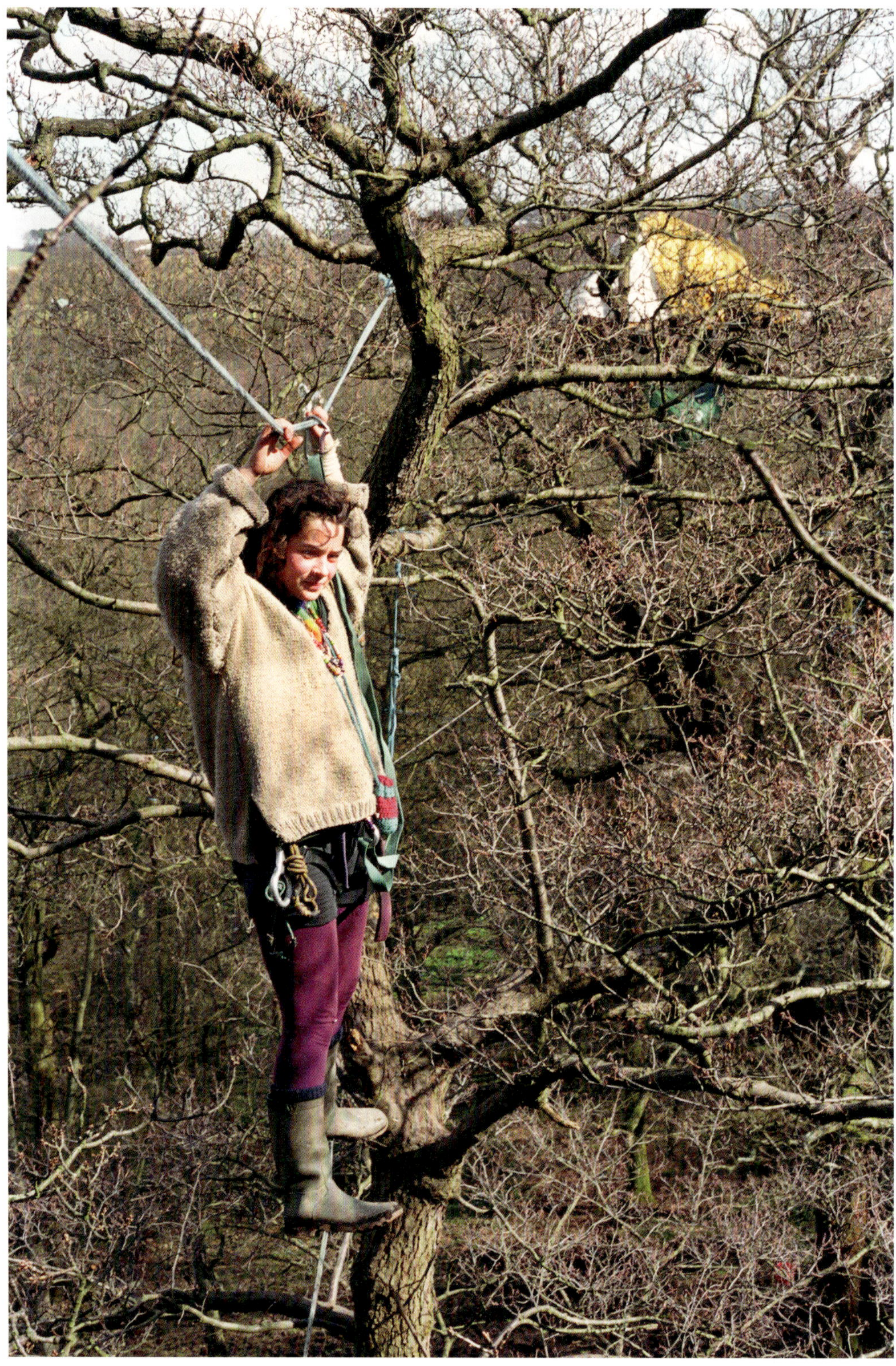

Stanworth Valley: M65

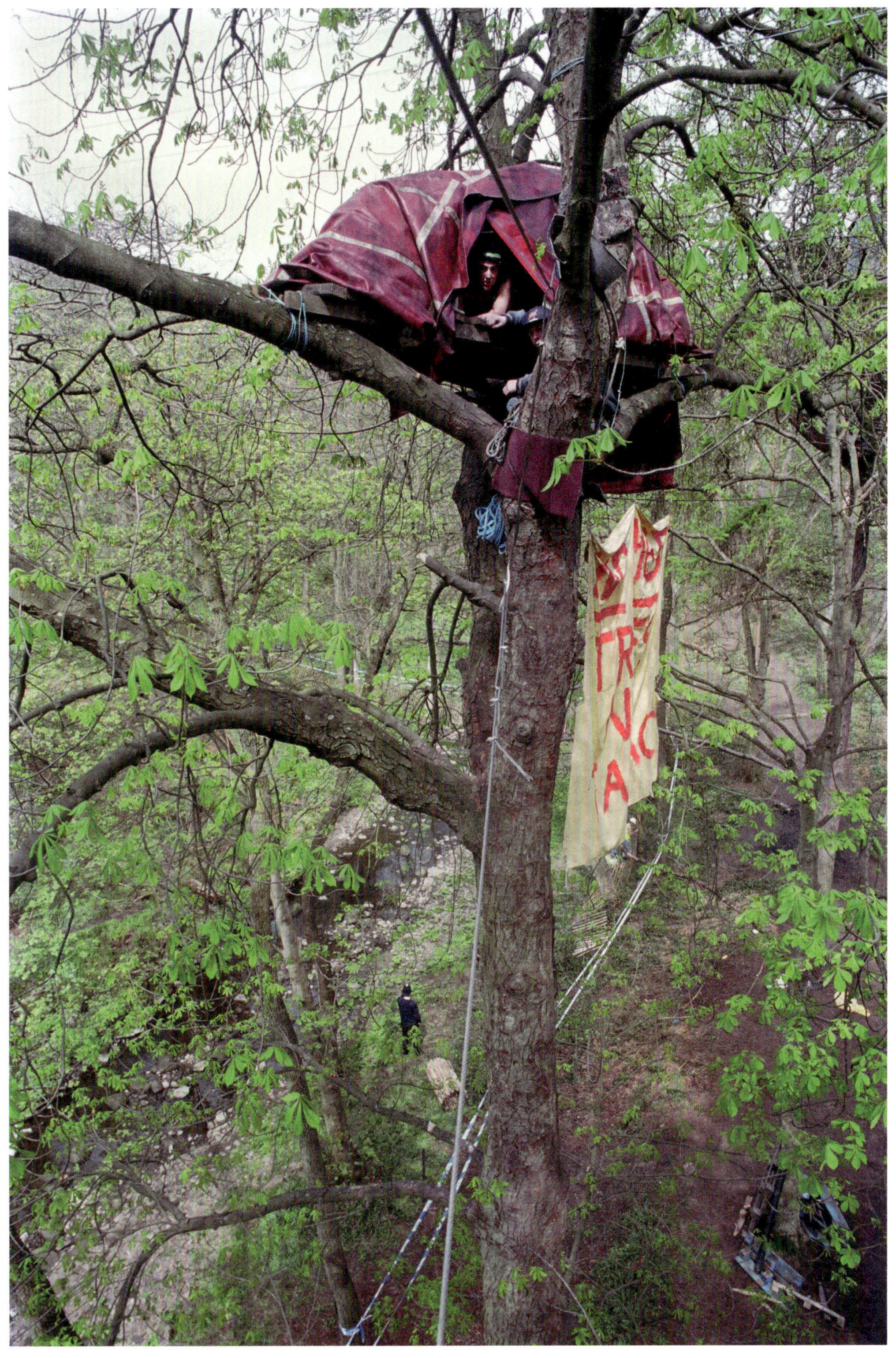

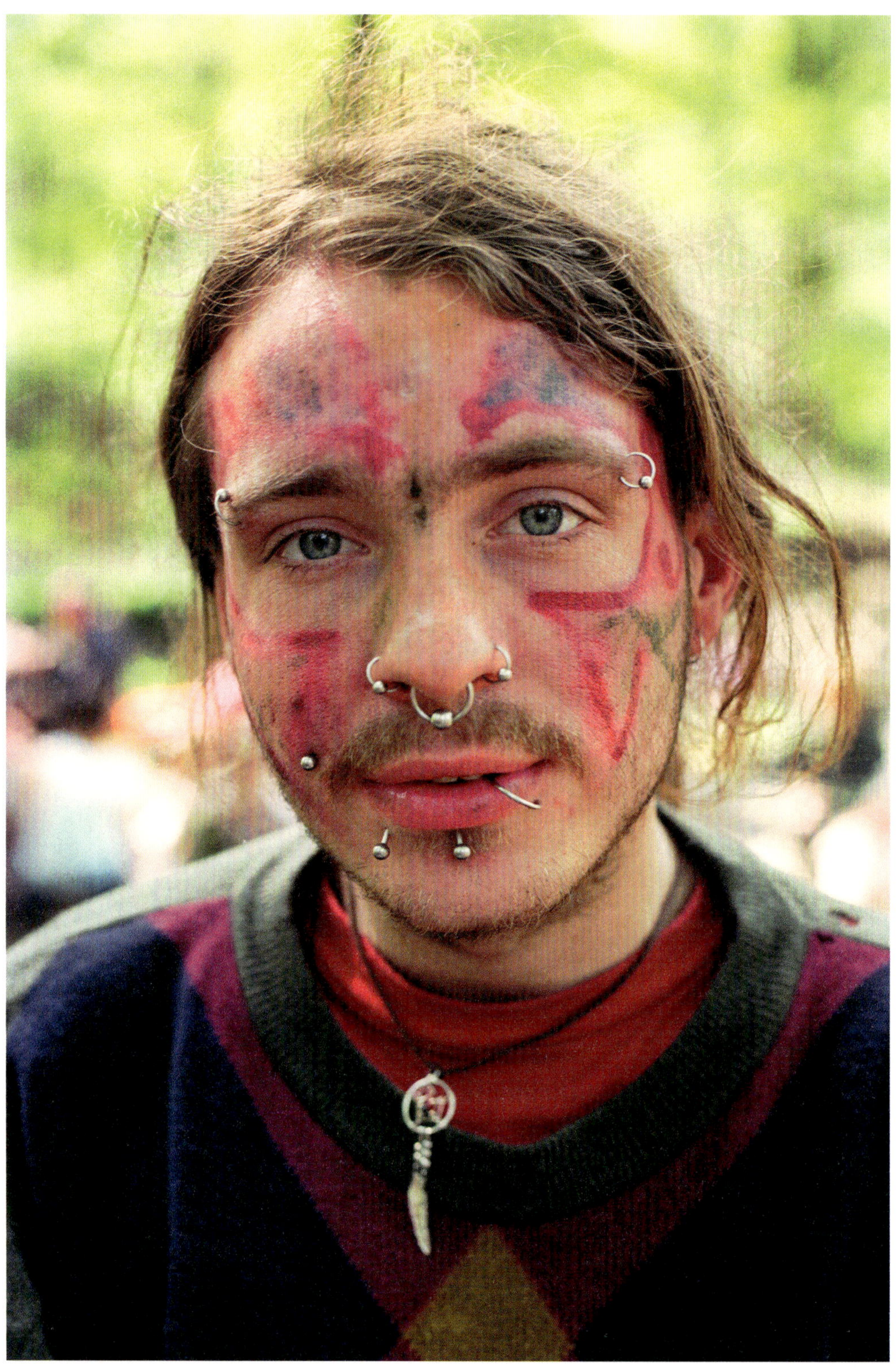

Stanworth Valley: M65

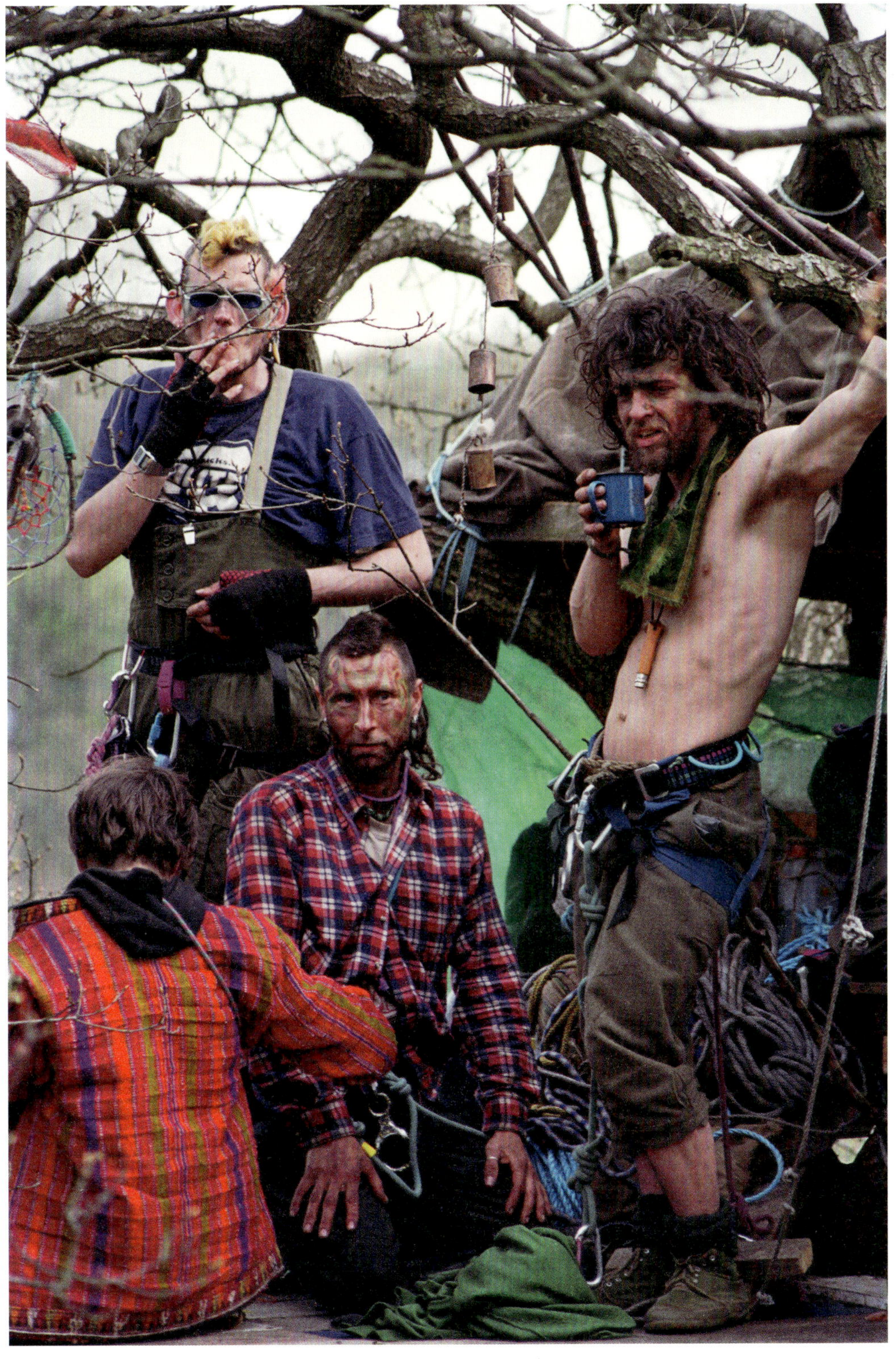

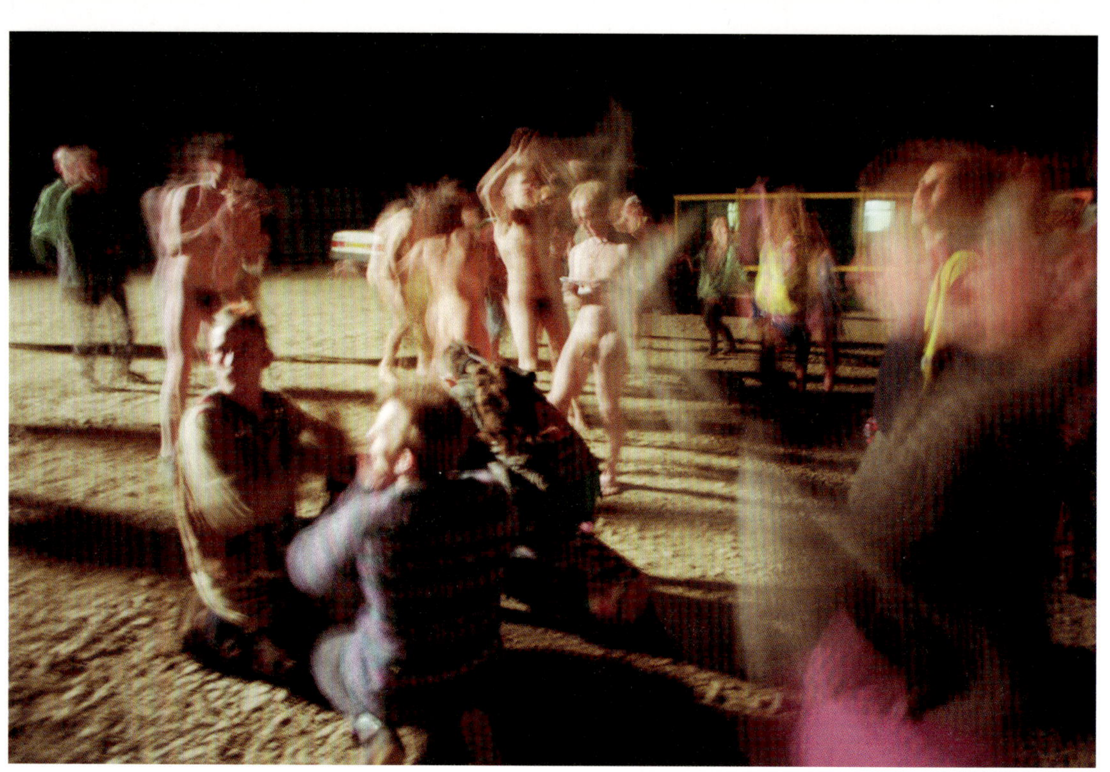

Stanworth Valley: M65

The night before the eviction began was 'Beltane' the Gaelic May Day festival. This celebration was strange and unknown to those who were there to ensure the destruction of the trees. The activists took this opportunity to come together in the cold fright of night, strip naked and dance to the beat of drums in a bid to psychologically unnerve the security and police – in a warning of the battle that was soon to commence.

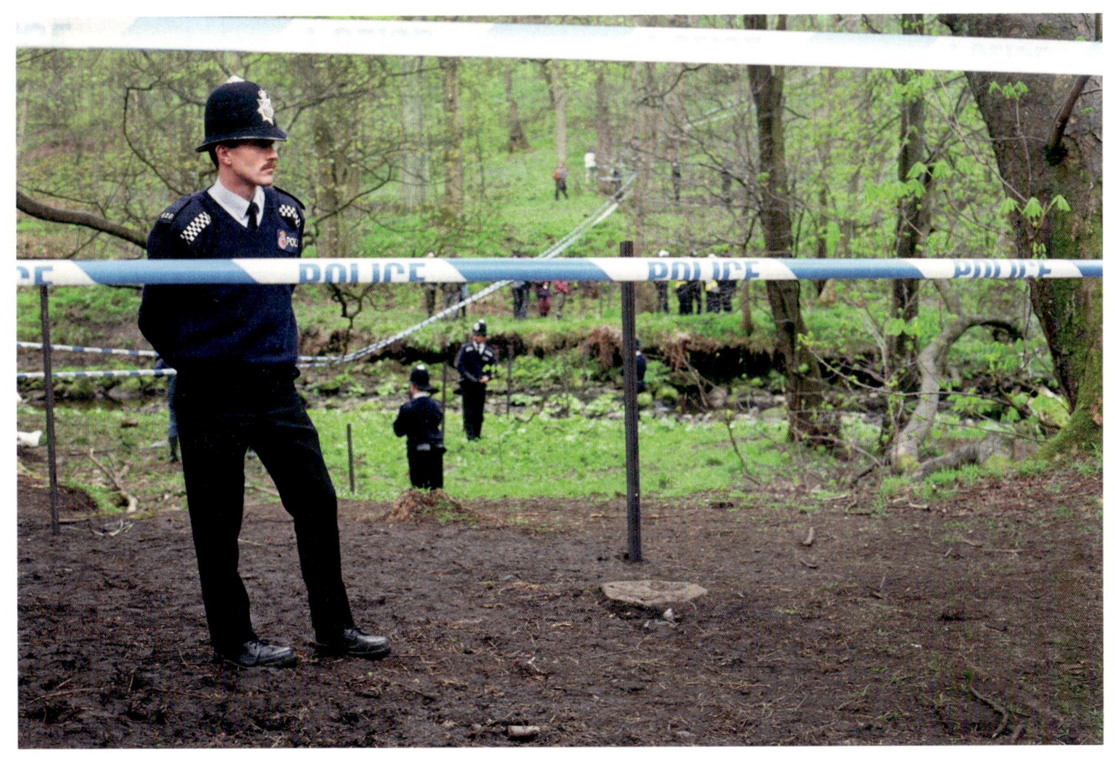

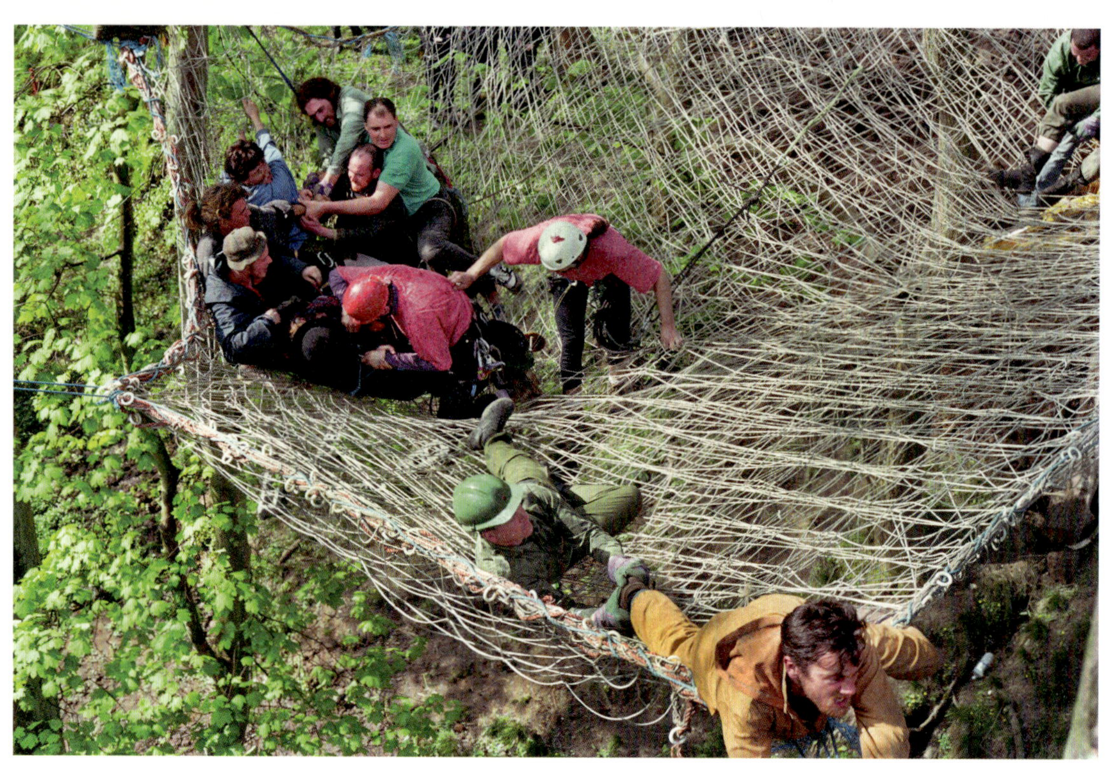

Stanworth Valley: M65

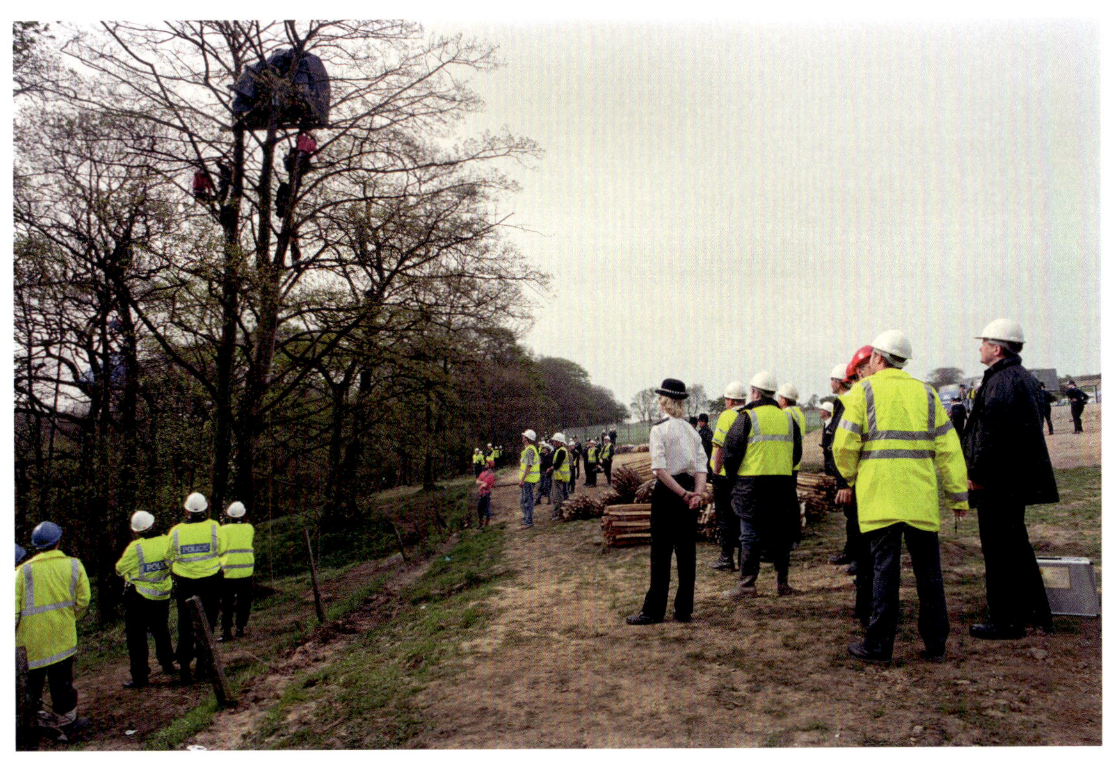
POLICE

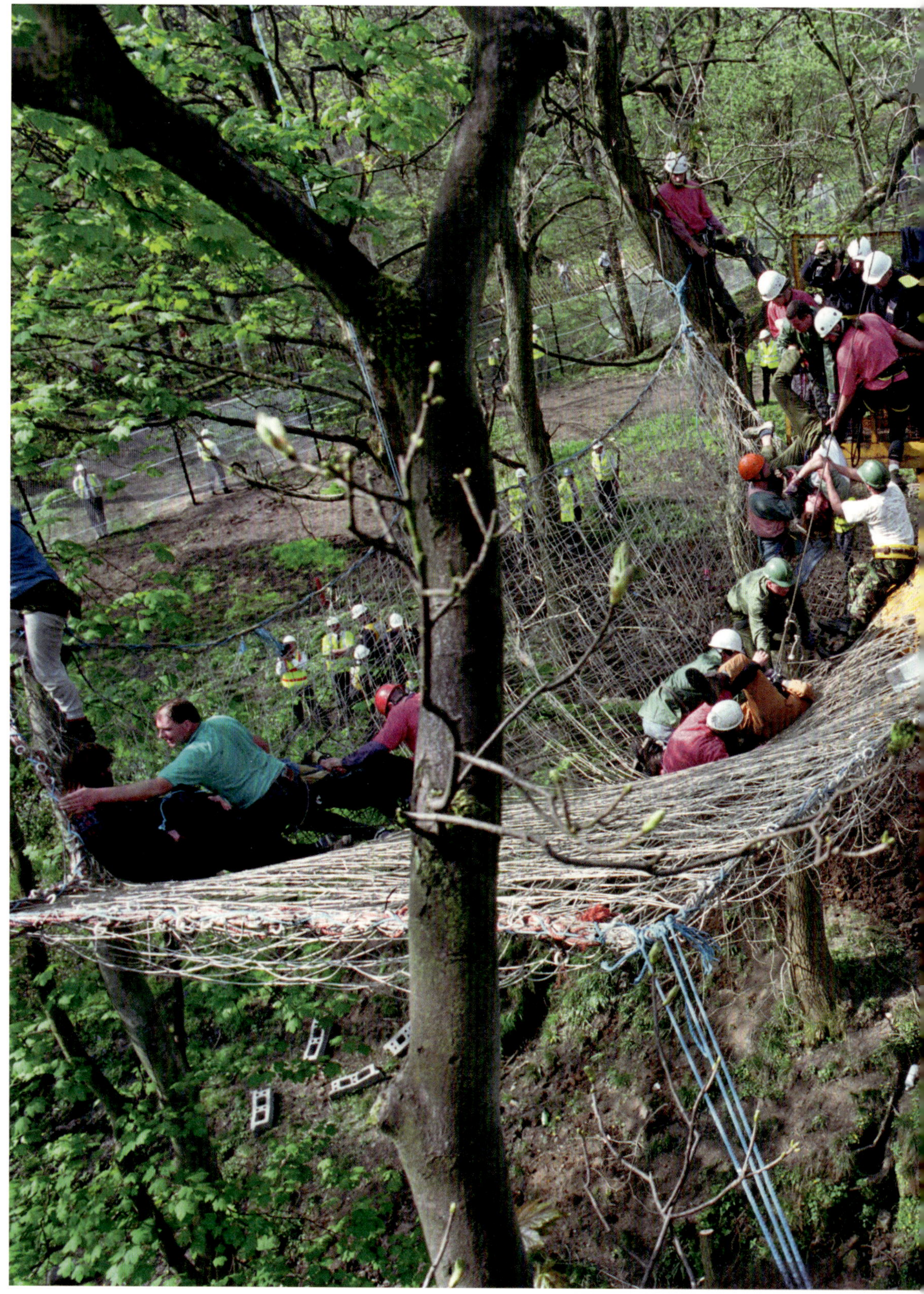

Stanworth Valley: M65

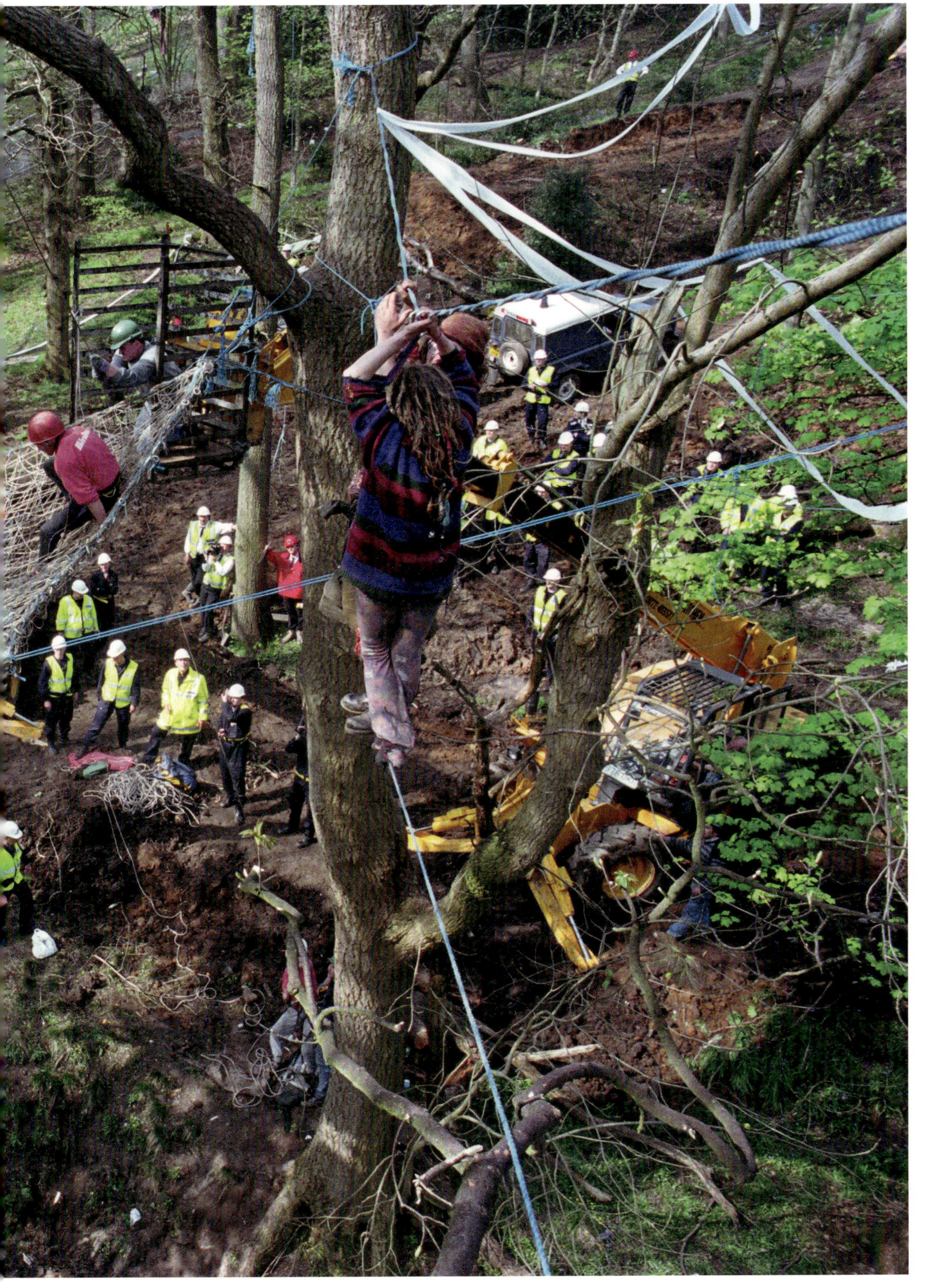

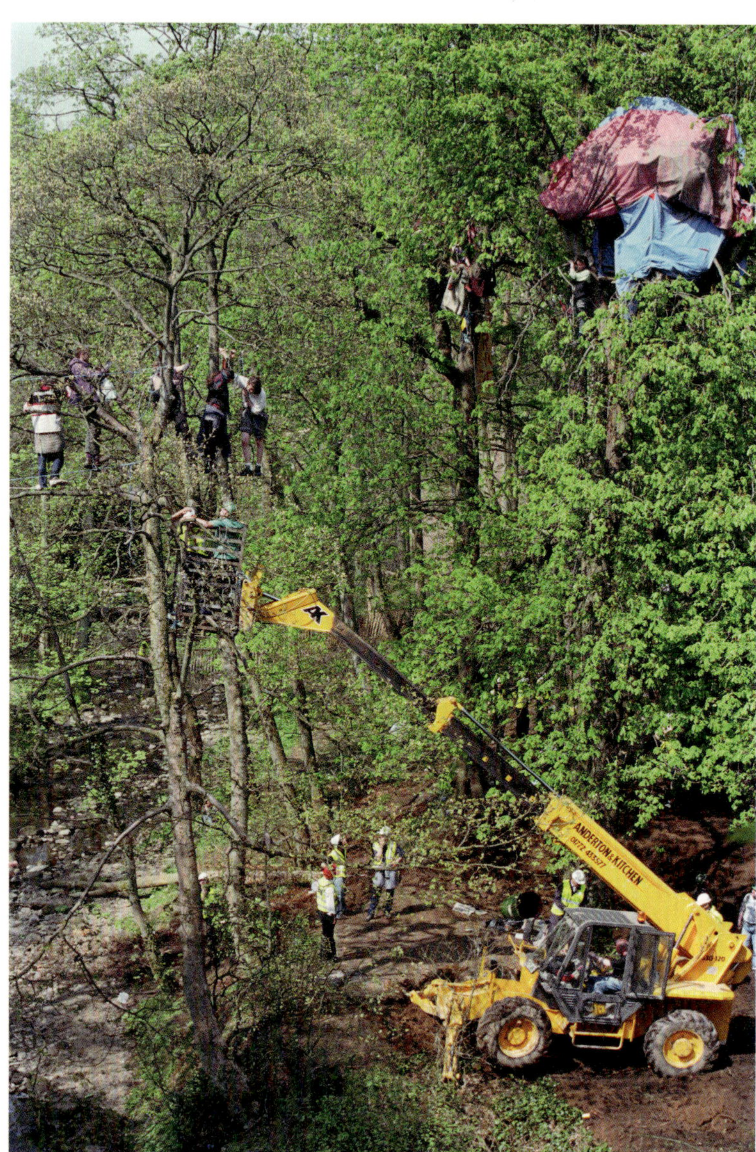

Stanworth Valley: M65

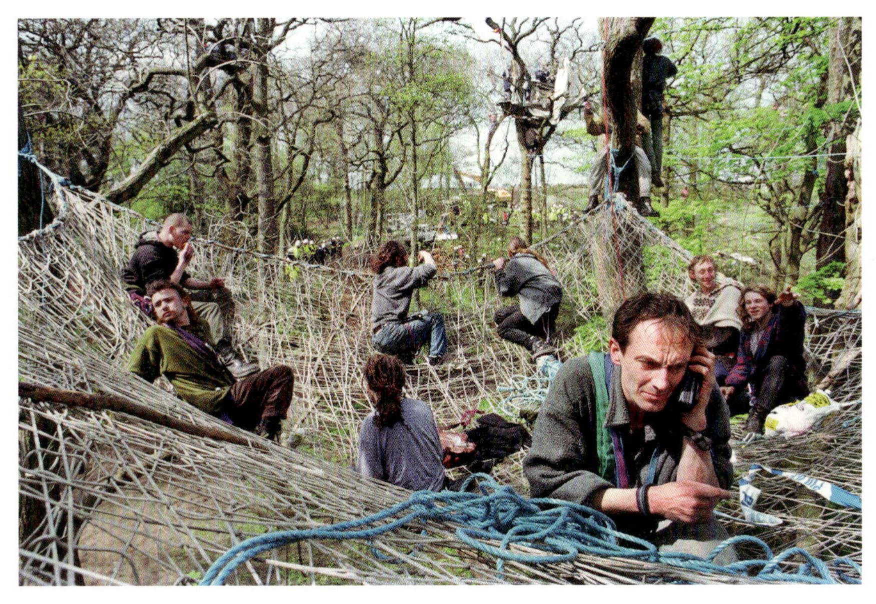

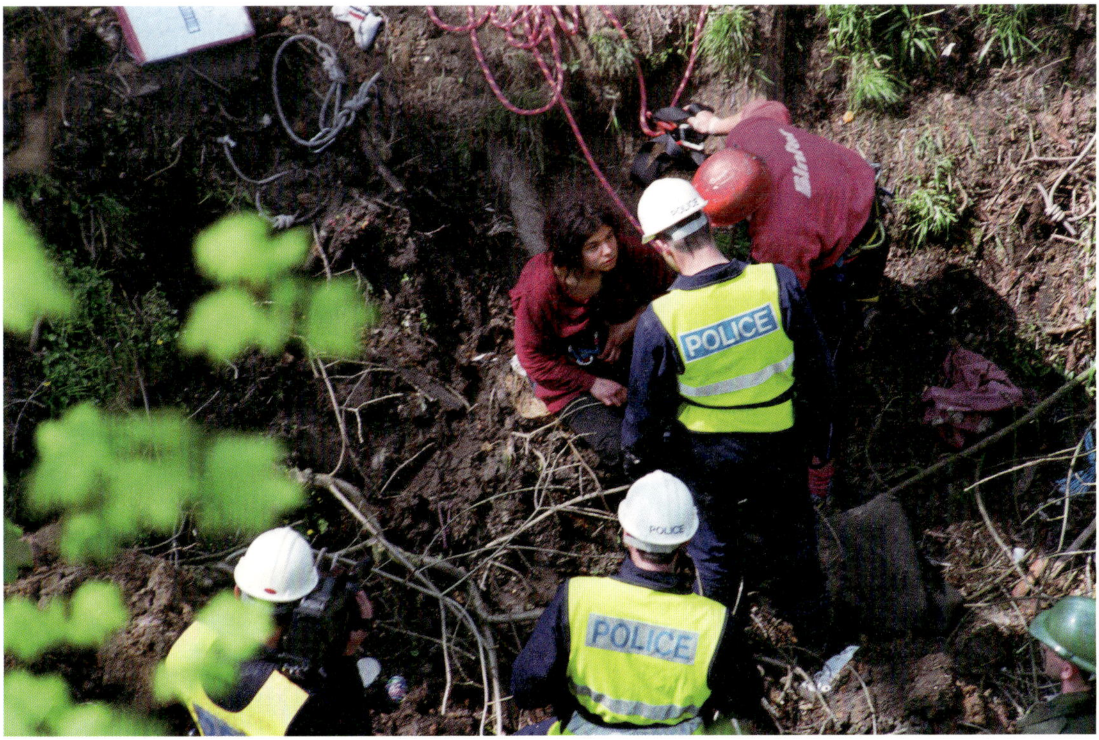

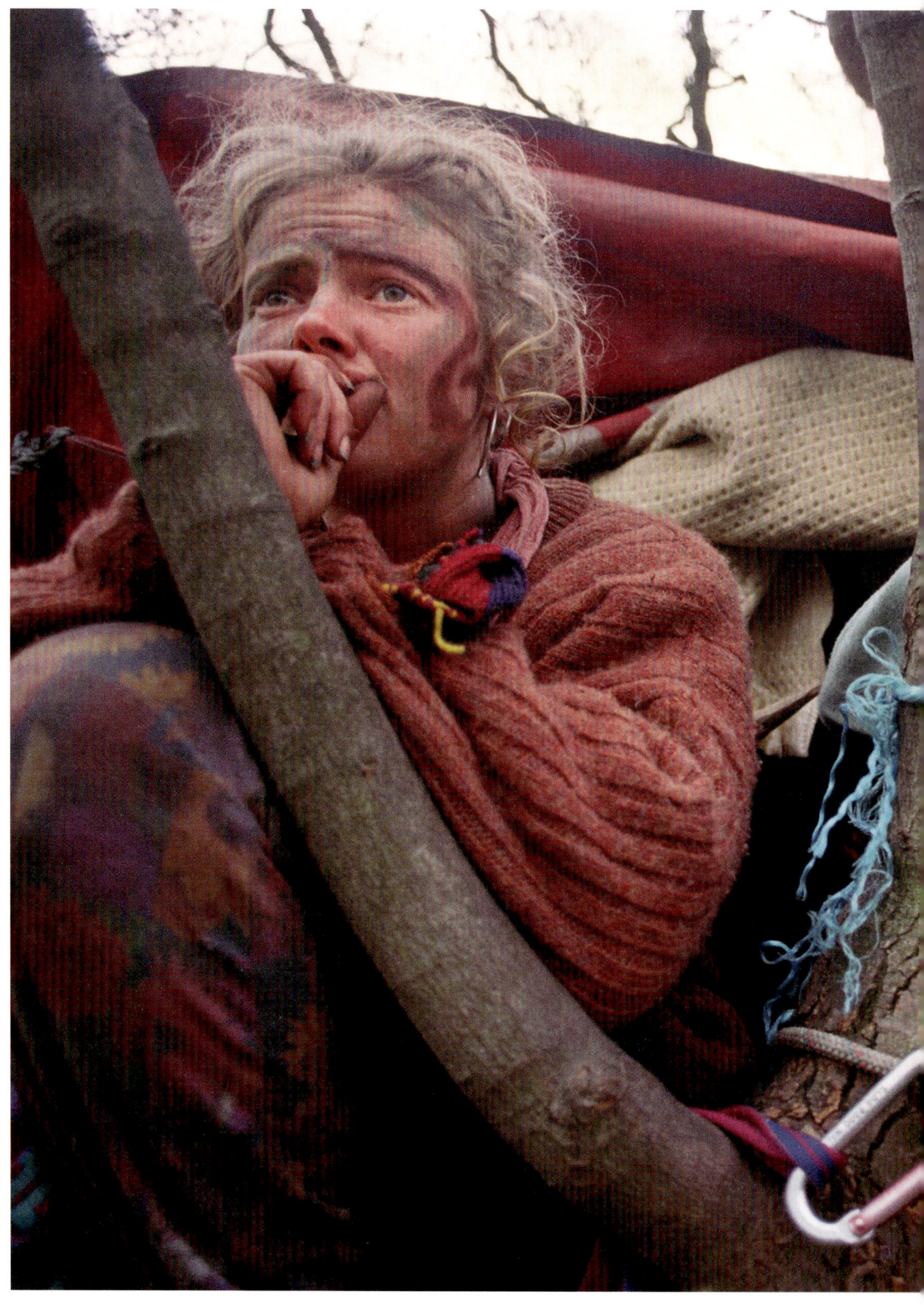

Stanworth Valley: M65

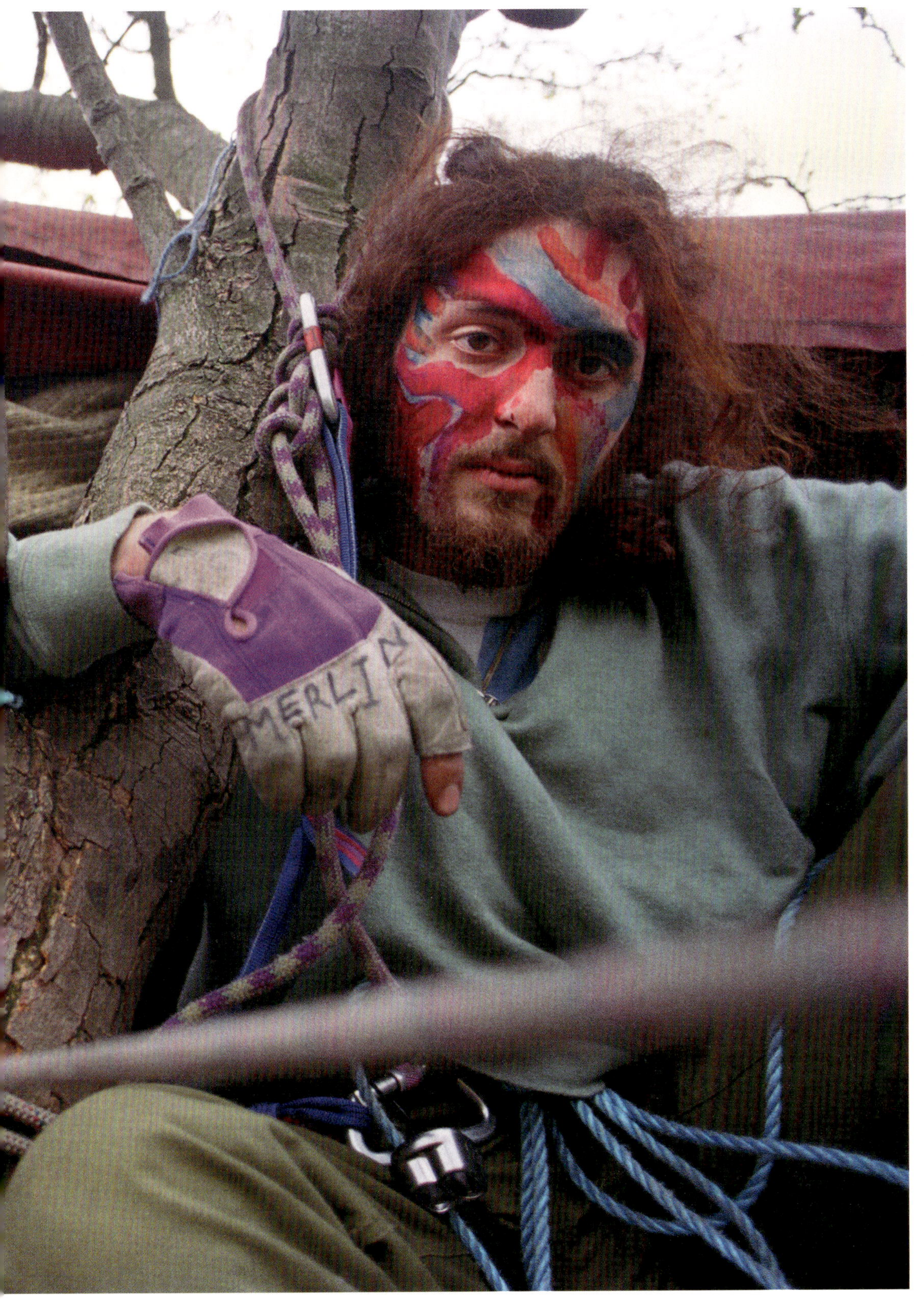
MERLIN

Days into the eviction and the sheer exhaustion had begun to show on the faces of those defending the trees. The scream of chainsaws, humans, and of trees, some centuries old, destroyed in mere seconds took its toll on everyone fighting for the old trees. There's a prophetic look in these haunted eyes, as if seeing into the future with its dystopian destruction of our beautiful planet. We are now living that future.

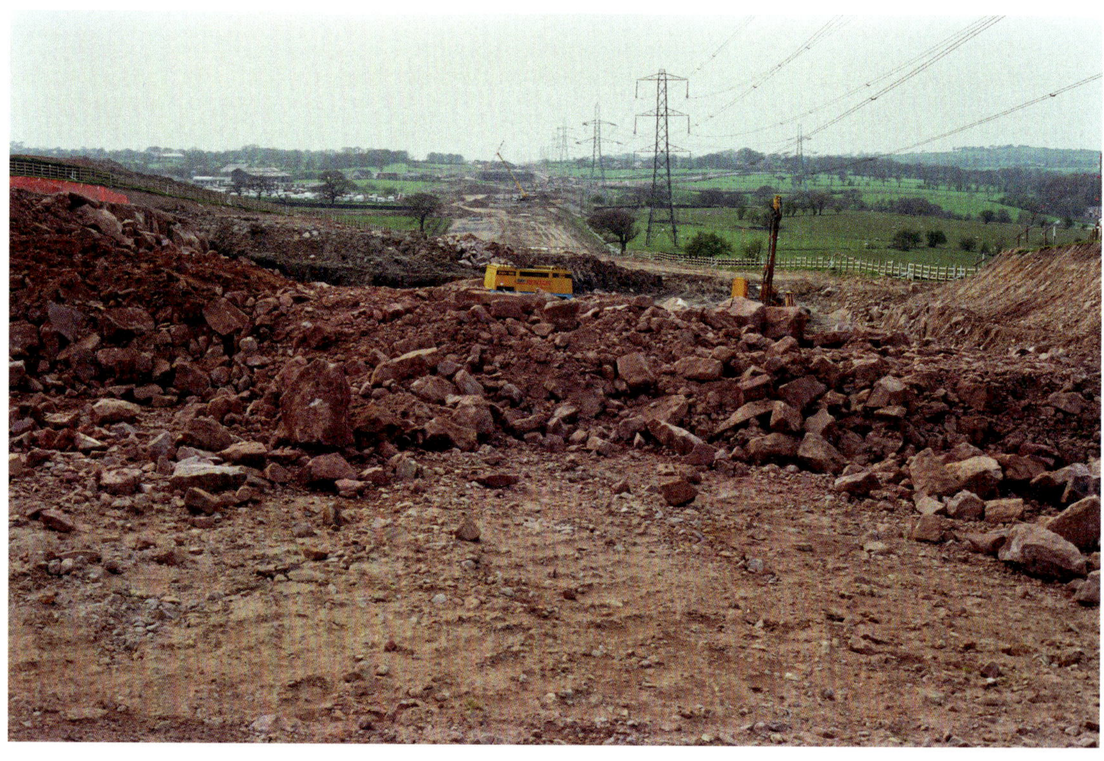

Stanworth Valley: M65

Reclaim the Streets: Camden May 1995

In a staged act of faux road rage two drivers got out of their vehicles on a sunny afternoon on Camden High Street and started smashing up each other's cars. A moment of absurdity combining simultaneous destruction and art – a new style of environmental protest never witnessed before.

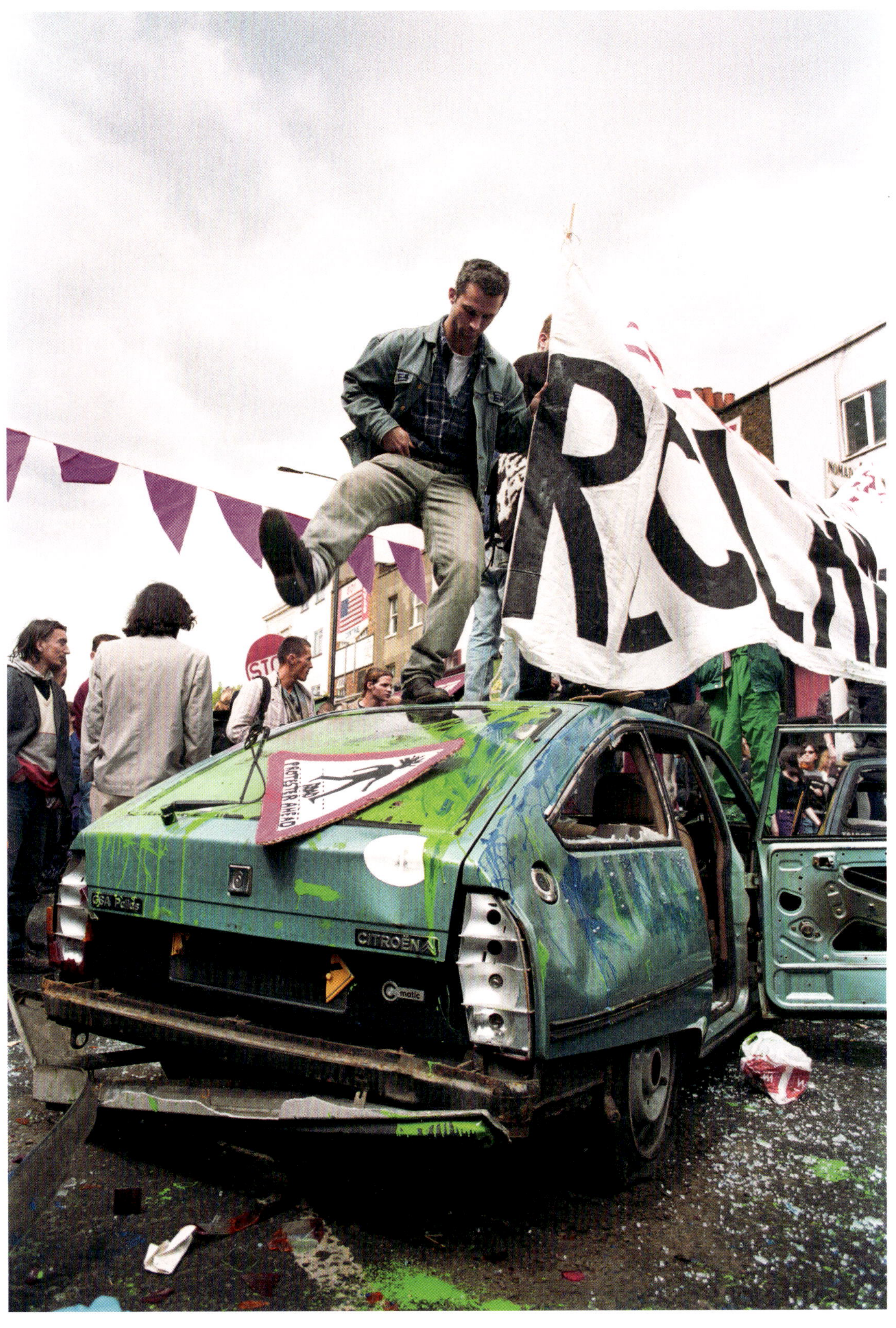
PROTESTER AHEAD
CITROËN

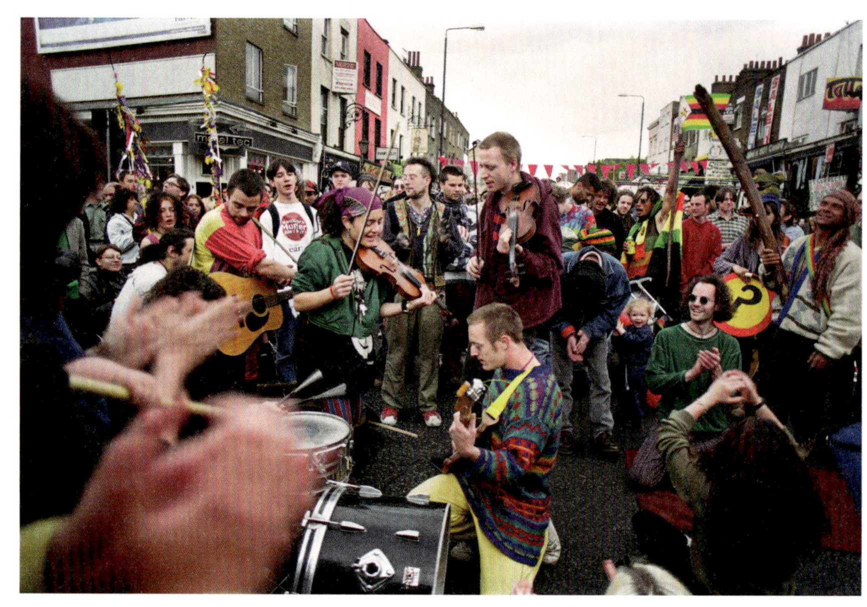

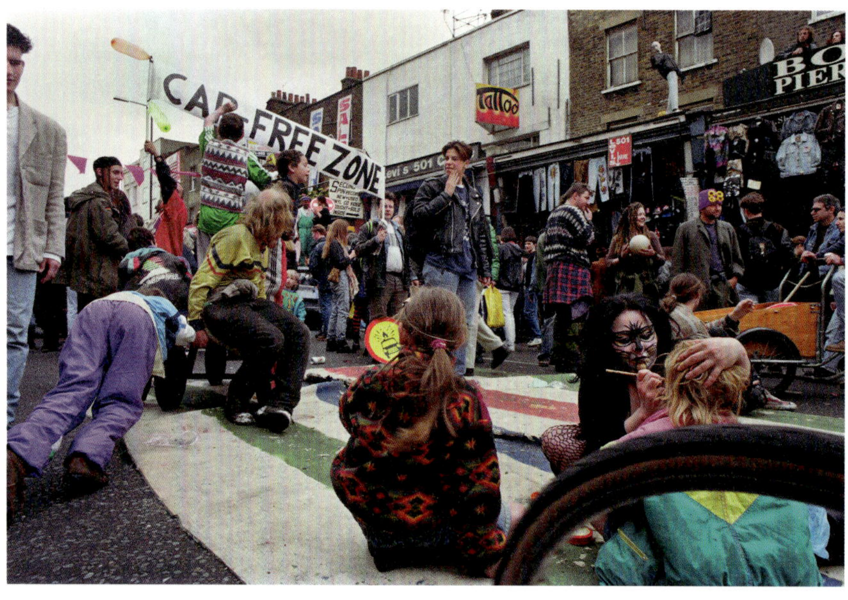

Reclaim the Streets: Camden

From down the street came the sound of music getting louder. Suddenly a fantastic machine came into view, built from rickshaws and bicycle parts like some make-believe fantasy that left a trail of love and joy in its wake. This pedal-powered contraption was the Rinky Dink Sound System and in no time those stood on the street began to move and jive to a beat that appeared as if by magic from its yellow conical speakers.

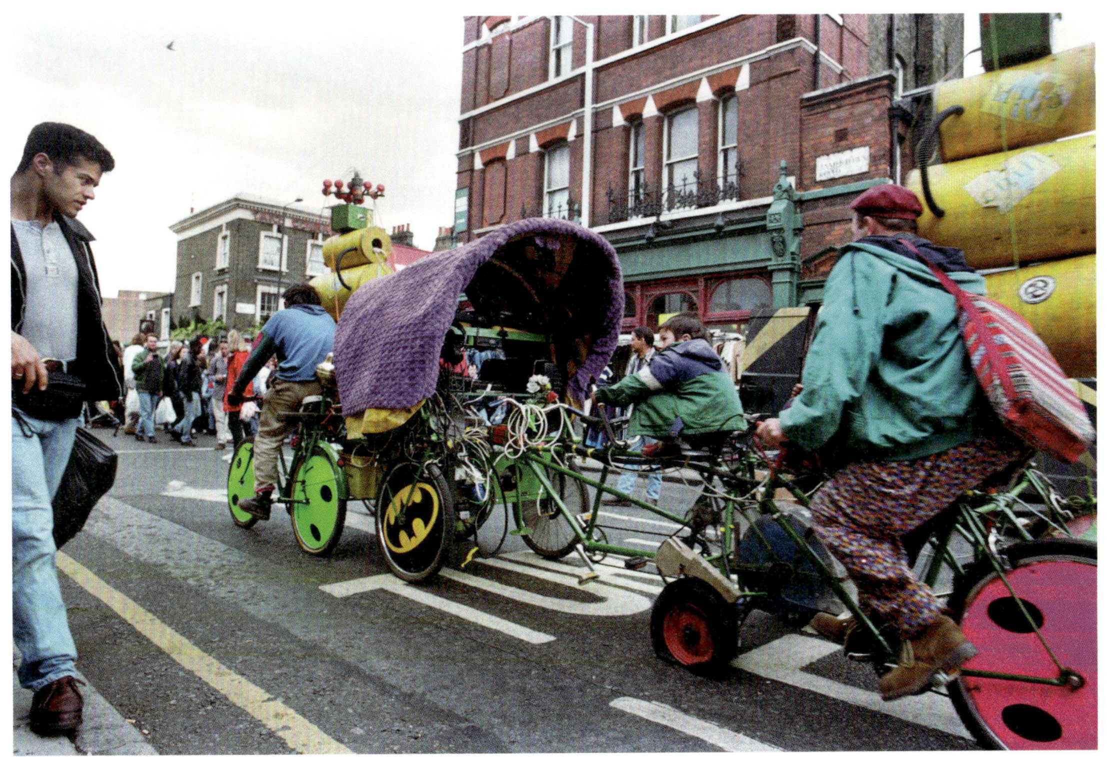

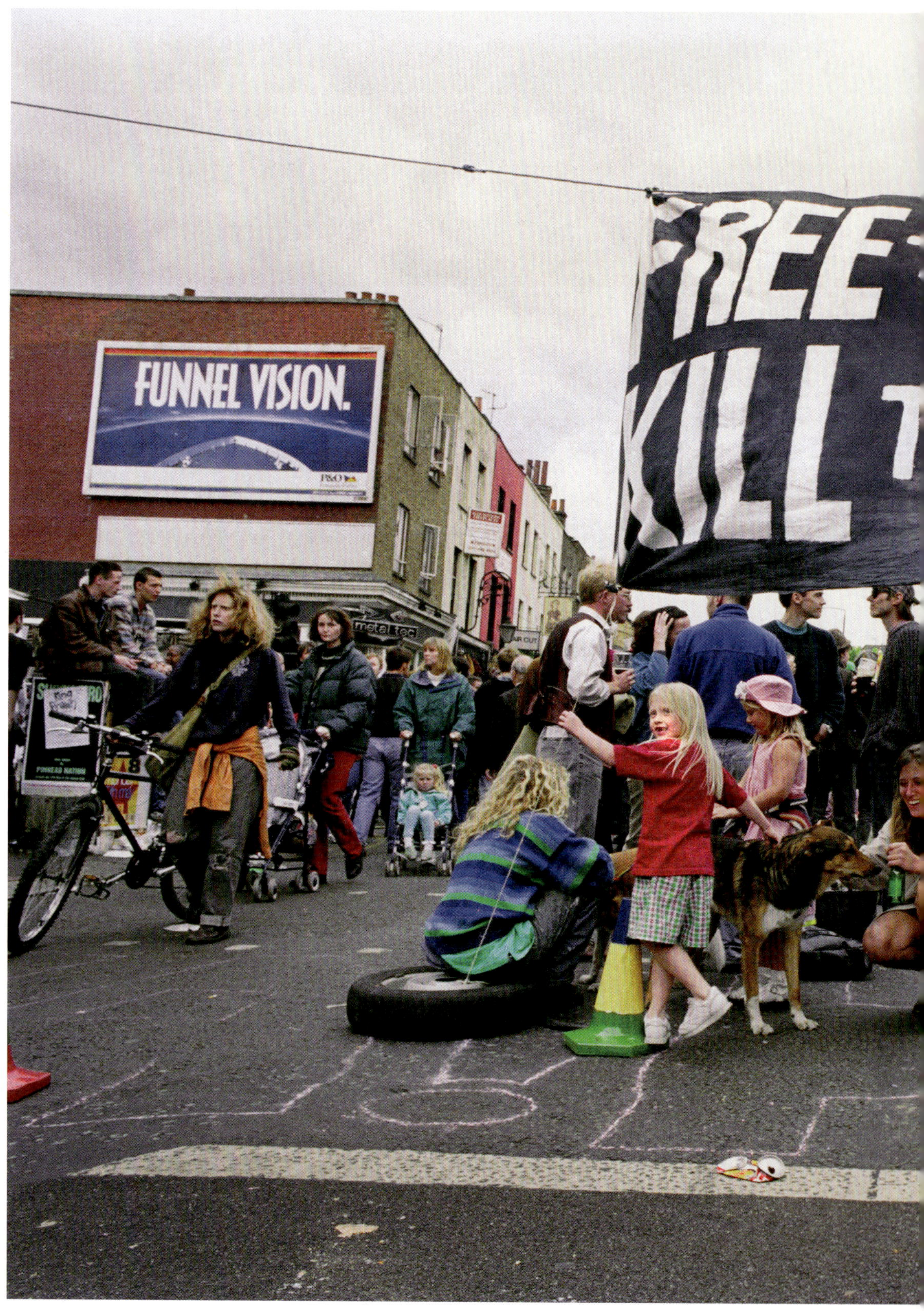

Reclaim the Streets: Camden

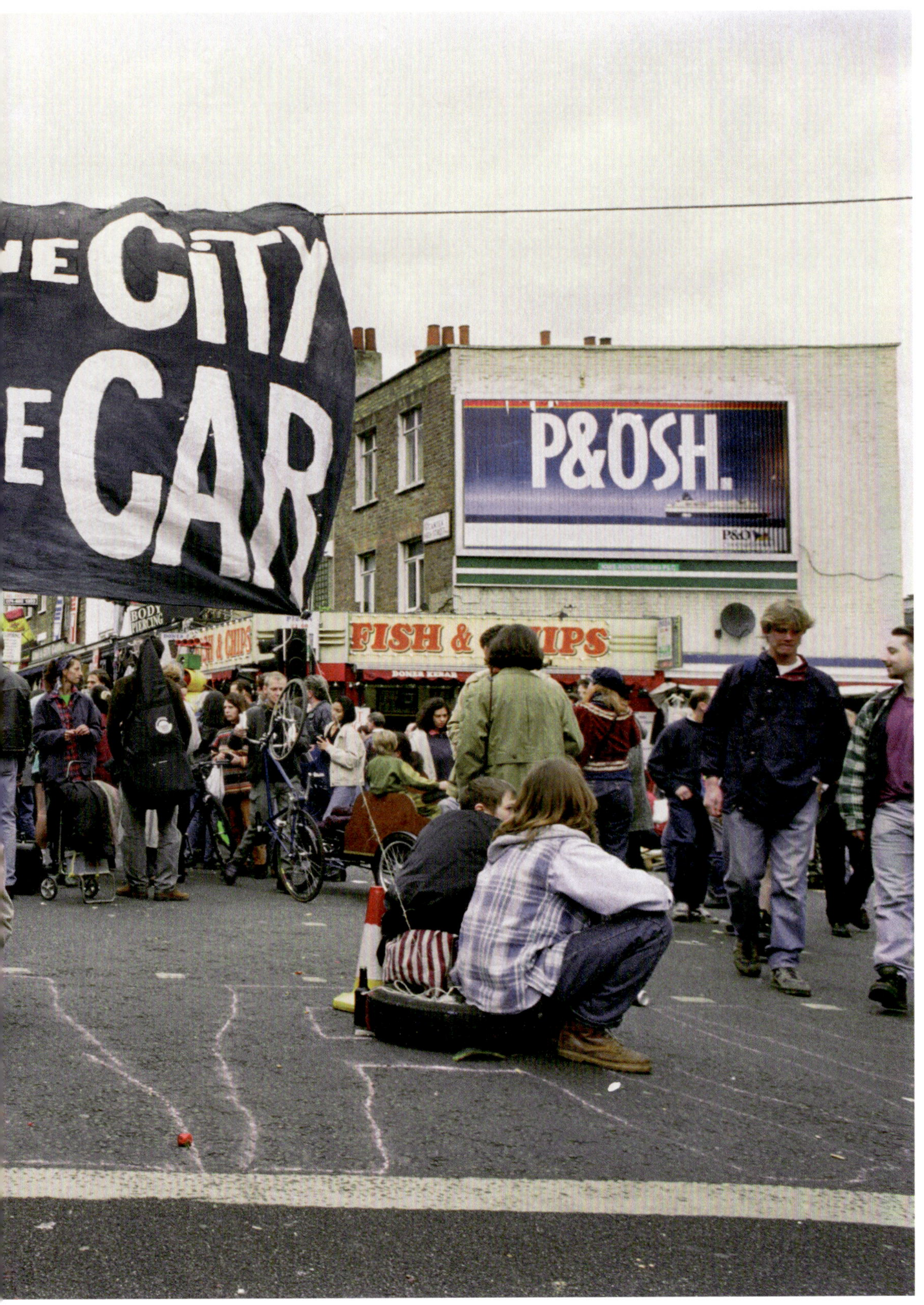
CITY
CAR
P&OSH.
FISH &
BODY PIERCING
DONER KEBAB

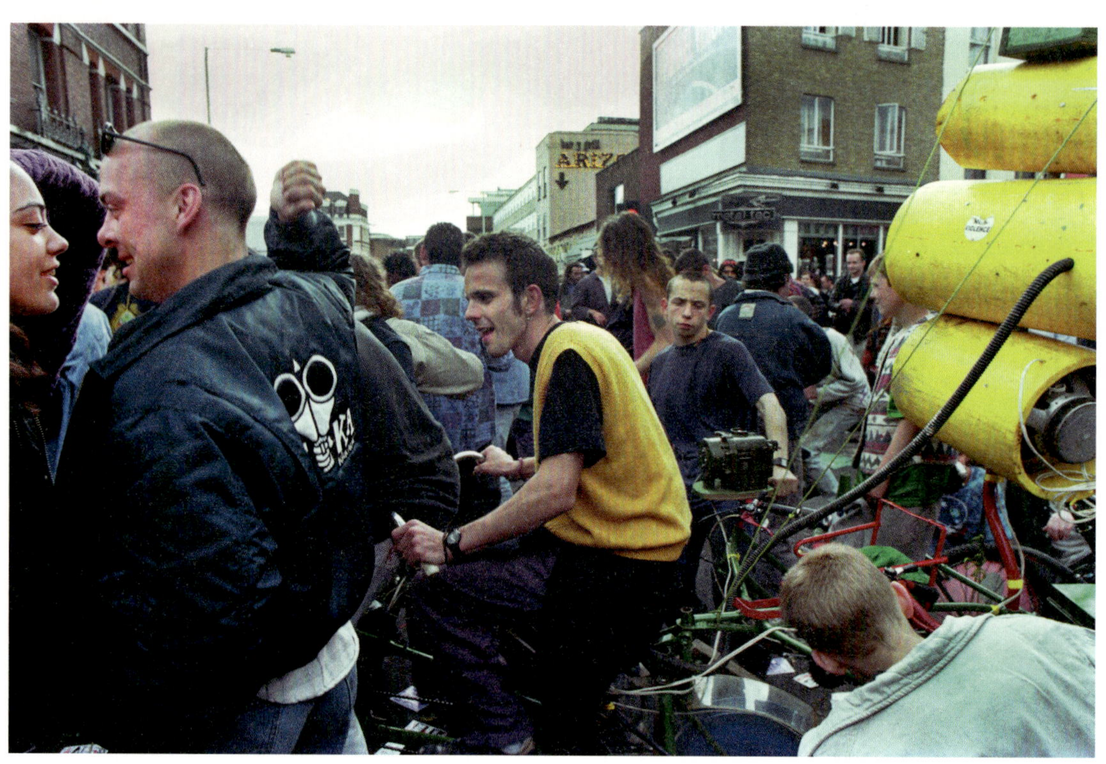

Reclaim the Streets: Camden

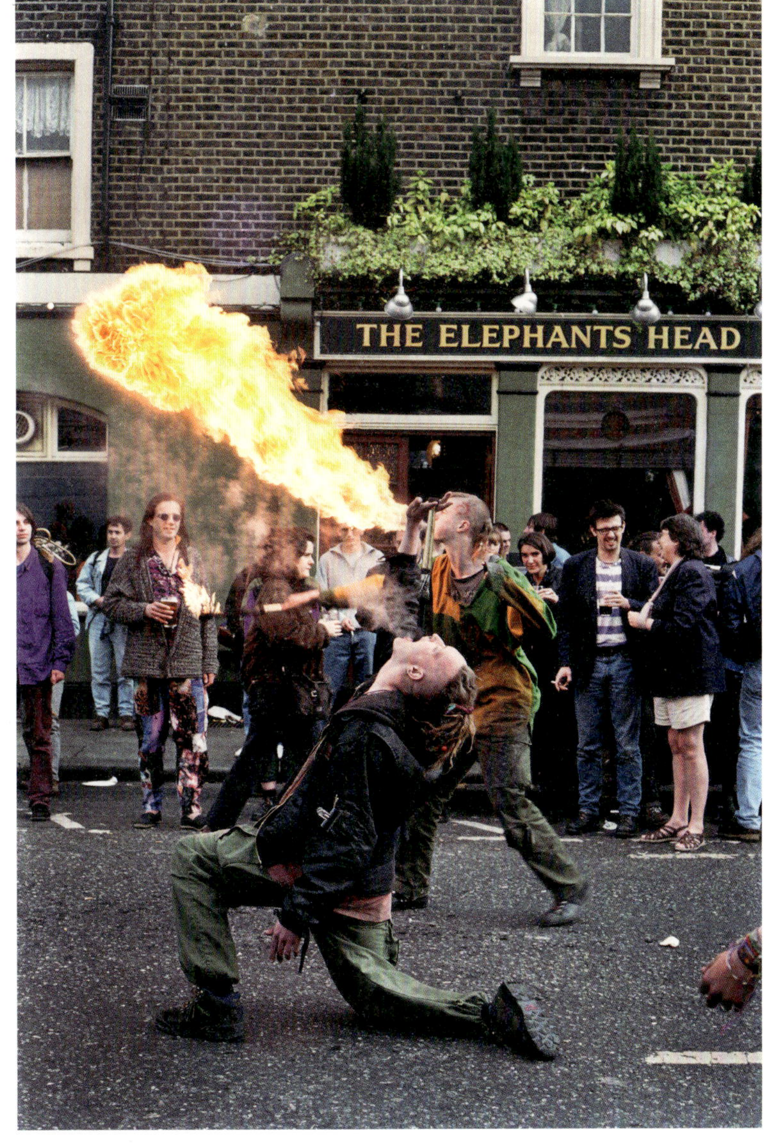
THE ELEPHANTS HEAD

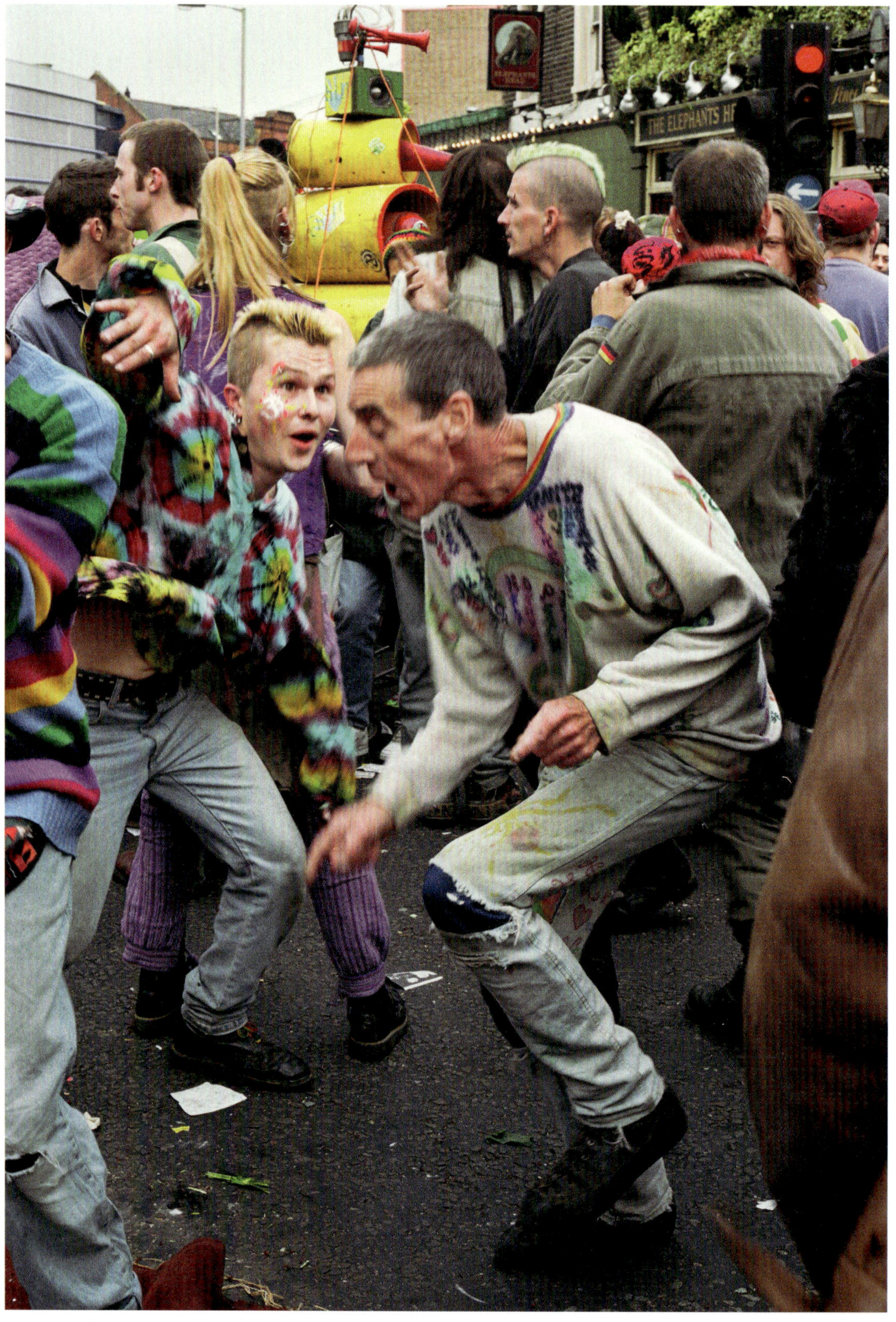

Reclaim the Streets: Camden

Reclaim the Streets: Islington July 1995

Meeting in Kings Cross the word went around to take the tube to Islington in North London. Hundreds crammed onto the platform, the atmosphere was electric: we knew we were about to shut down an important London road as an act of environmental protest. A man appeared from nowhere with a dog wrapped around his neck.

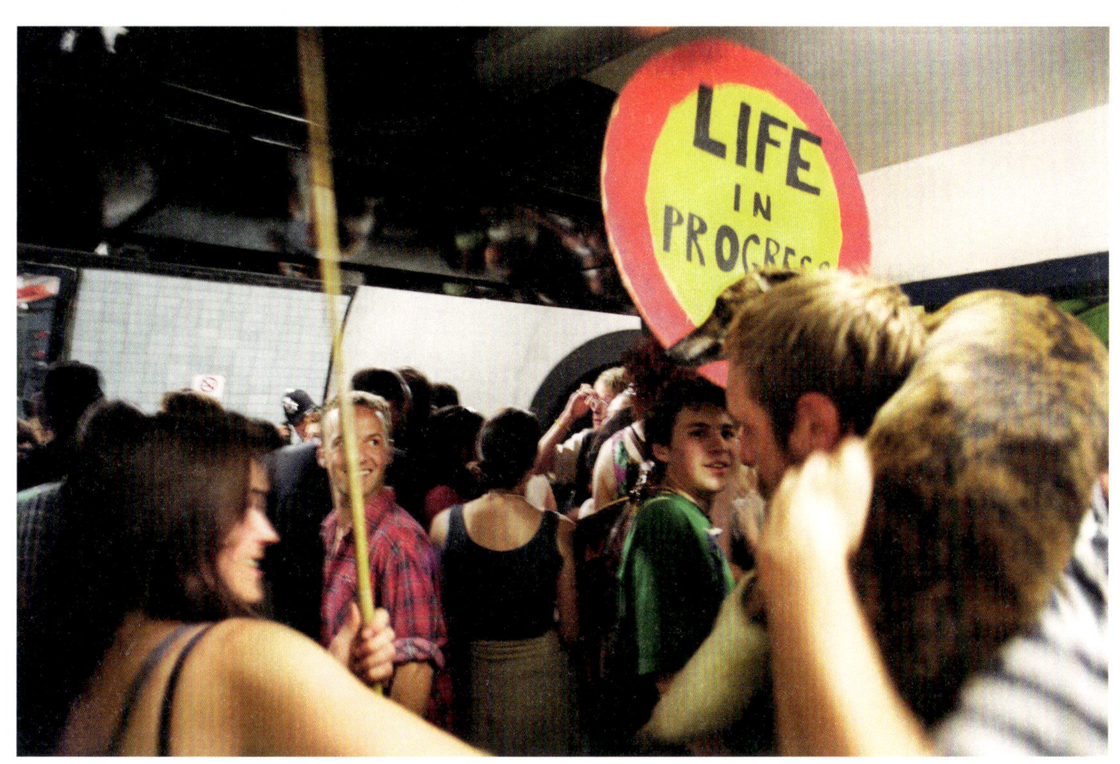
LIFE
IN

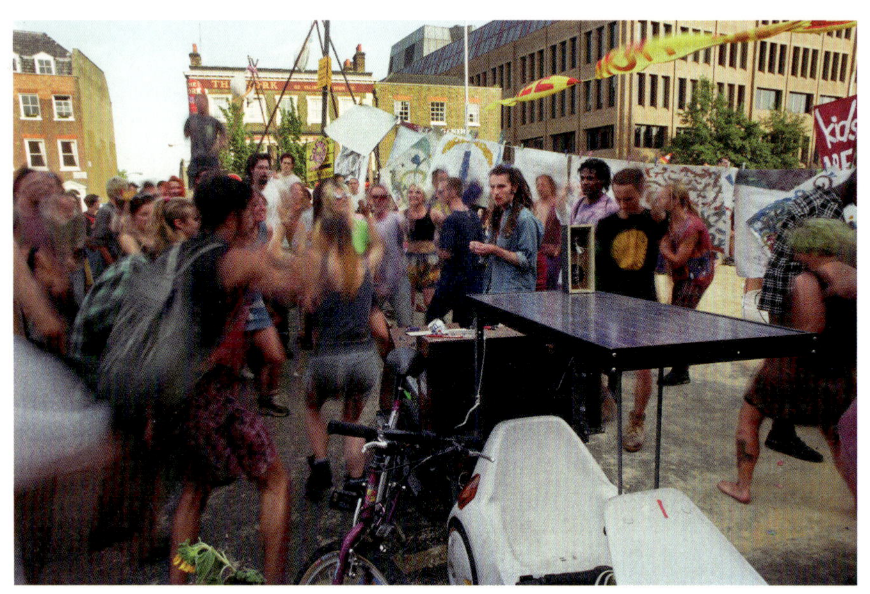

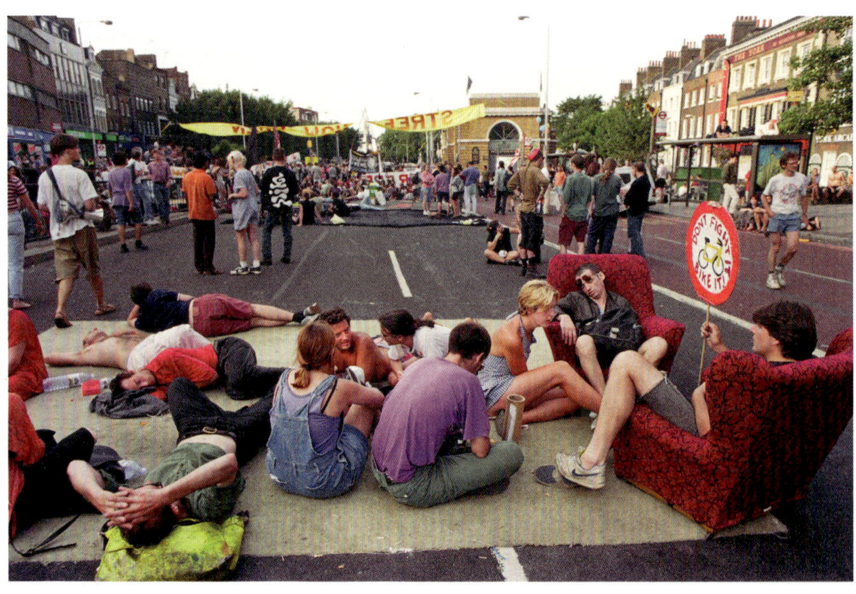

Reclaim the Streets: Islington

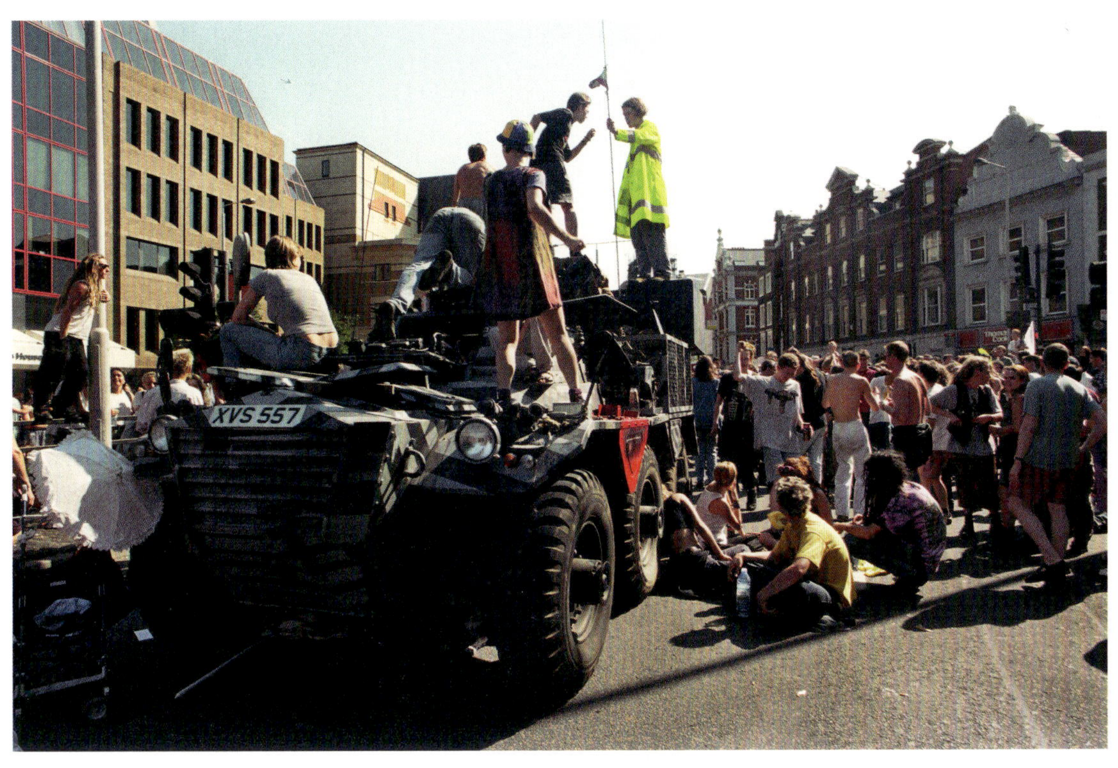

Once at Islington everyone spilled out on the street, stopping the traffic. A strange military vehicle appeared with a massive sound system playing Louis Armstrong's 'What a wonderful world'. Inside the tank-like structure was Jimmy Cauty from the KLF who started to DJ. At different points when the music was pumping he'd mix in what sounded like someone scrolling through different radio stations on an old fashioned knob radio dial. It was simultaneously surreal, arty, fun and annoying.

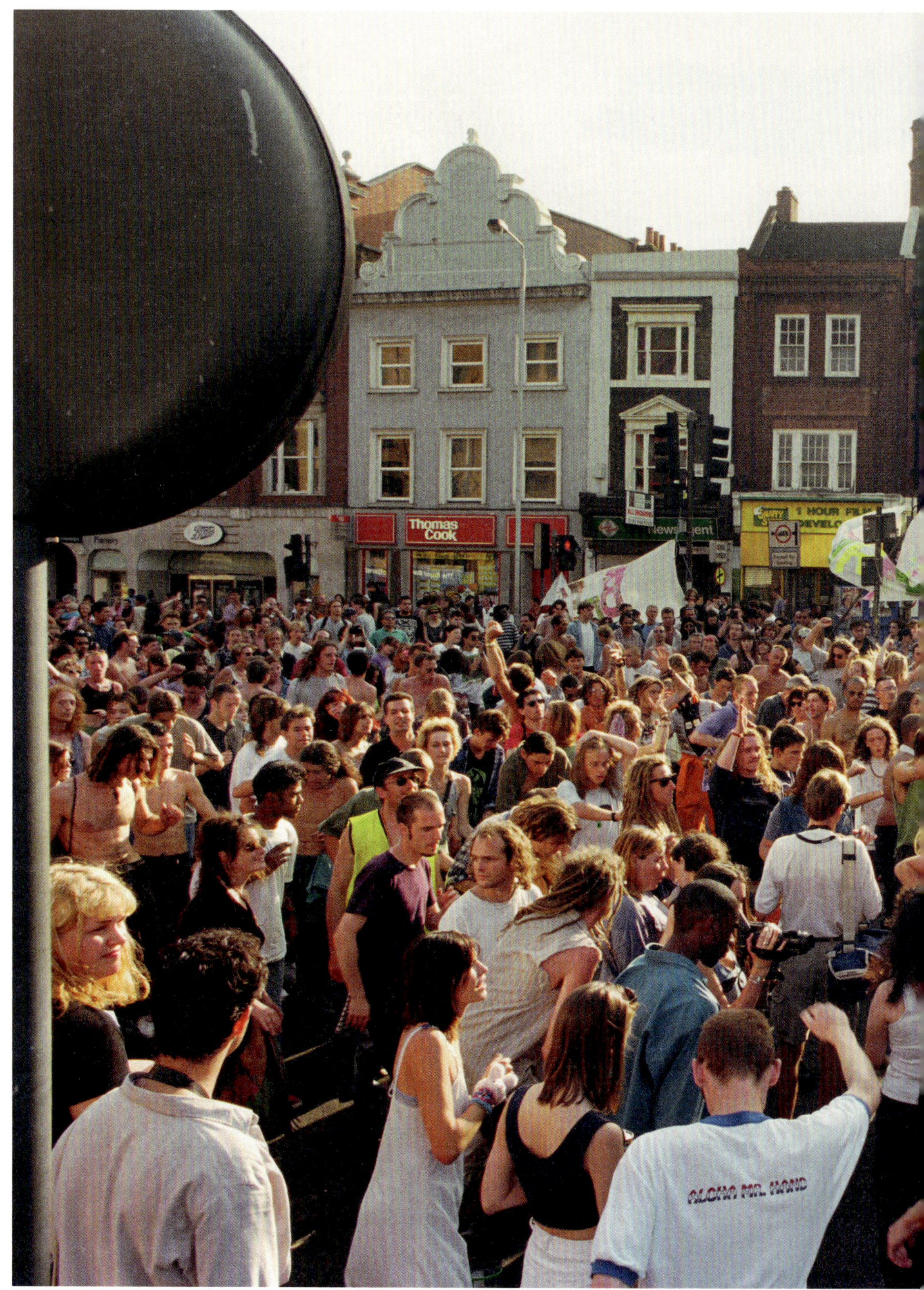

Reclaim the Streets: Islington

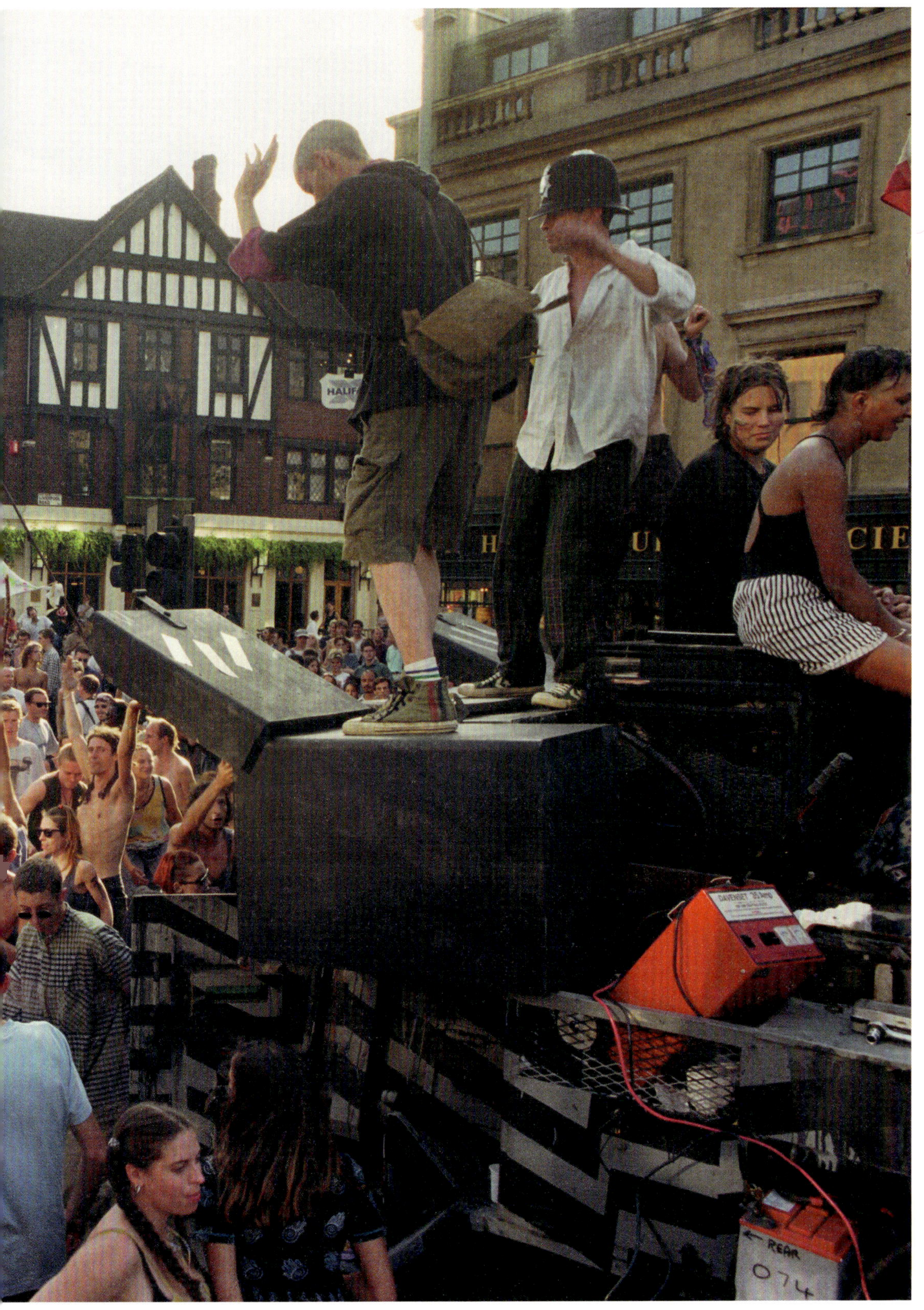
REAR
074

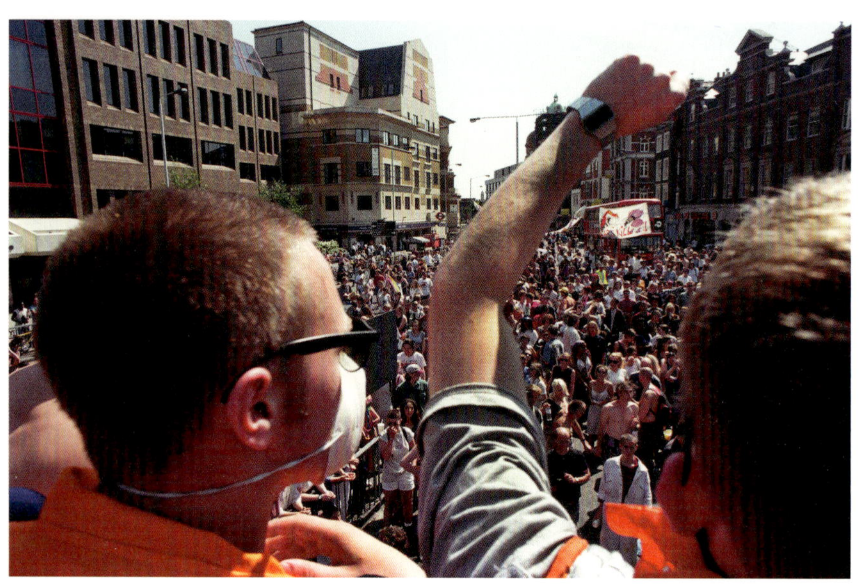

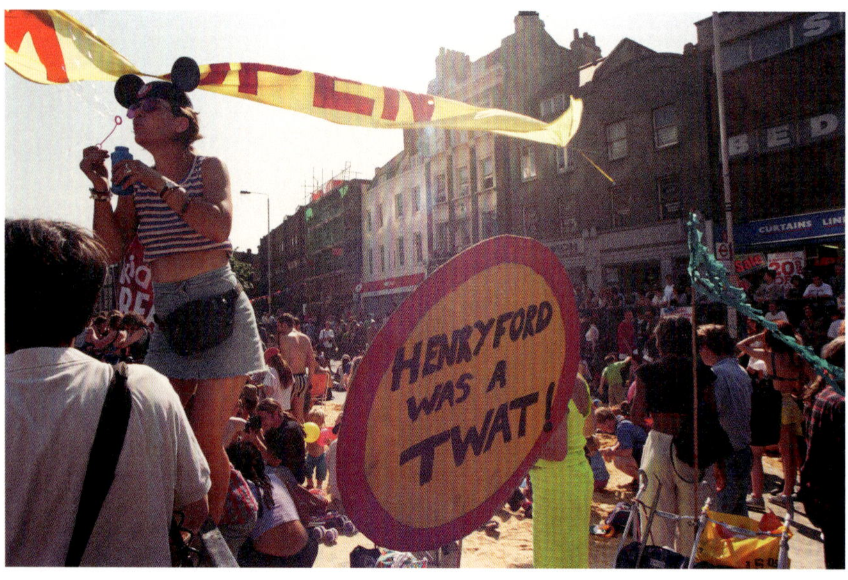

Reclaim the Streets: Islington

A couple of hours earlier it had been a road rammed with cars choking those who walked it with a toxin all too familiar on London's streets. Now it was a sandpit for children who looked out into a world of adults celebrating a car-free zone with laughter and dancing.

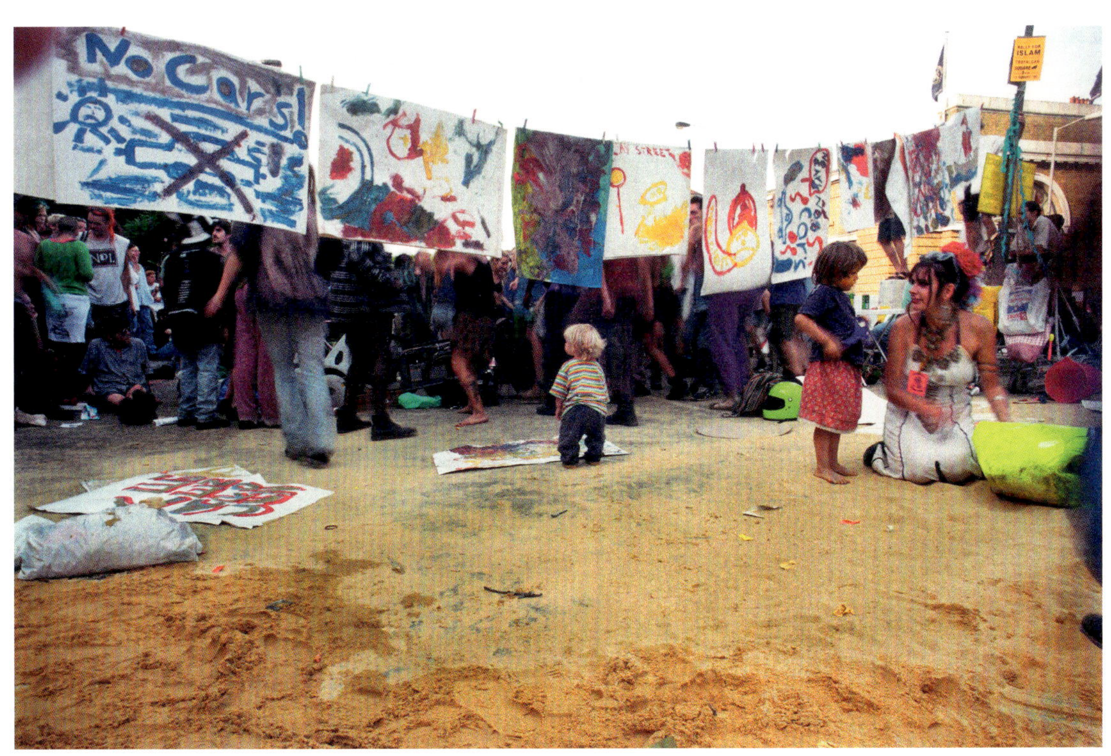

Reclaim the Streets: Streatham
August 1995

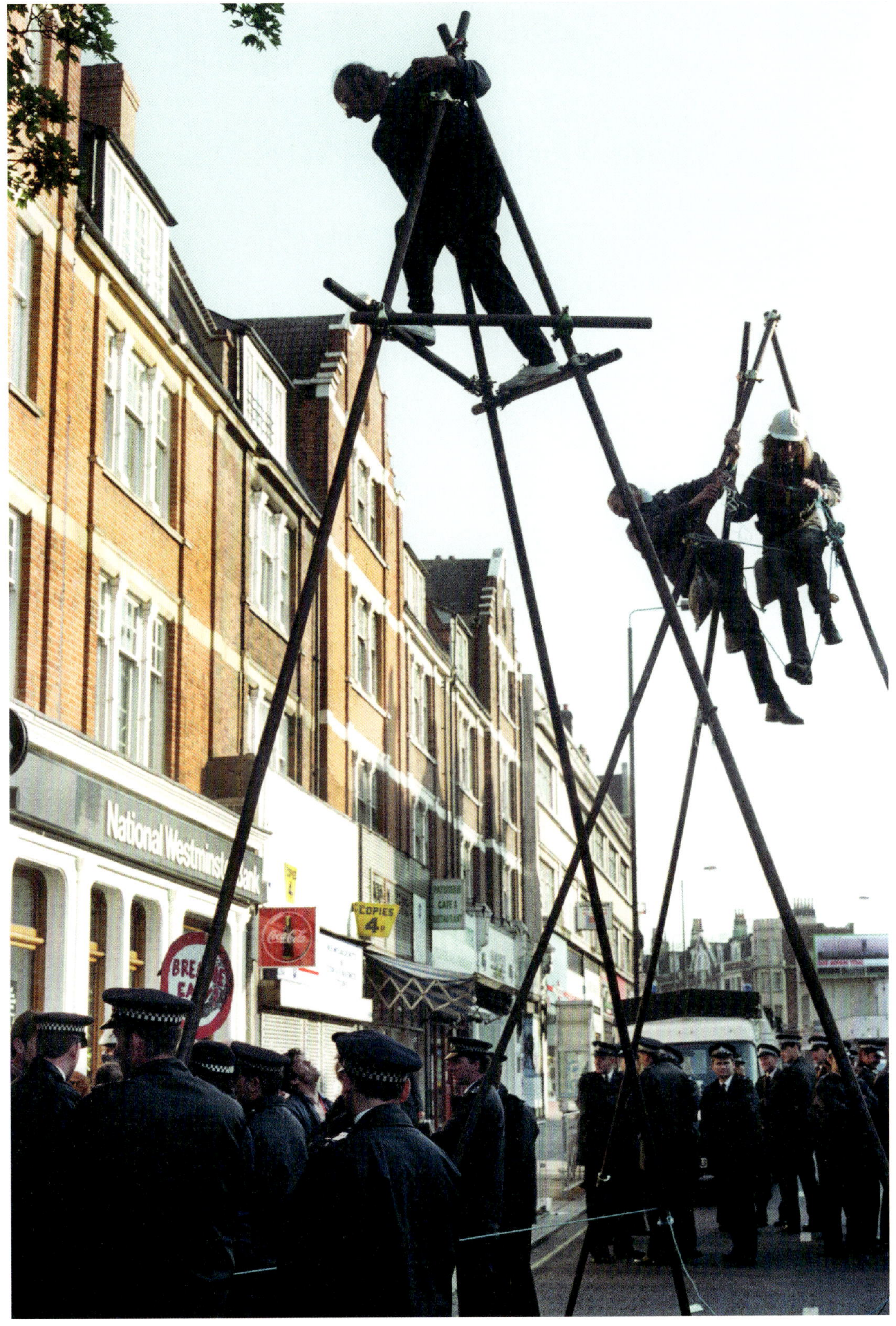
Coca-Cola
COPIES
4p

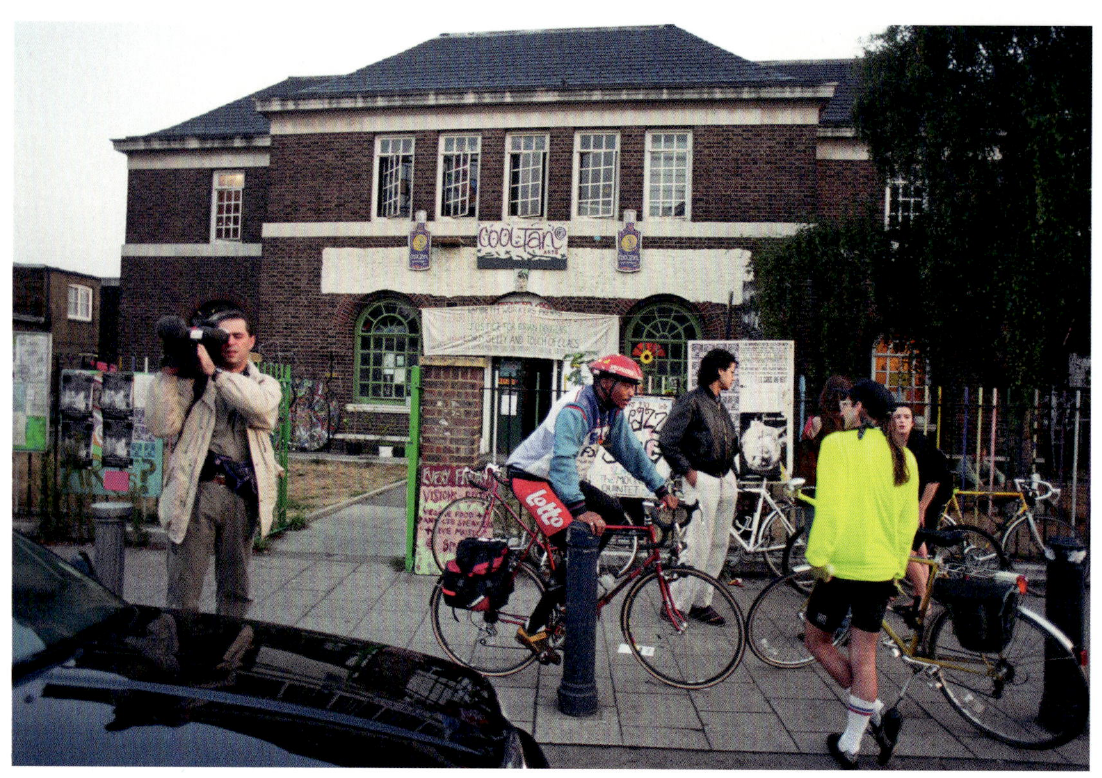

Early one summer morn before an action we met at the infamous Cool Tan Arts Centre, a squatted former unemployment benefit office in Brixton. This important building played an essential role in the activist movement of the 90's. A rambling space with a unique and vibrant atmosphere it allowed Reclaim the Streets and other activist movements like EarthFirst! to coordinate direct action campaigns from its base. Within its walls plotting, scheming and coordinating all took place with the occasional inspiration from one of Cool Tan's legendary techno parties.

Reclaim the Streets: Streatham

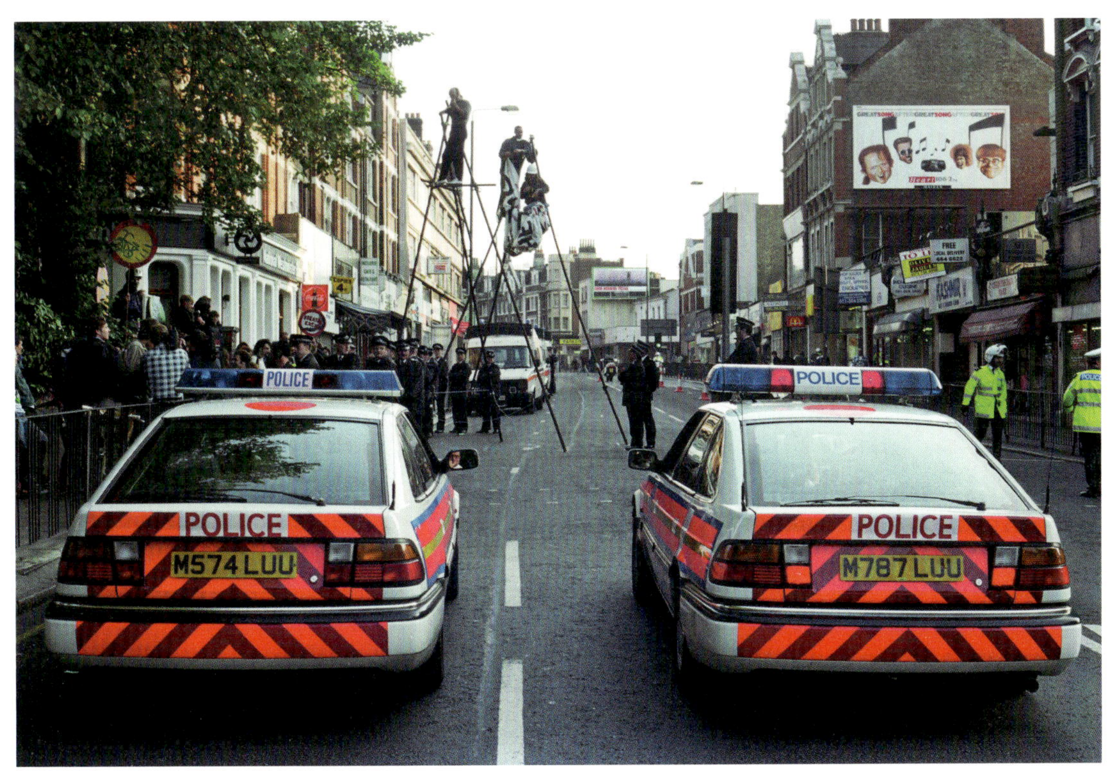
POLICE
POLICE
M574 LUU
POLICE
POLICE
M787 LUU

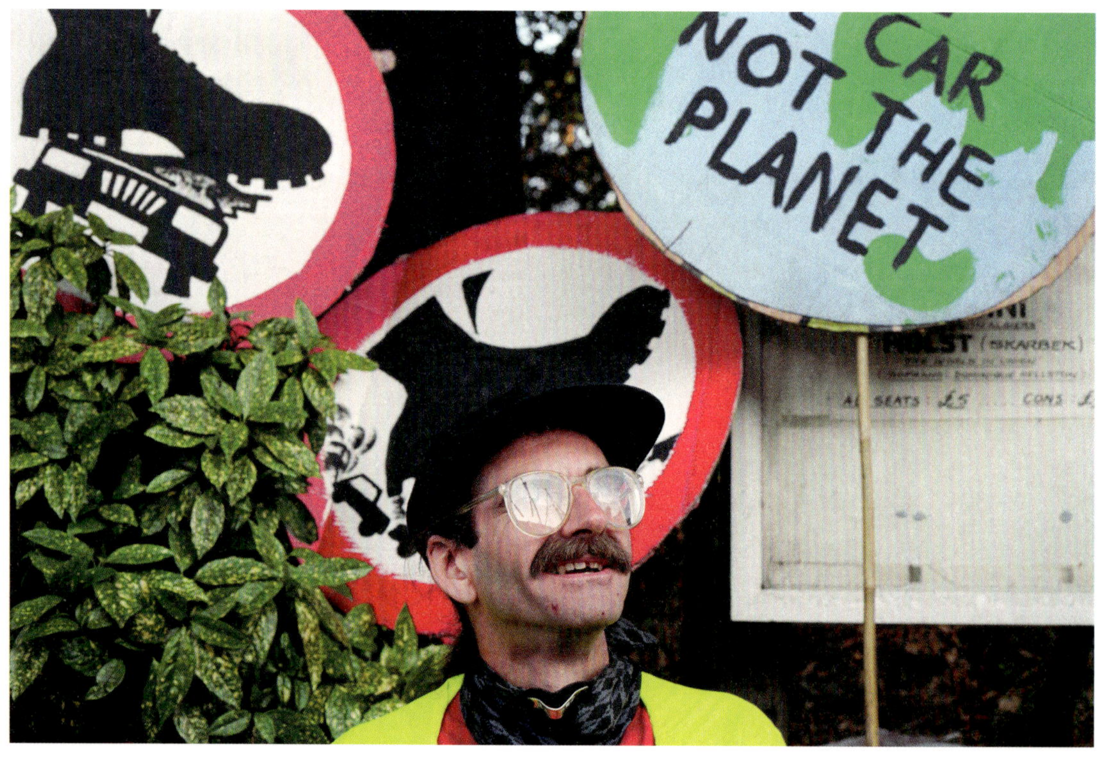

Reclaim the Streets: Streatham

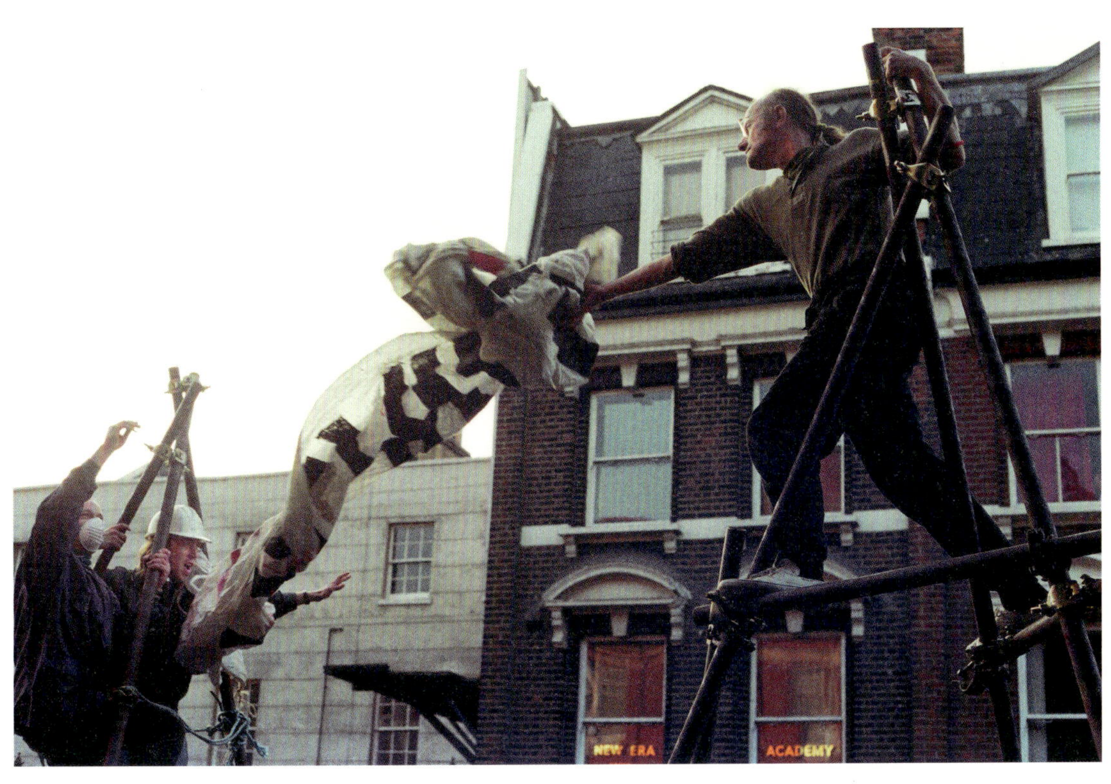

In the early rush hour morning traffic on one of the main arteries into South London a committed group of activists lay in wait for the sound of a whistle. As soon as its shrill call punctuated the fume-laden air those taking action jumped out into the road with scaffolding poles that were erected into neat tripods with exact movements in less than two minutes. The police who were already present made a desperate attempt to stop the action. Reclaim the Streets, with their military precision, were one step ahead.

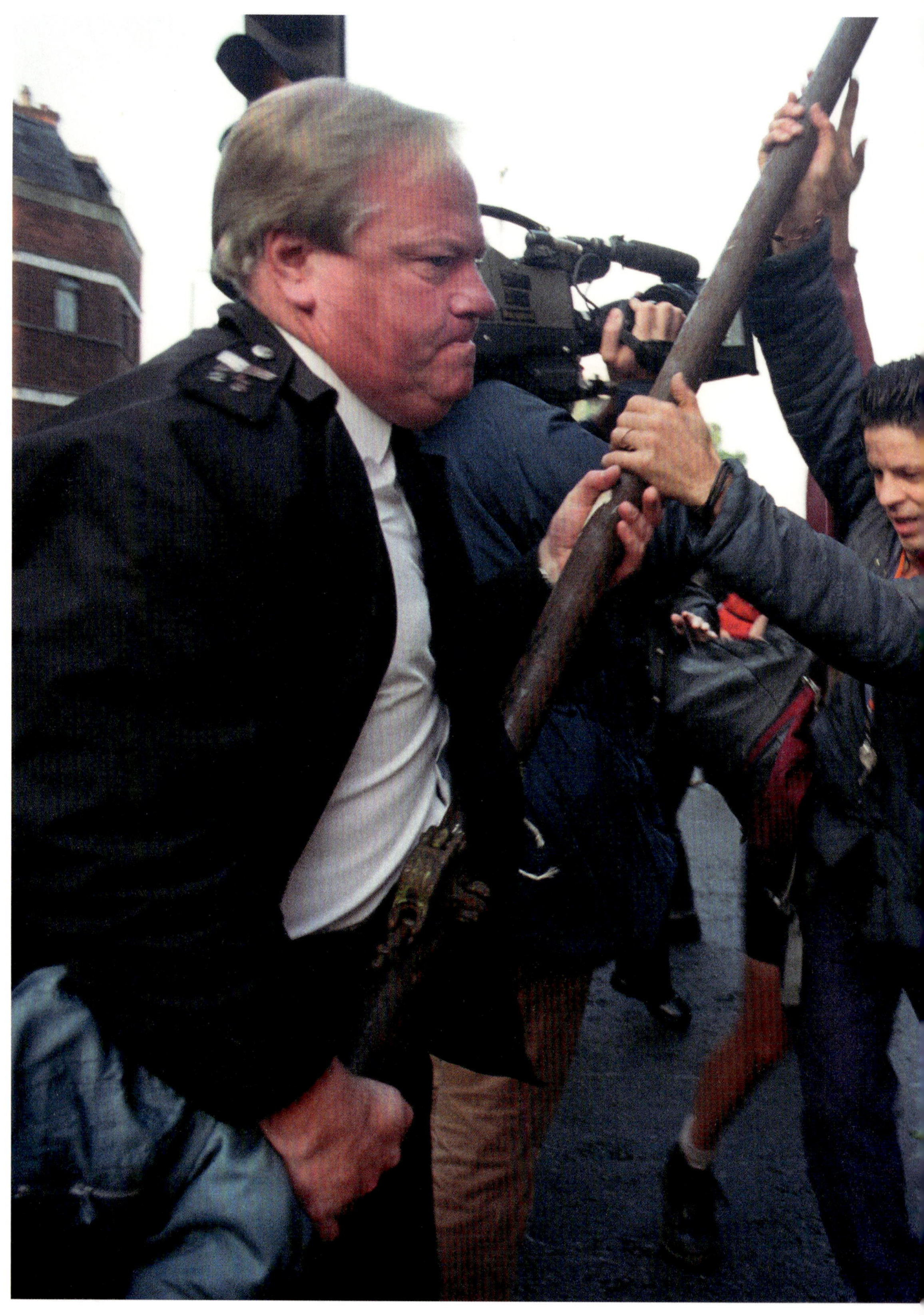

Reclaim the Streets: Streatham

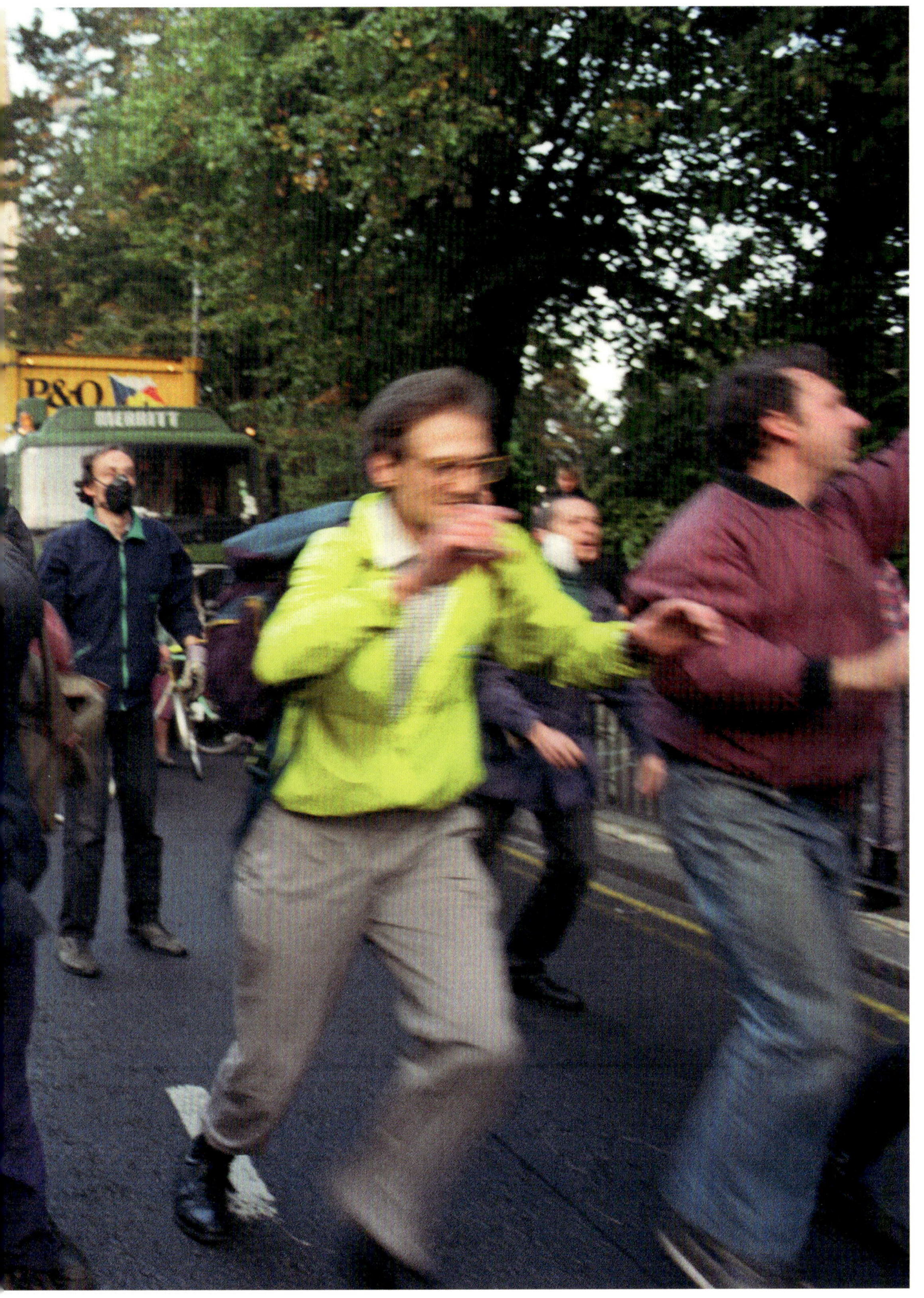
P&O

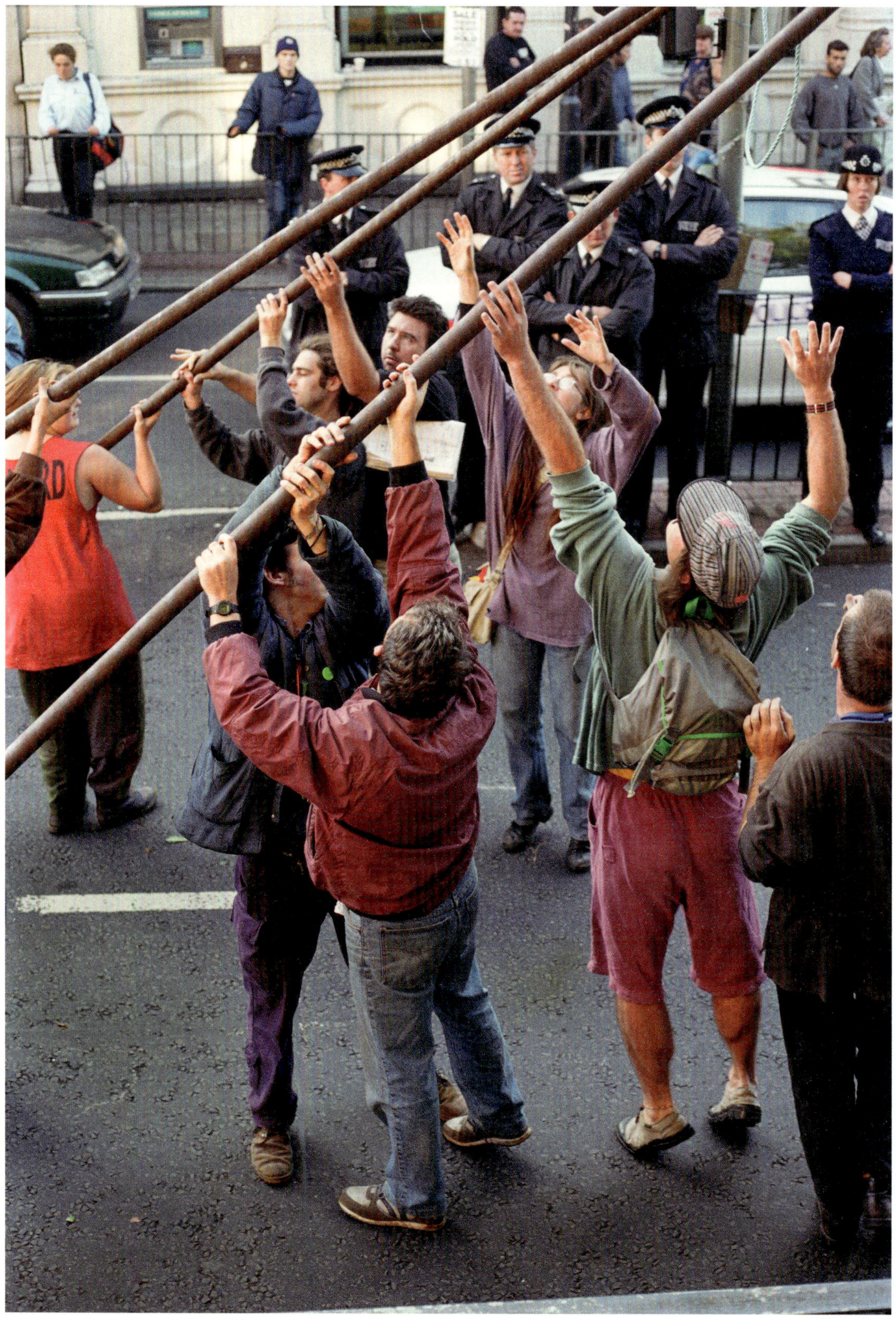

Reclaim the Streets: Streatham

East London: M11
September 1995

The final days of the M11 campaign in Leyton was a reminder that all too often governments from across the world oppose the desperate cries drawing attention to the slow destructive death our precious planet is being exposed to. Those forces can be seen here, ever oppressive, shutting down and arresting dissent, locking up those who could see the insanity of what we were doing. Understanding where our world is heading won't be found looking to the mainstream of society. Instead look to those on the fringes, among the oddballs, the strange ones, those who see the world with a vision: they'll be the ones that have the answers.

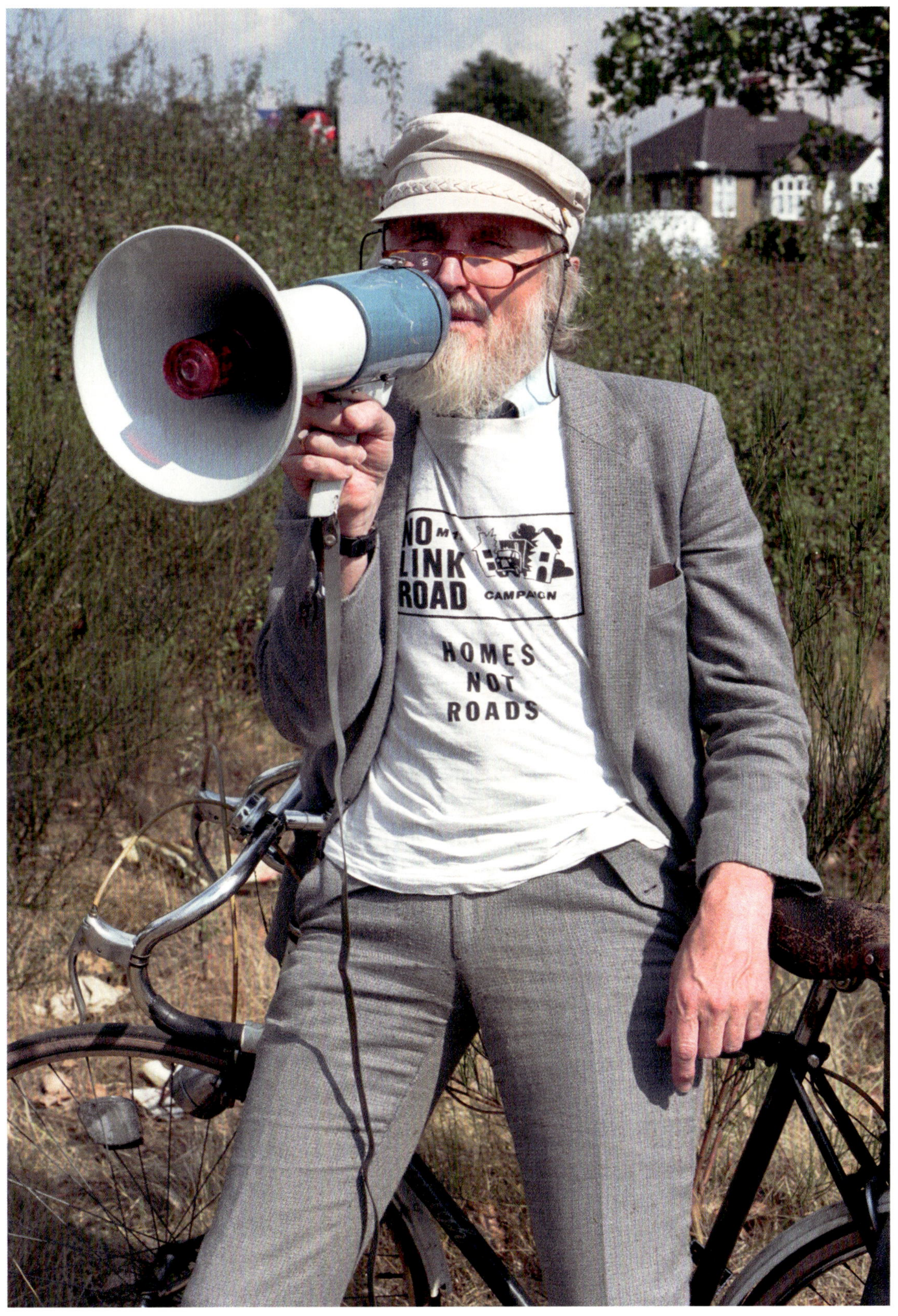
NO M11 LINK ROAD CAMPAIGN
HOMES NOT ROADS

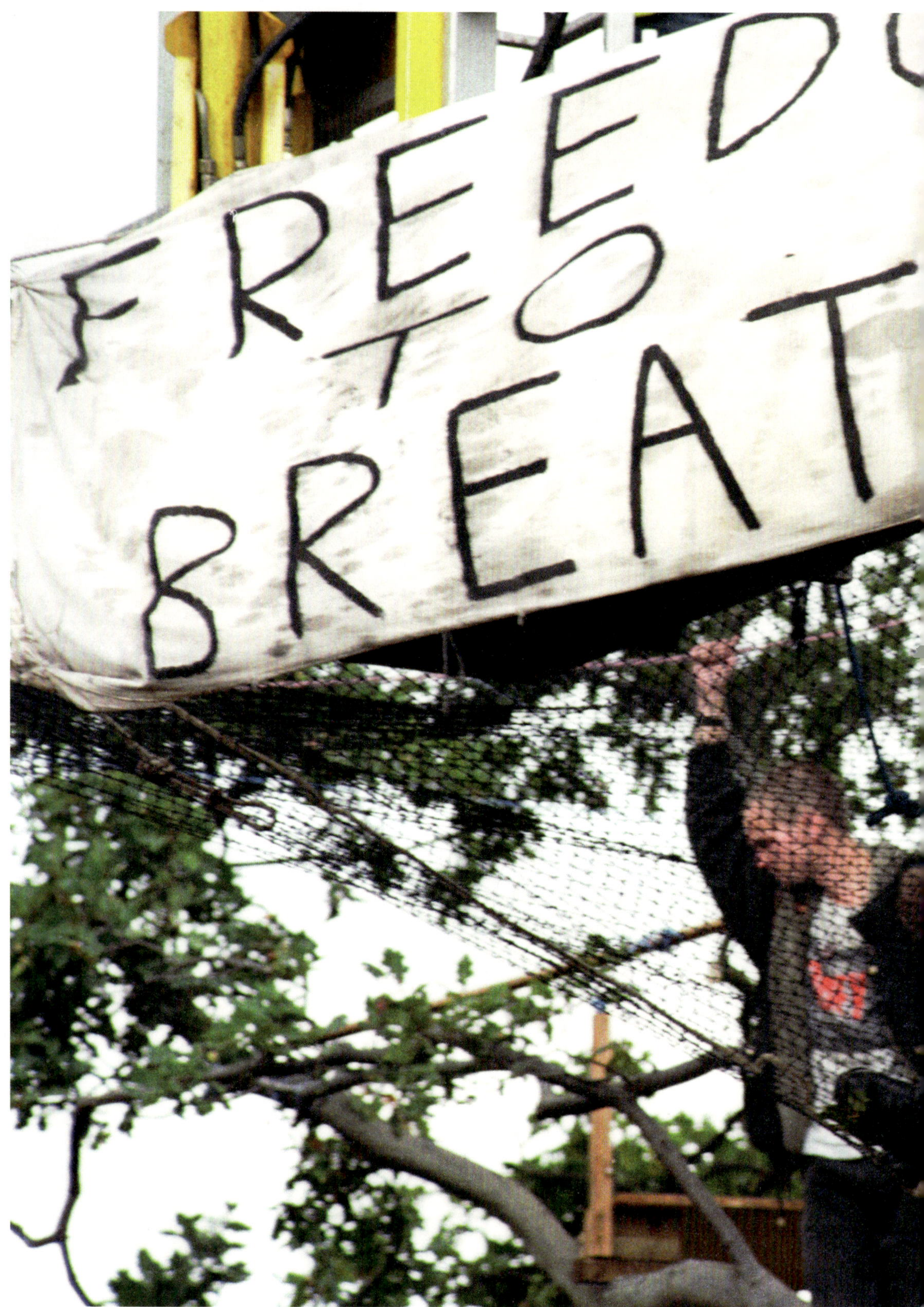

East London: M11

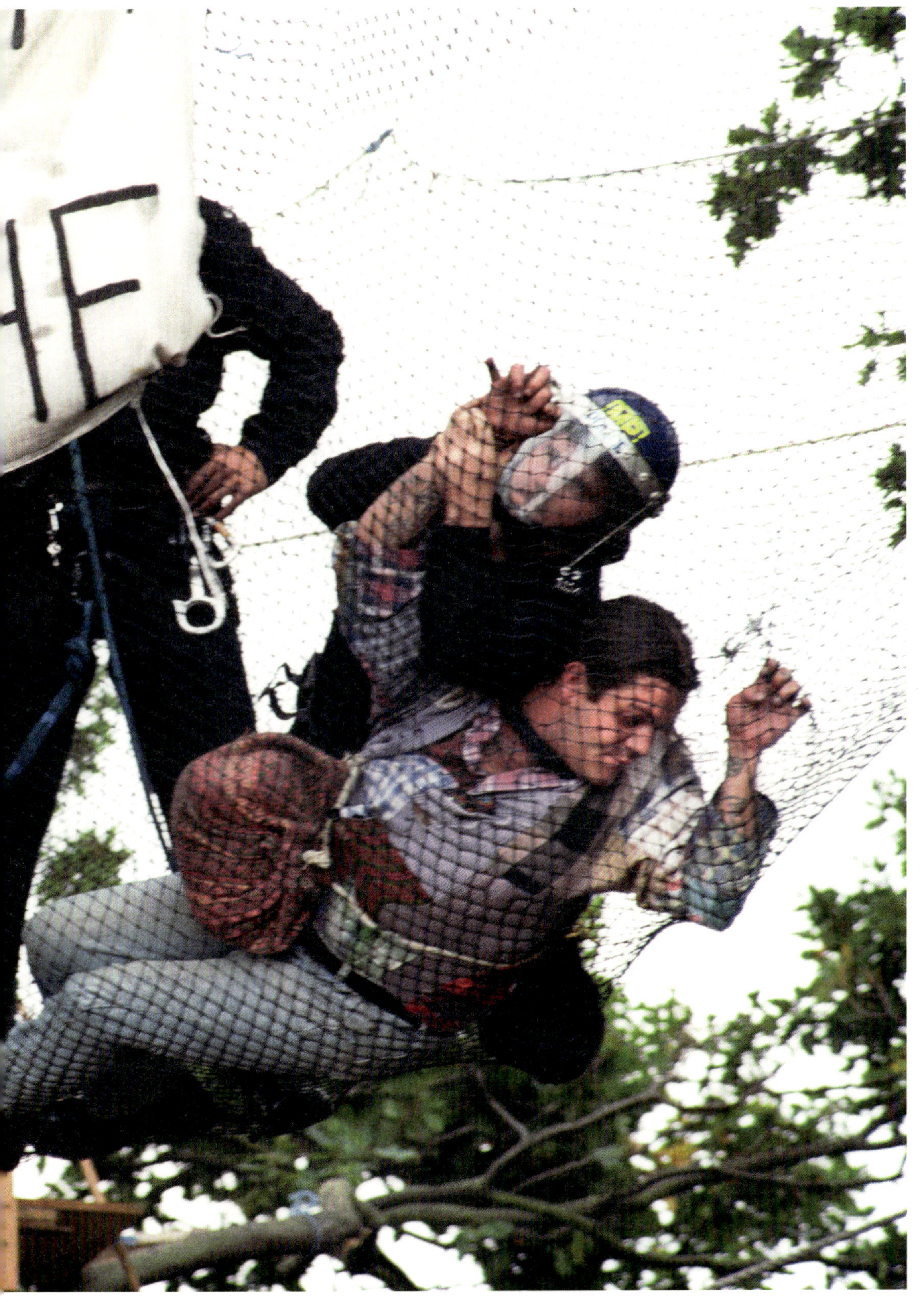

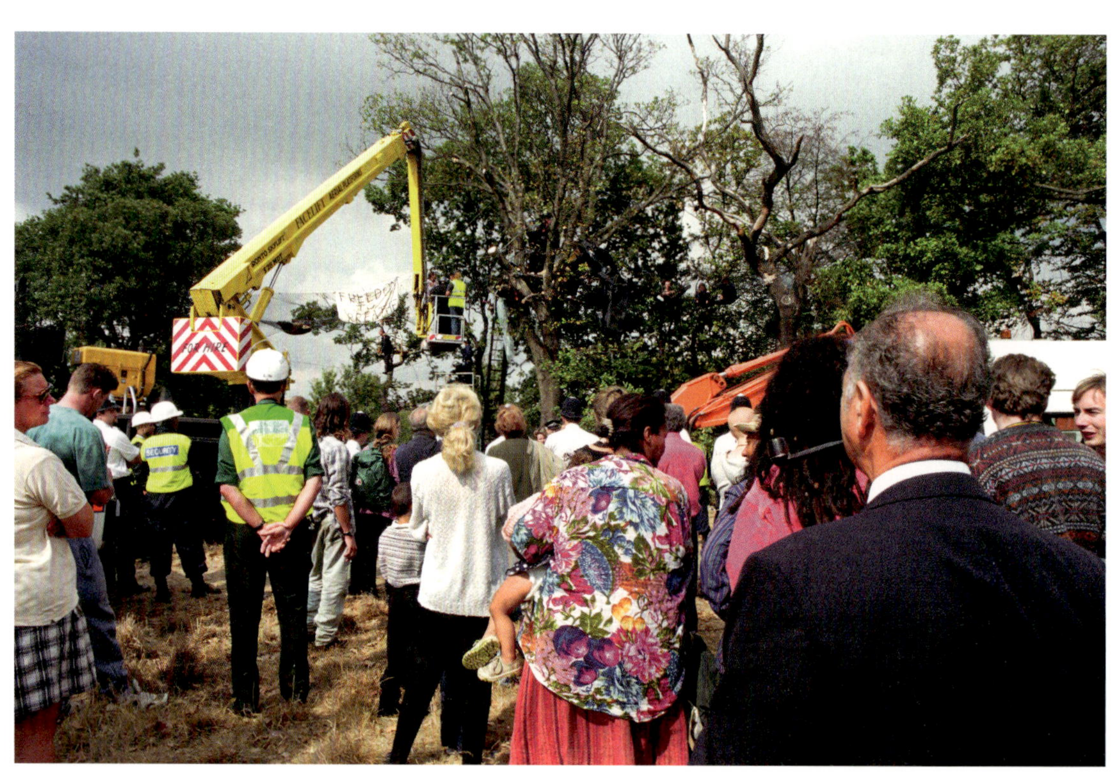

East London: M11

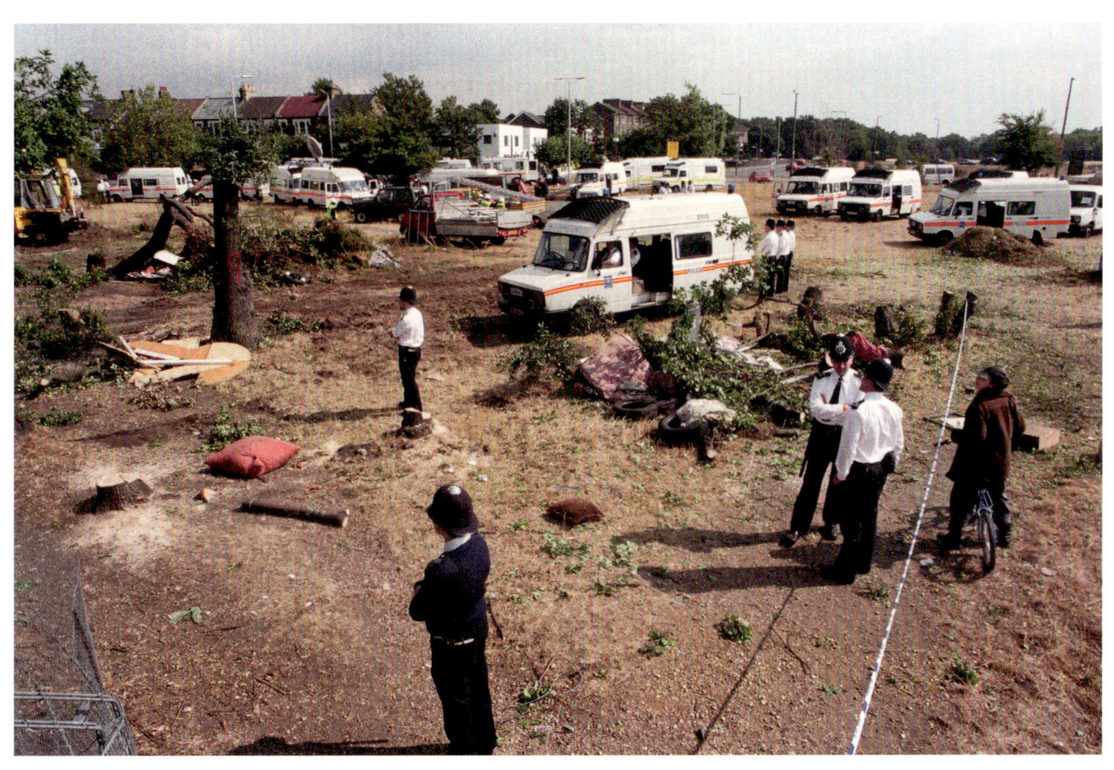

Newbury Bypass
August 1995 – April 1996

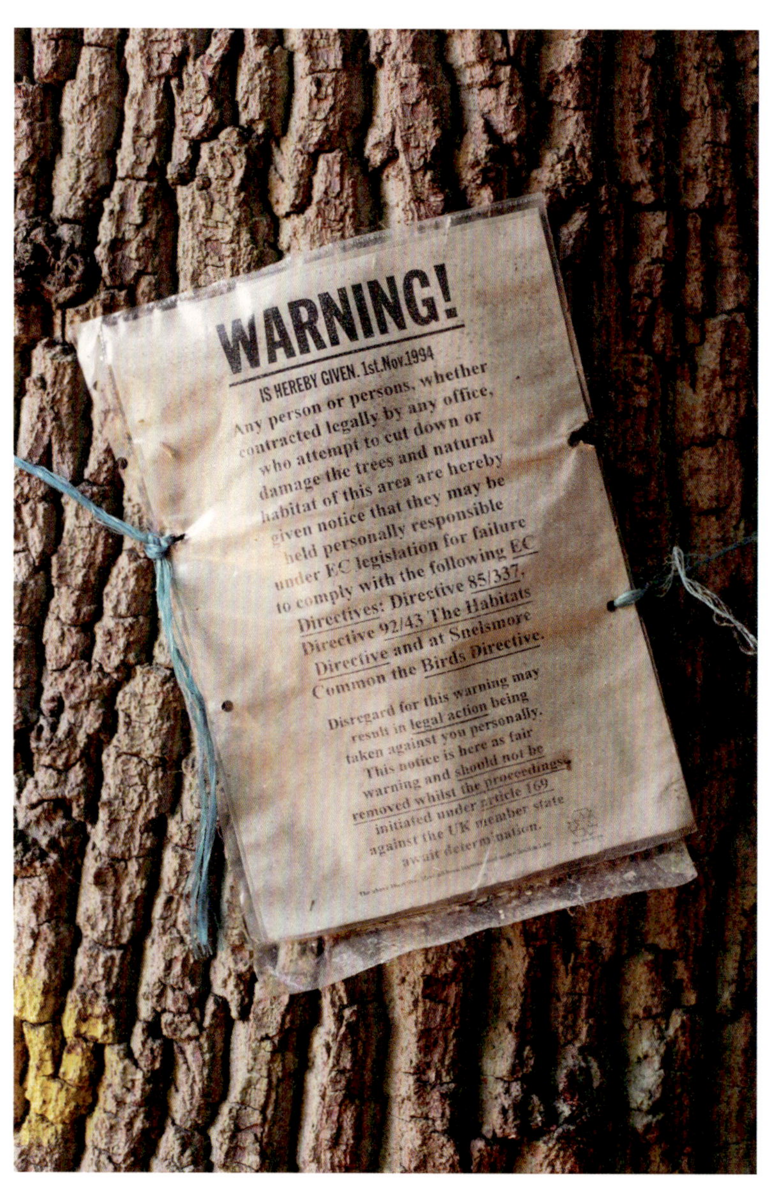

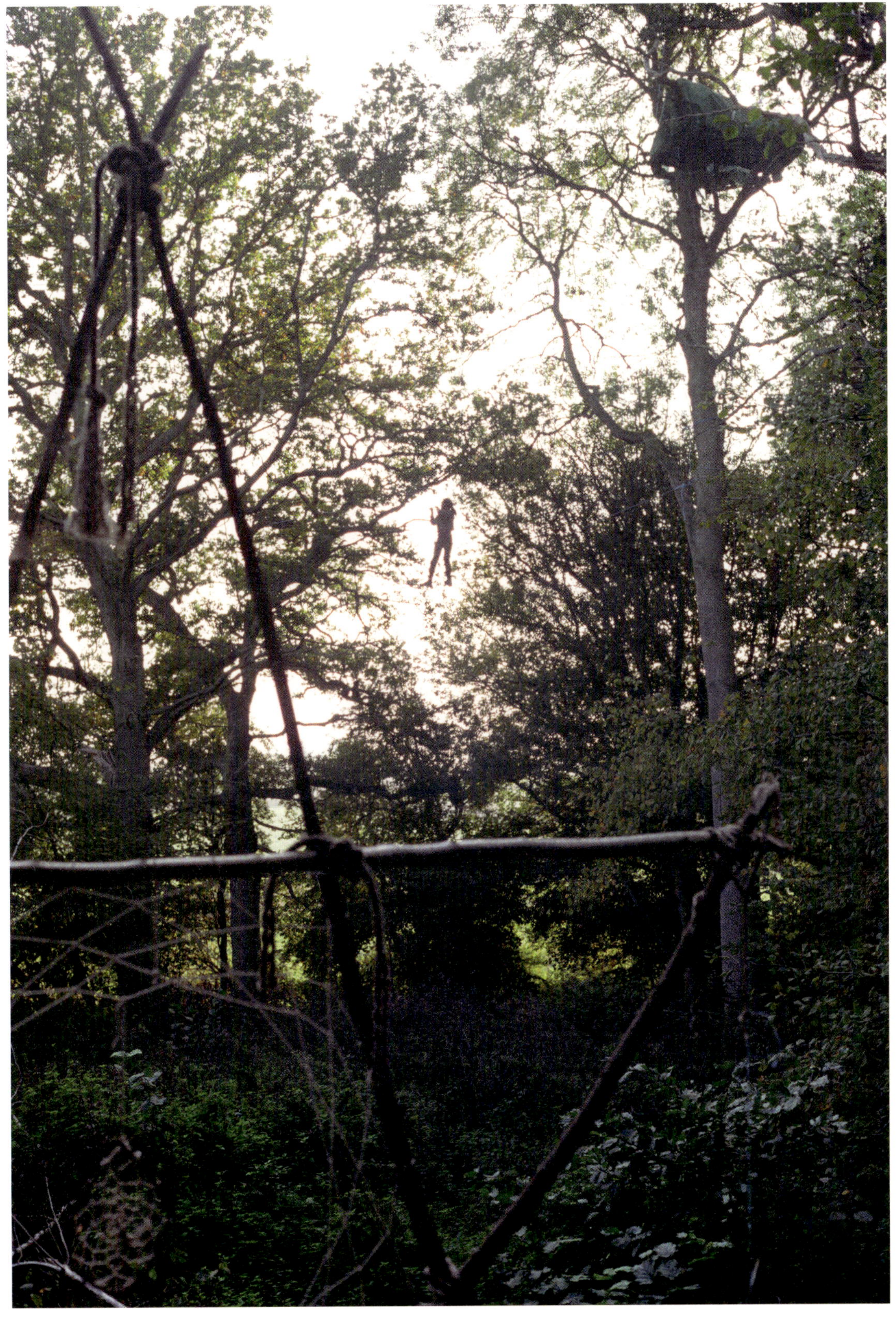

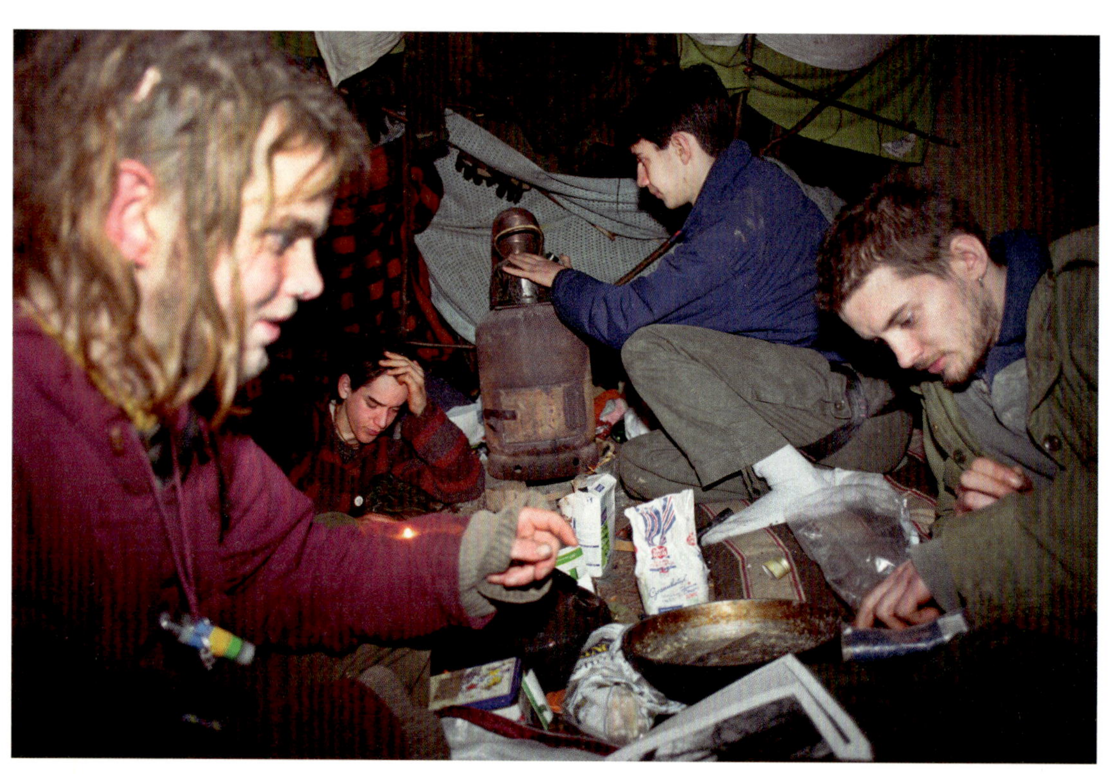

Newbury Bypass

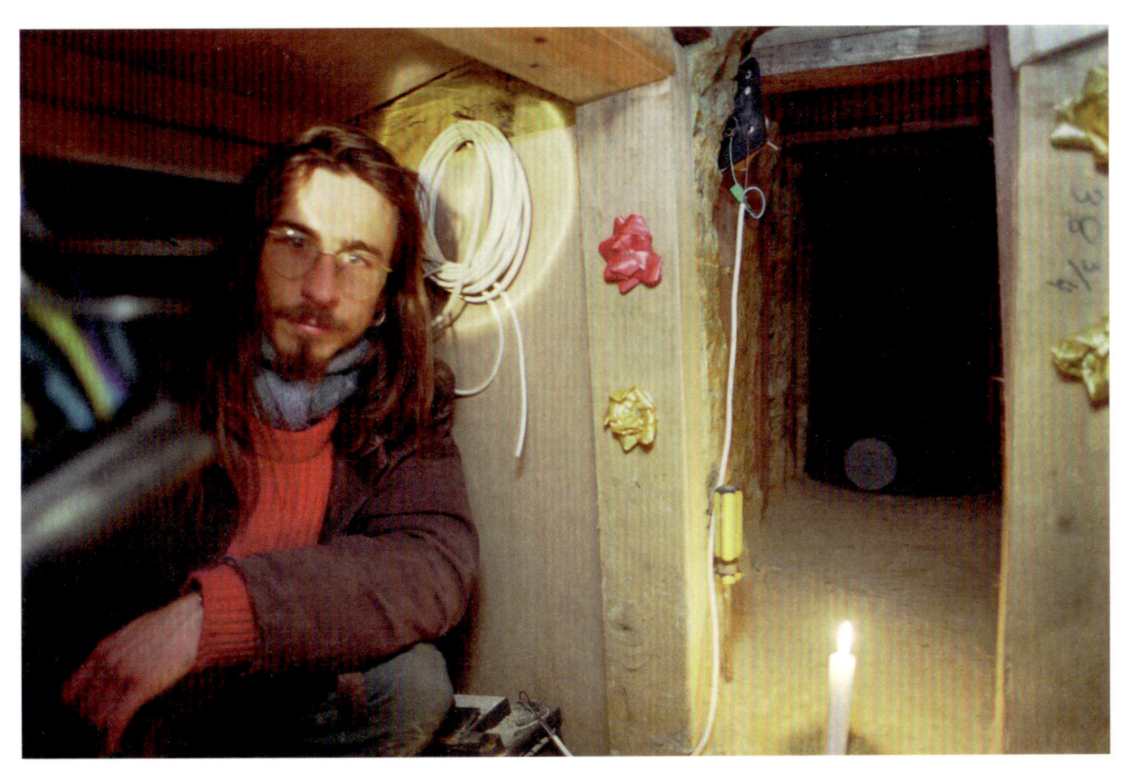

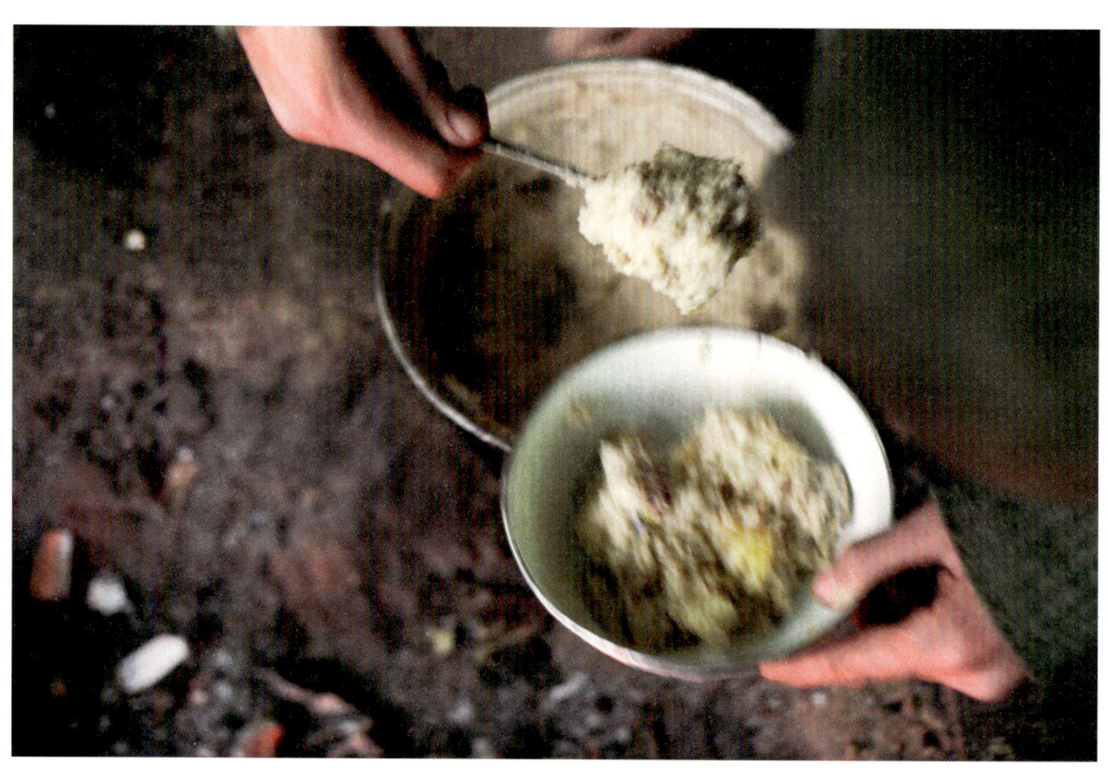

Newbury Bypass

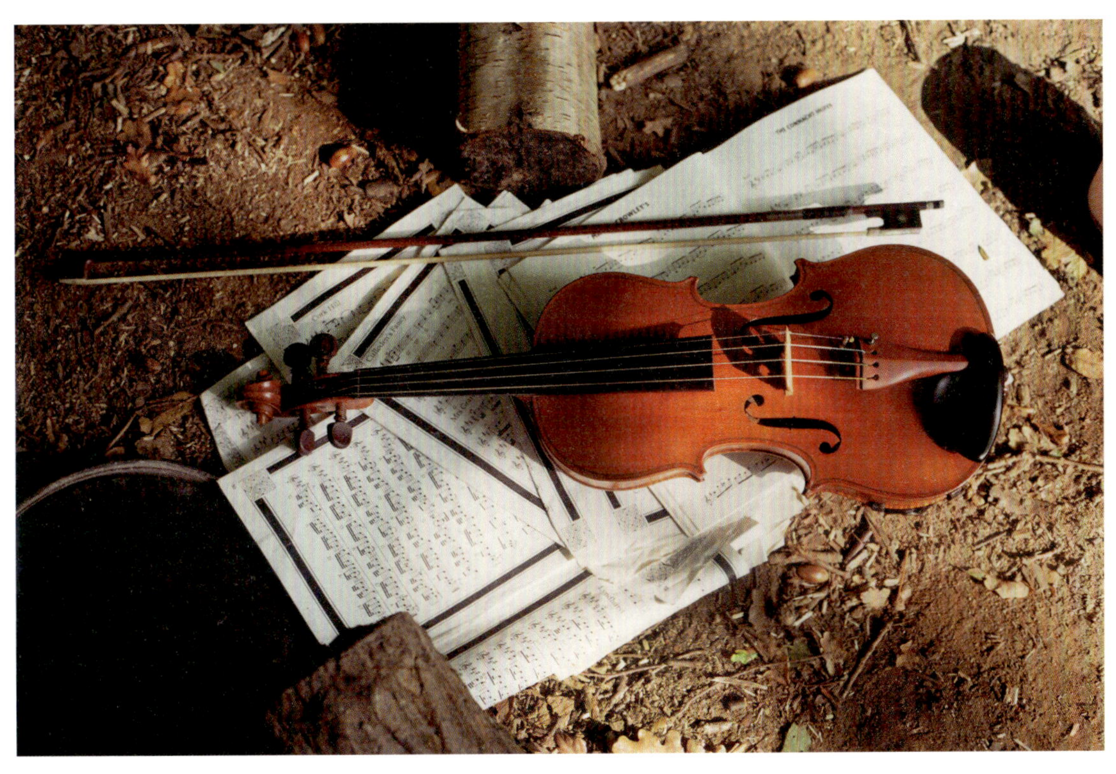

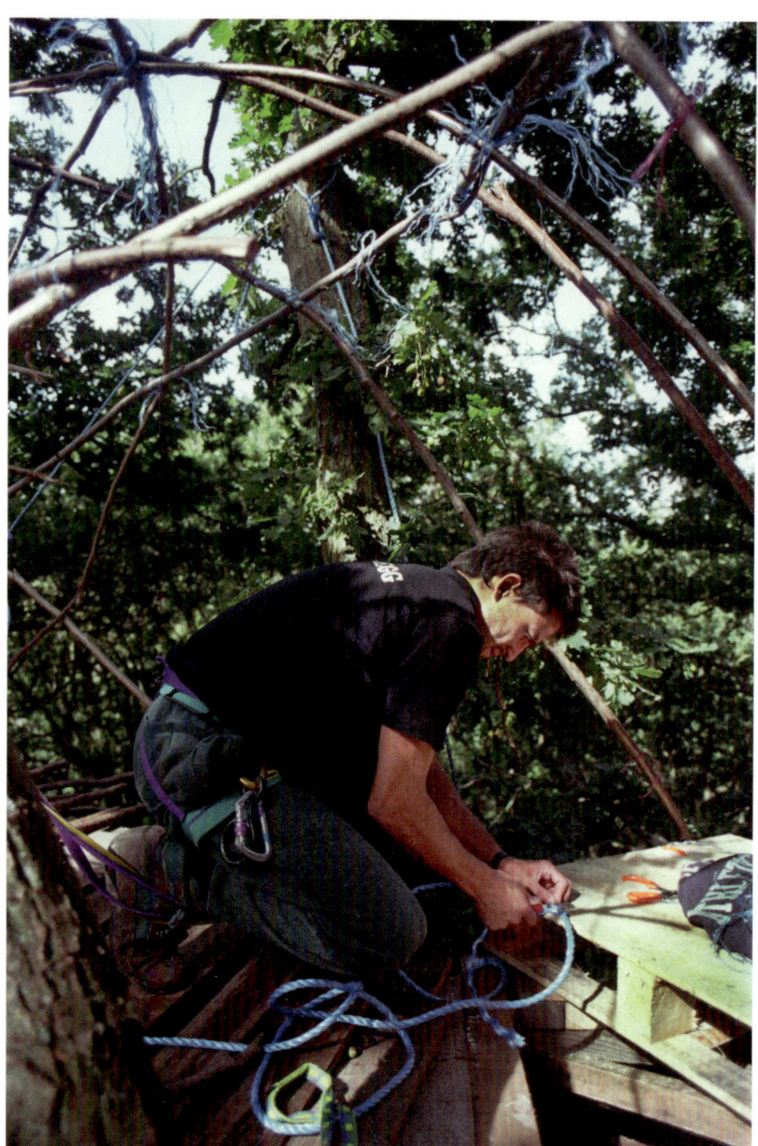

Newbury Bypass

Tree hugging I suspect has gone on for centuries. It's that moment of wrapping your arms around a living organism so big and powerful it can only calm and reassure you. As if embracing an ancestor, a many times great-grandparent from hundreds of years past, whispering into your ear: 'Don't worry, it's going to be okay'. Strange how such a profound moment of connection with nature became a derogatory term used to poke fun at those who fought for the planet. No-one's laughing now.

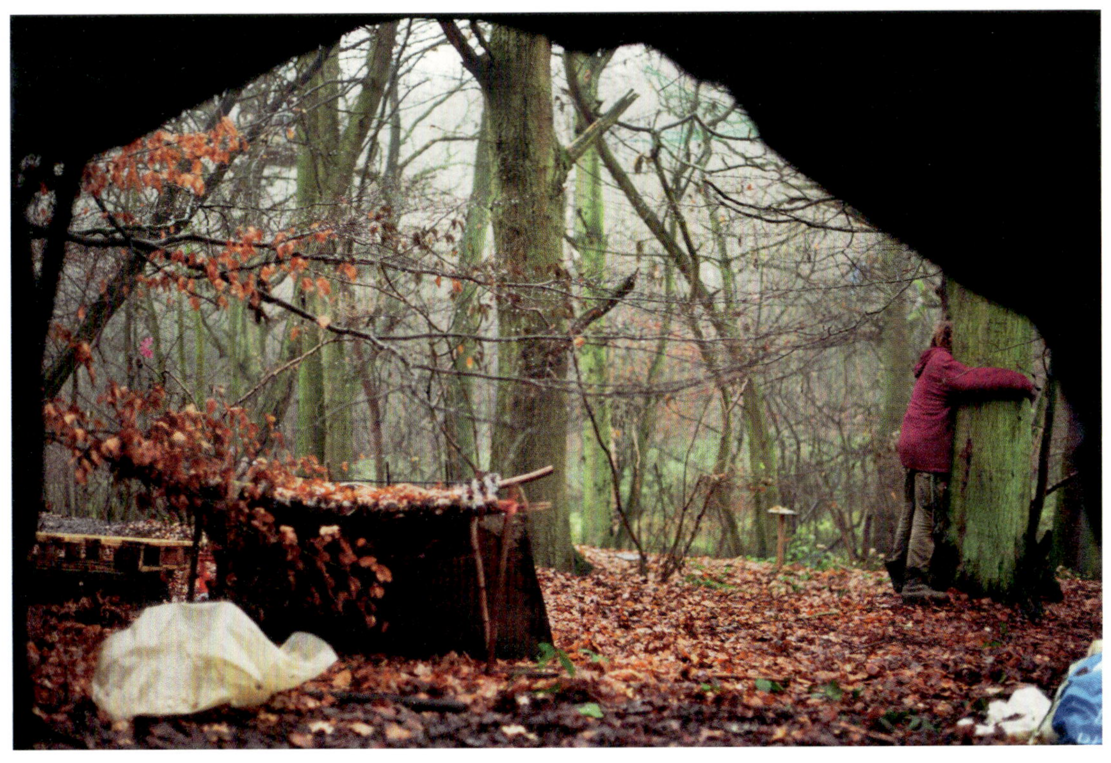

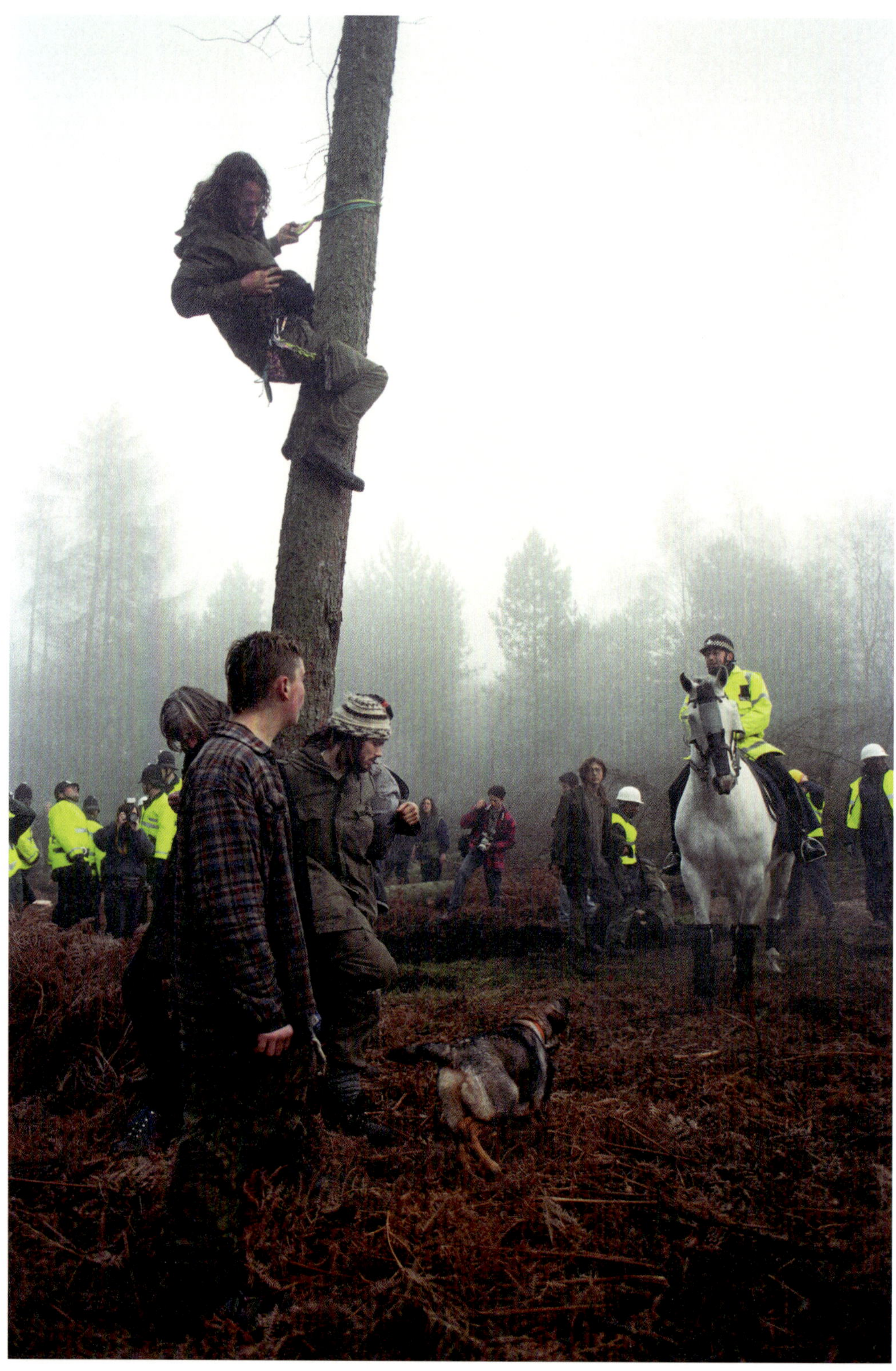

Newbury Bypass

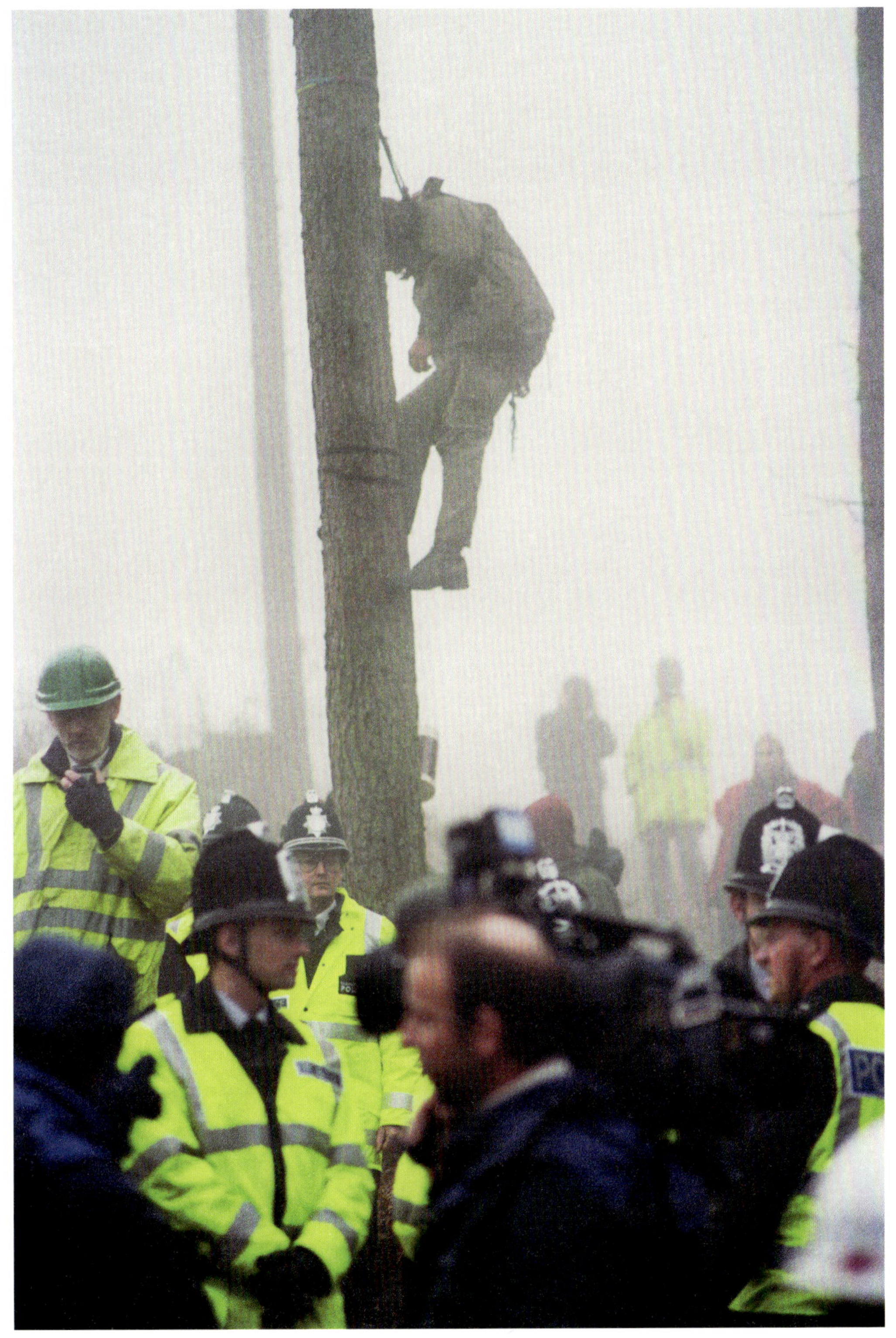

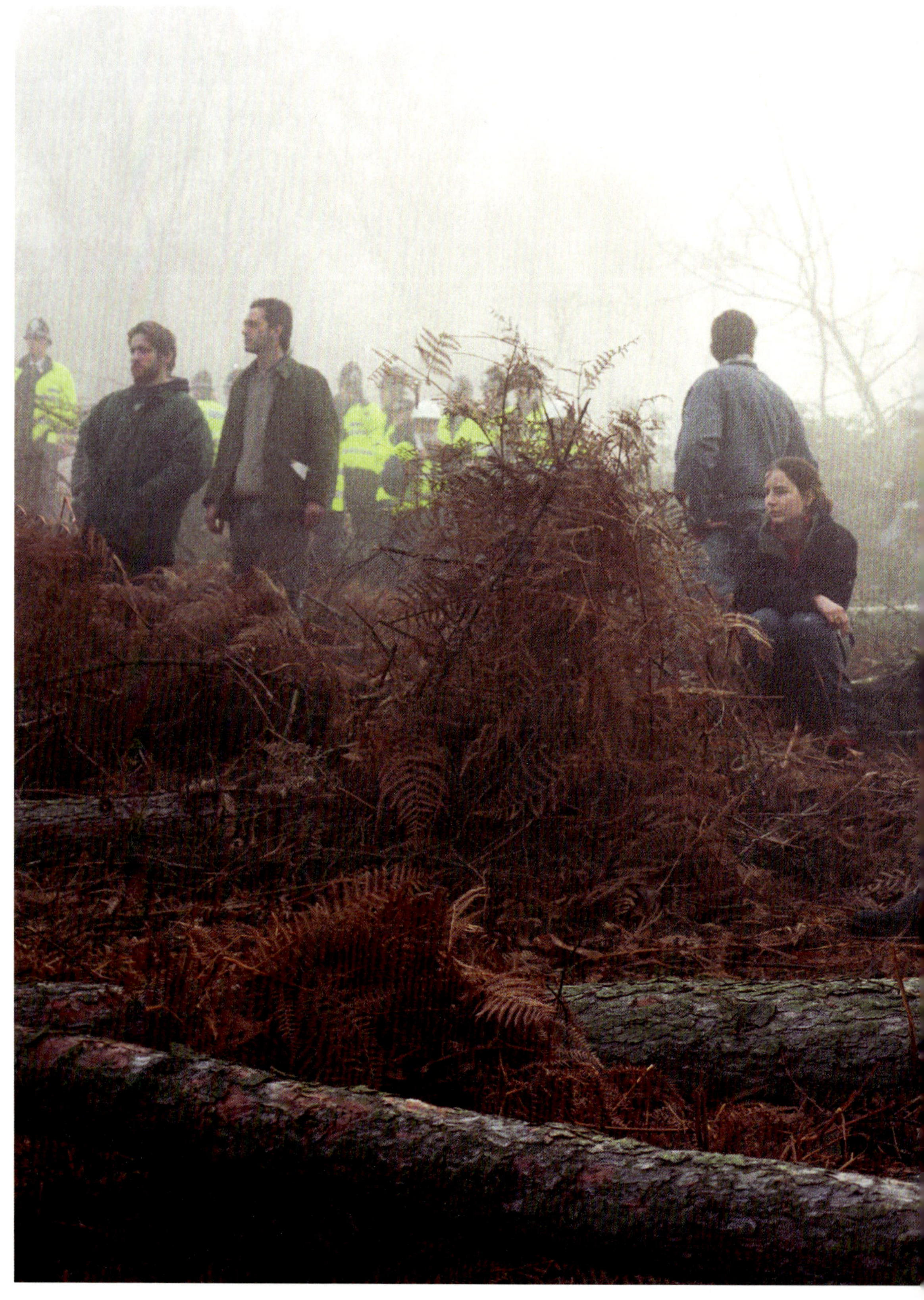

Newbury Bypass

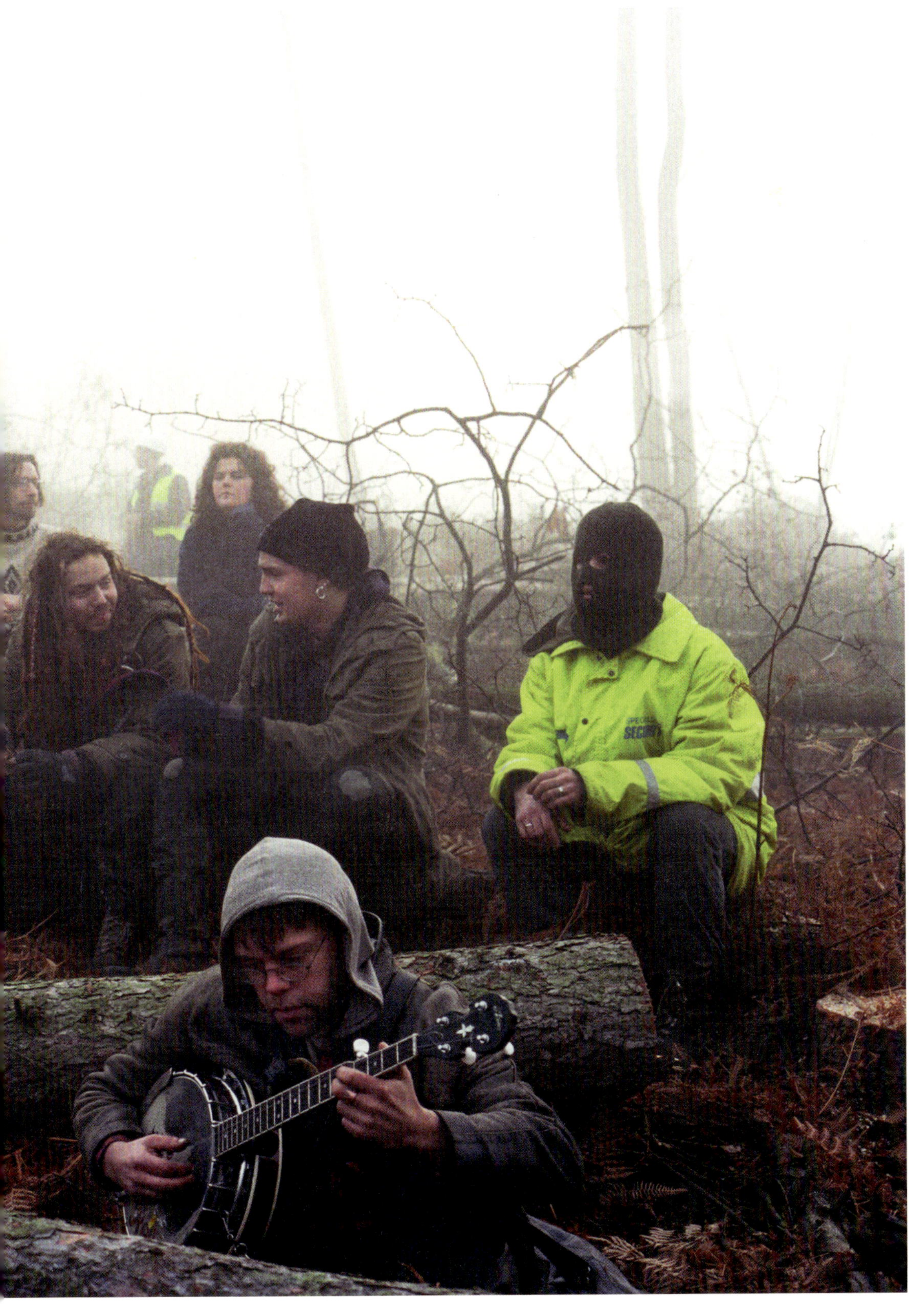

There were an estimated 10,000 trees that needed to be cut down by the state in order to build the Newbury Bypass. It took an inordinate amount of security just to protect one chainsaw so its dirty work could be ensured. Here lies the power of direct action activism. Yes the Newbury Bypass was built however the protest drew so much negative attention to the Government's road building plan and cost such an eye-watering amount in policing and security that the next year, in 1997, transport minister Steven Norris went on flagship British news program Panorama to say the Newbury Bypass should never have been built. The government, spooked by the idea of future battles, then scrapped the other 77 other new roads they had originally proposed.

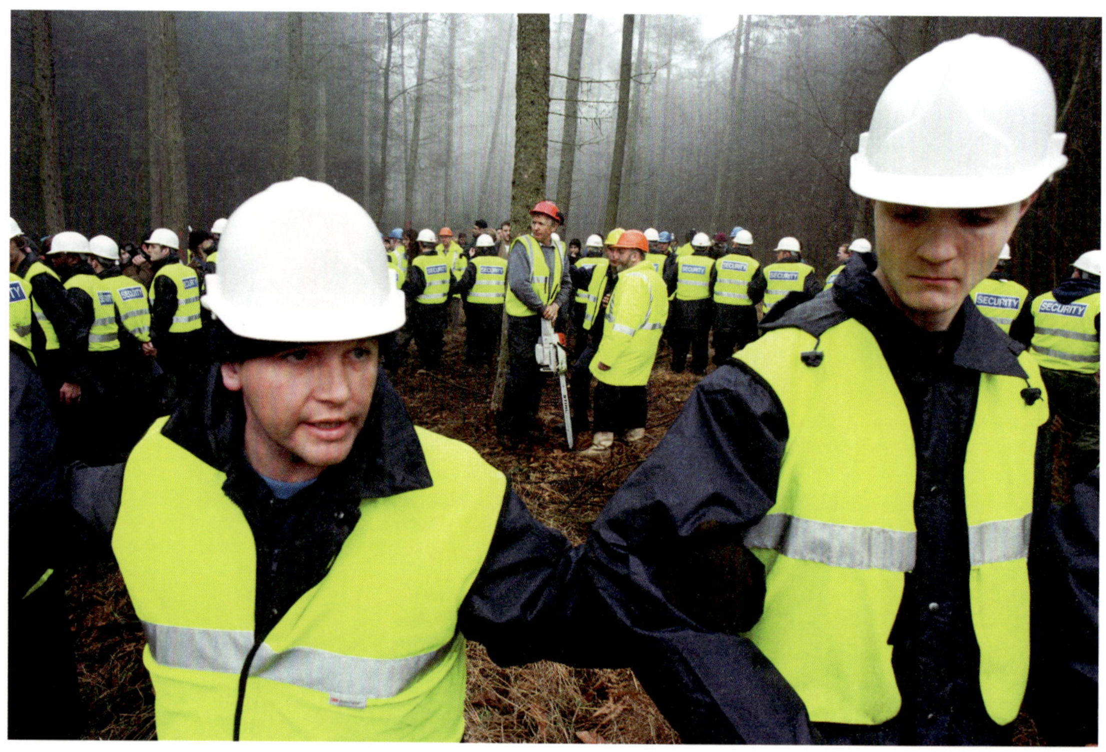

Newbury Bypass

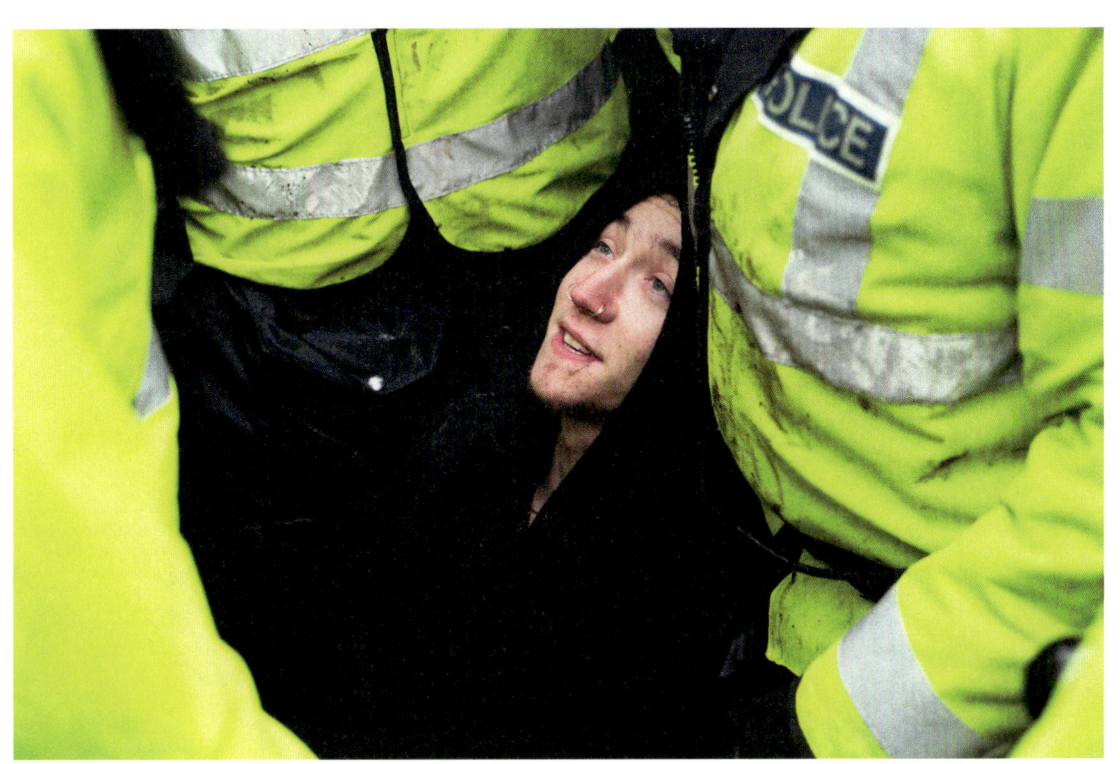
OLICE

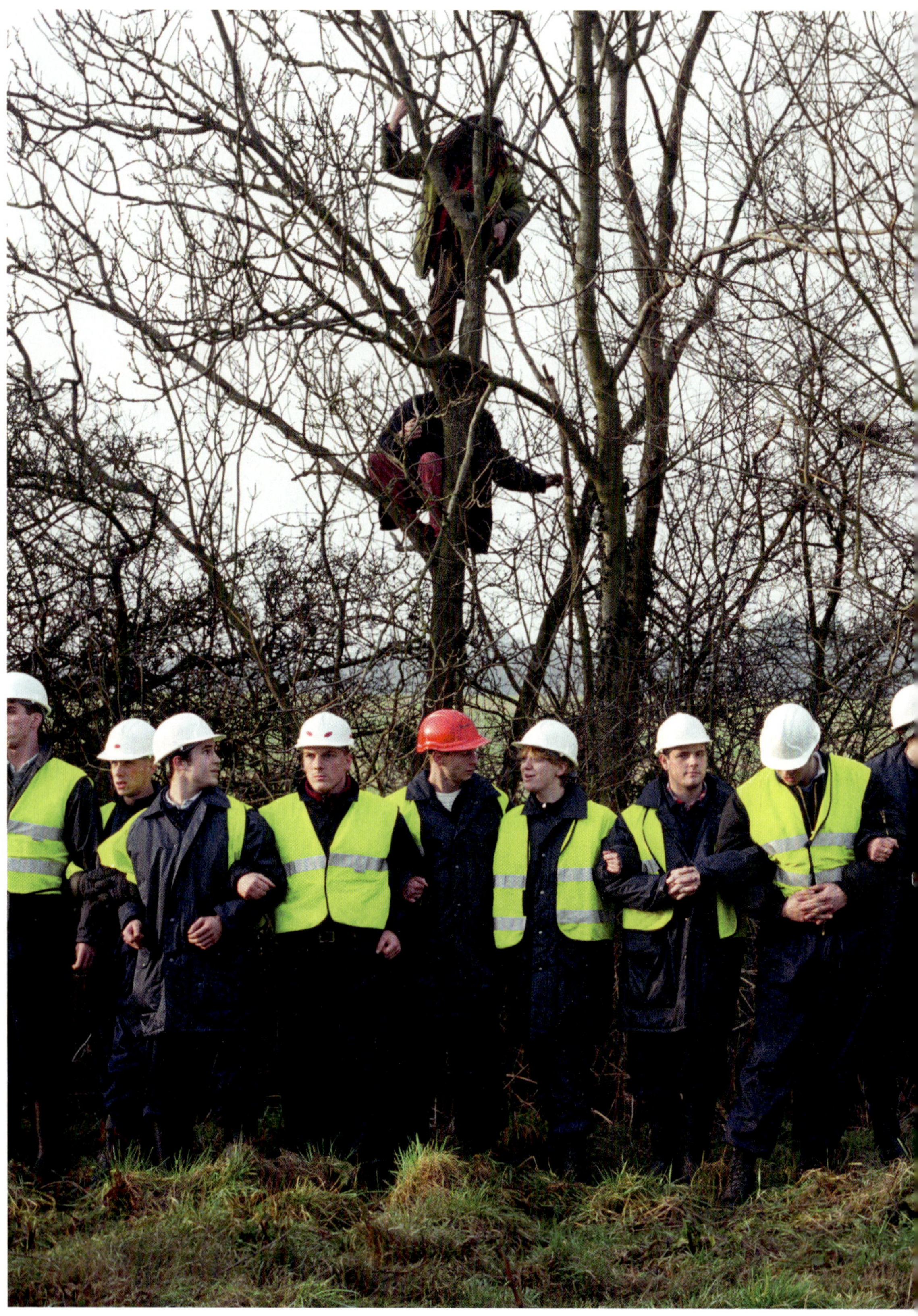

Newbury Bypass

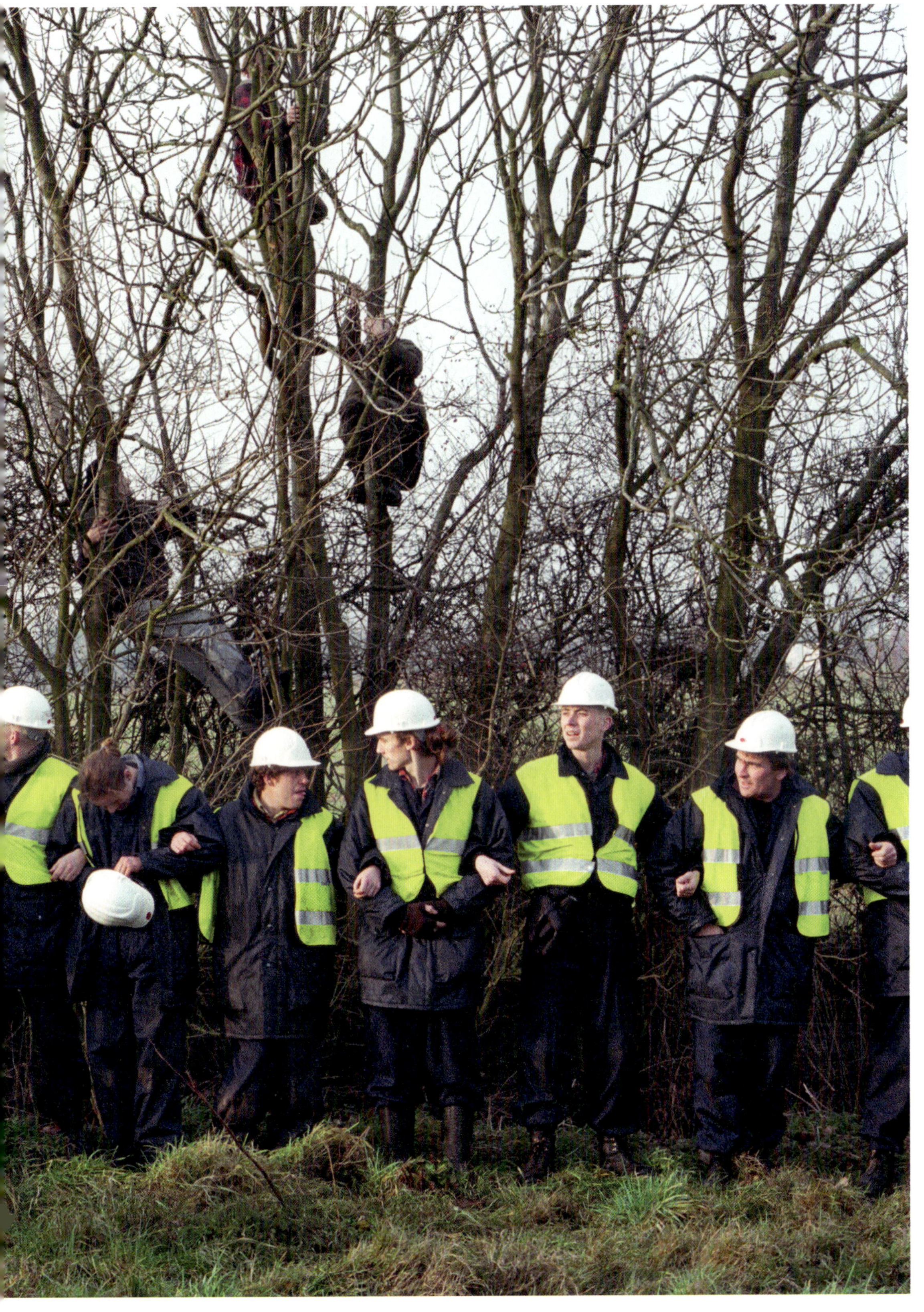

The third battle of Newbury – the first two having occurred during the English civil war – began on a very cold day in January 1996. Those first days were absolutely nuts with bodies flying everywhere. Activists would run for any tree they could while the government-employed security would throw heavy arms out in an attempt to catch them and hand them on to the police for arrest. All too often it resembled a rugby scrum with no rules as one person would desperately cling to a small tree only to be ripped off some time later.

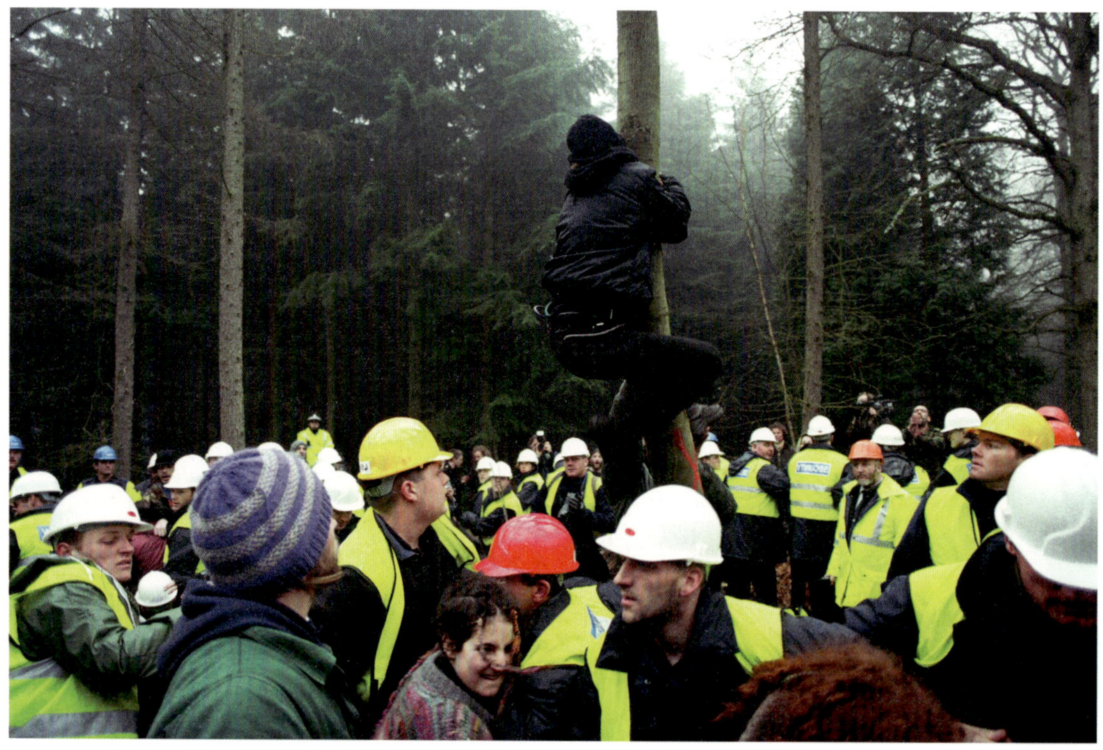

Newbury Bypass

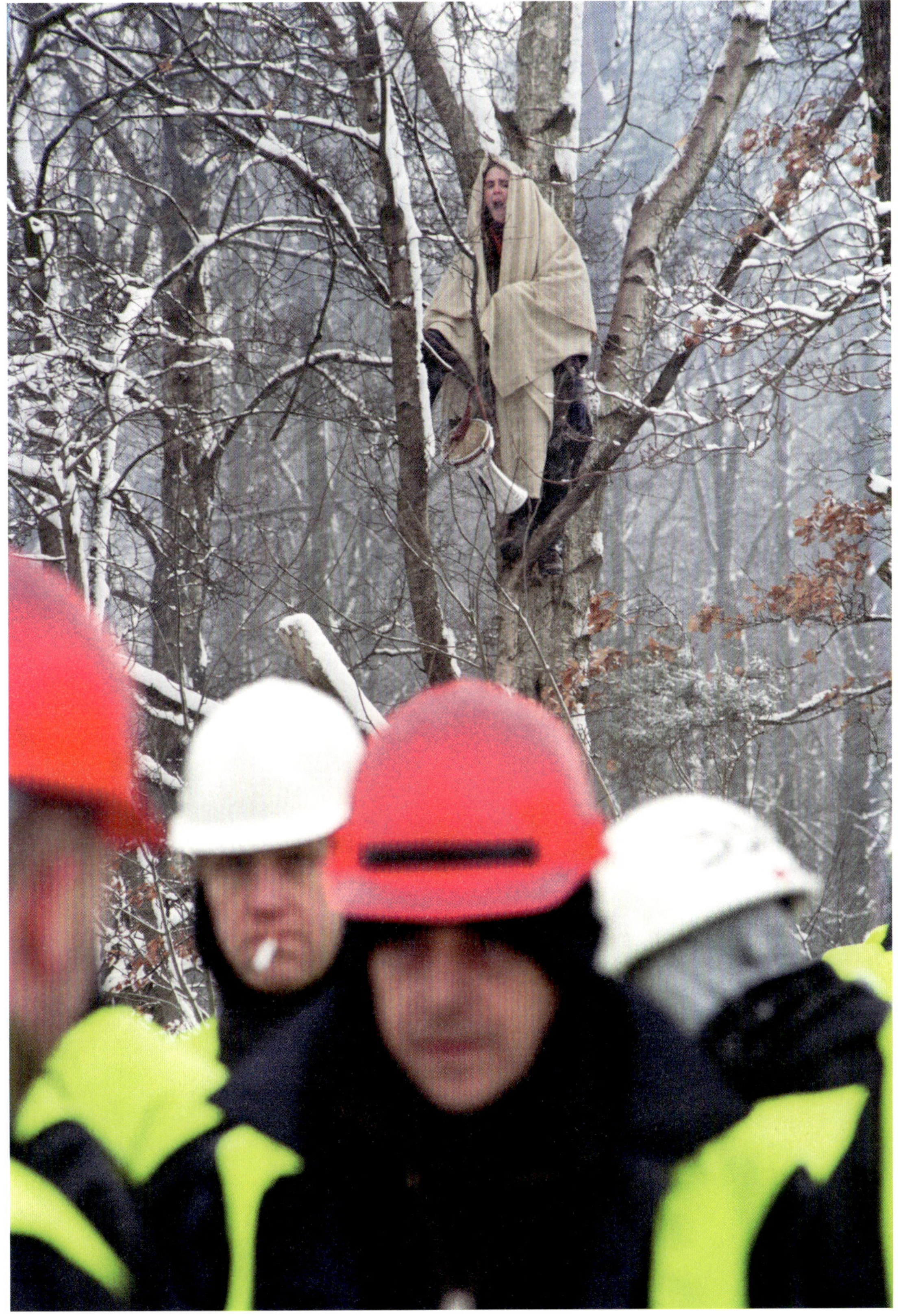

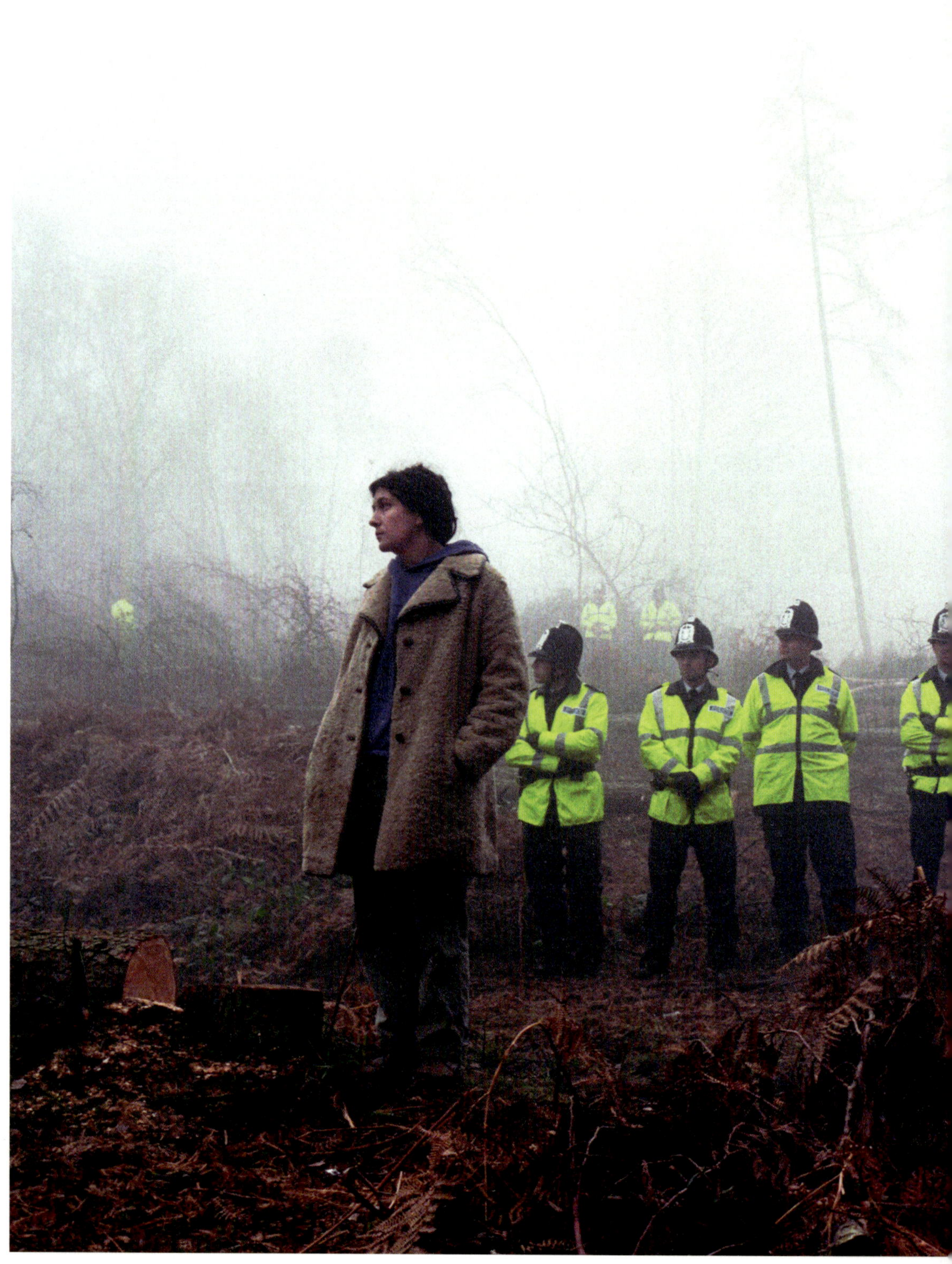

Newbury Bypass

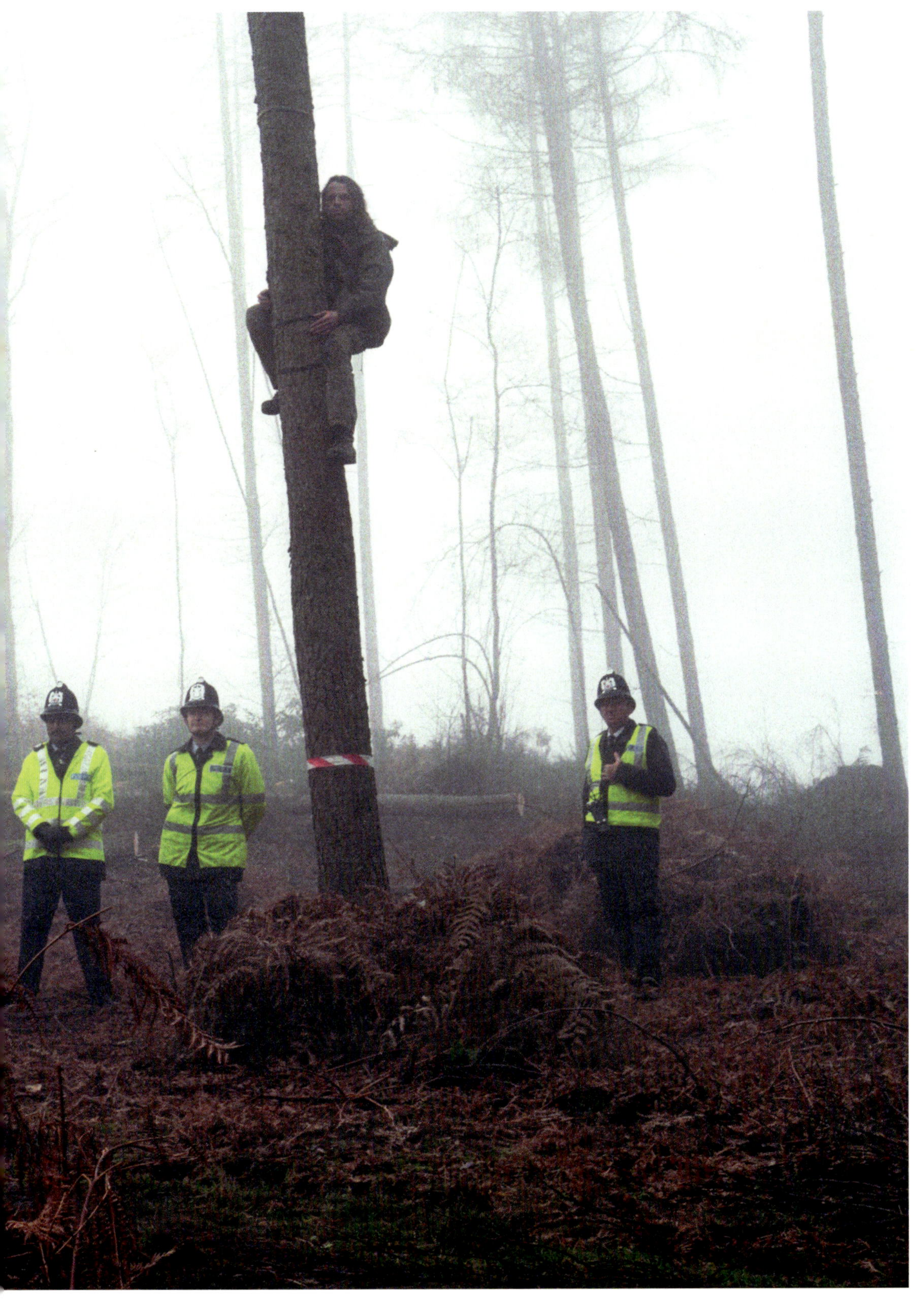

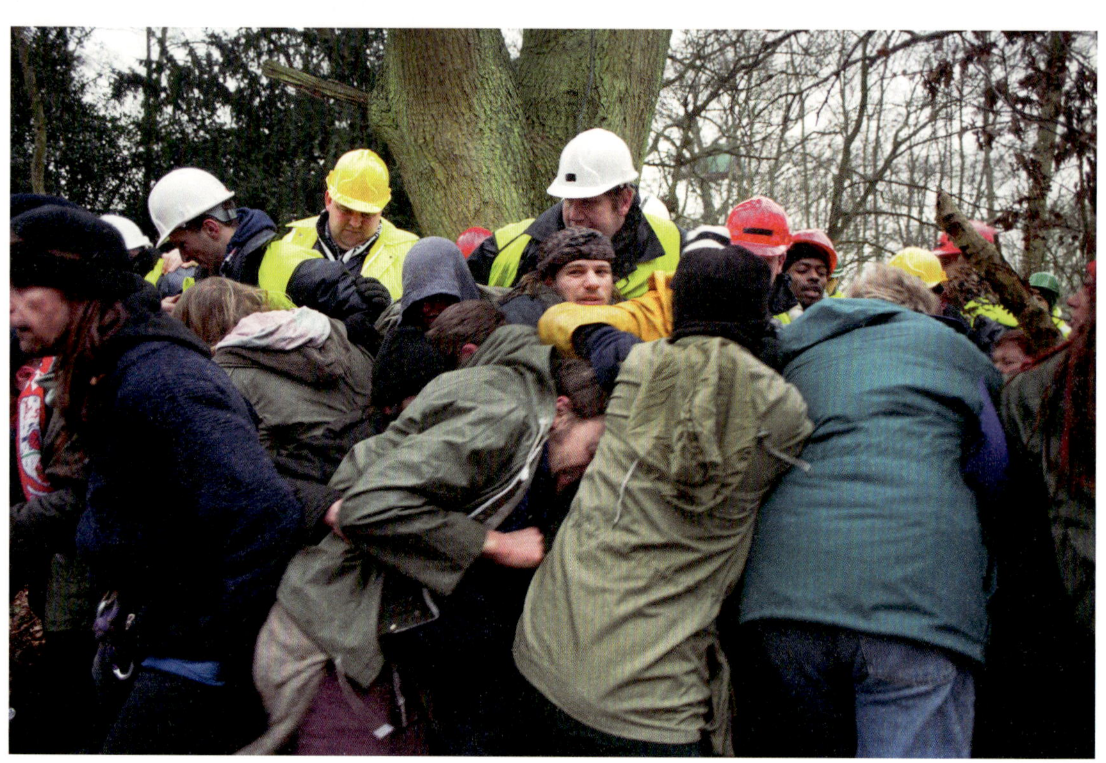

Newbury Bypass

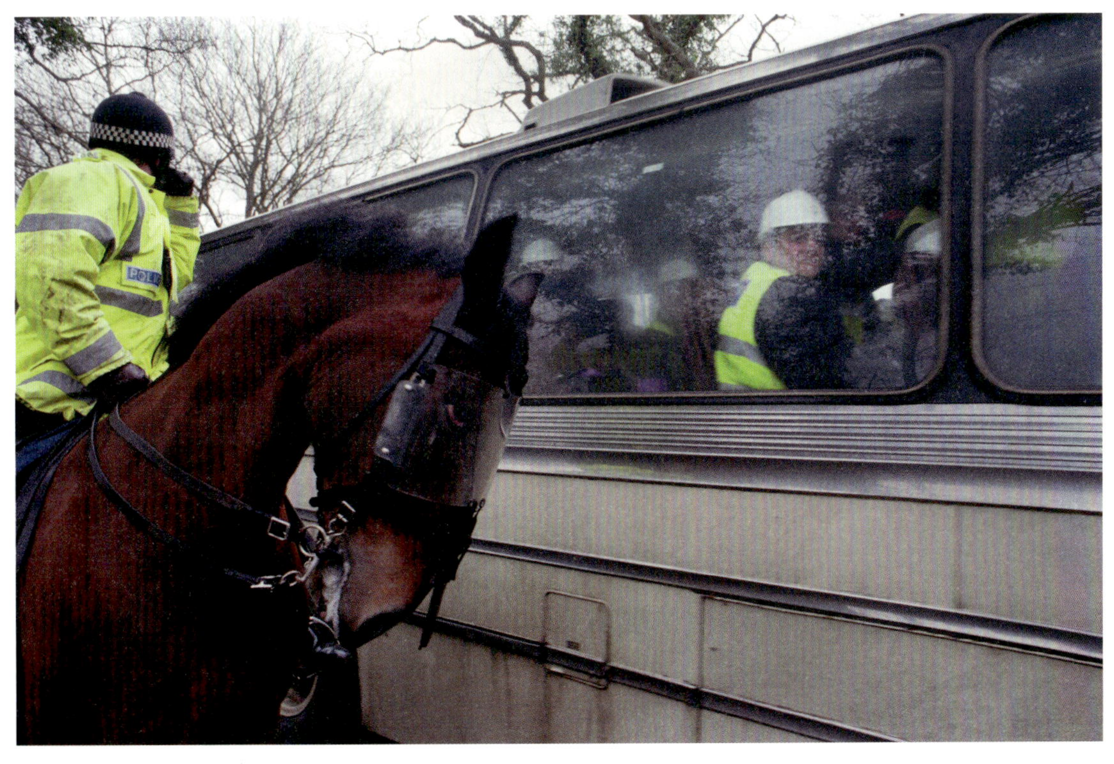

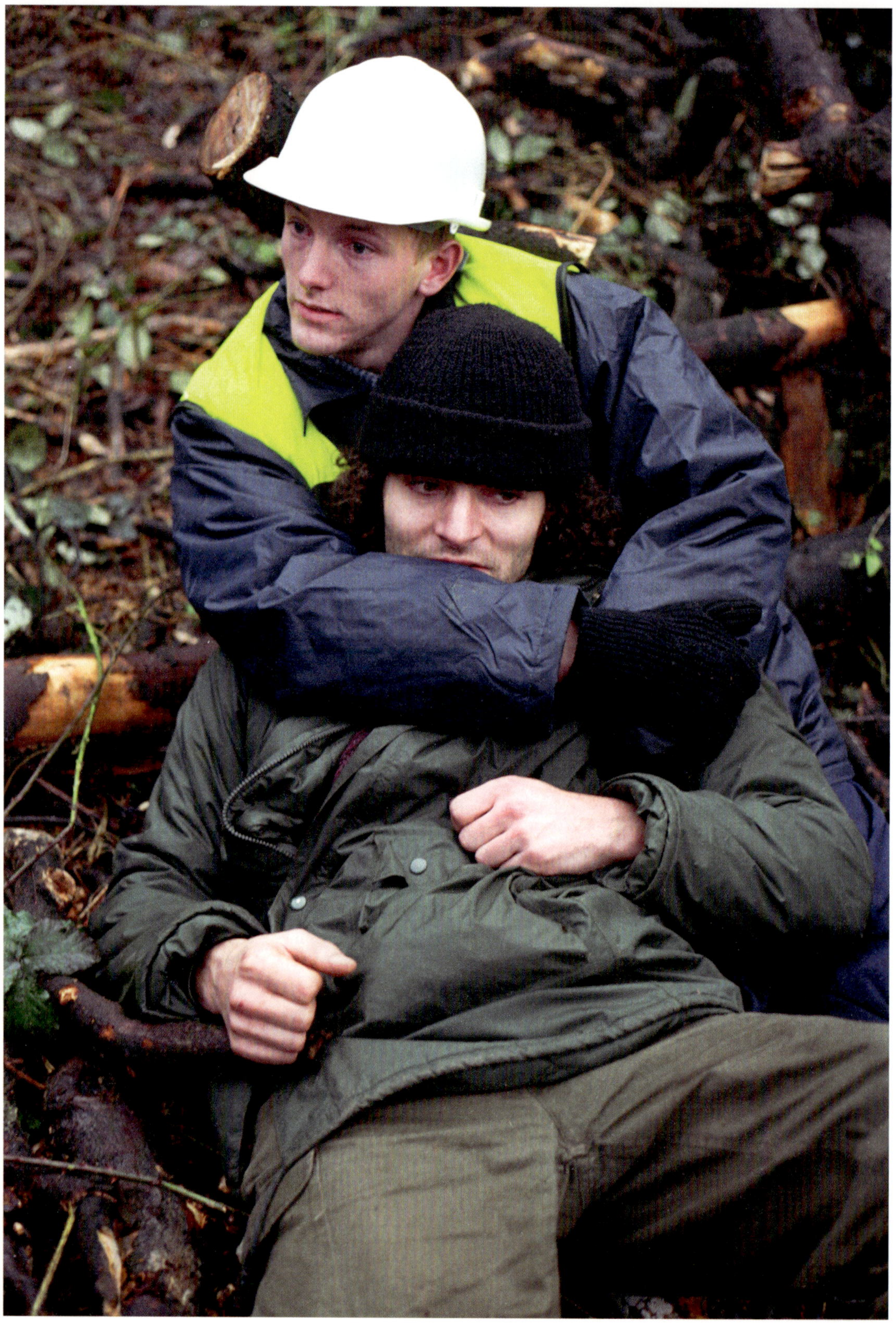

Newbury Bypass

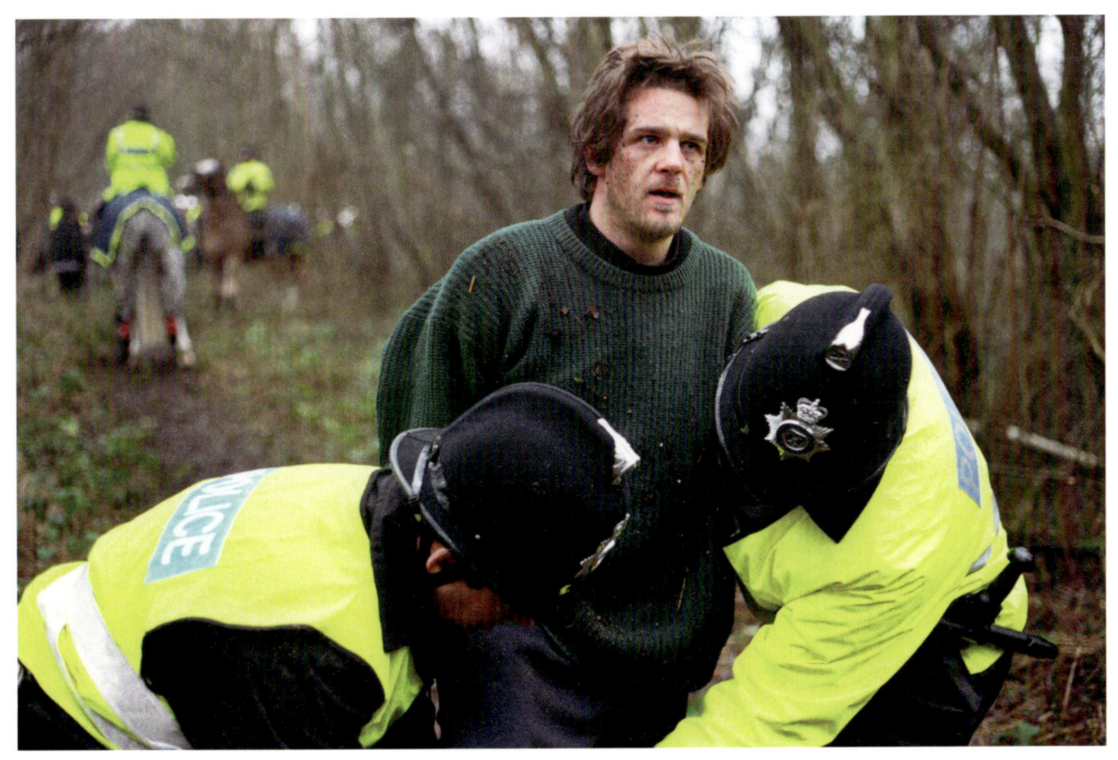

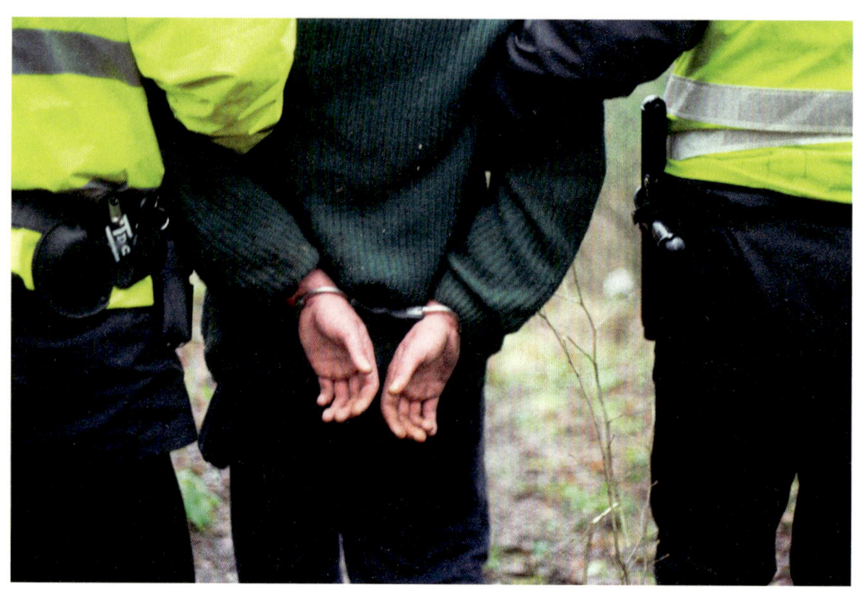

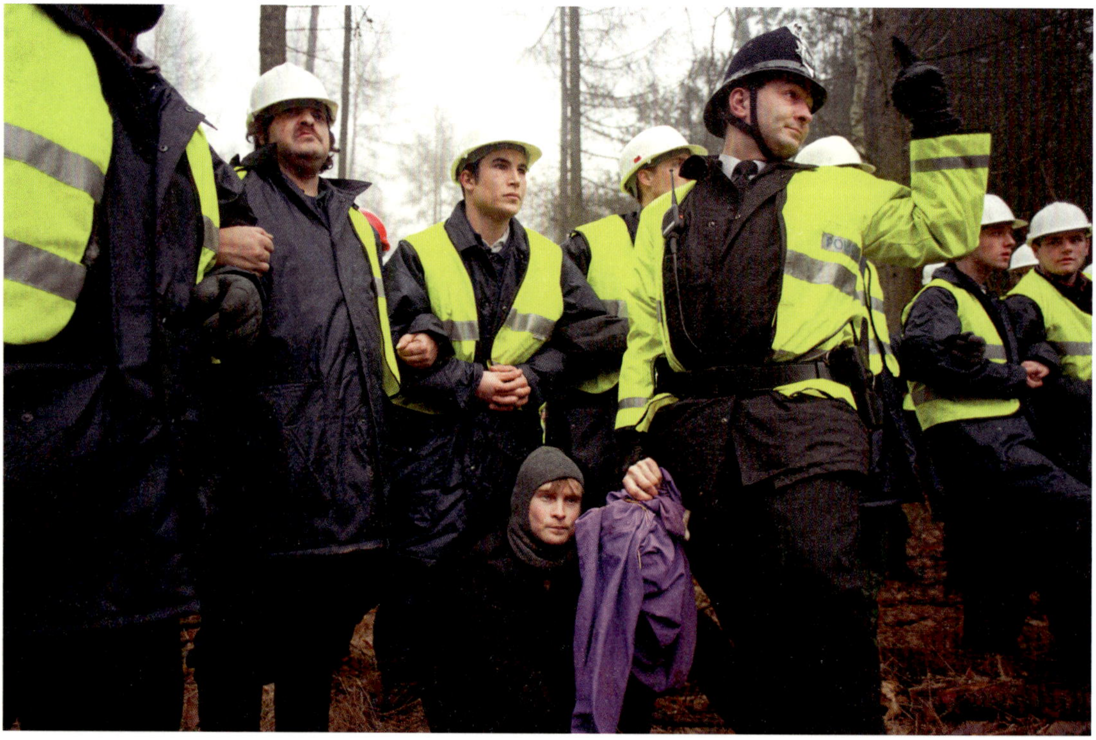

Newbury Bypass

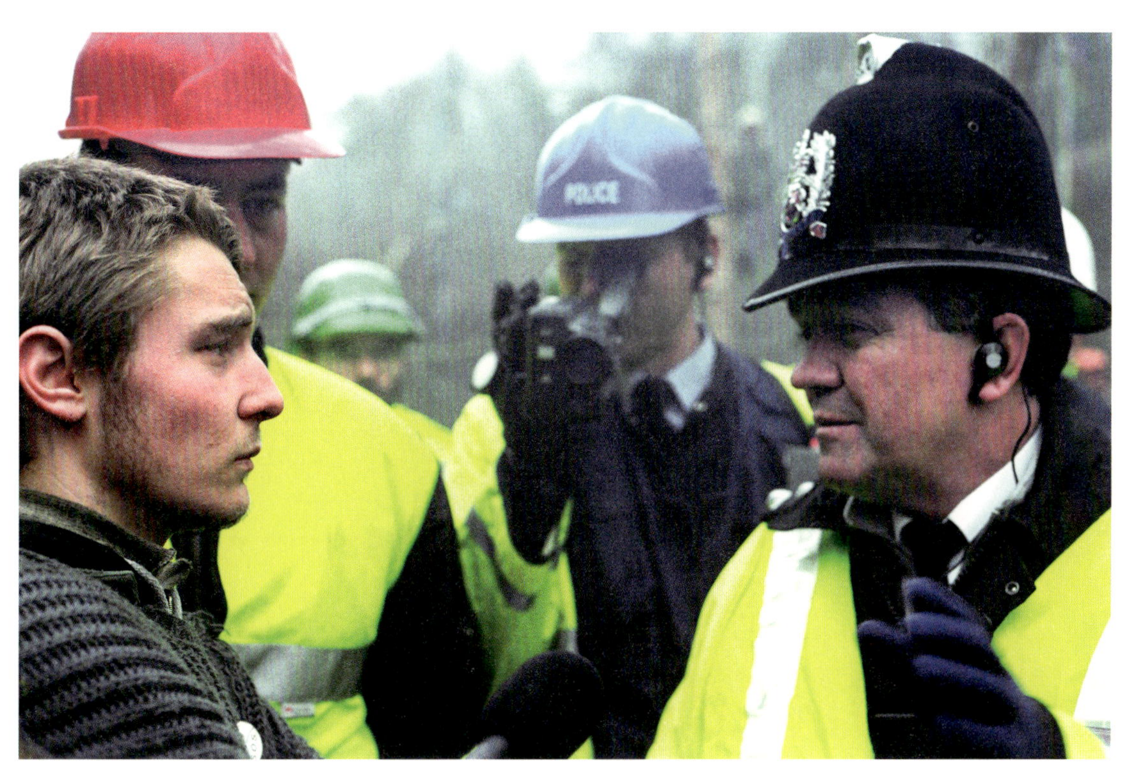
POLICE

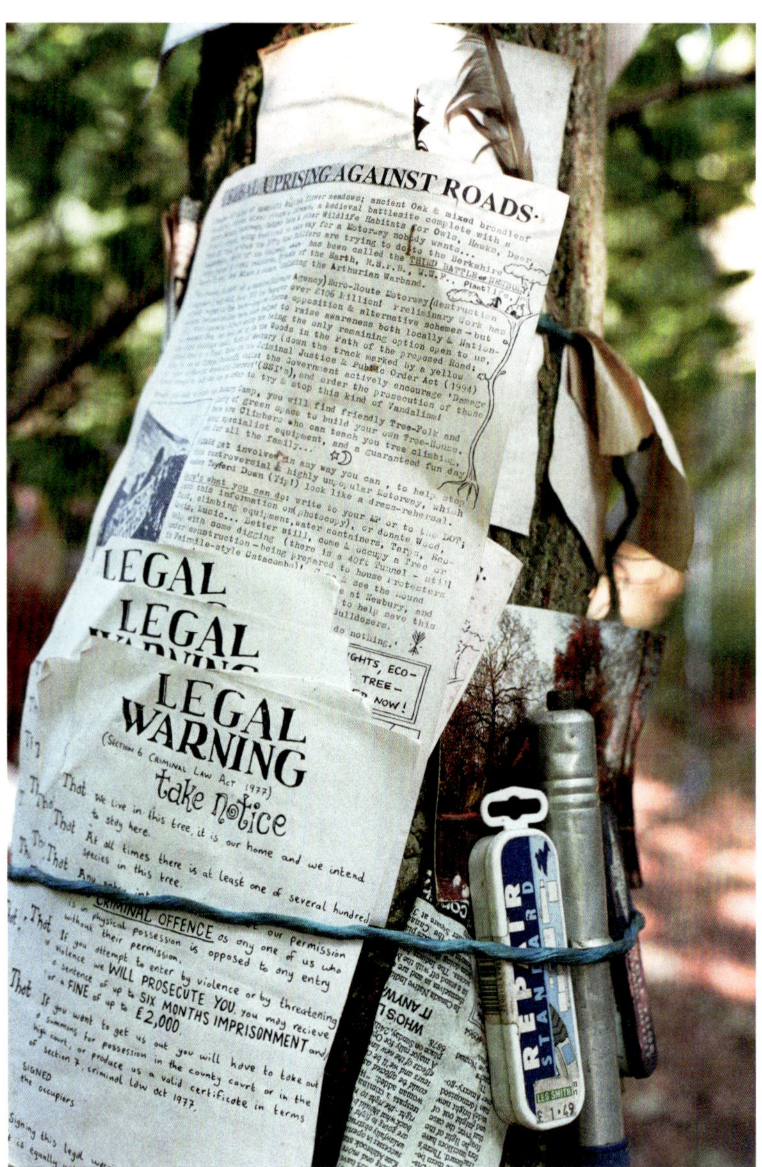

Newbury Bypass

The activists at Newbury went to extraordinary lengths to draw attention to the campaign and how we, as a society, were treating the environment. Balin in his determination spent 16 days in the tripod only coming down to defecate and eat.

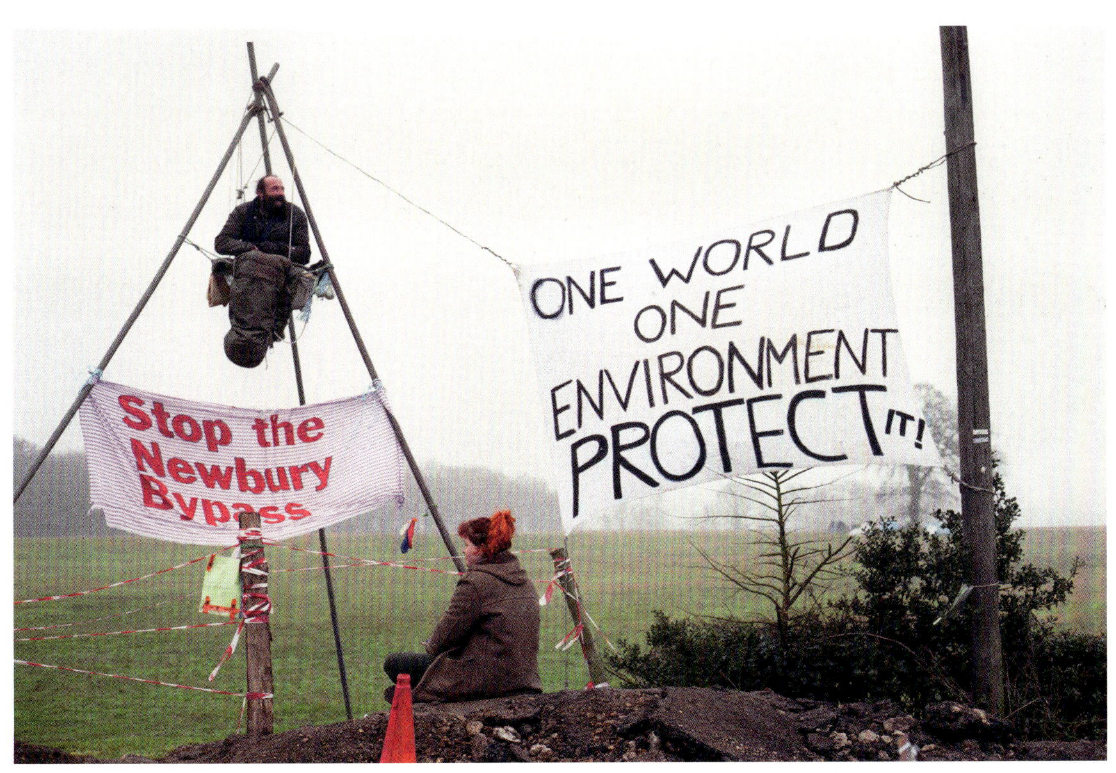

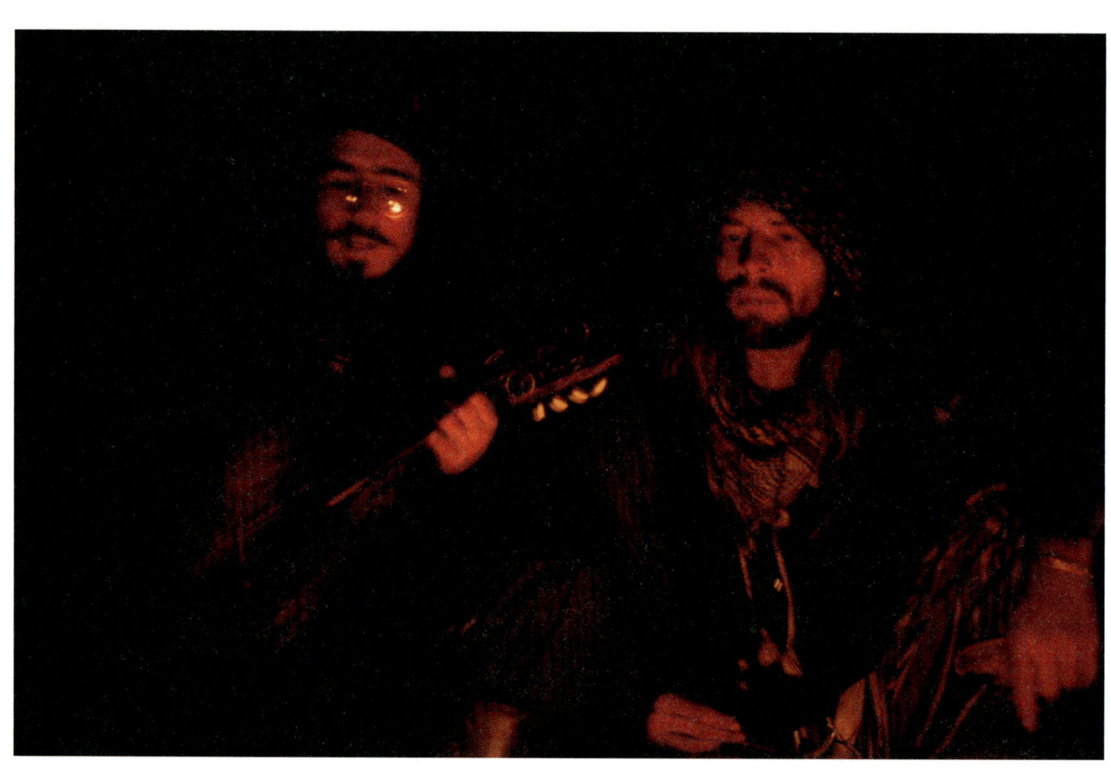

Newbury Bypass

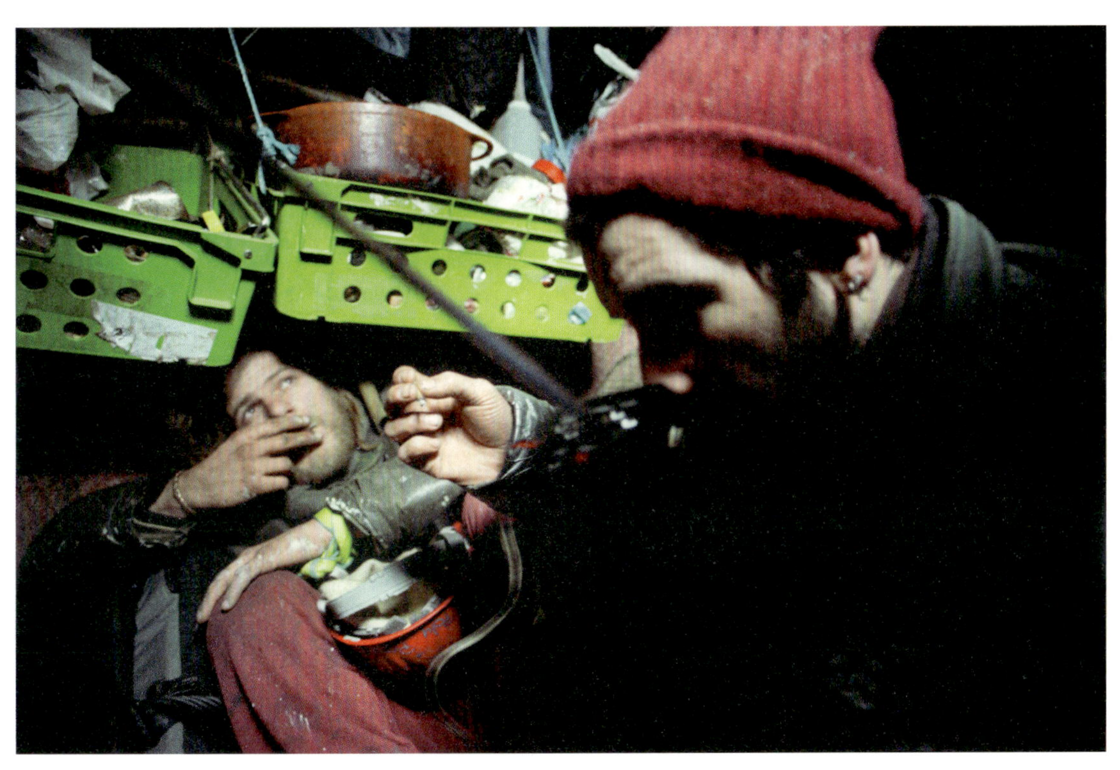

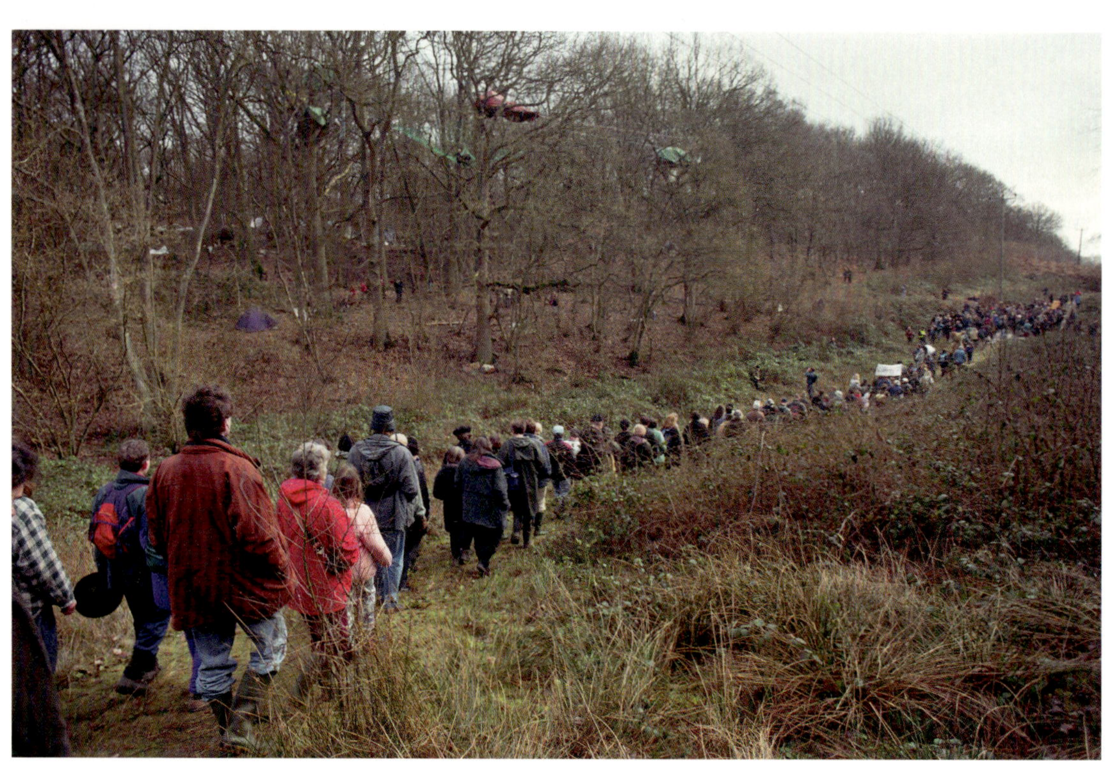

Newbury Bypass

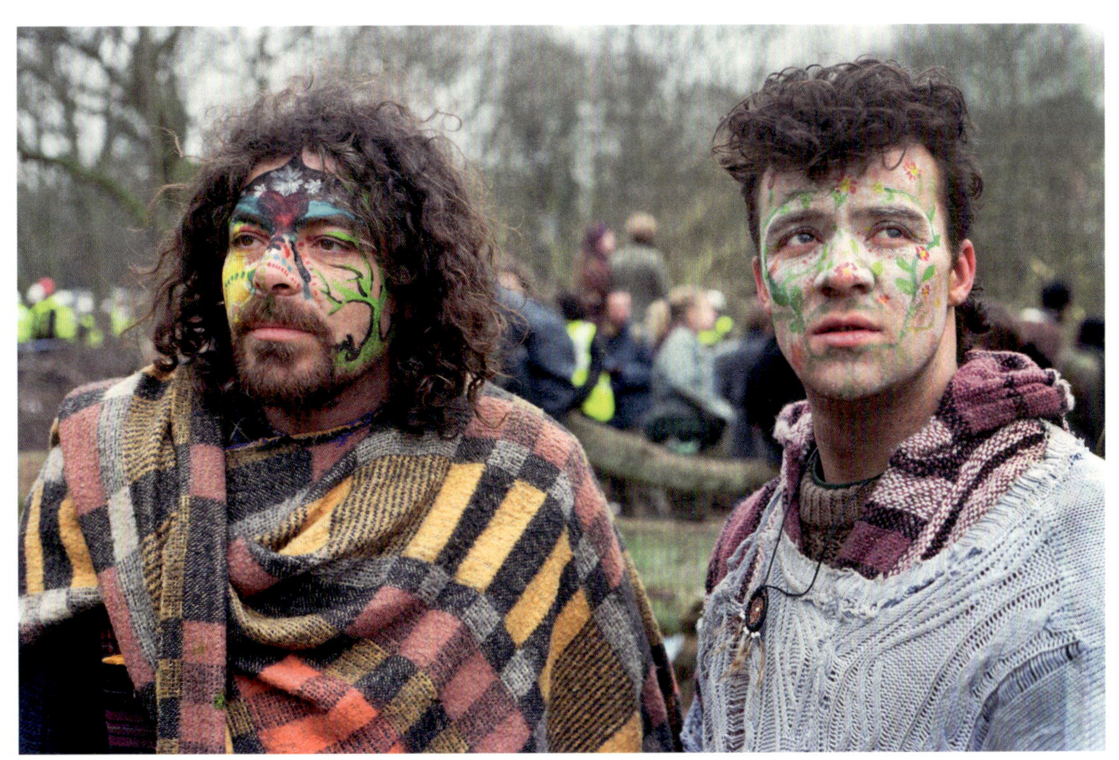

David Bellamy talking at the Newbury Green party meeting. An outspoken and at the time controversial figure who nevertheless was one of the first to embrace direct action environmental activism. In 1983, he was imprisoned for blockading the Australian Franklin River in a protest against a proposed dam and in his 1989 book 'The Greenhouse Effect' he said: 'The profligate demands of humankind are causing far-reaching changes to the atmosphere of planet Earth, of this there is no doubt. Earth's temperature is showing an upward swing, the so-called greenhouse effect, now a subject of international concern. The greenhouse effect may melt the glaciers and ice caps of the world, causing the sea to rise and flood many of our great cities and much of our best farmland.' Sadly his words fell on deaf ears.

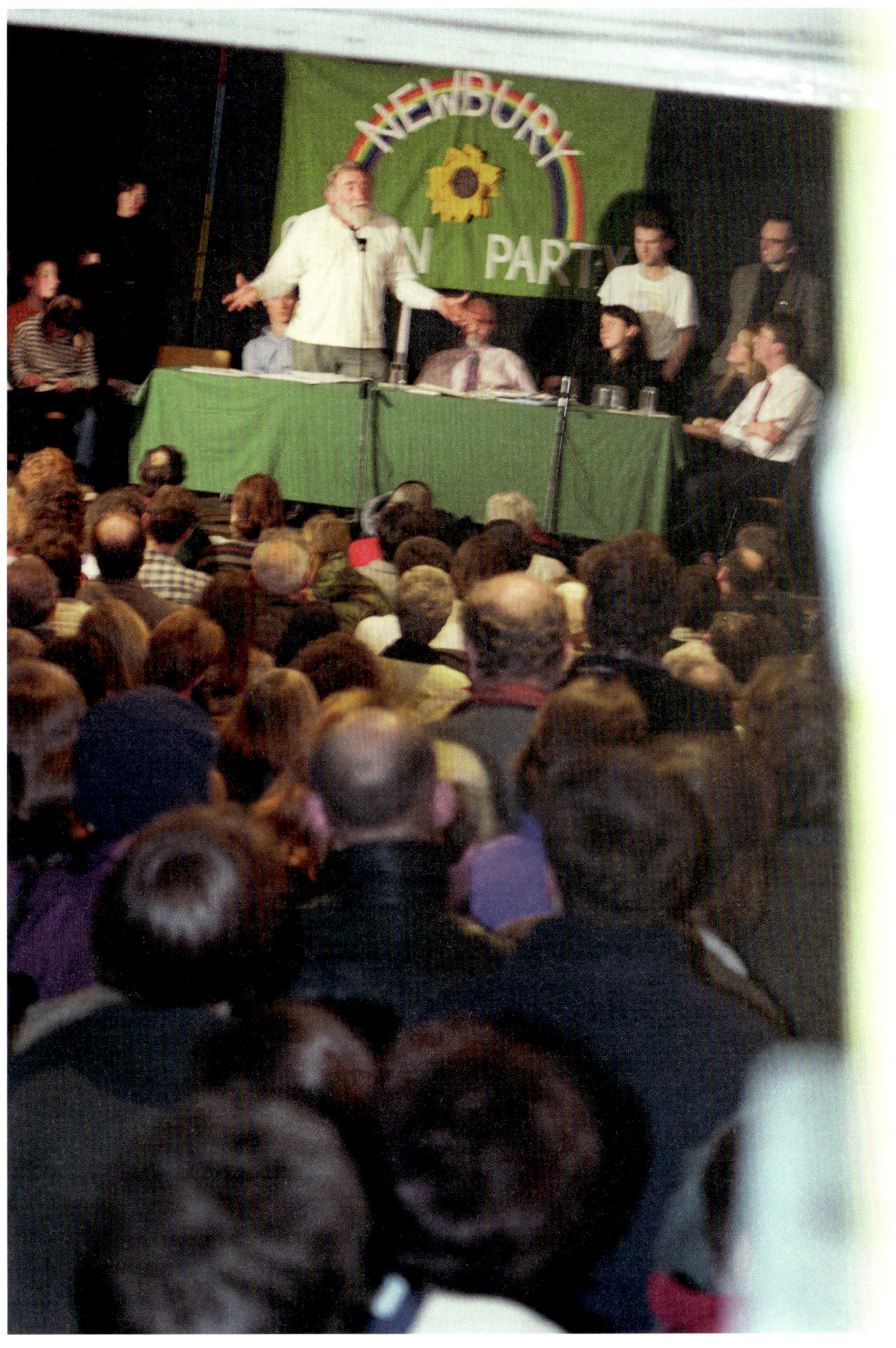
NEWBURY
PARTY

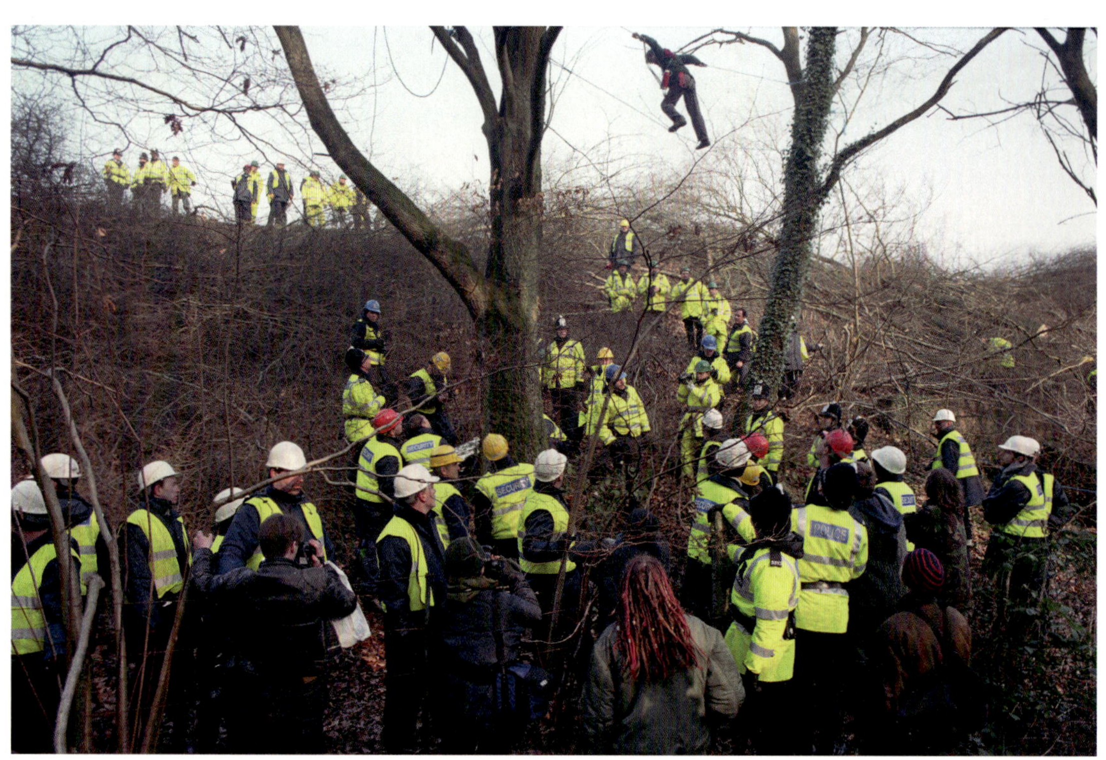

Newbury Bypass

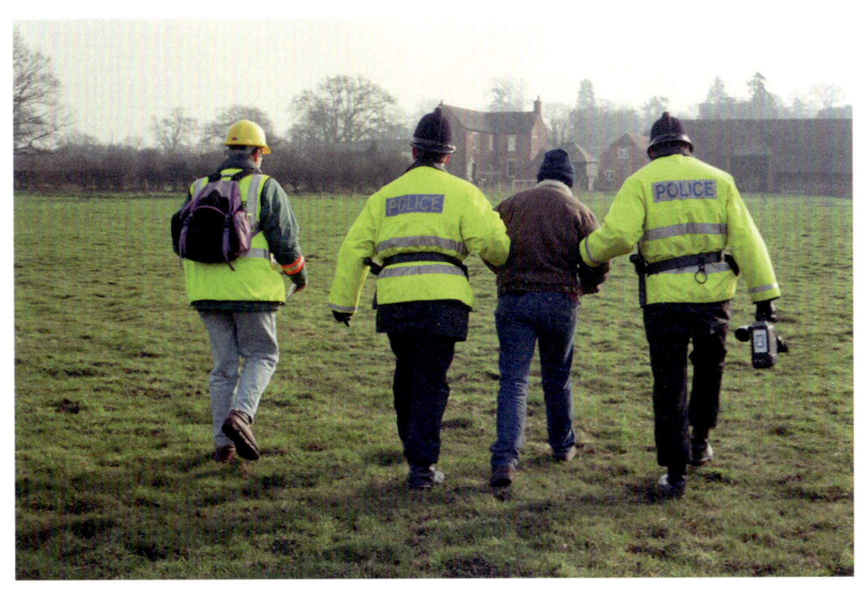
POLICE
POLICE

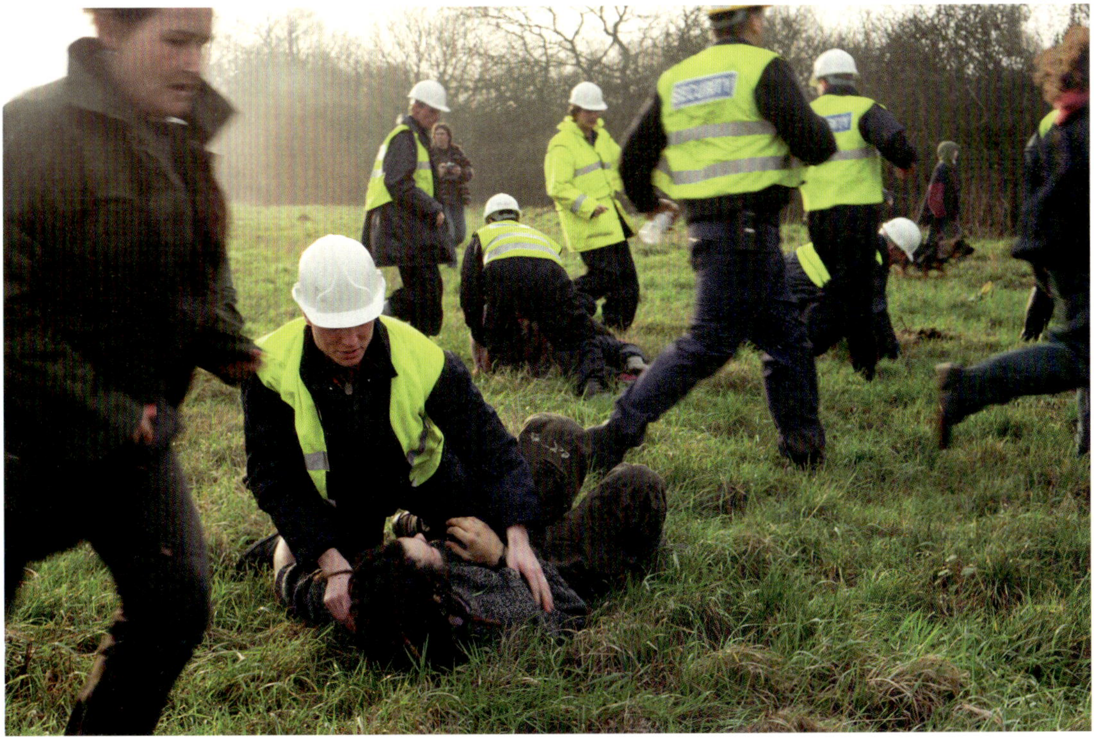

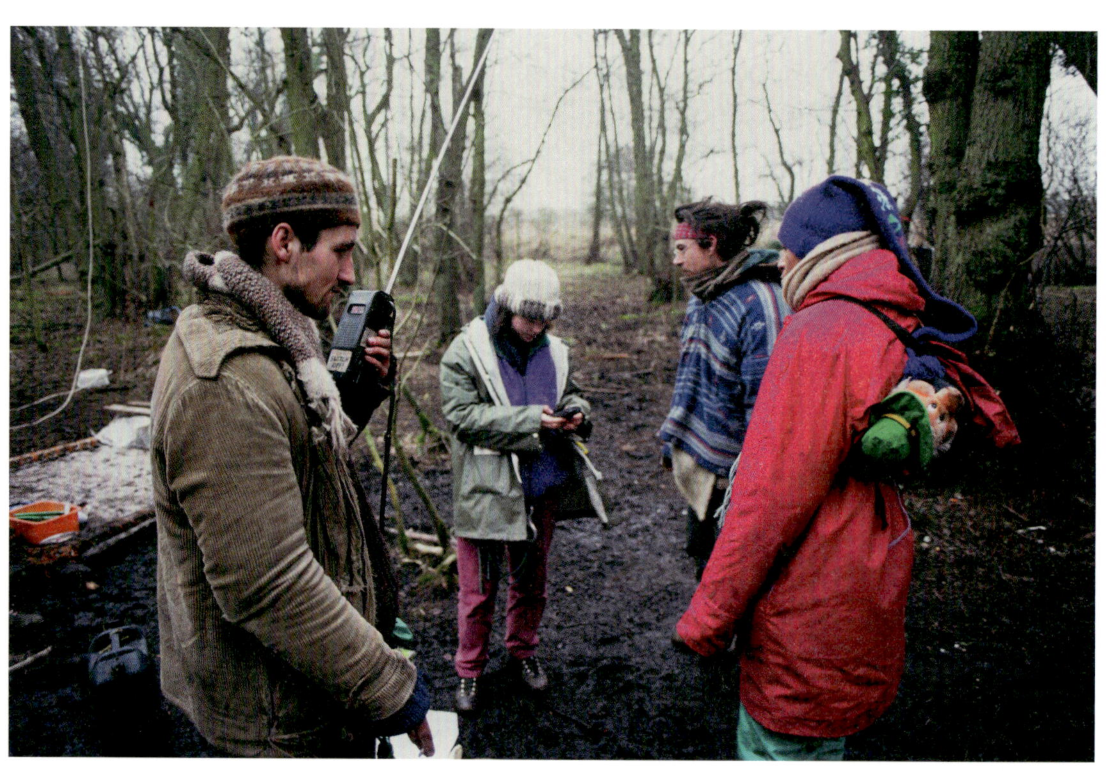

Newbury Bypass

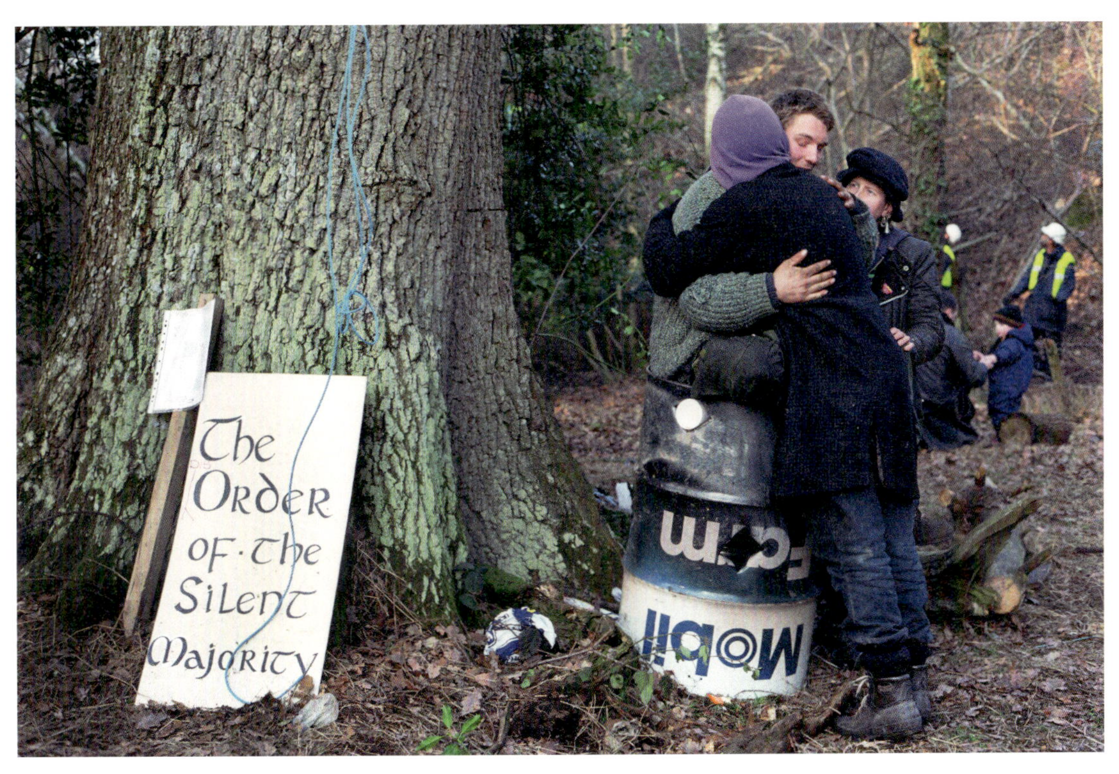
The
Order
of · the
Silent
Majority

A winter's scene typical of a day at the protest. One man juggles as another plays a folk melody while behind them an activist engages with the security to explain why as activists they're so passionate about saving the trees. In the distance someone stands among the snow covered branches as the cold bites further into their body all the while guarding the wood from the ever-present threat of government destruction.

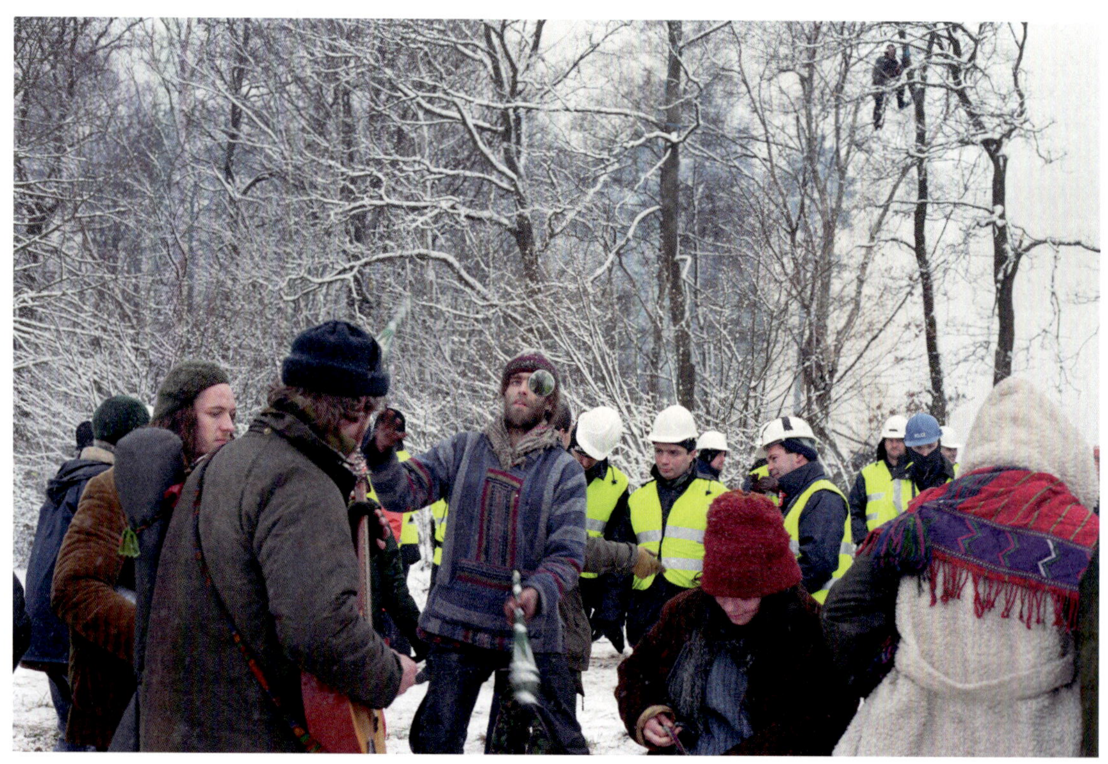

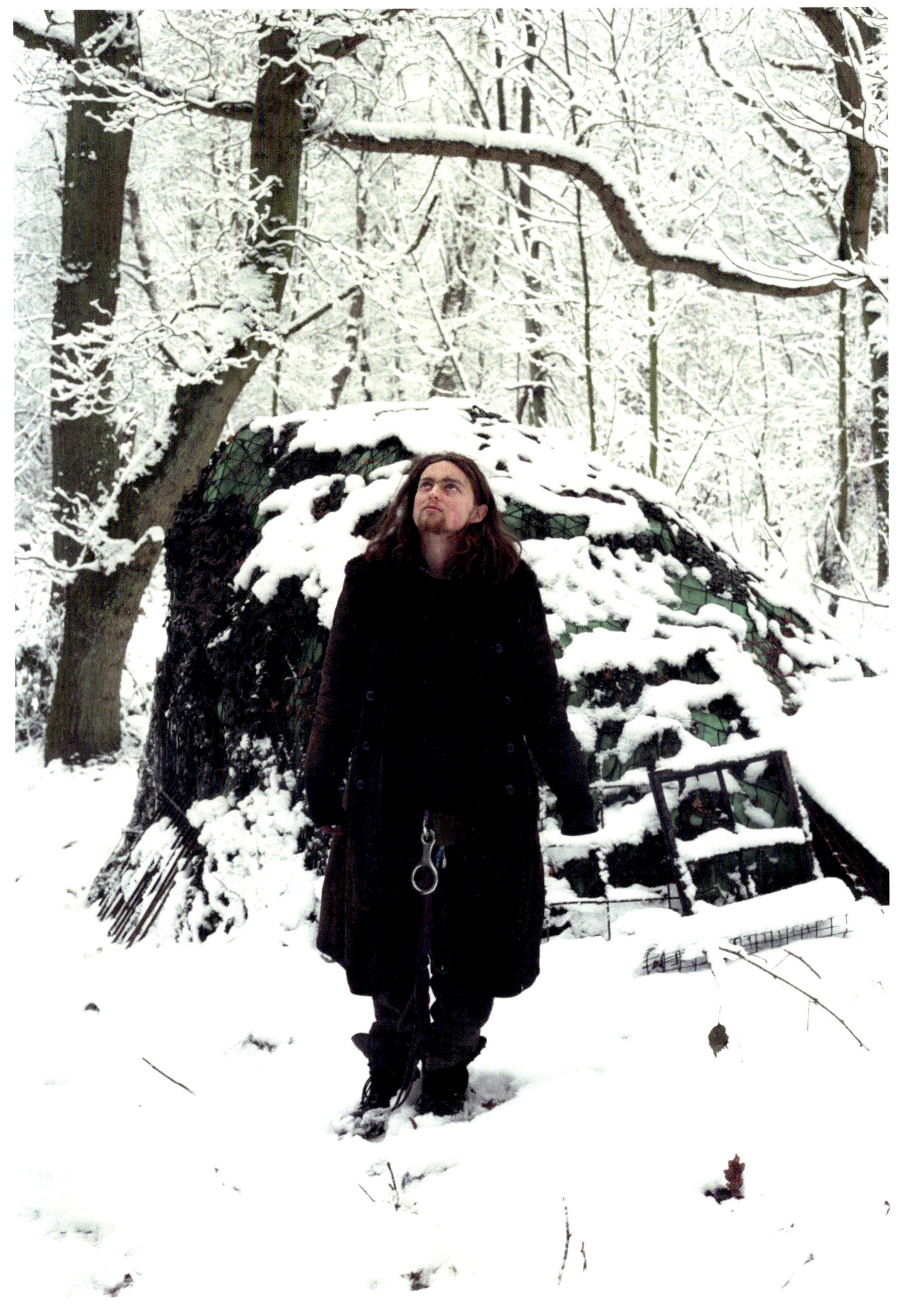

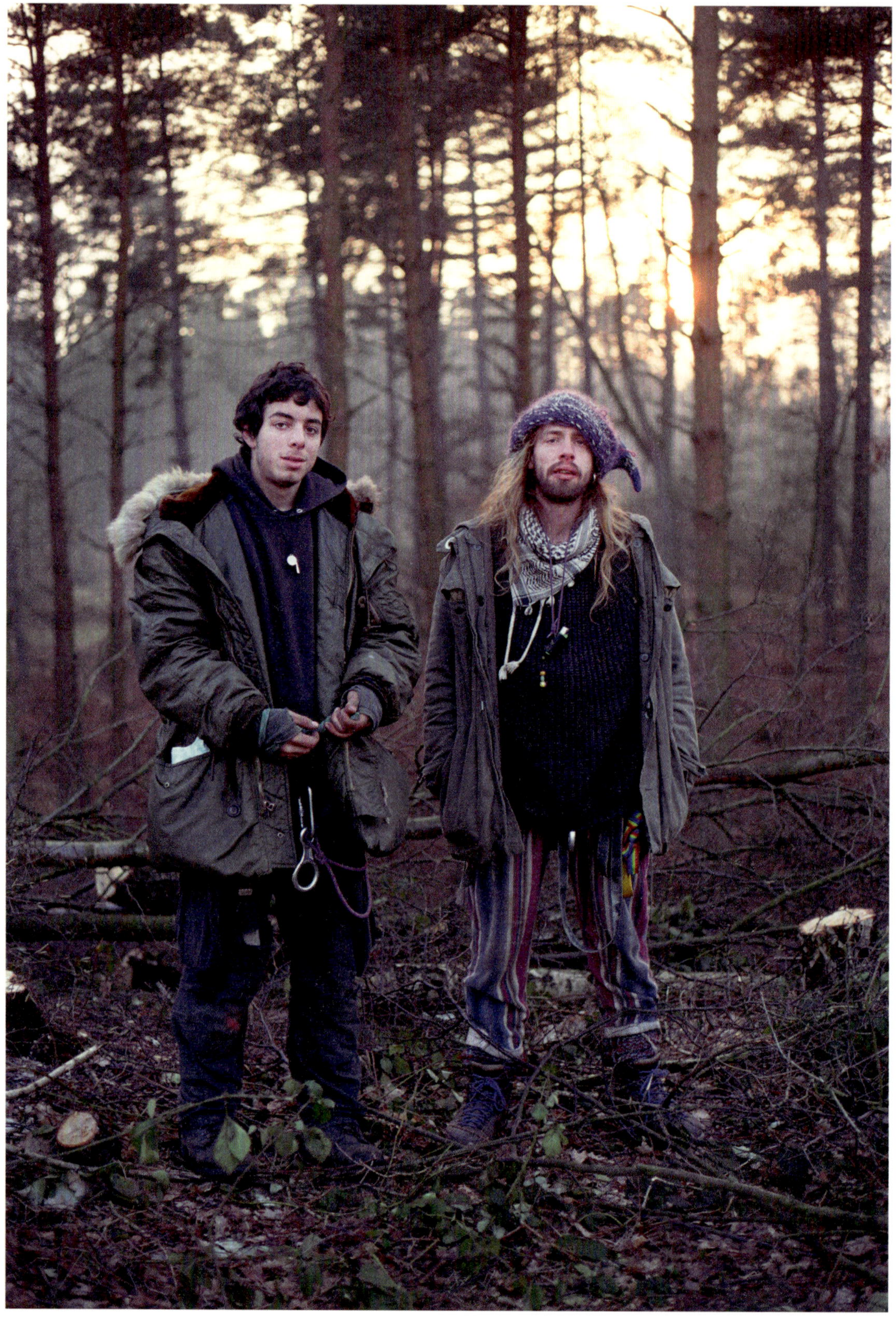

Newbury Bypass

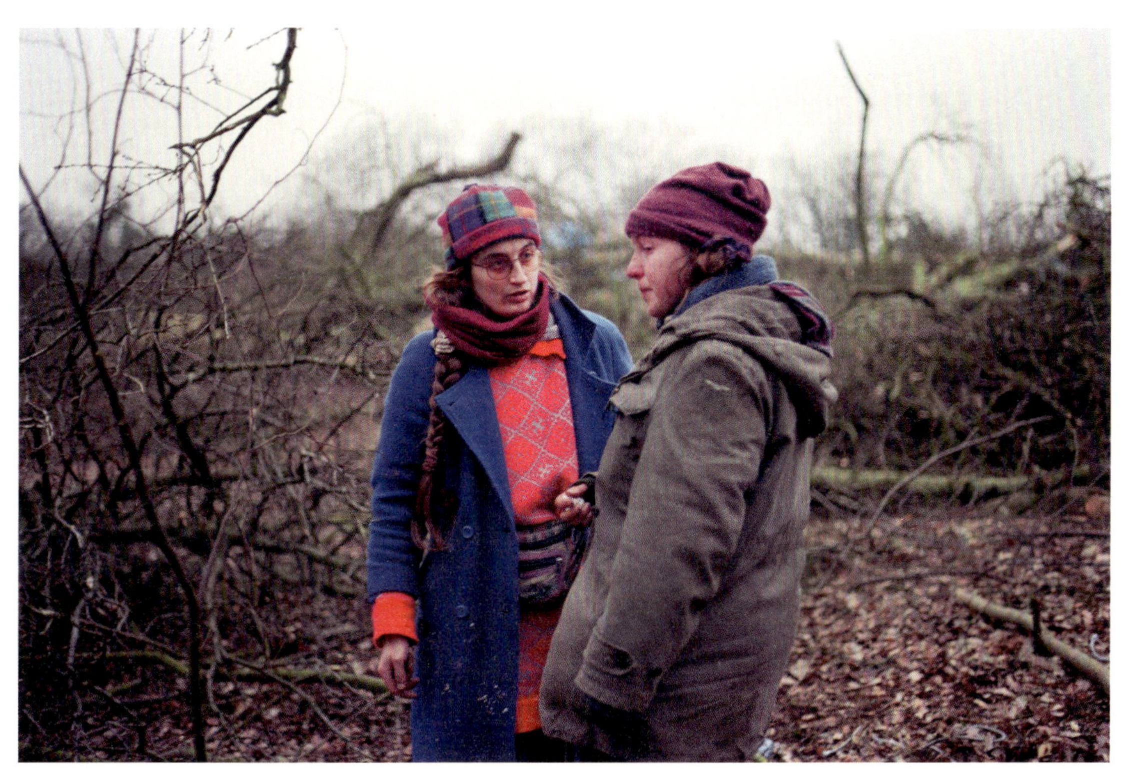

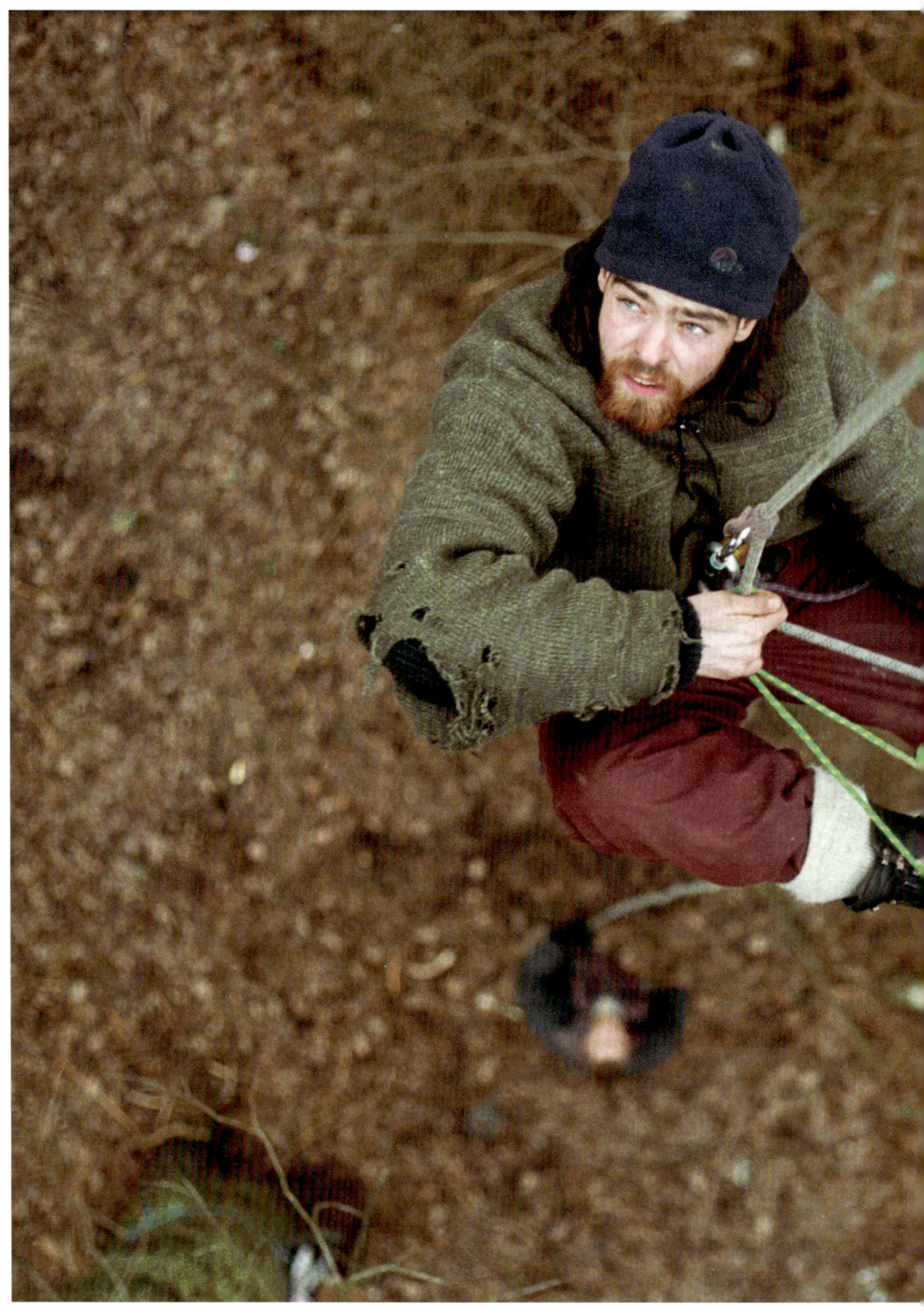

Newbury Bypass

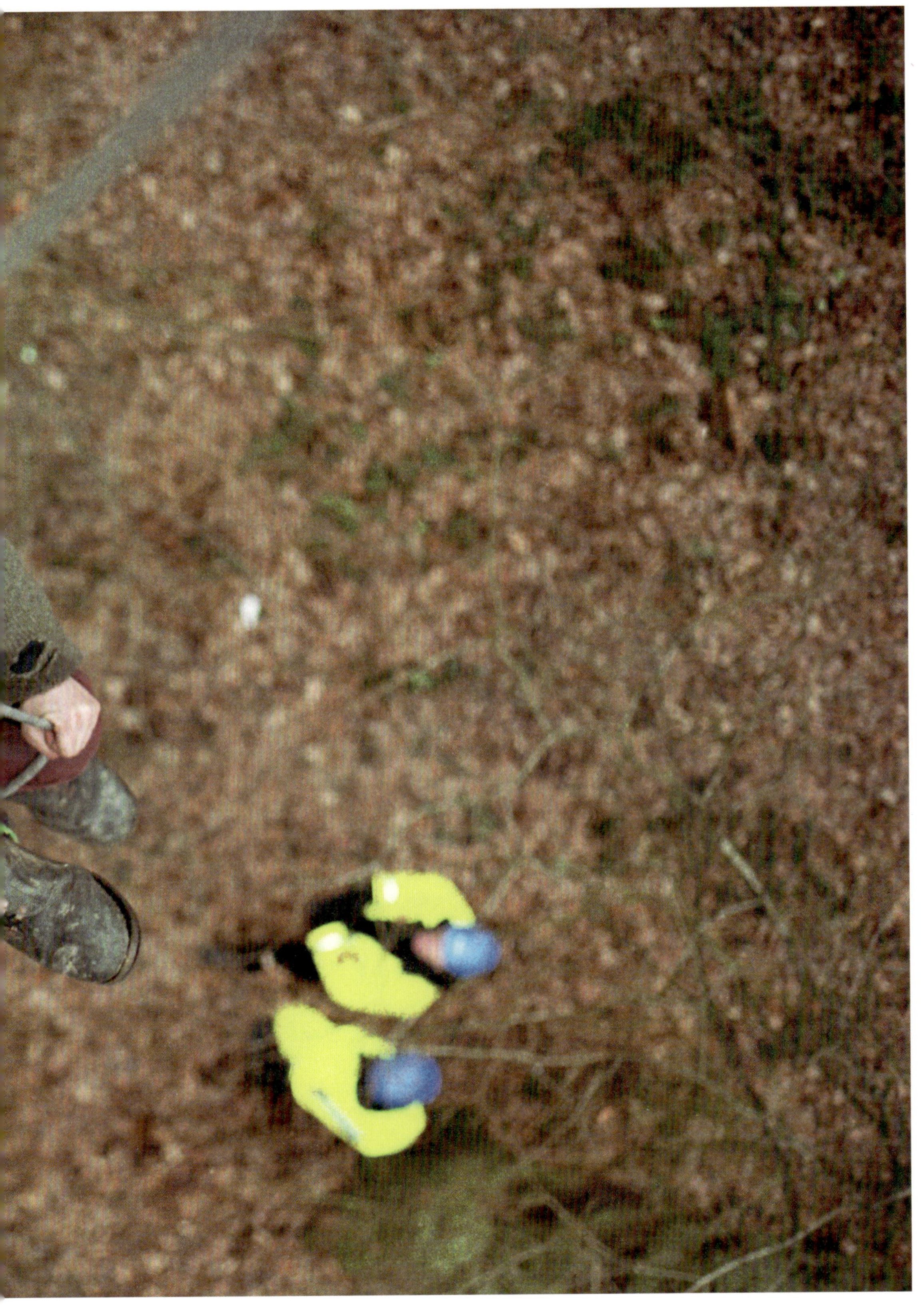

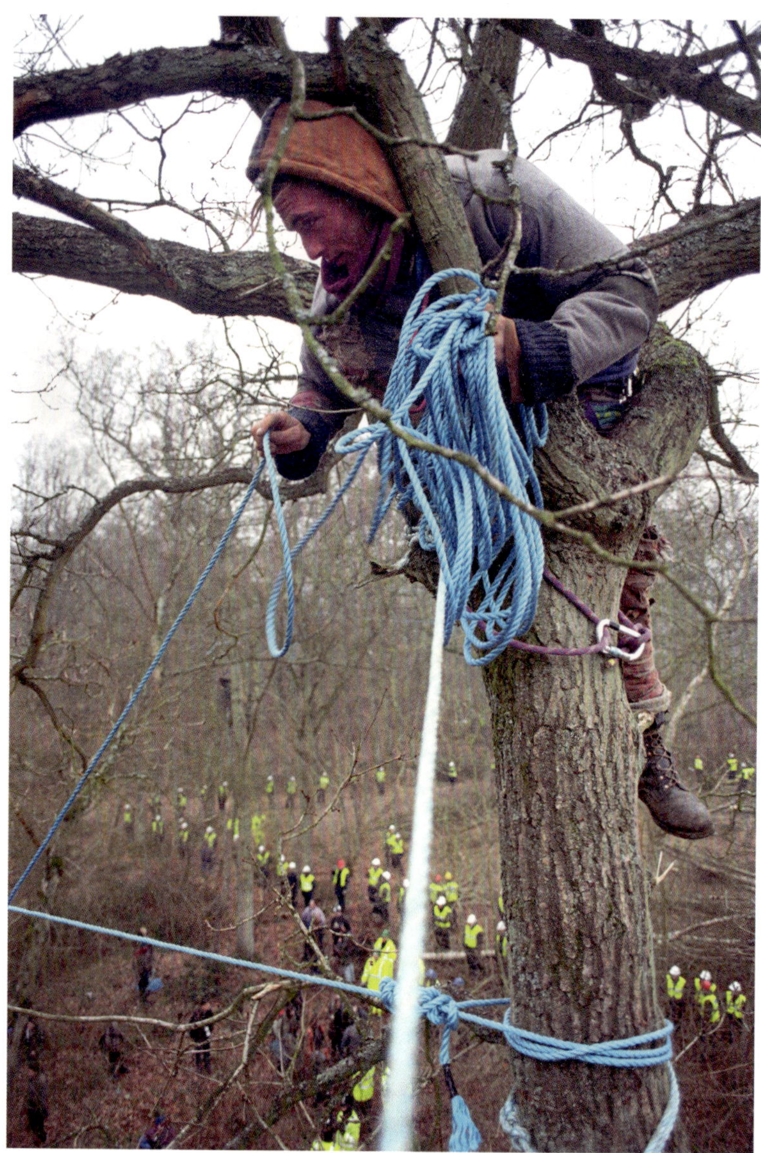

In the early morn a CB radio check-in informs activists where the police, security, eviction climbers and chainsaws are heading. Long before the ubiquitous presence of mobile phones these simple radio devices allowed the different camps to keep in contact and organise according to the movements of those slicing their way through the English countryside.

Newbury Bypass

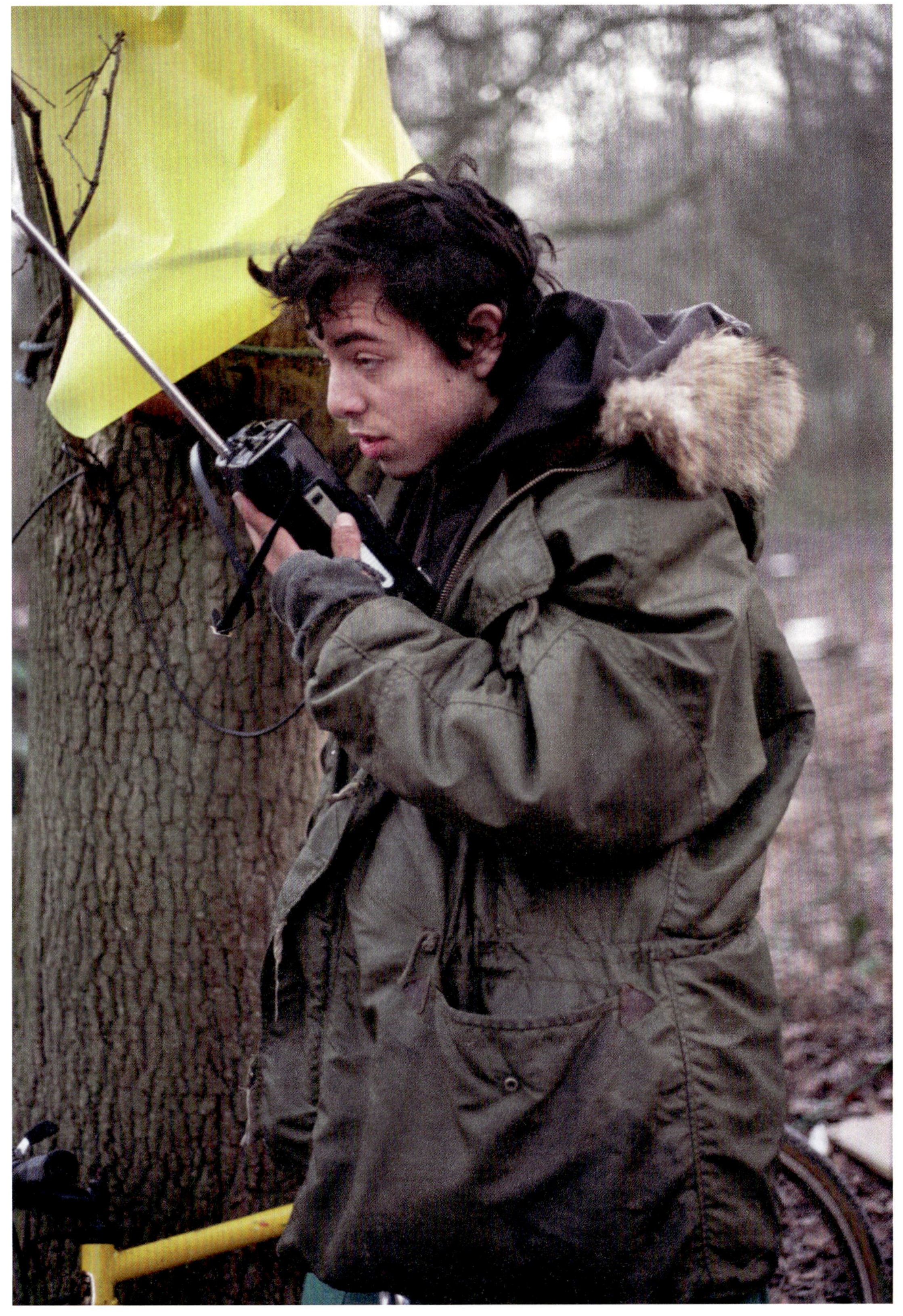

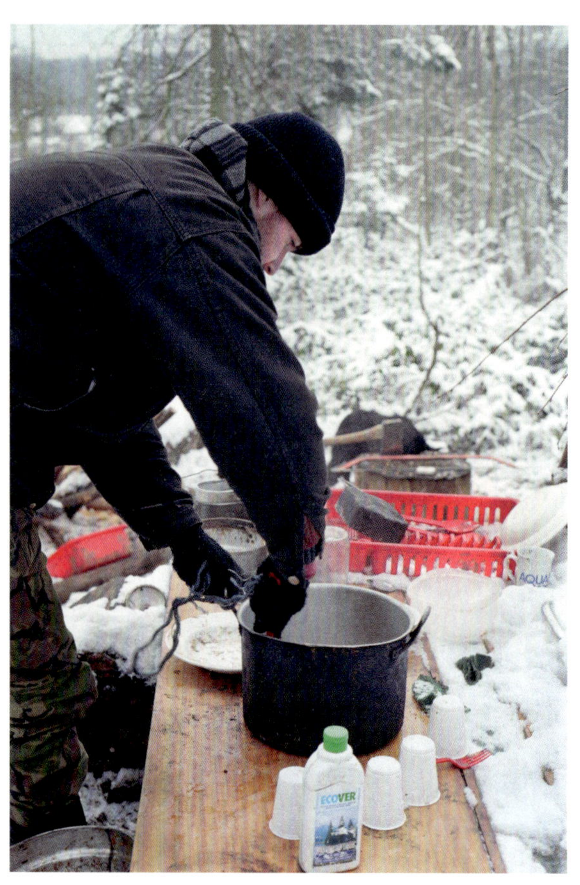

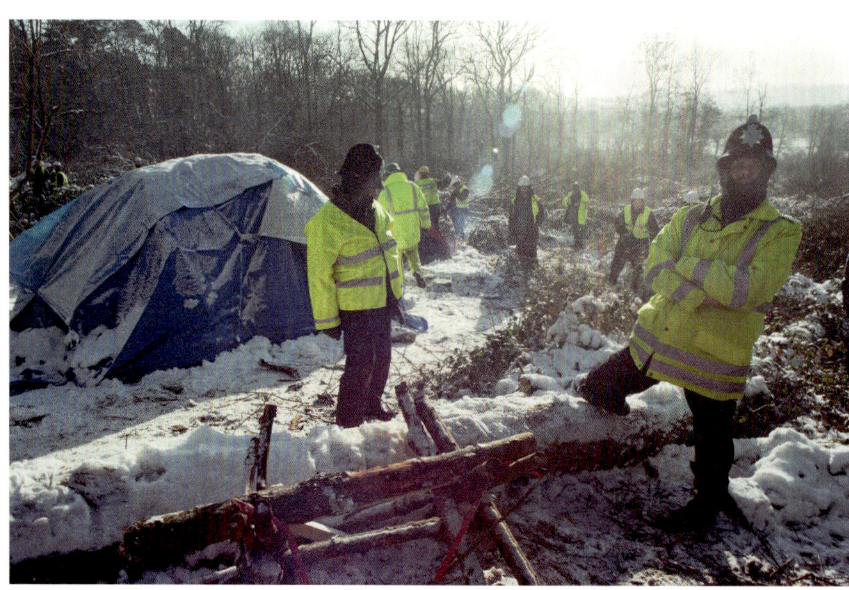

Newbury Bypass

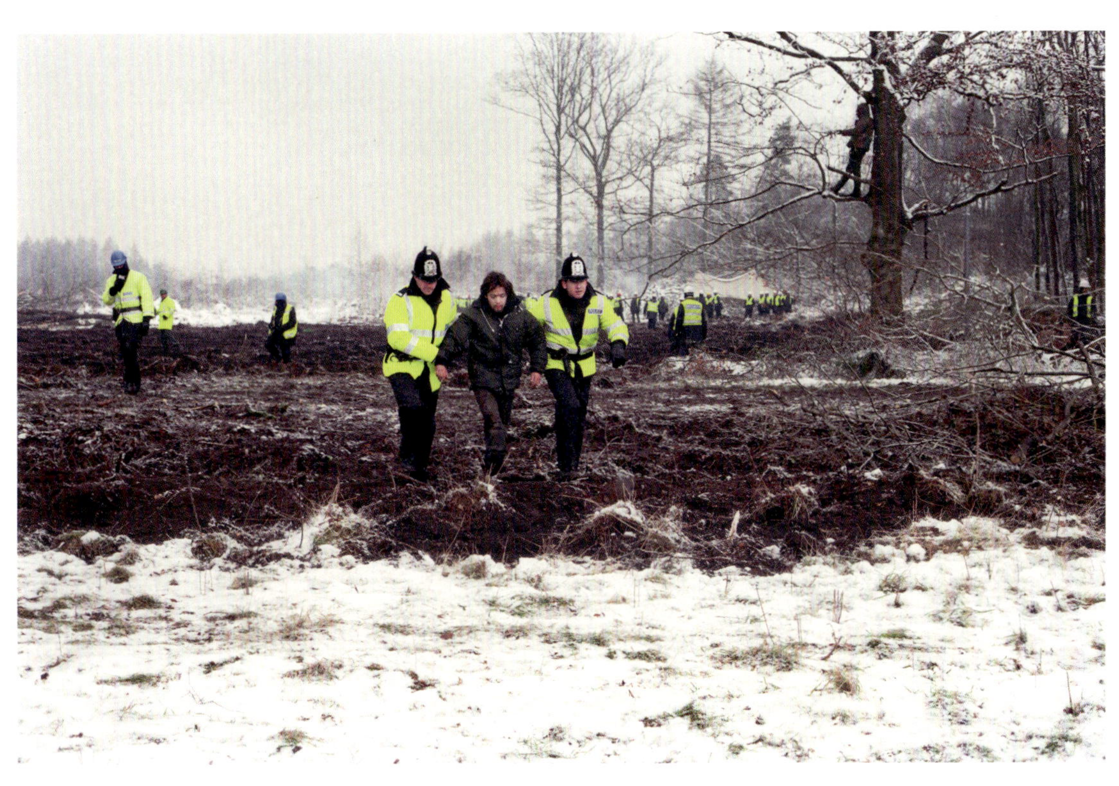

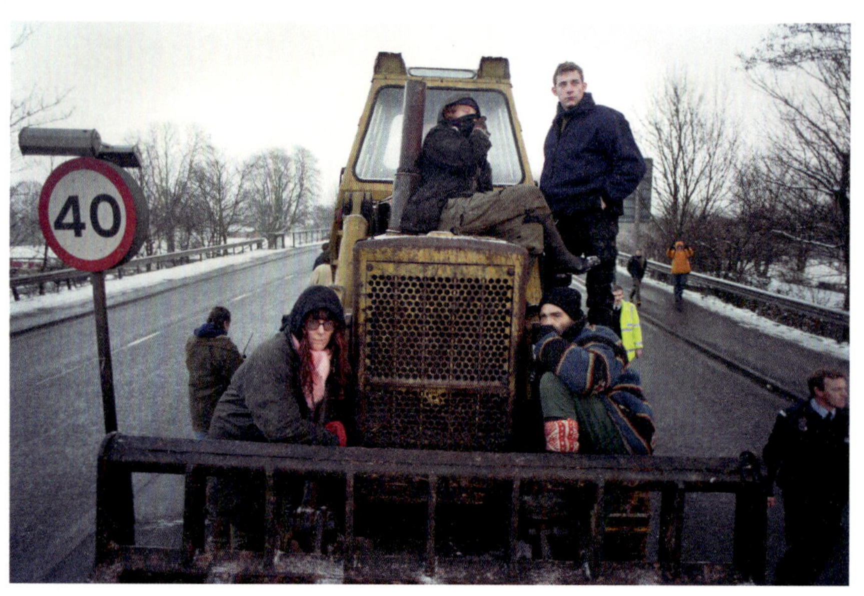

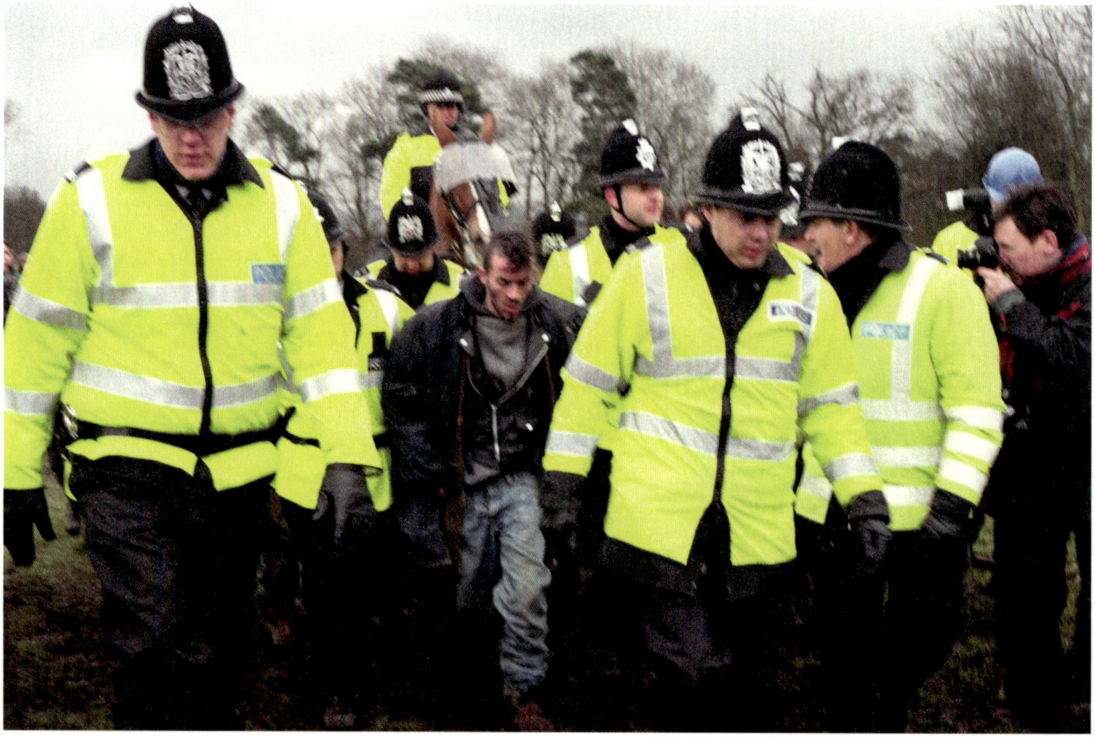

Newbury Bypass

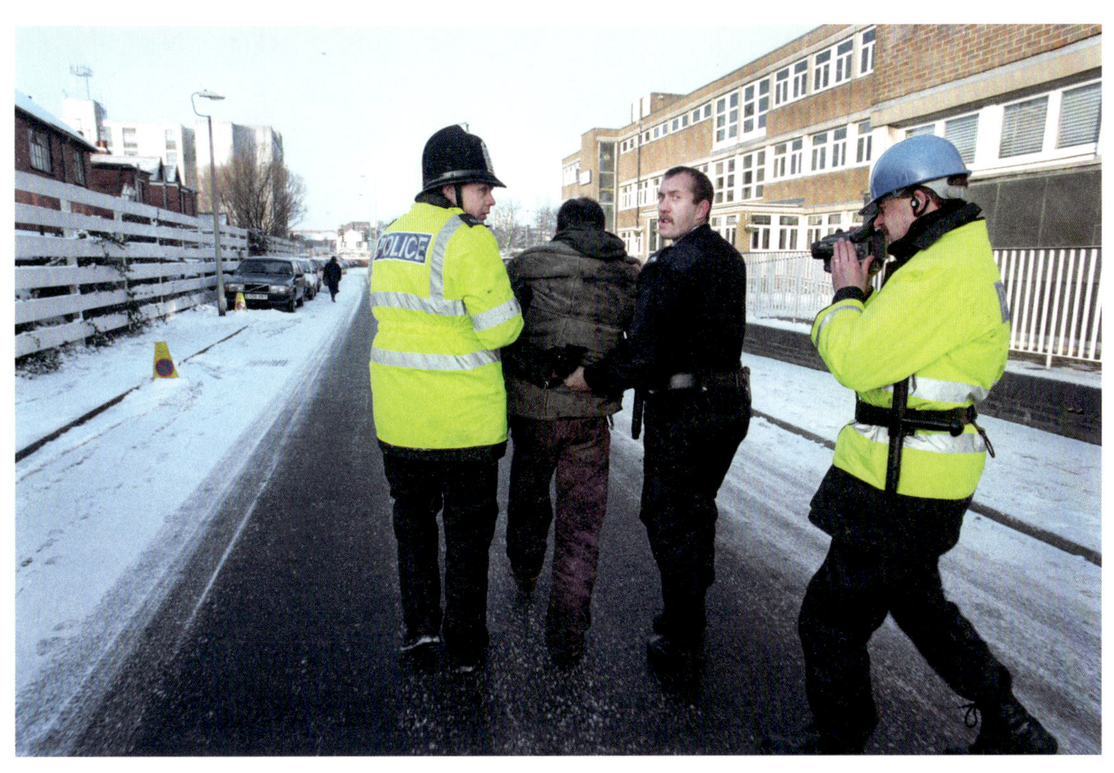

Lying in wait in the dawn light the convoy of heavy works vehicles approached, much like tanks in a war raged against nature. At a given moment activists ran onto the road and clambered onto the cold steel machines. The plain-clothes police, having failed to stop the action, were driven by rage. A slow strangulation is an effective way to remove someone from a digger. The policeman in yellow looks away so as not to witness his colleague's brutality.

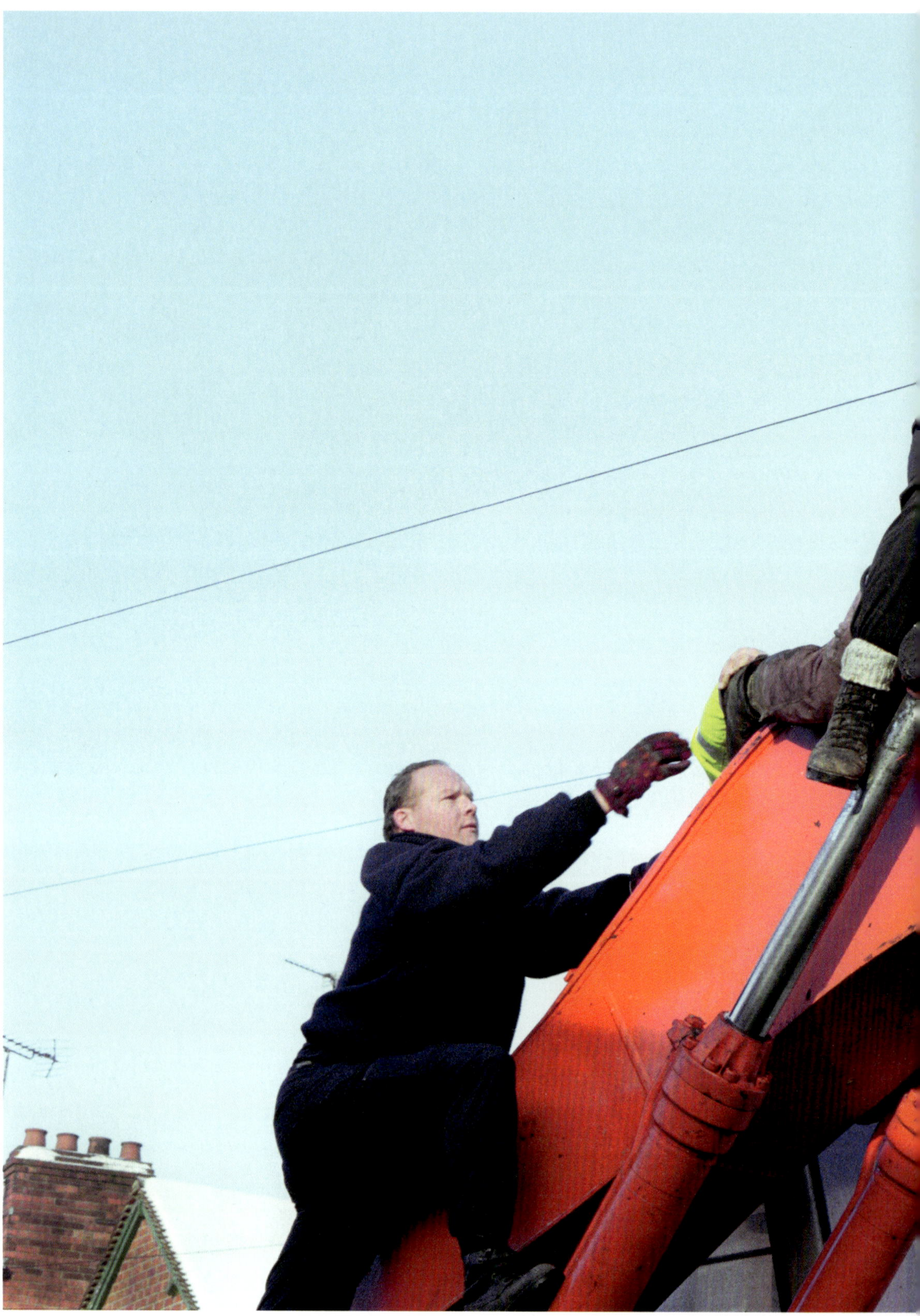

Newbury Bypass

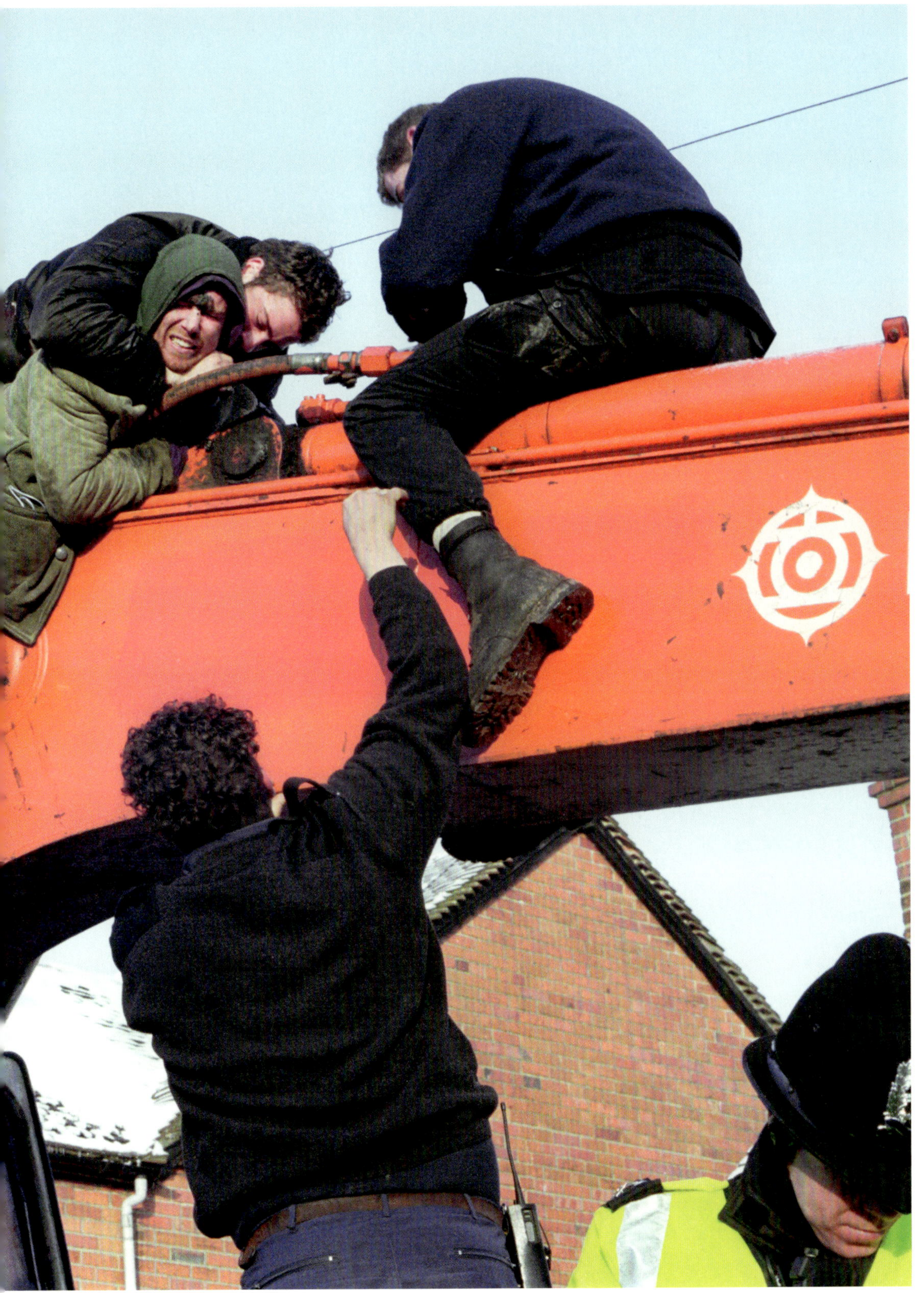

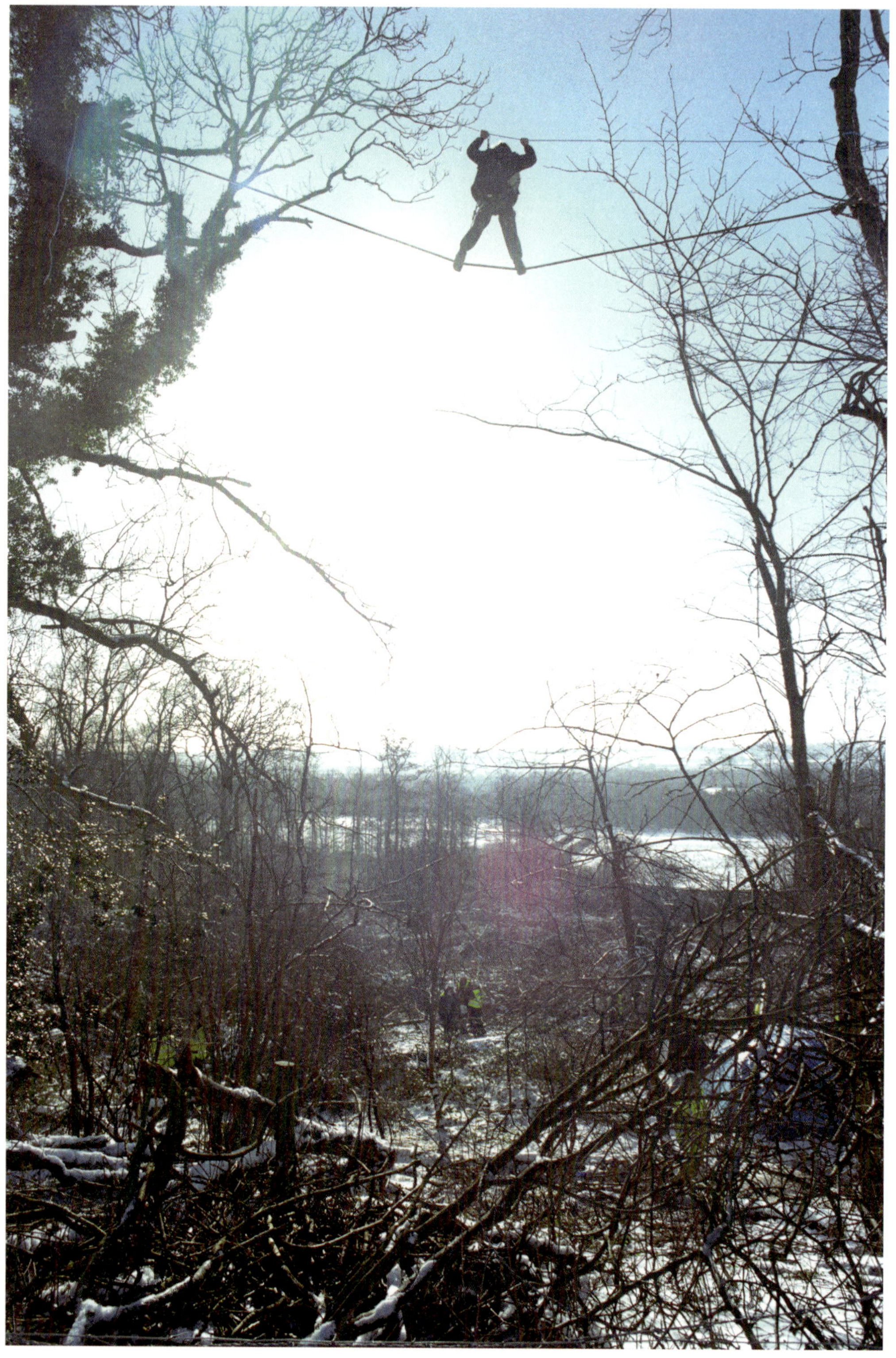

Newbury Bypass

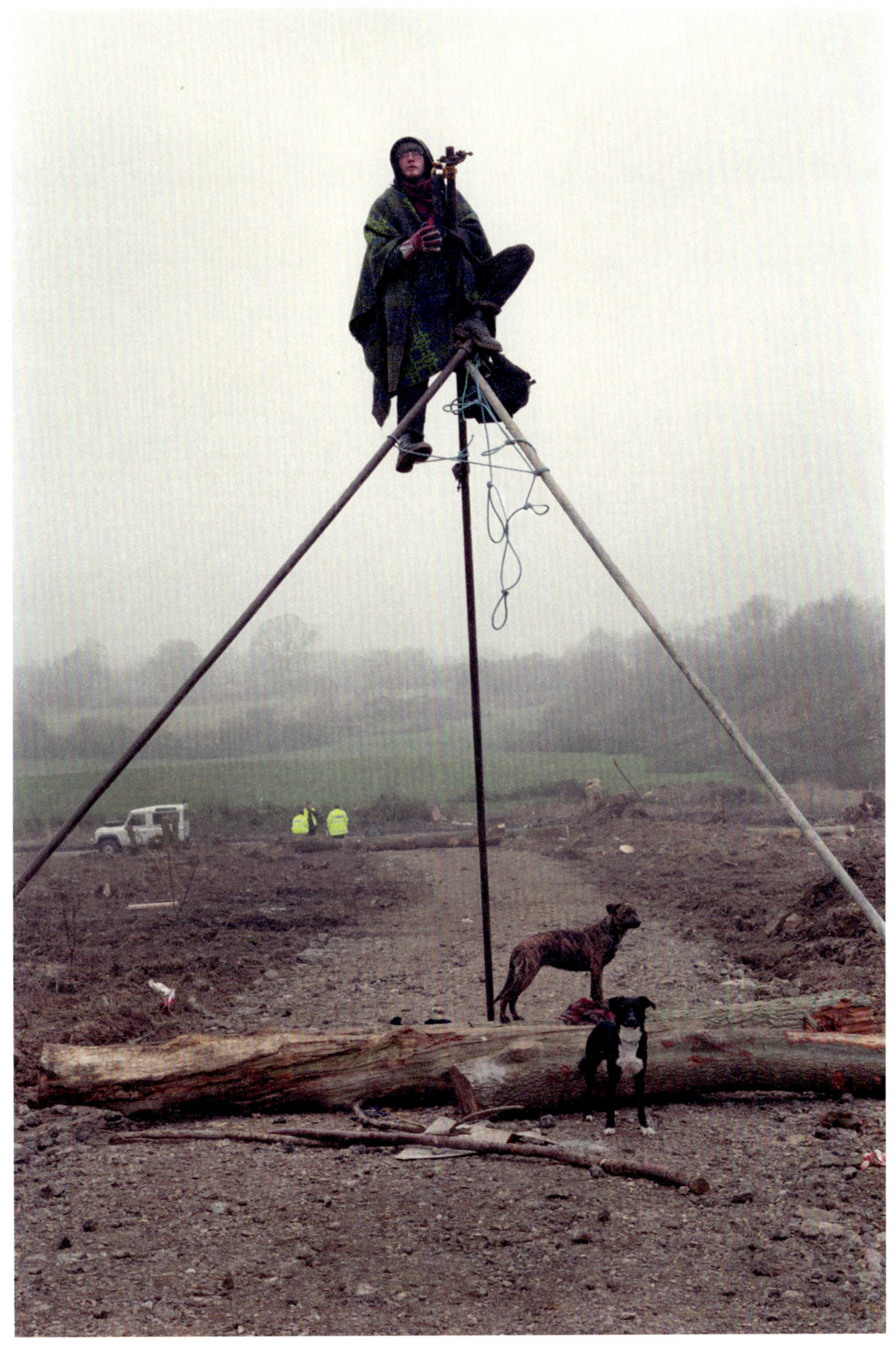

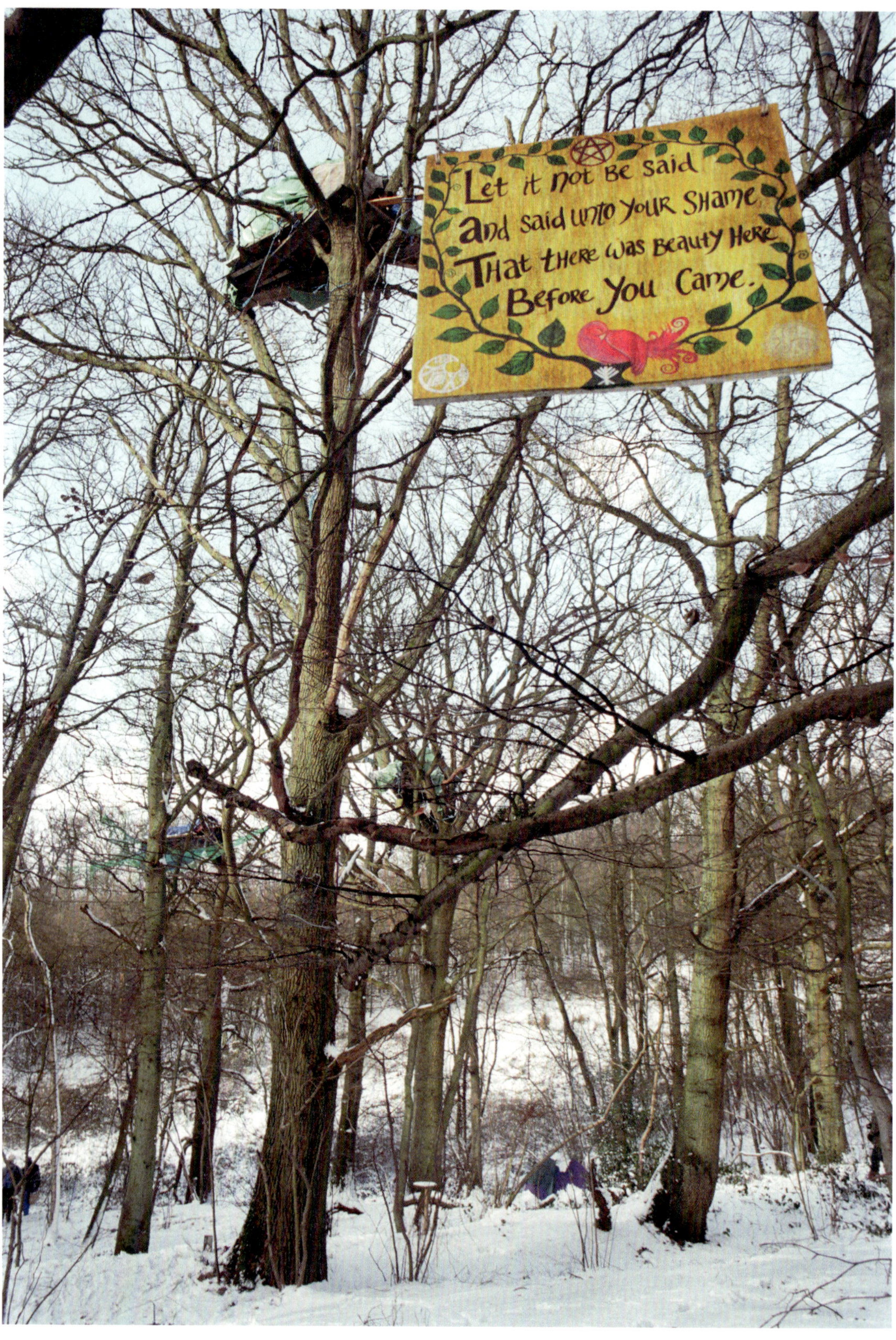

Newbury Bypass

That winter was the coldest in memory with temperatures plunging to -13. Living in the Newbury camps in such conditions was a tough insight into how many lived for centuries before us. The water would freeze making even simple chores like making tea a challenge while holding onto frozen branches for hours defending a tree would bring some close to frostbite. I'd never really understood the importance of the first kiss of spring until I'd spend much of that winter living outside. The deep death of those months was replaced by a twinkling vivaciousness of exploding new life.

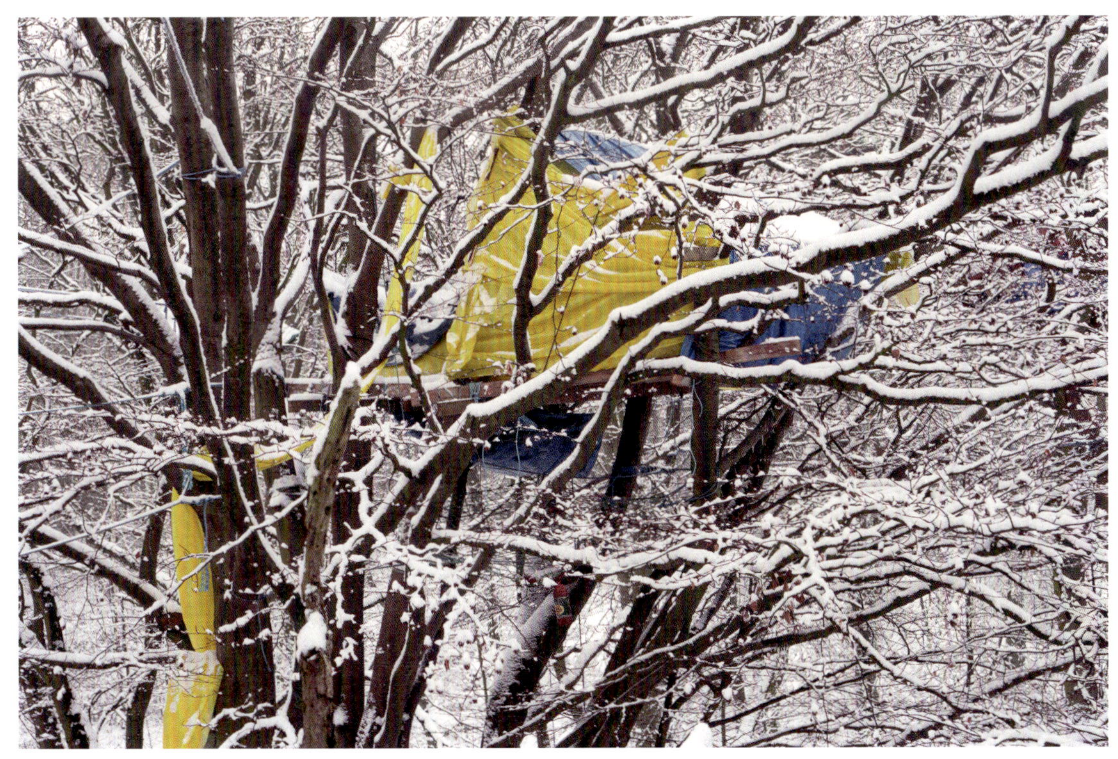

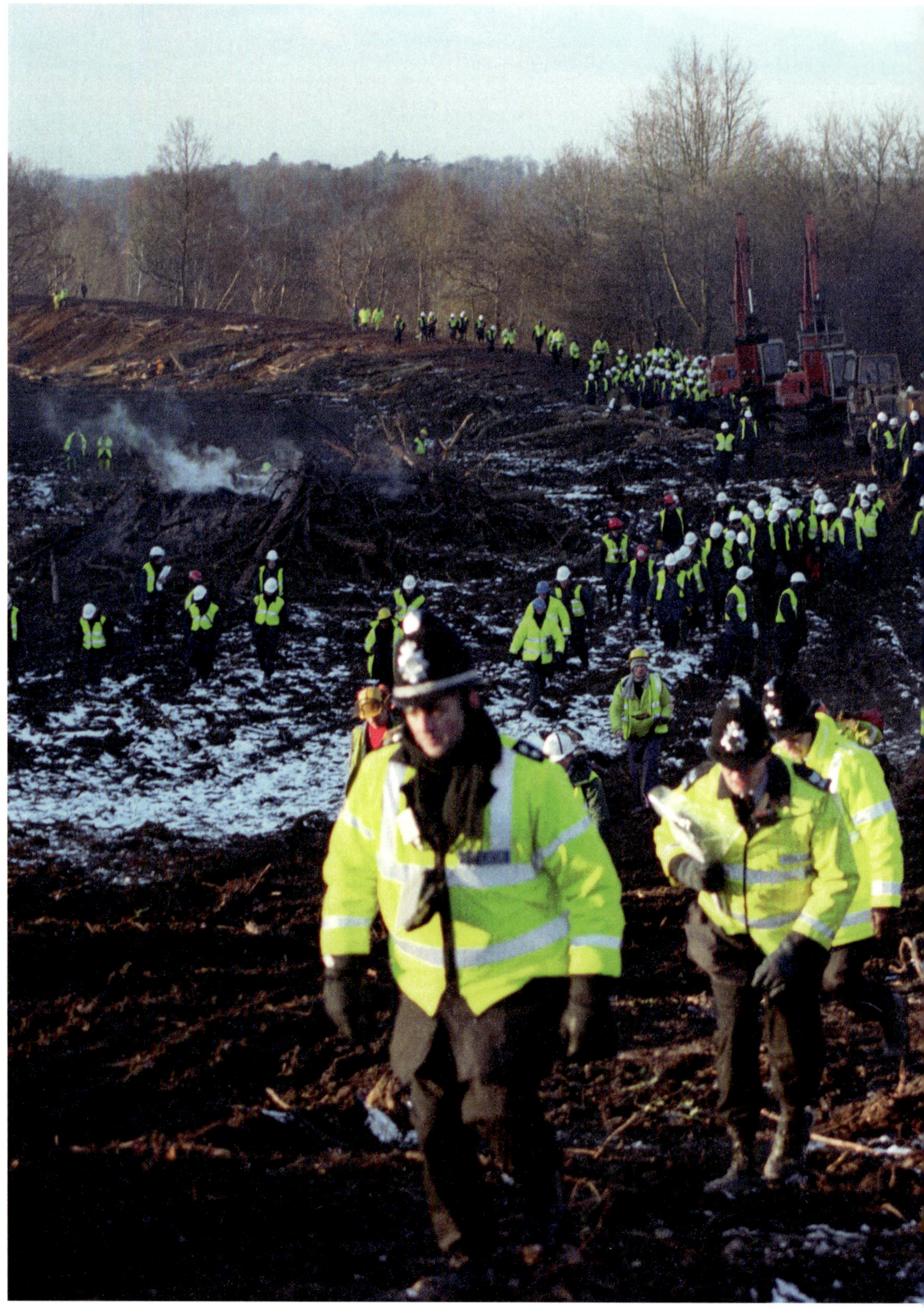

Newbury Bypass

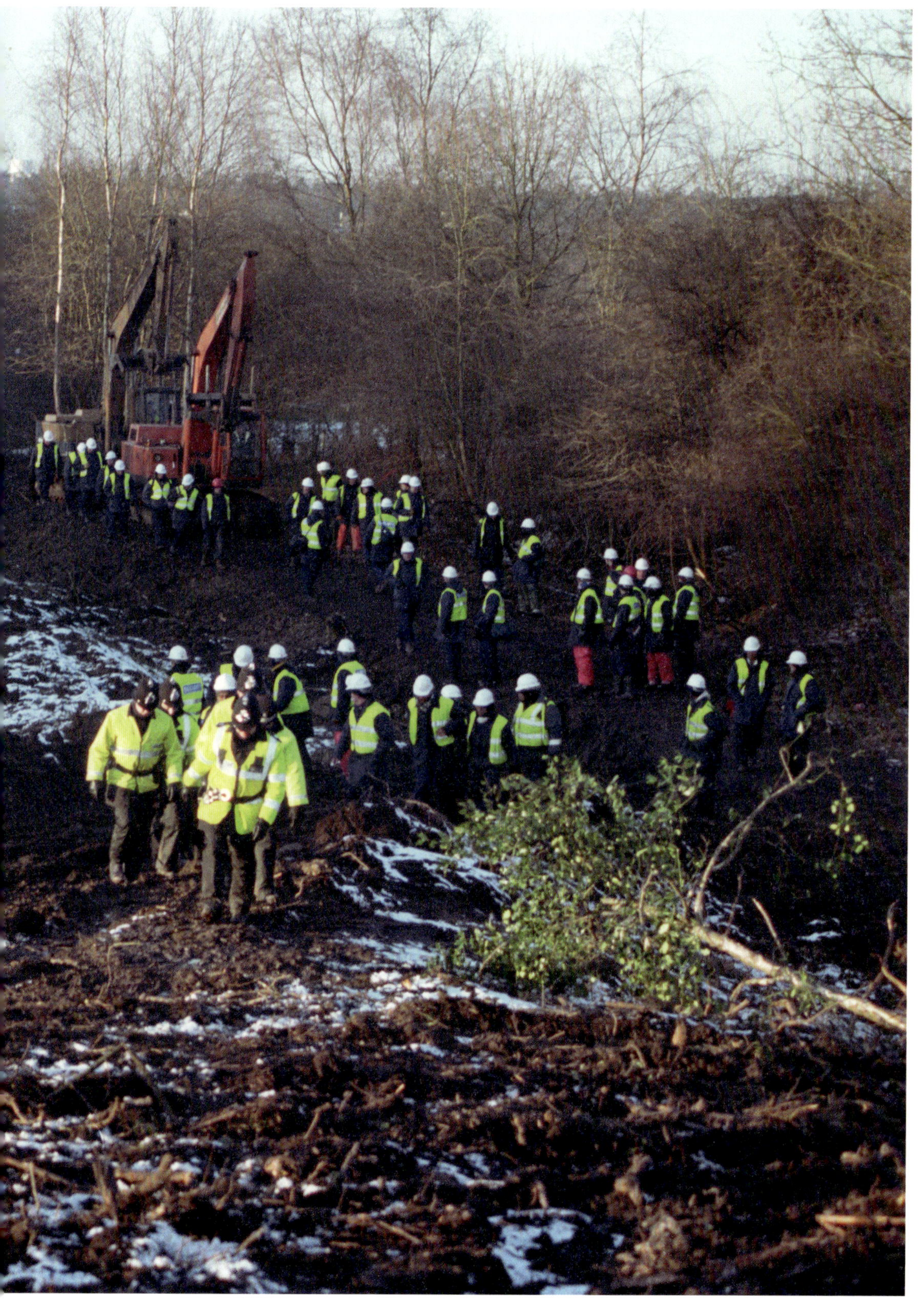

Much like an army leaving the battle scene, a convoy of diggers is escorted by its footsoldiers, determined to protect all that which was ripping, shredding and tearing its way through a world that has sustained us for millennia.

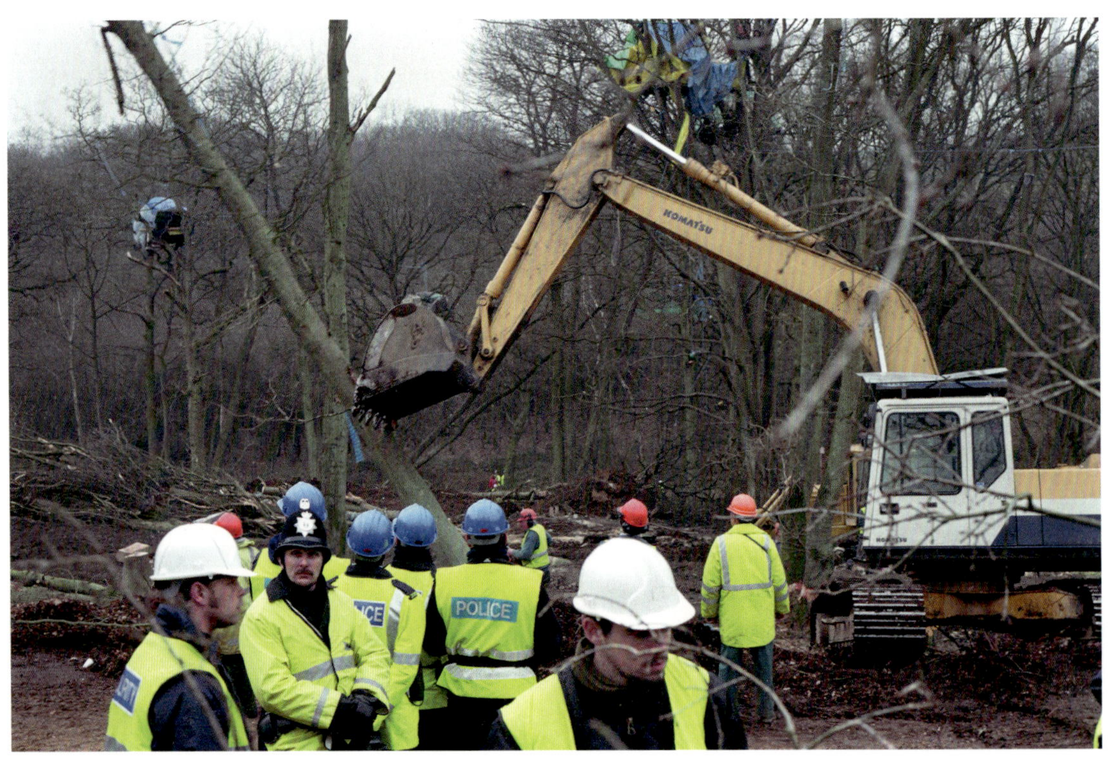

Newbury Bypass

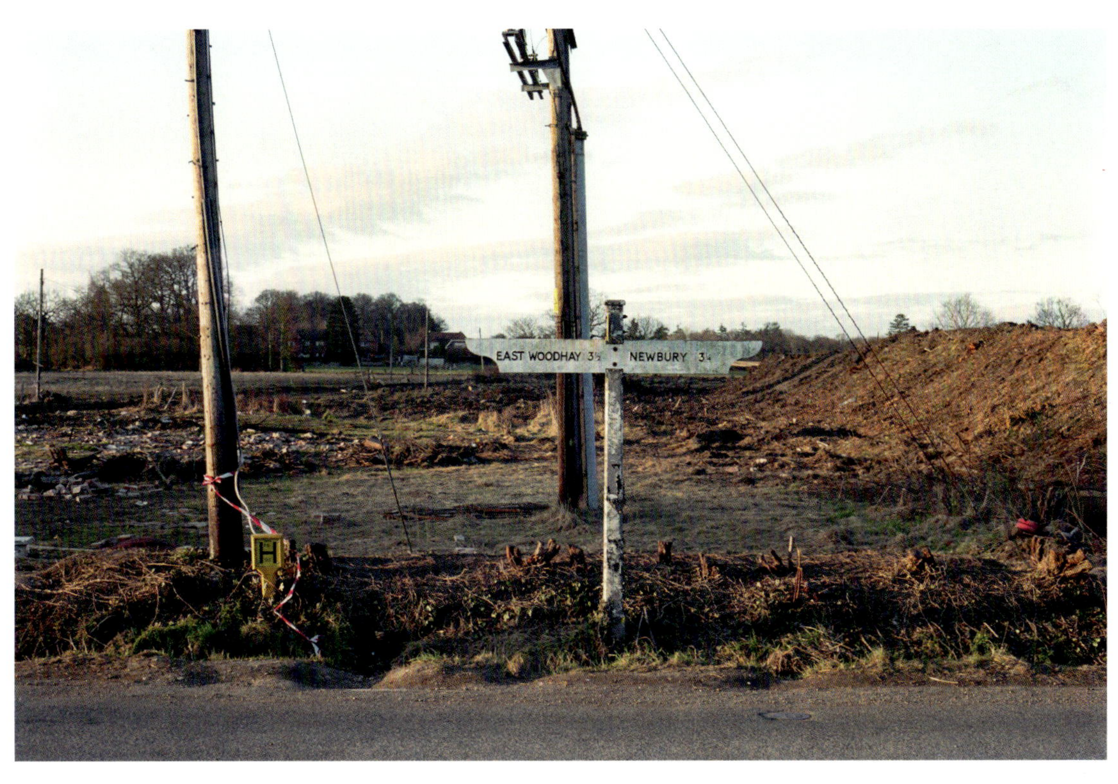

The violence against man, woman and ancient landscape took its toll on everyone. The constant scream of chainsaws and humans ripped from the trees left a heavy mark on the psyche of those there. Some suffered from PTSD for a long time afterwards – unable to forget the horrors of a government blind to the destruction it was inflicting on a gentle old land. No one who fought against the Newbury bypass will ever forget those experiences: they are etched into our memory forever.

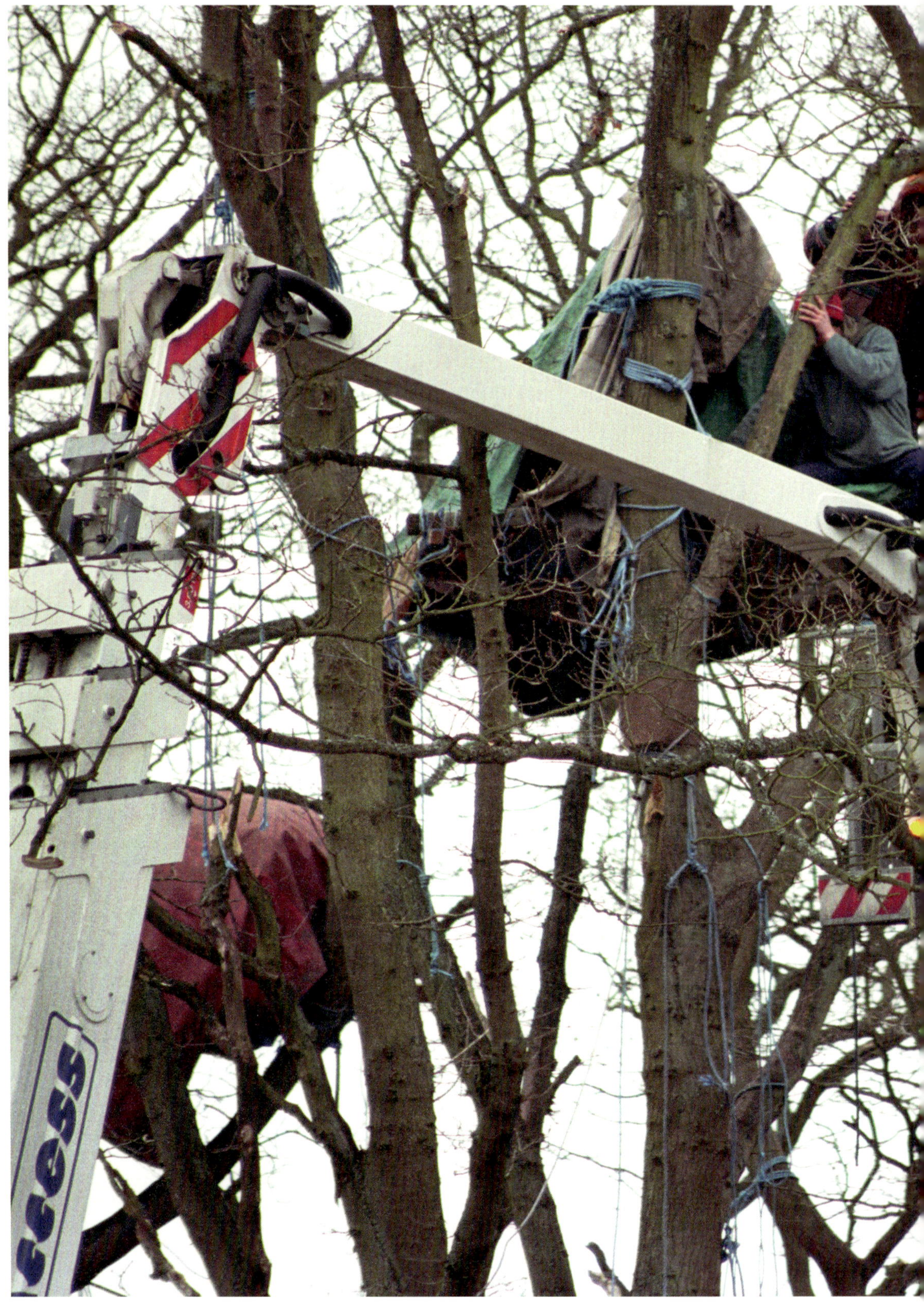

Newbury Bypass

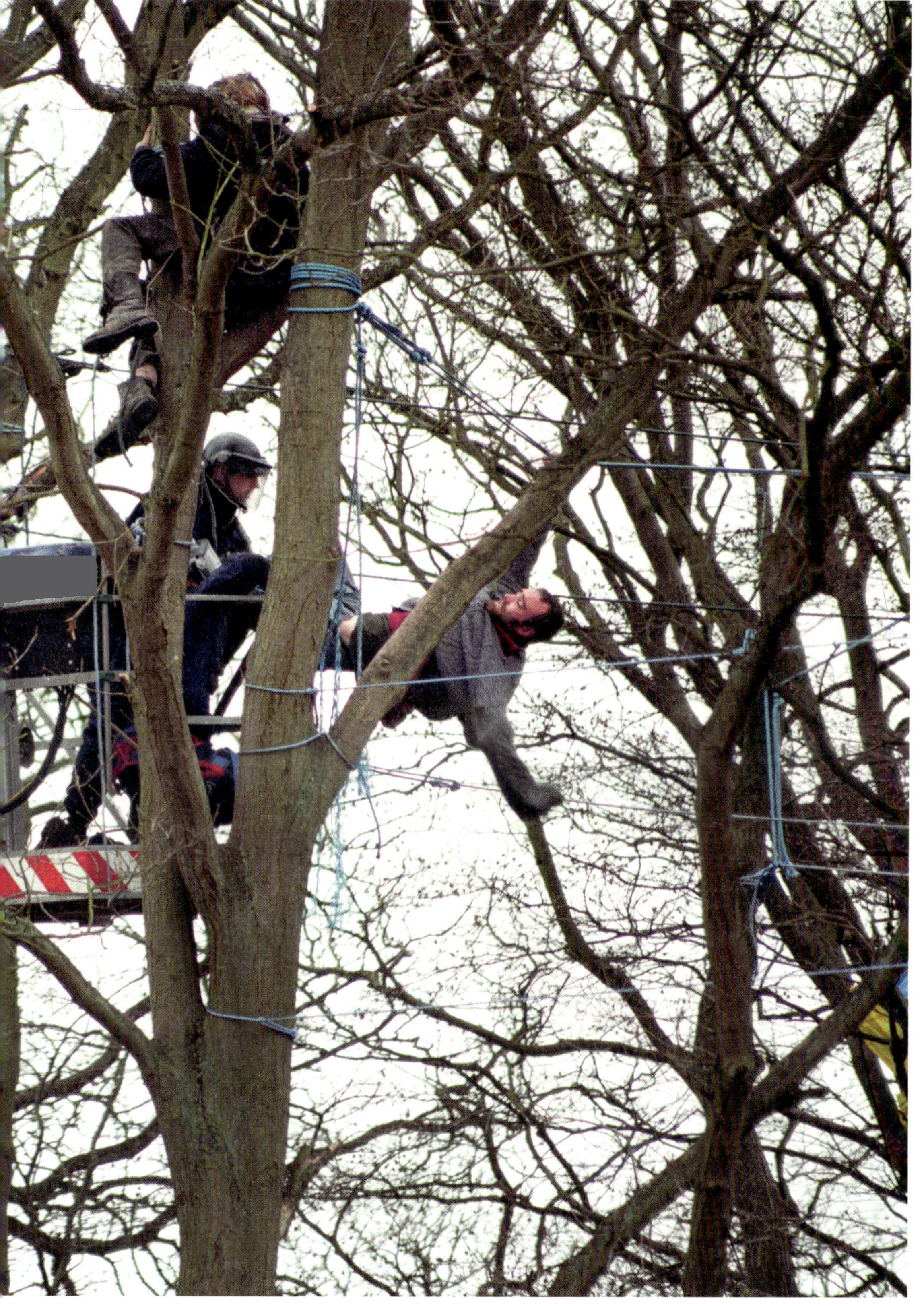

You can see the tension and anxiety etched onto the faces of those witnessing another brutal eviction from the trees. The shouting, screaming and sheer violence of the experience lingered in the mind long after the last tree had been felled.

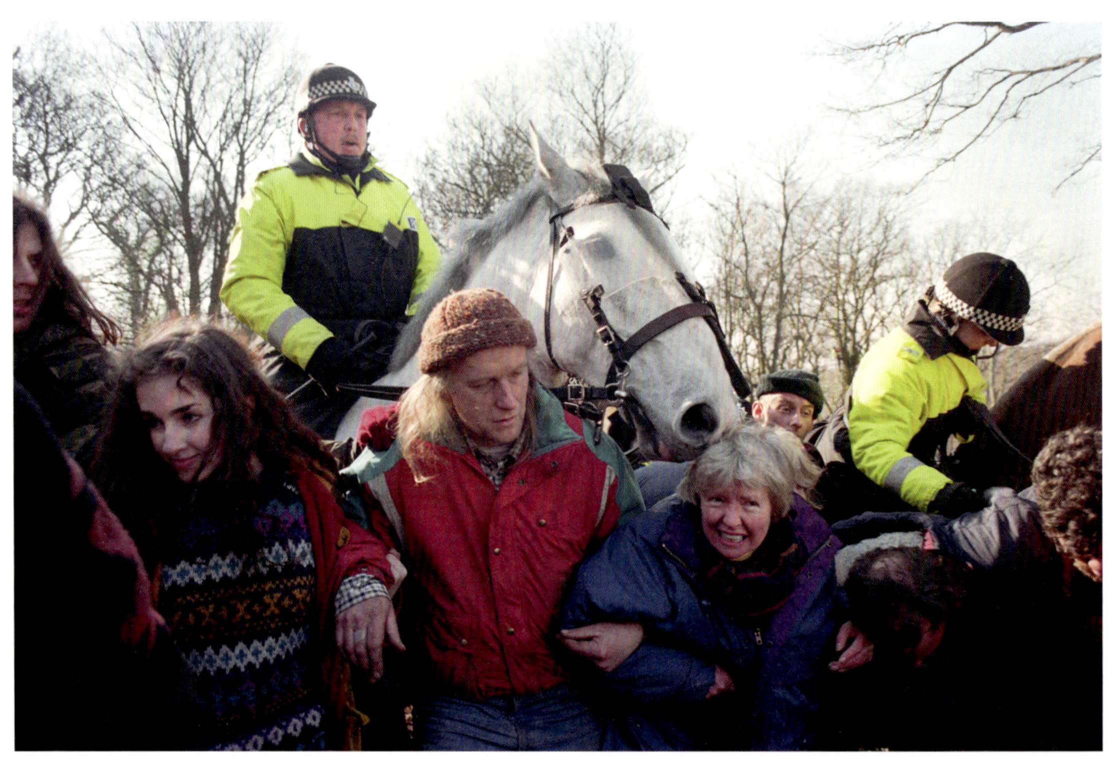

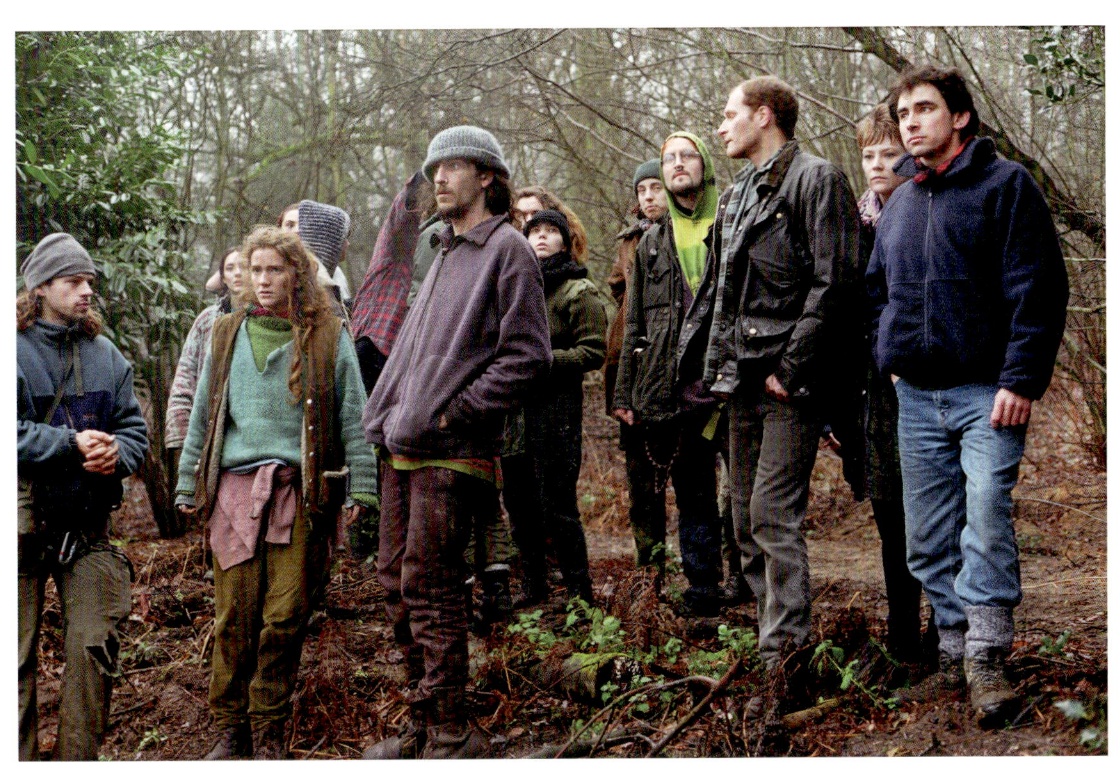

There were moments at Newbury where we were sure we were about to witness the death of an activist. The man desperately clung on with arms wrapped around the branch whilst the digger pushed over a tree in an act of wanton violence. It passed so close to the branch it chopped its end clean off. It is nothing short of a miracle that no one died during those intense months at the third battle of Newbury.

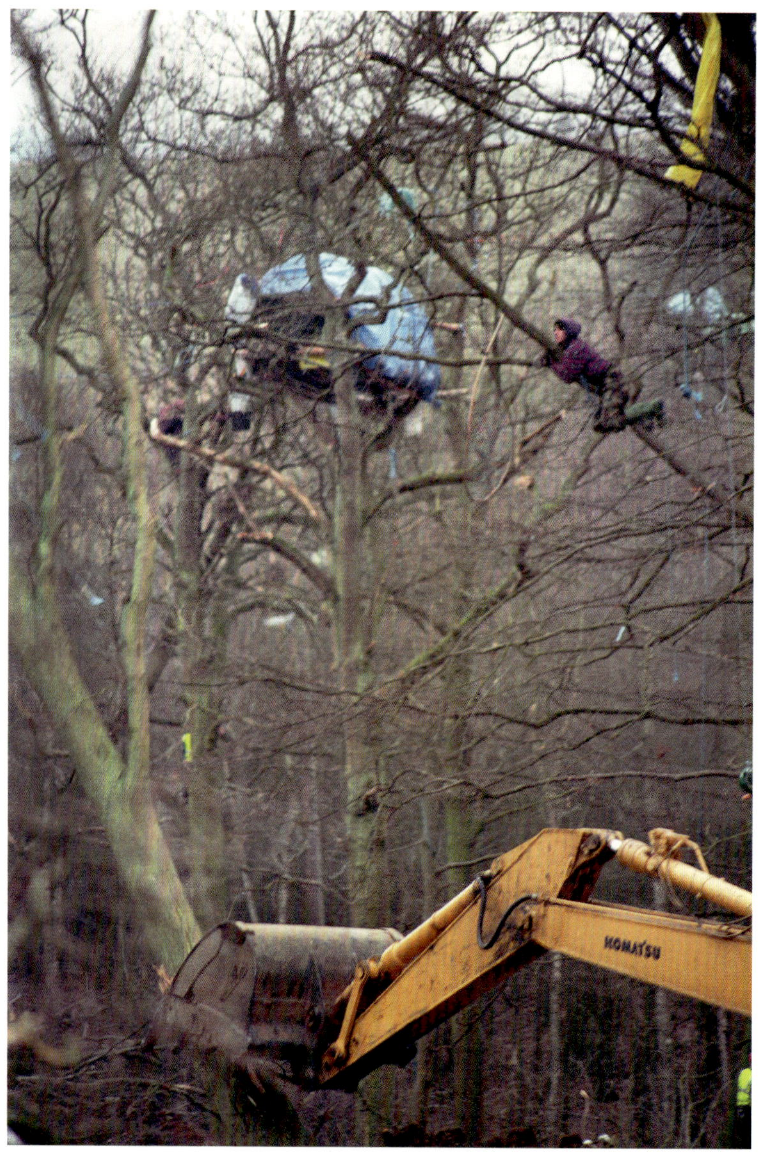

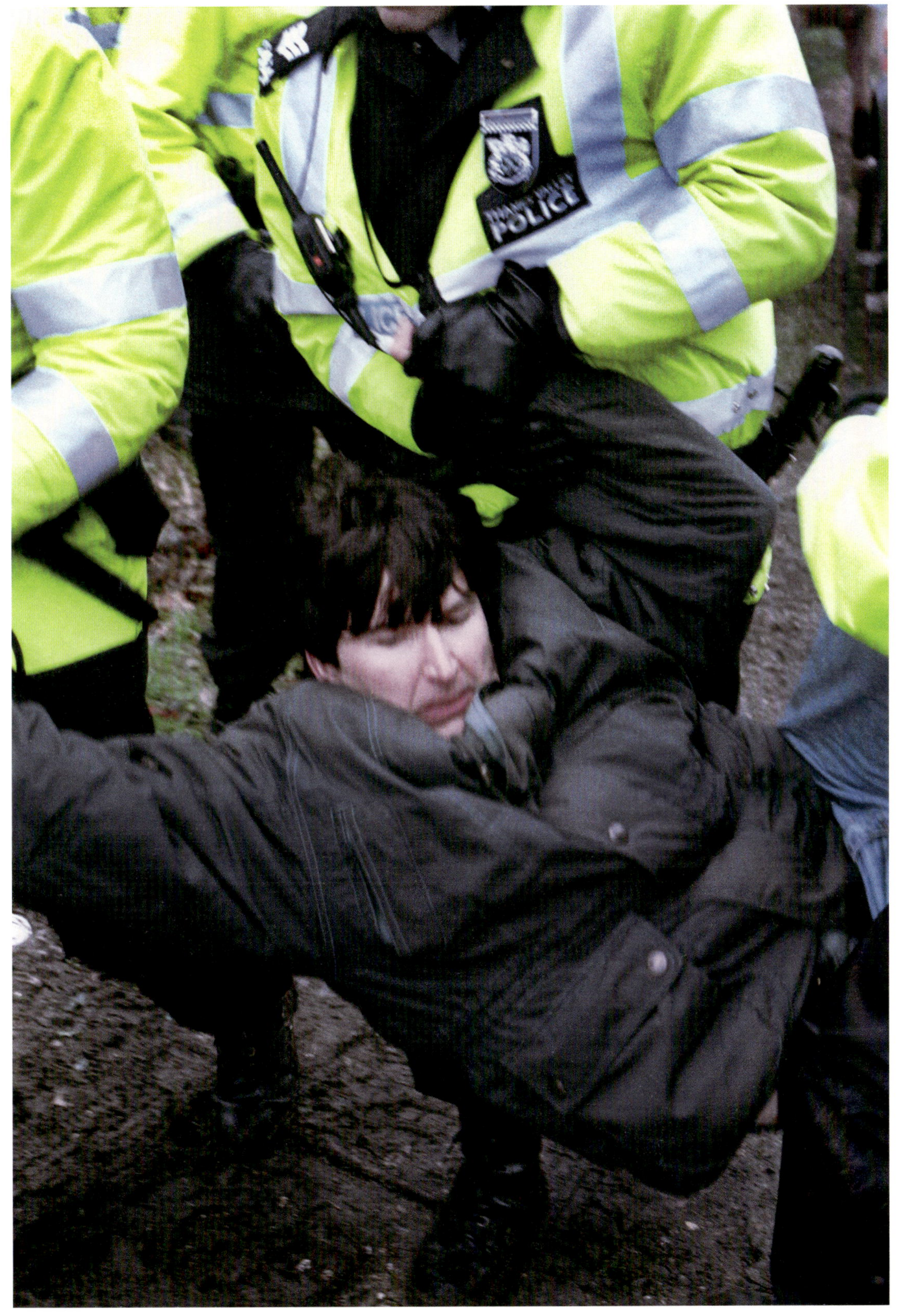
POLICE

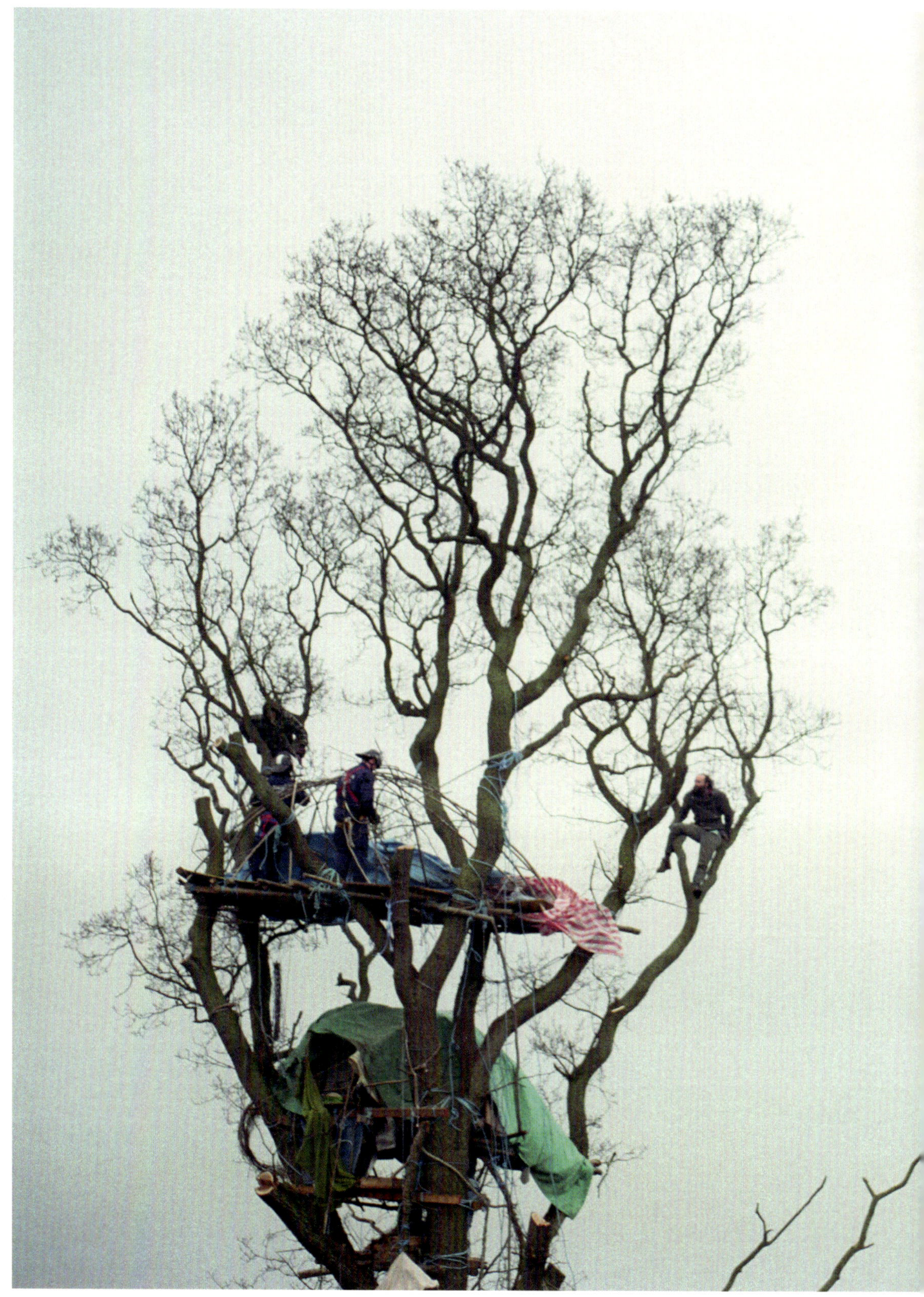

Newbury Bypass

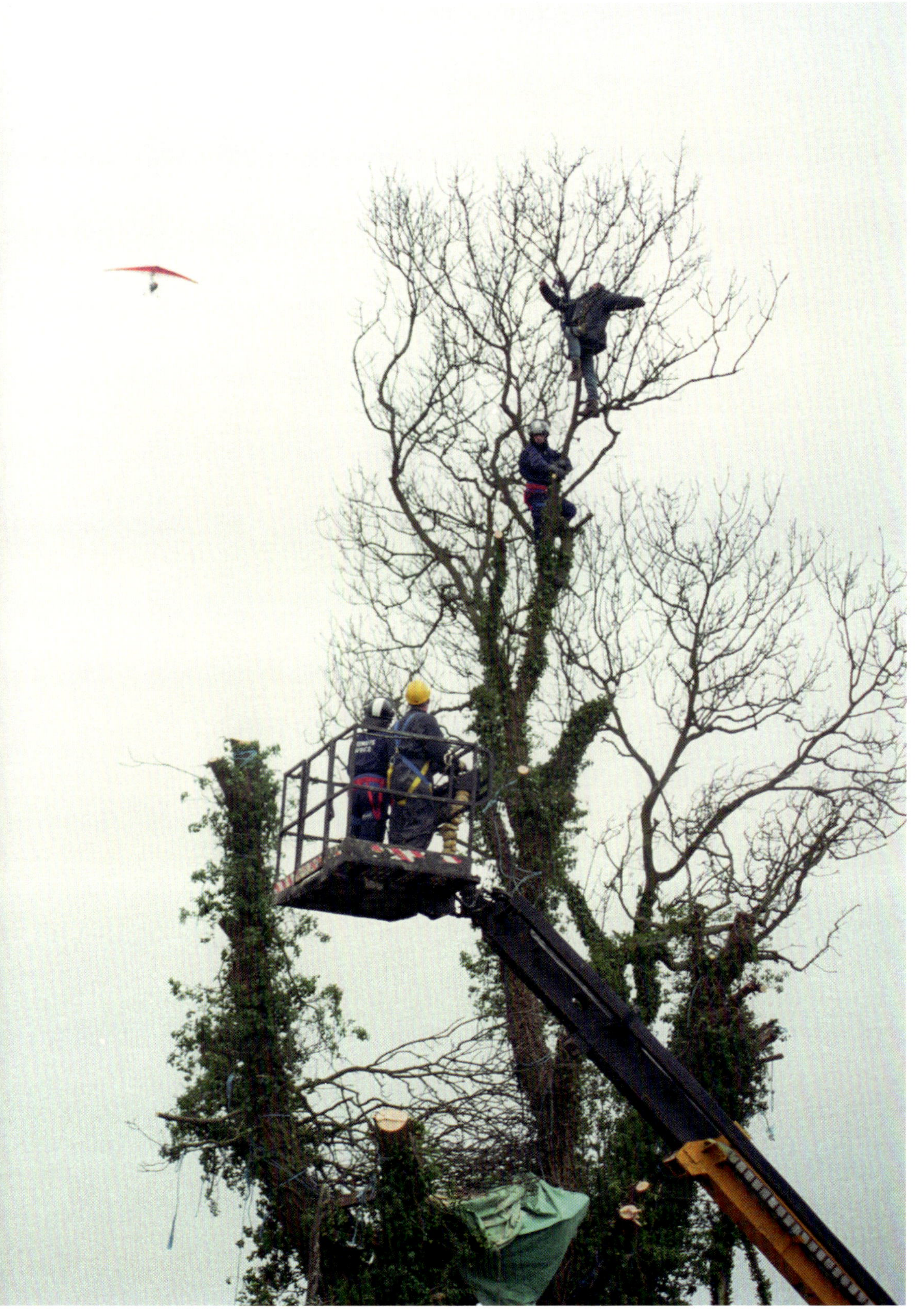

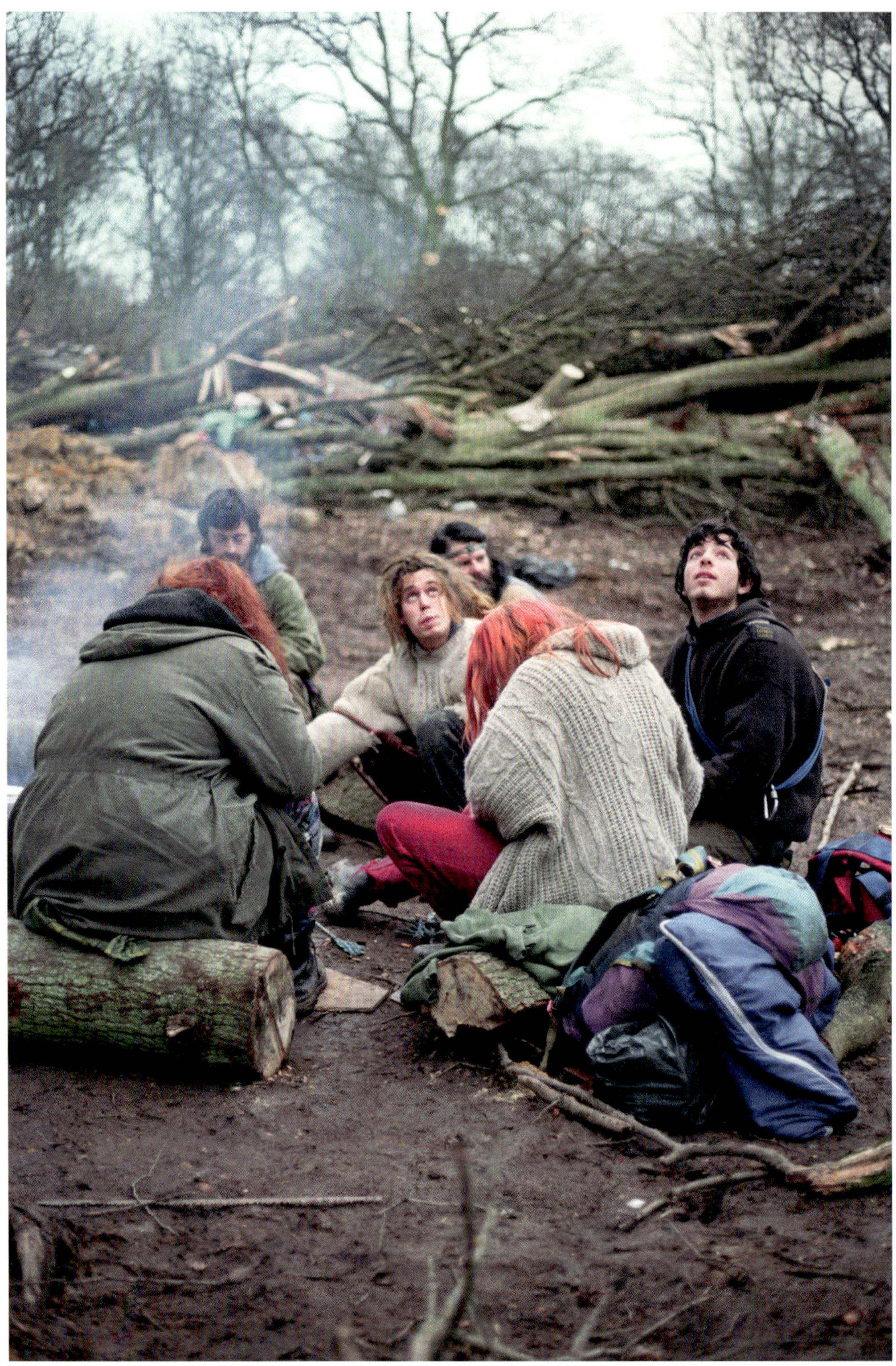

Newbury Bypass

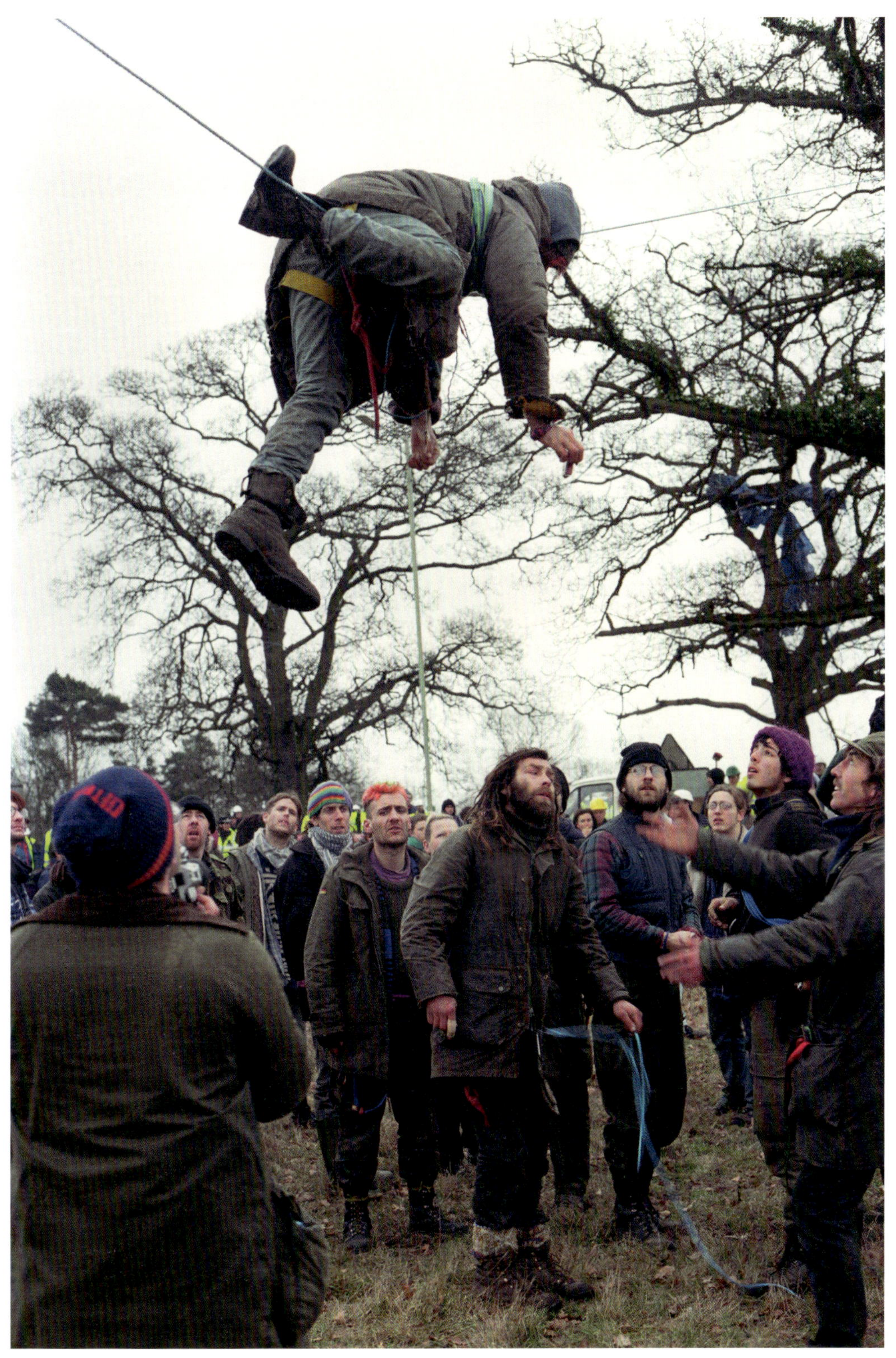

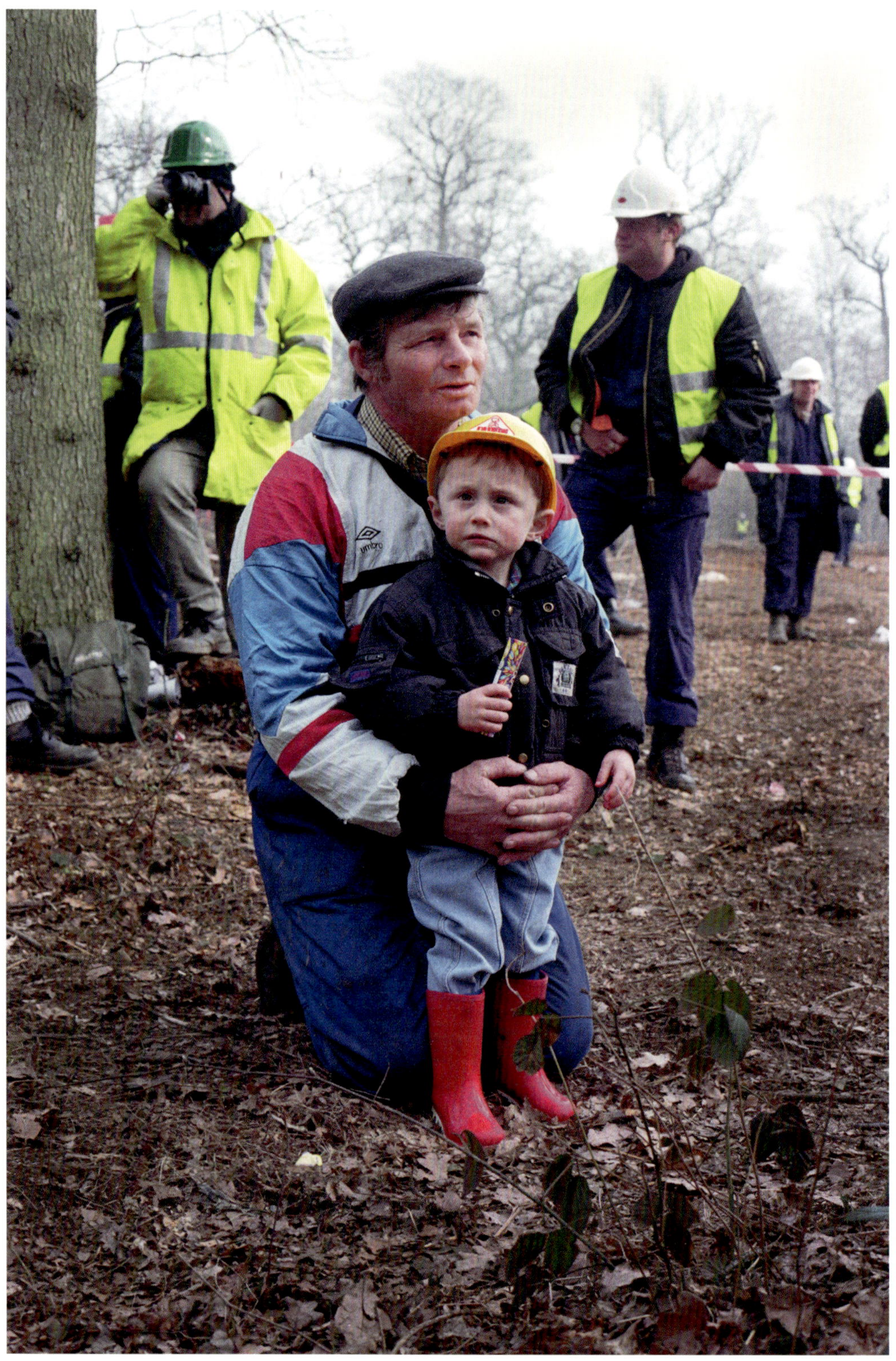

Newbury Bypass

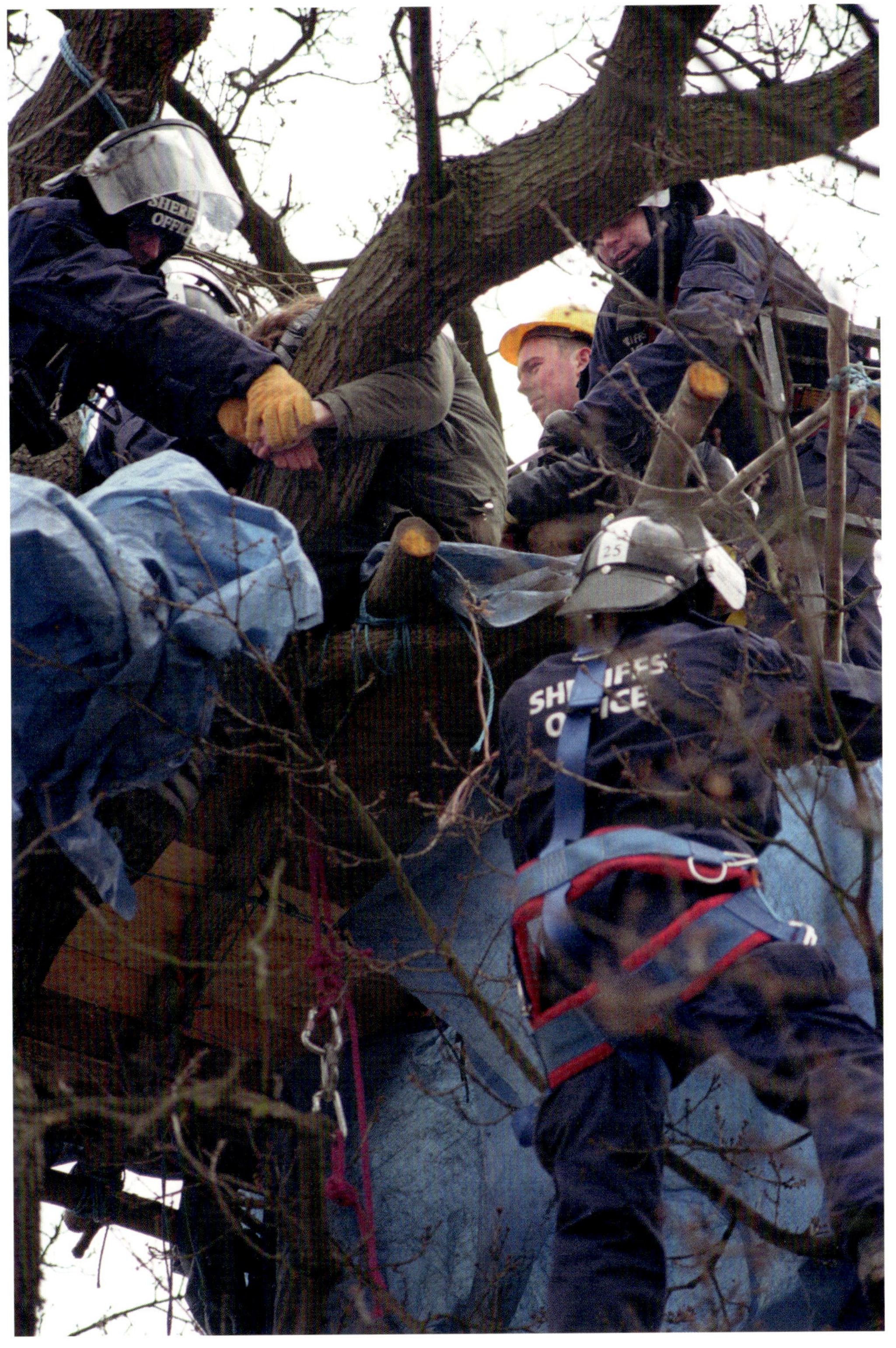
25

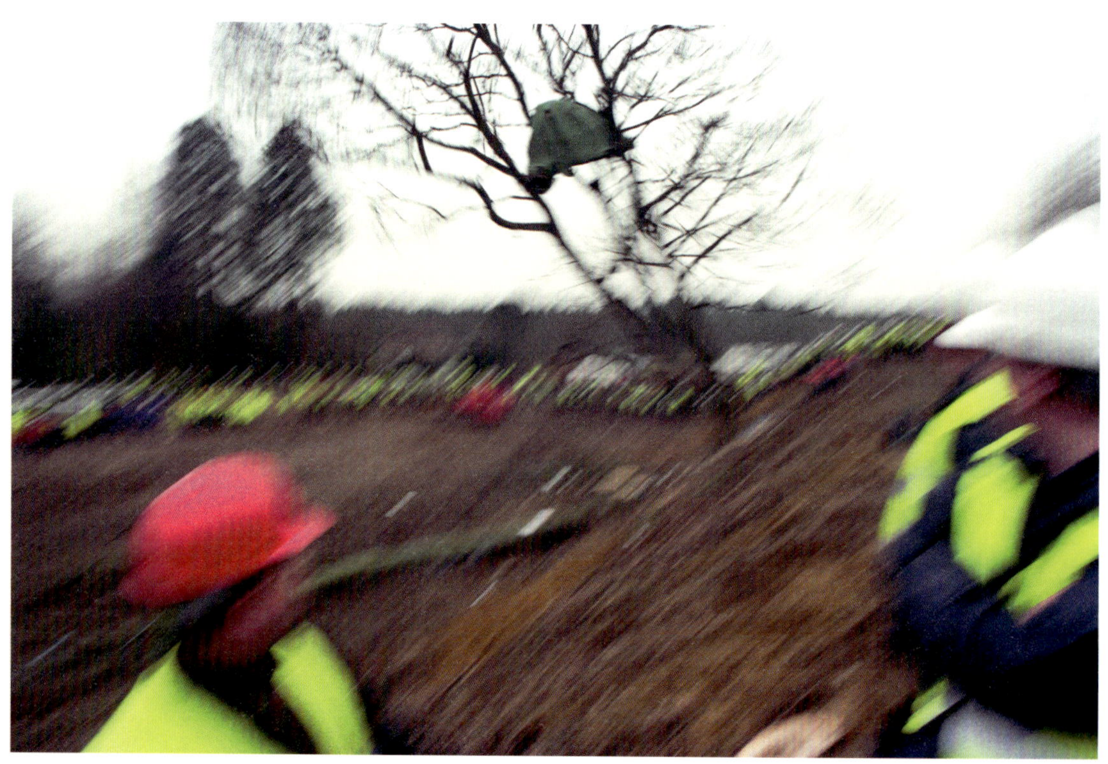

Newbury Bypass

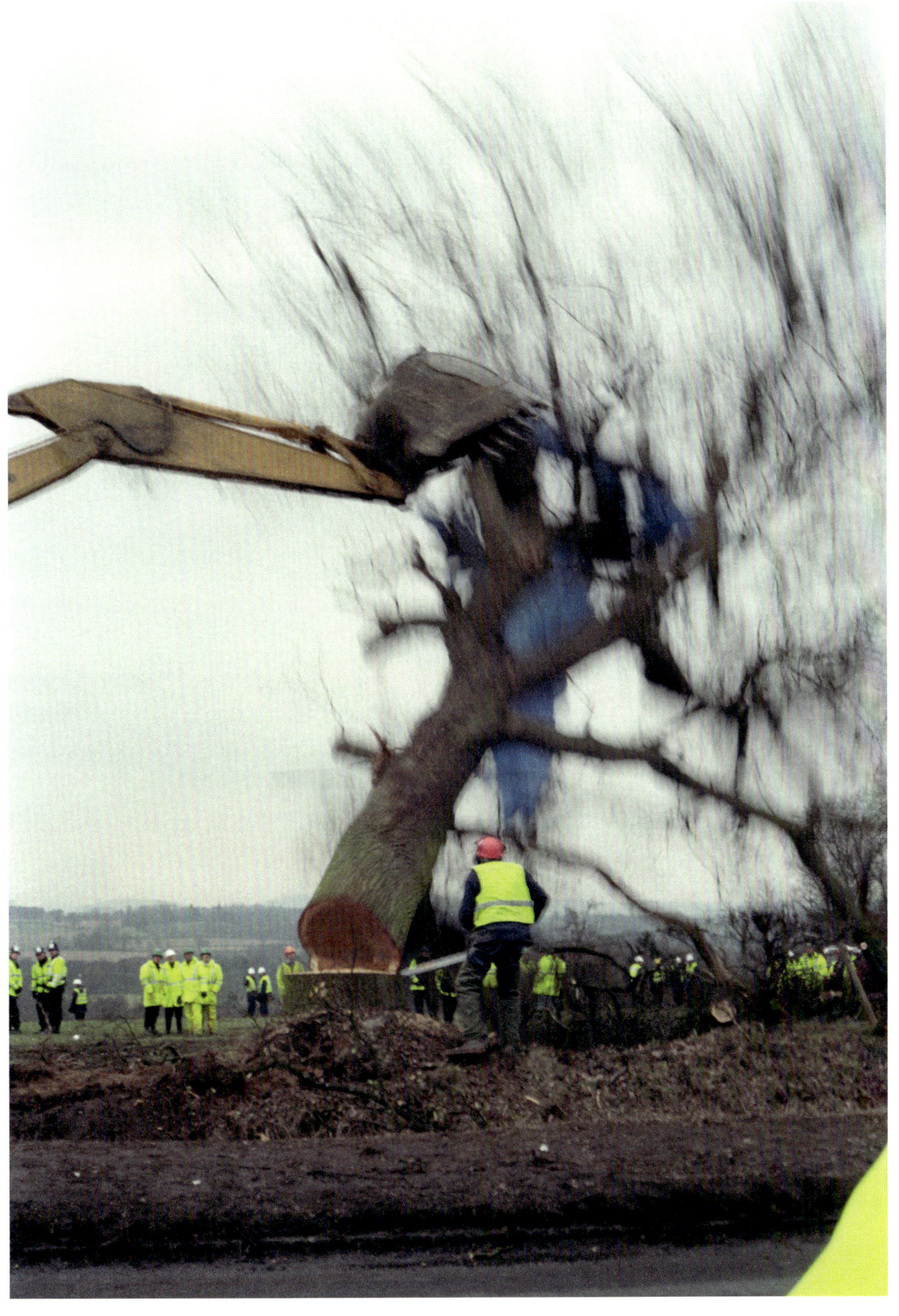

A young woman called Cake climbed a Silver Birch so she could prevent it from being toppled. In a cherry-picker crane came the sheriff's men removing all the branches other than those surrounding Cake. For close to three hours, in the bitter cold wind, she was left hanging onto branches not much bigger than twigs, praying they would not snap.

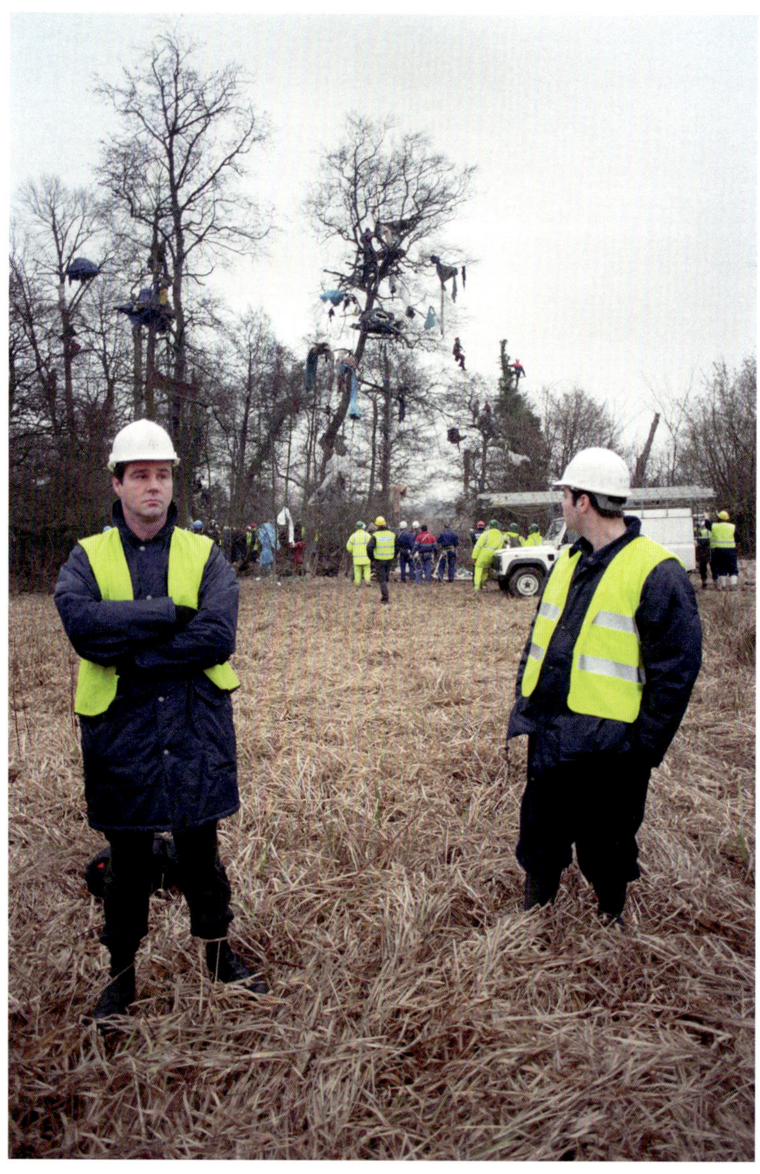

Newbury Bypass

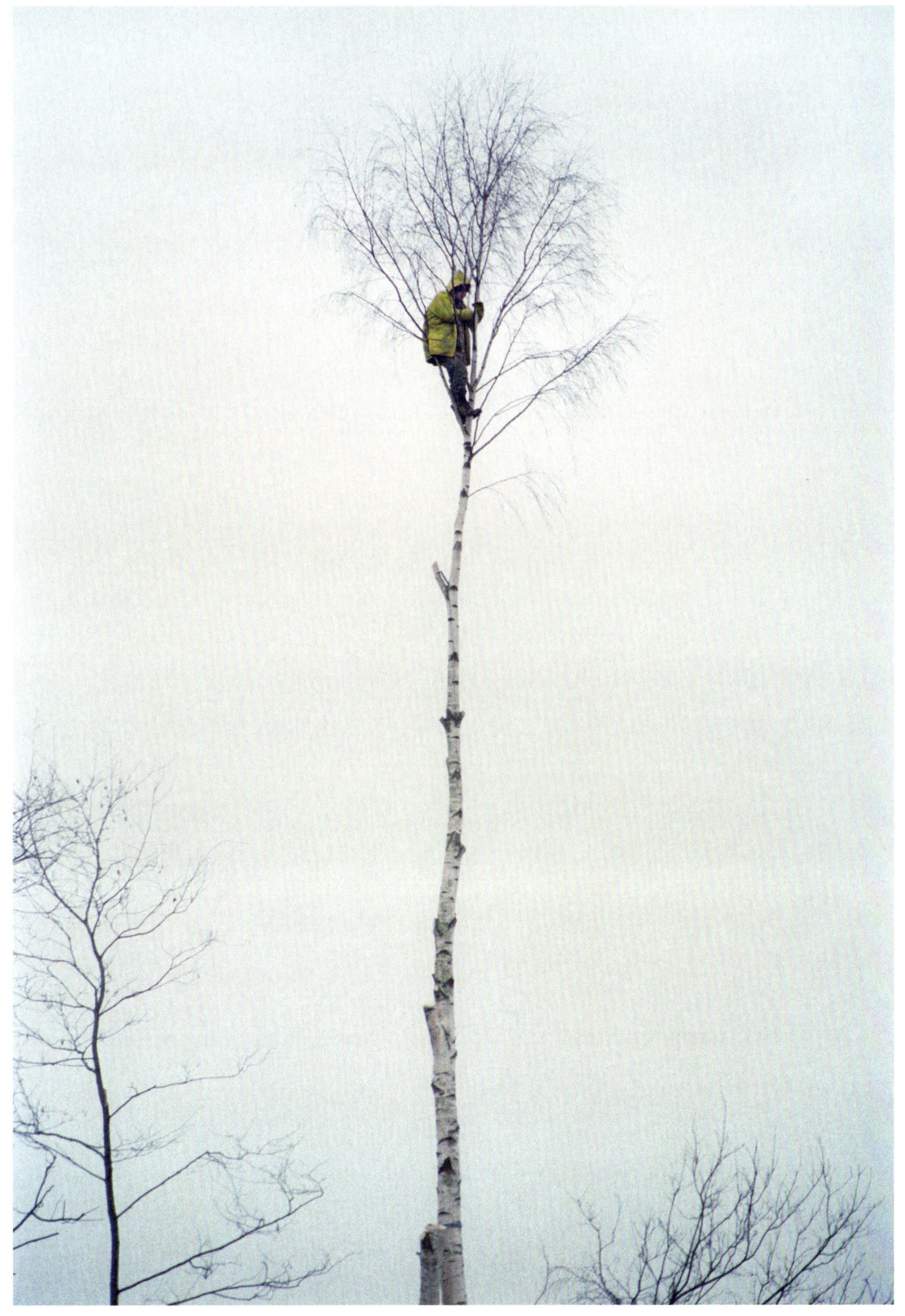

King Arthur Pendragon would make regular appearances to entertain those present with his quickfire banter. Some weeks later, during high-ariel drama in an old tree, Arthur's sword Excalibur was forcibly removed from him and in an act of victory was unceremoniously plunged to the ground more than 50 feet below by the Sheriff of Newbury's man. King Arthur was arrested for possession of an offensive weapon, one of over 30 arrests during his time fighting the bypass.

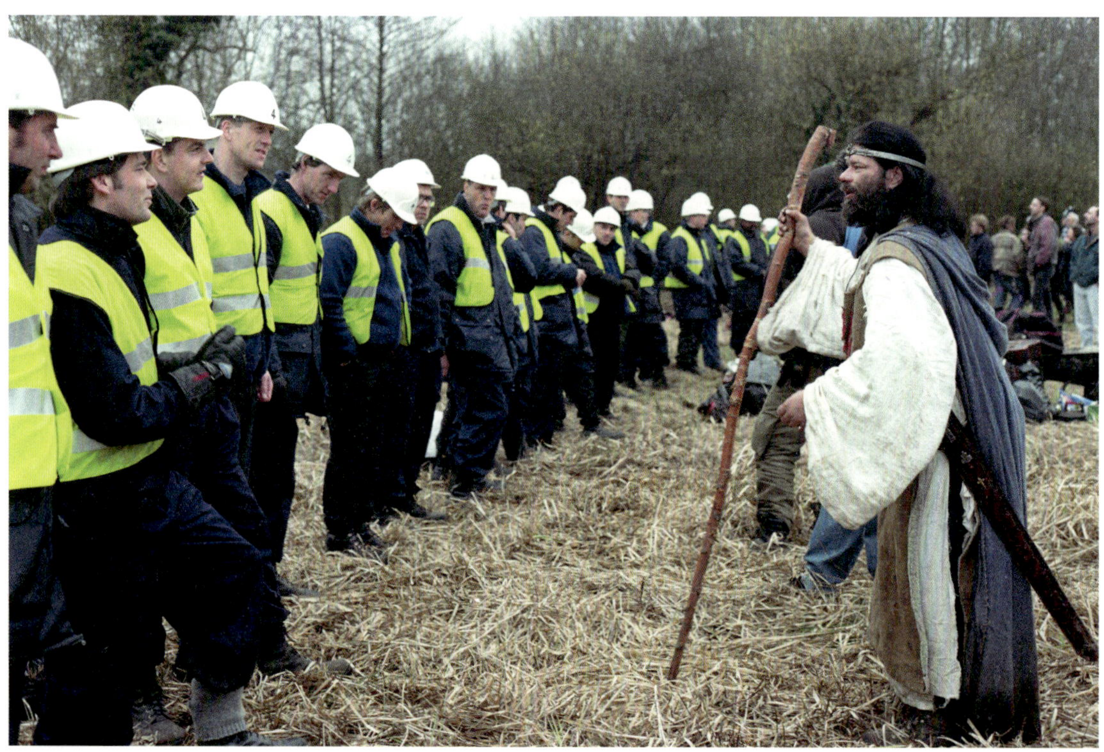

Newbury Bypass

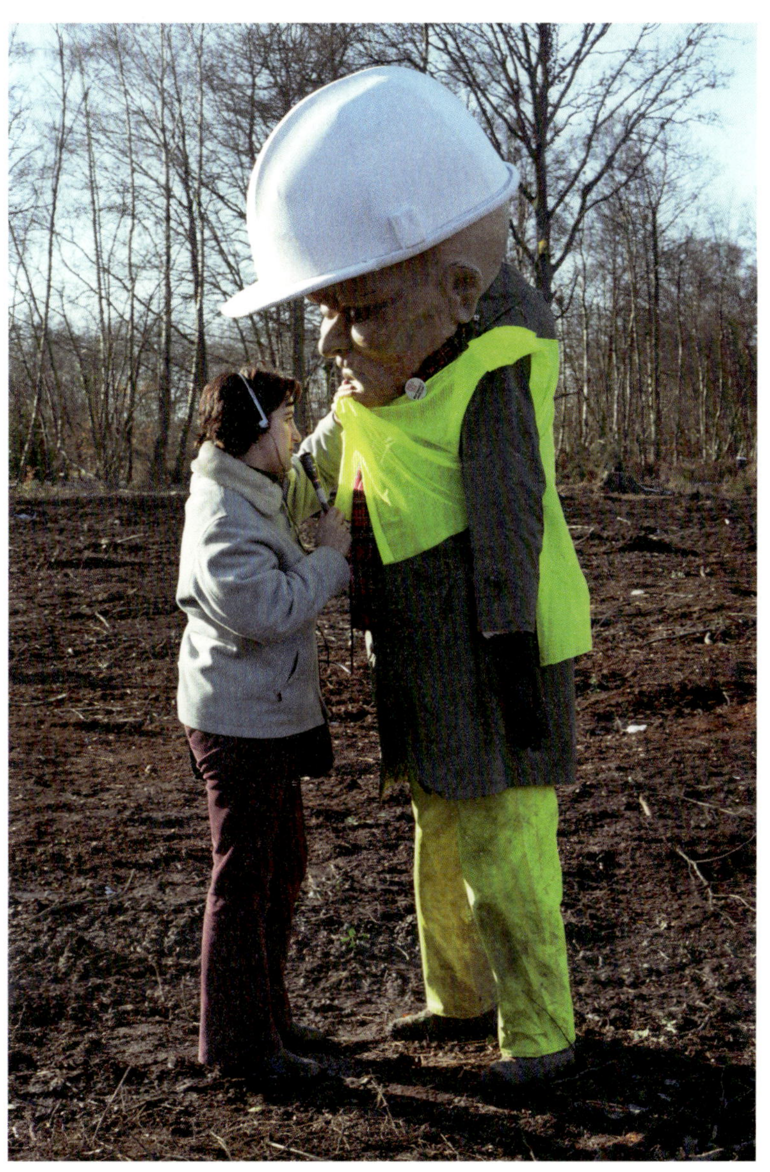

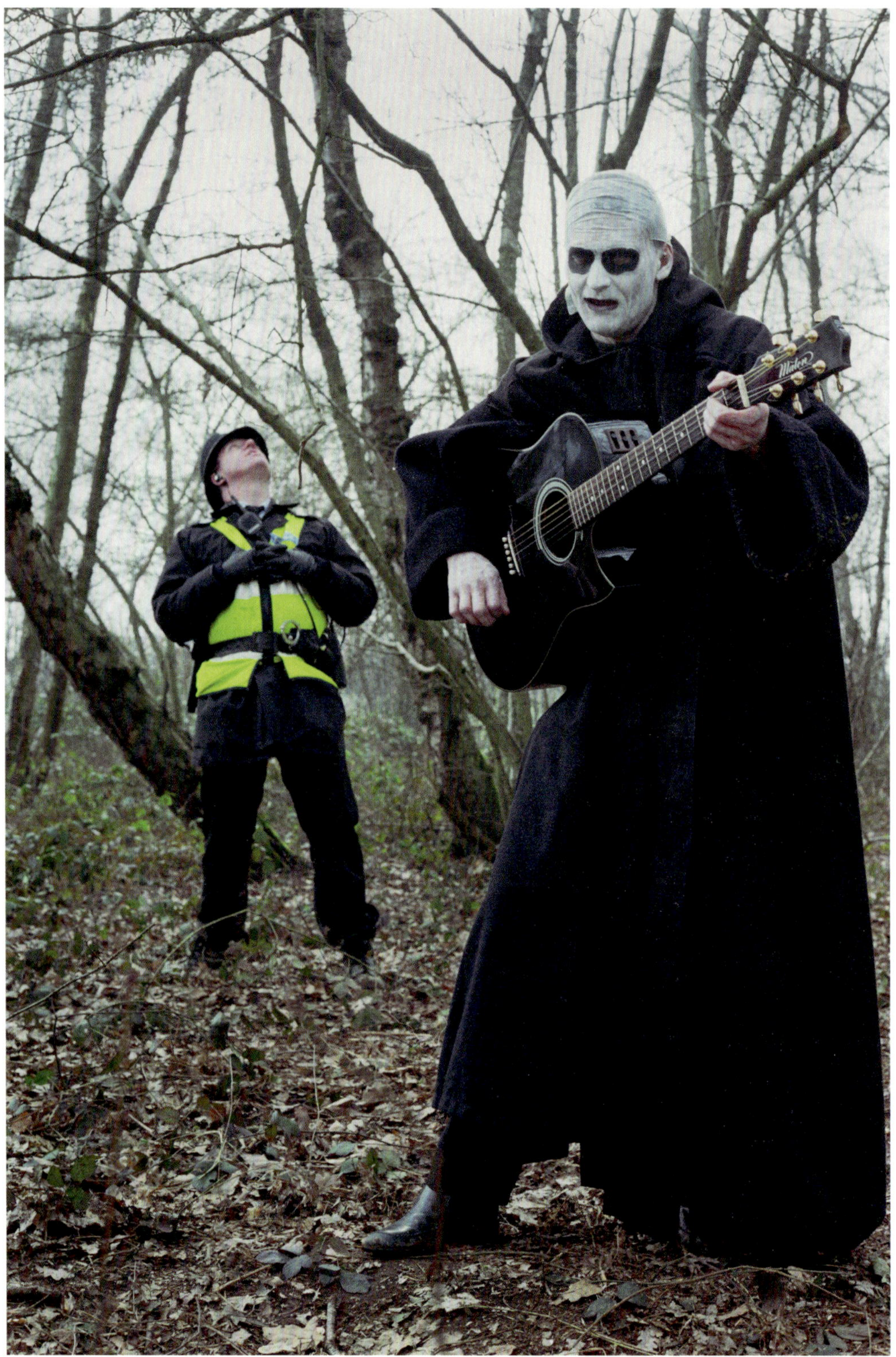

Newbury Bypass

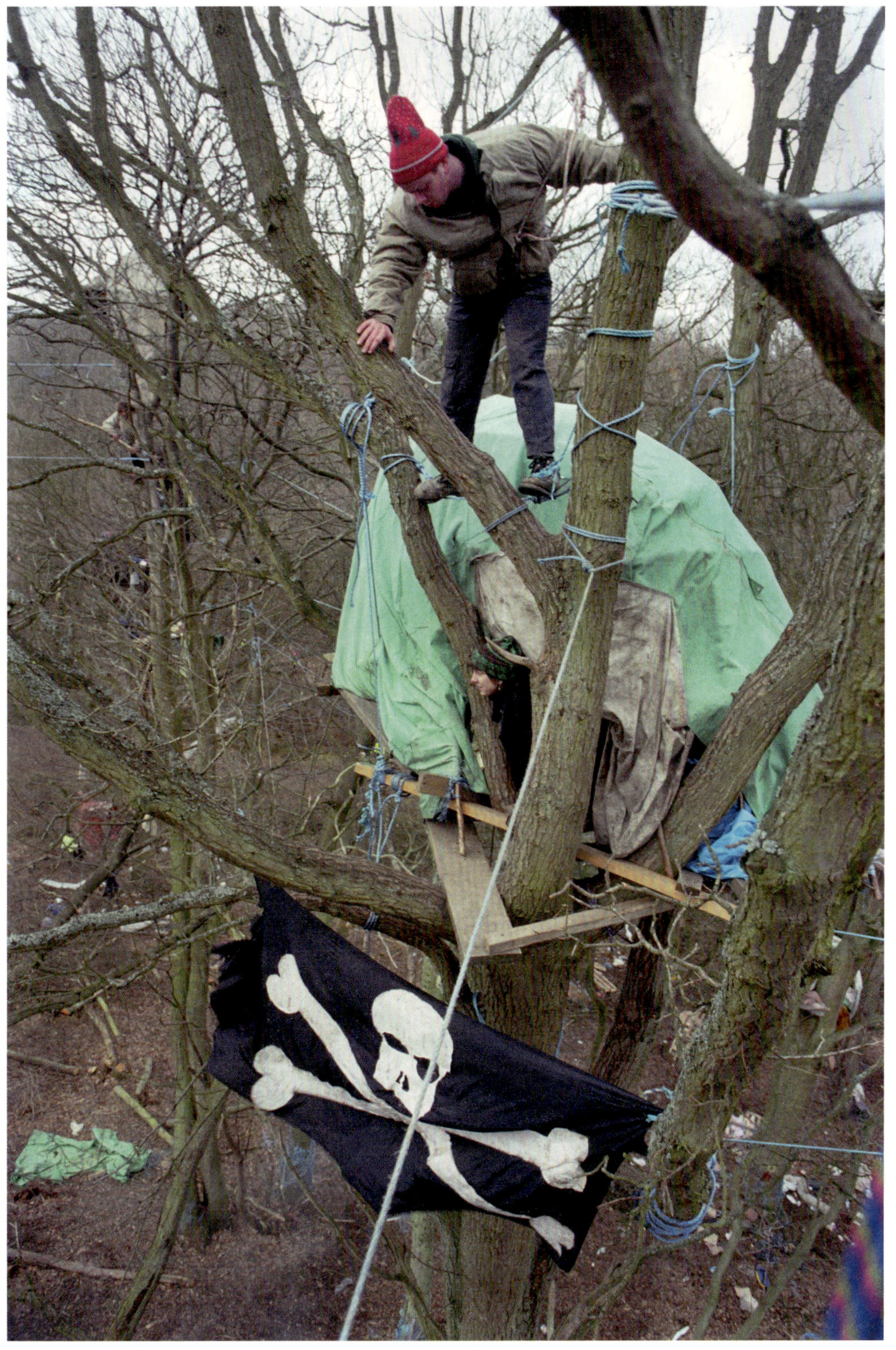

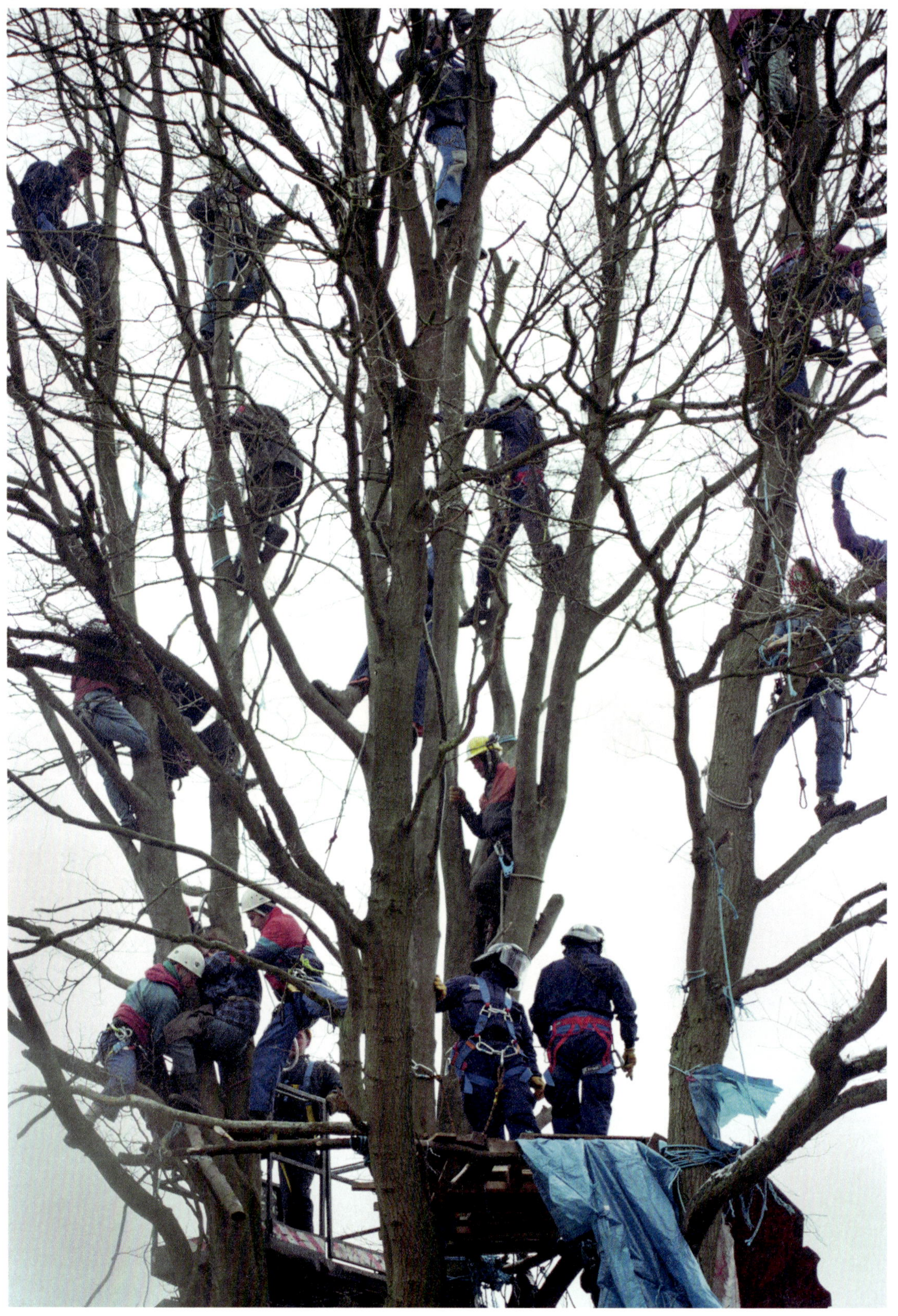

Newbury Bypass

They came on a cold March morning, several hundred security guards and policemen, a sea of illuminous yellow and black uniforms surrounding Snelsmore camp. By hook and claw they began to remove the activists one by one. Manoeuvring the cherry-picker crane they struck again: this time it was Kostas with his Vibe Tribe hat. With a 60-foot drop below him he desperately hung on with hands tightly wrapped around a branch. The sheriff's man pulled and pulled until eventually with a yell Kostas was ripped from the old beech and the tree's fate was sealed.

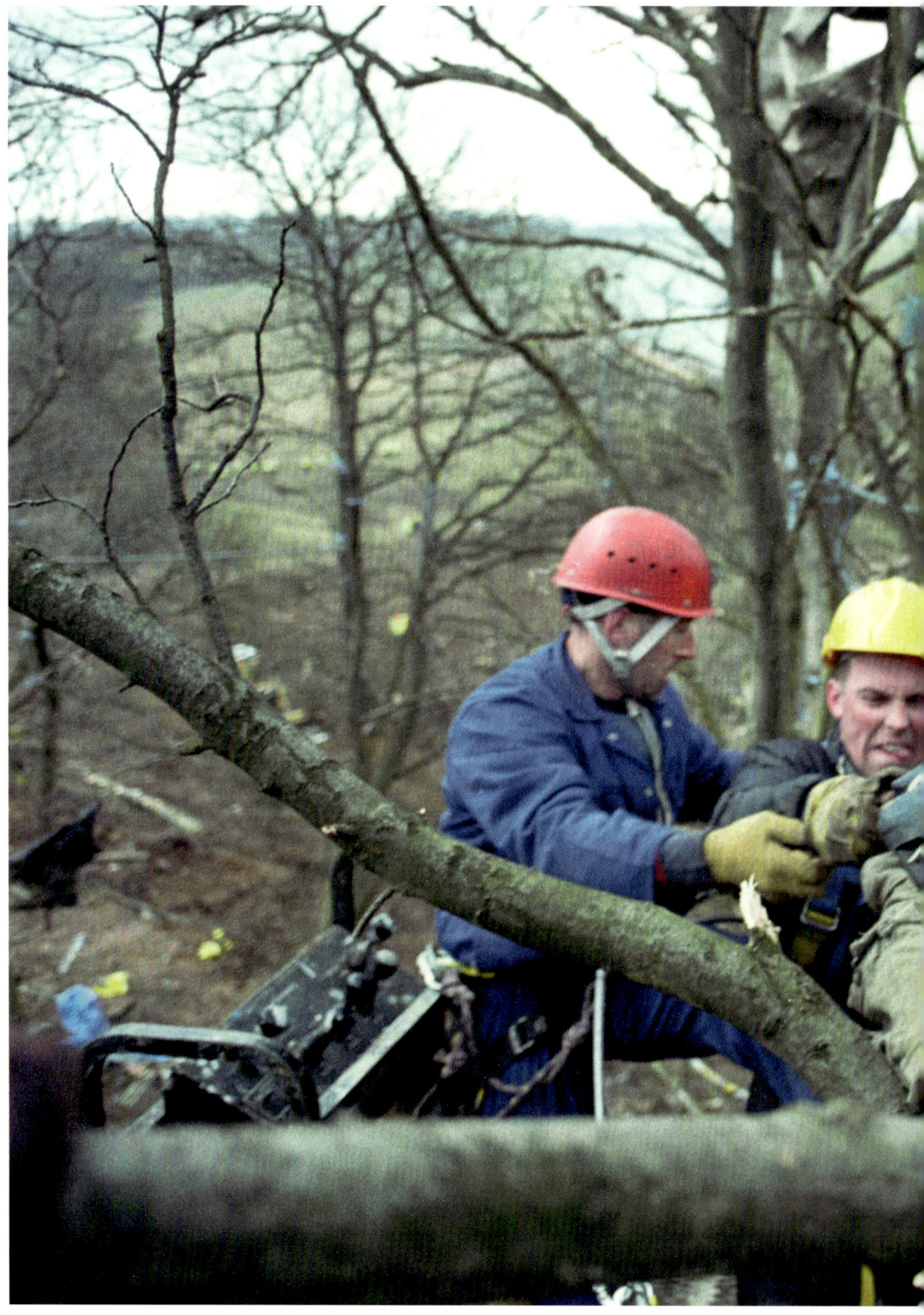

Newbury Bypass

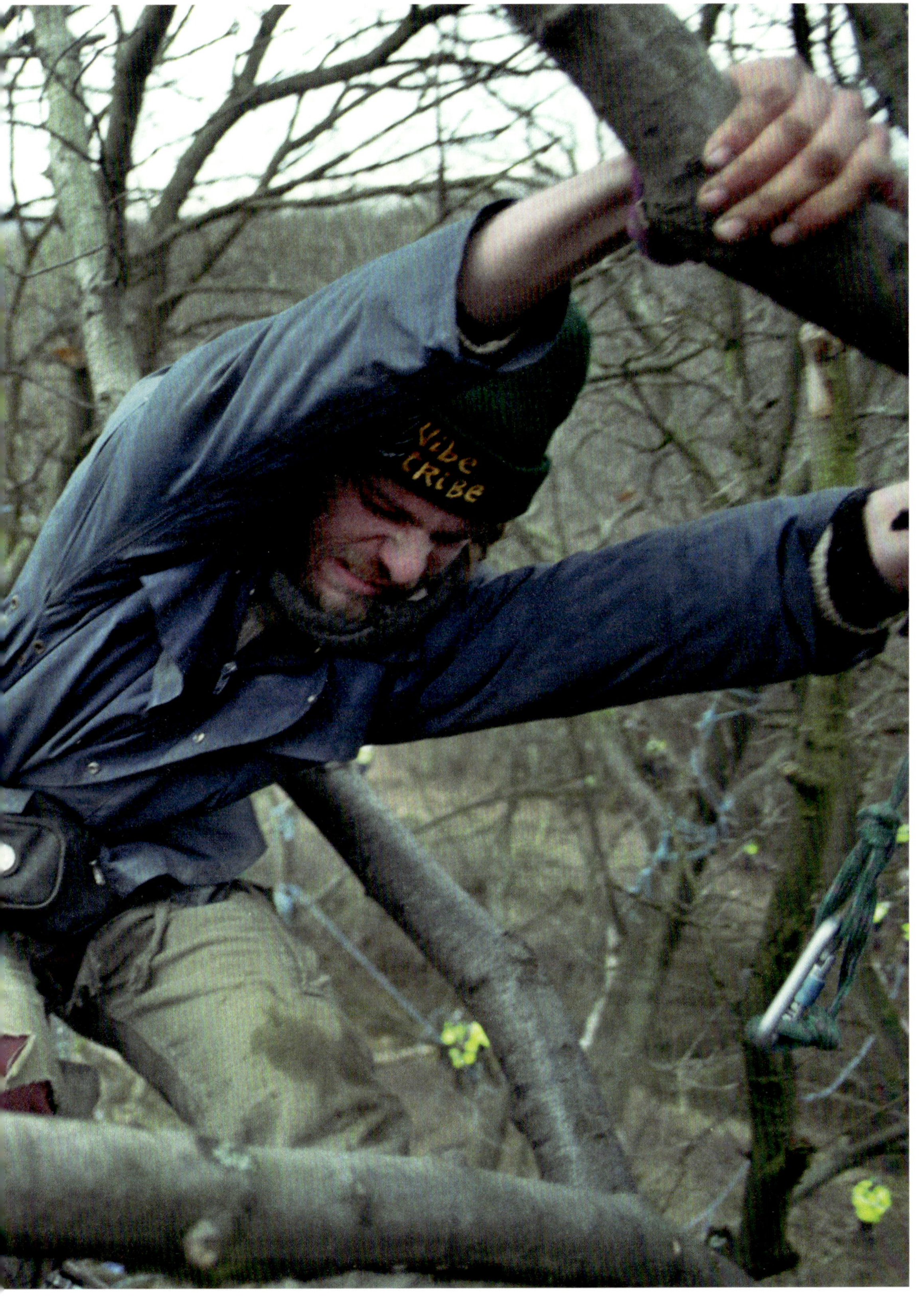
Vibe
tRiBe

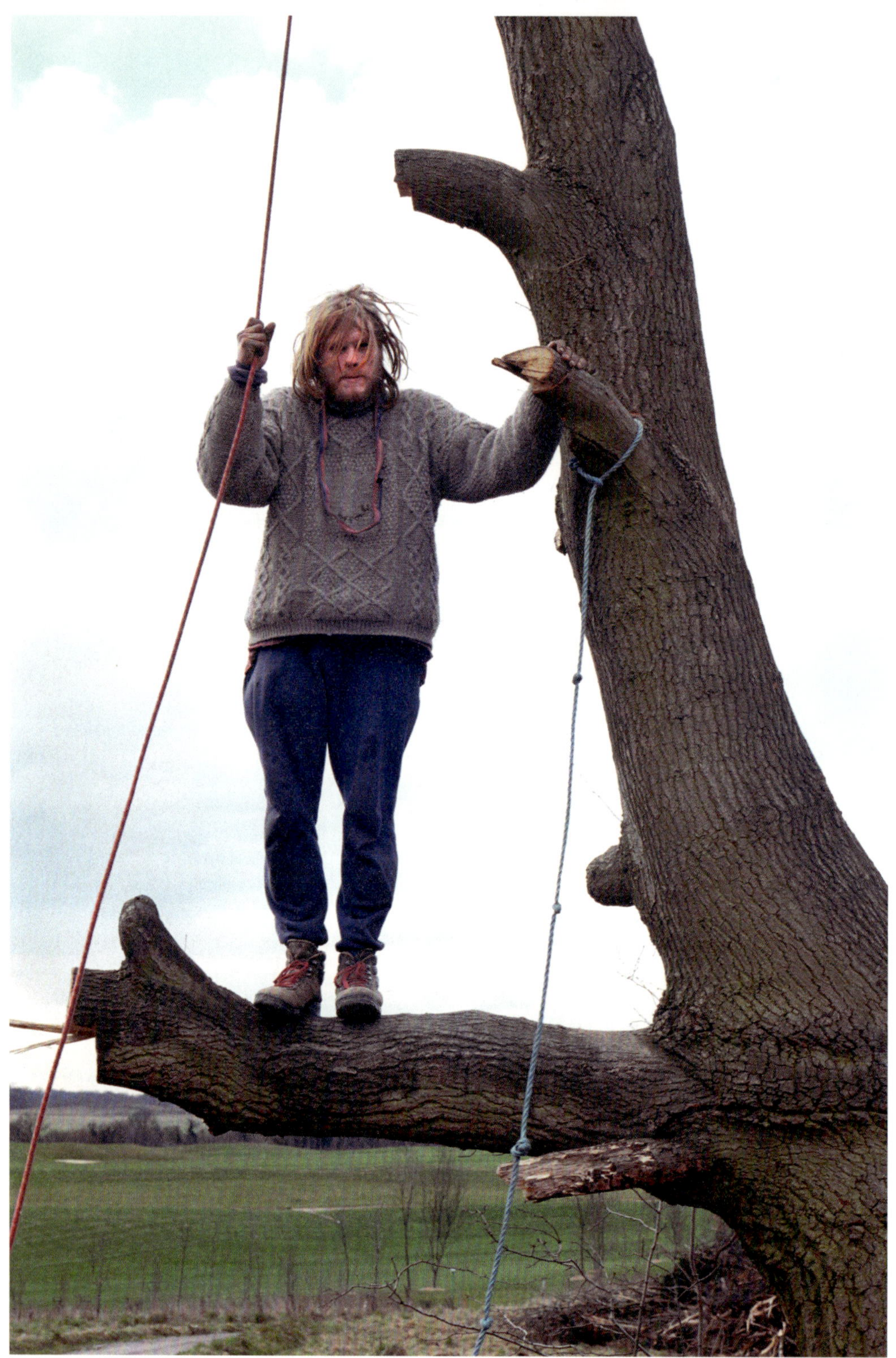

Newbury Bypass

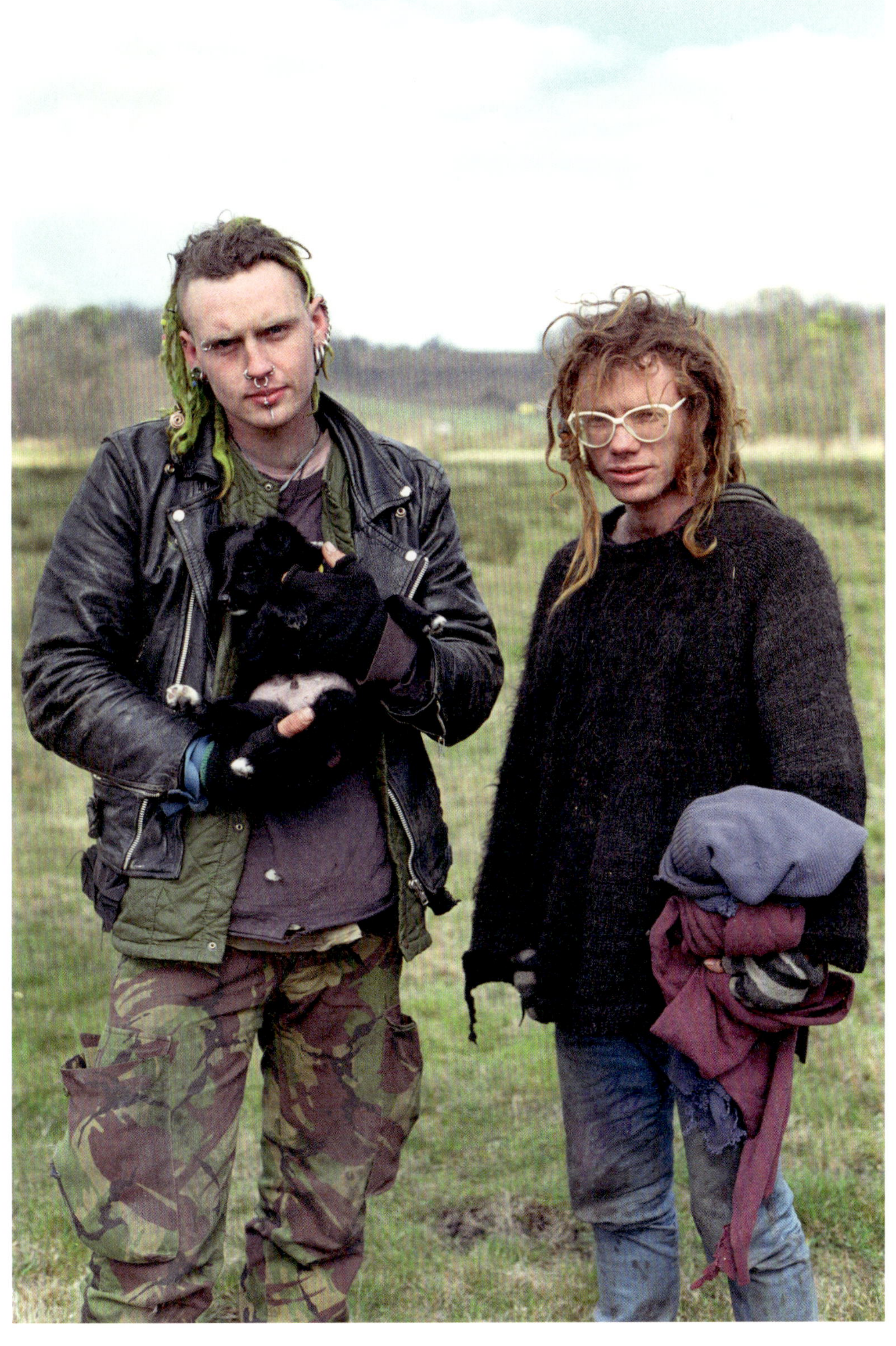

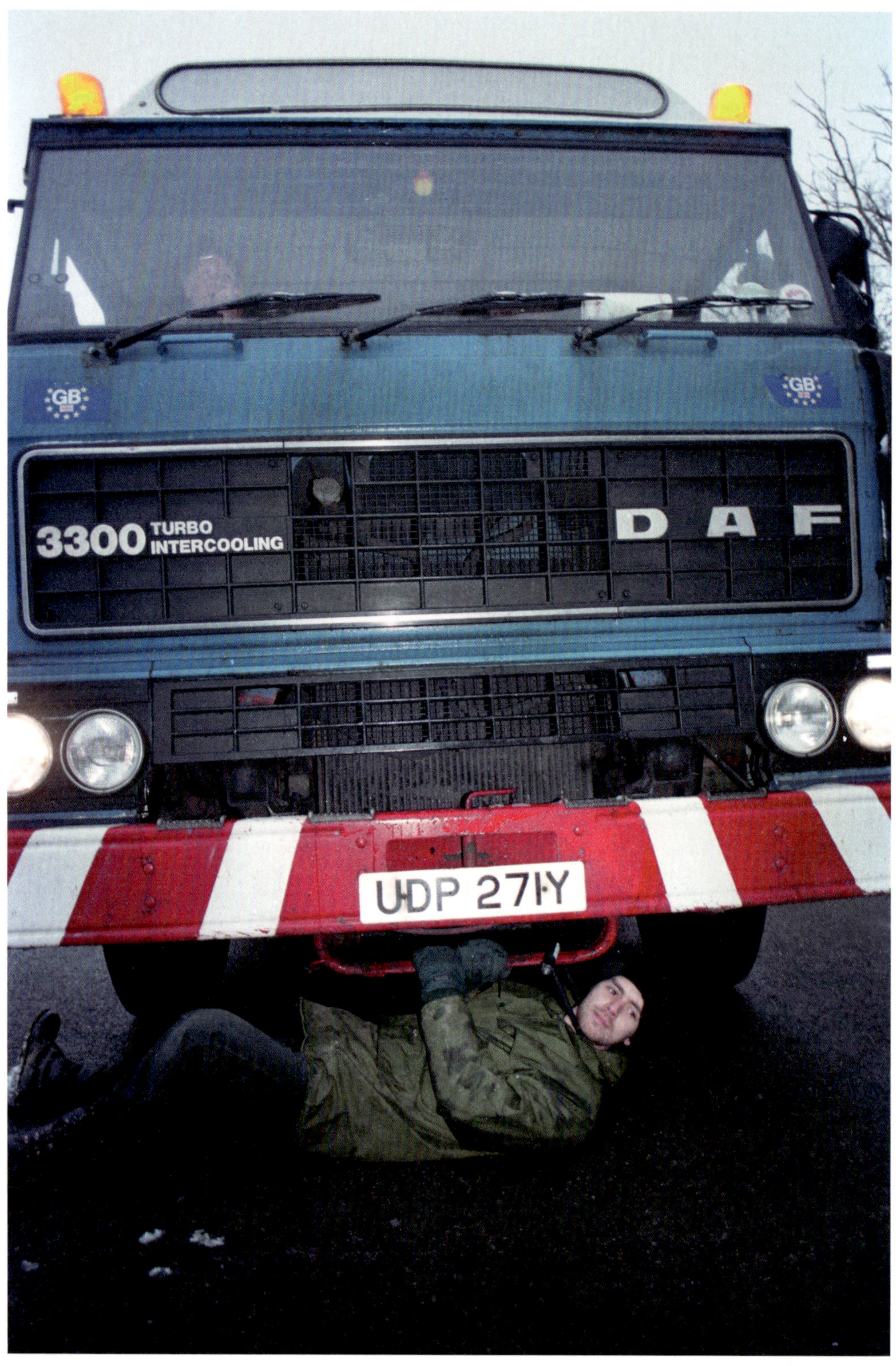

Newbury Bypass

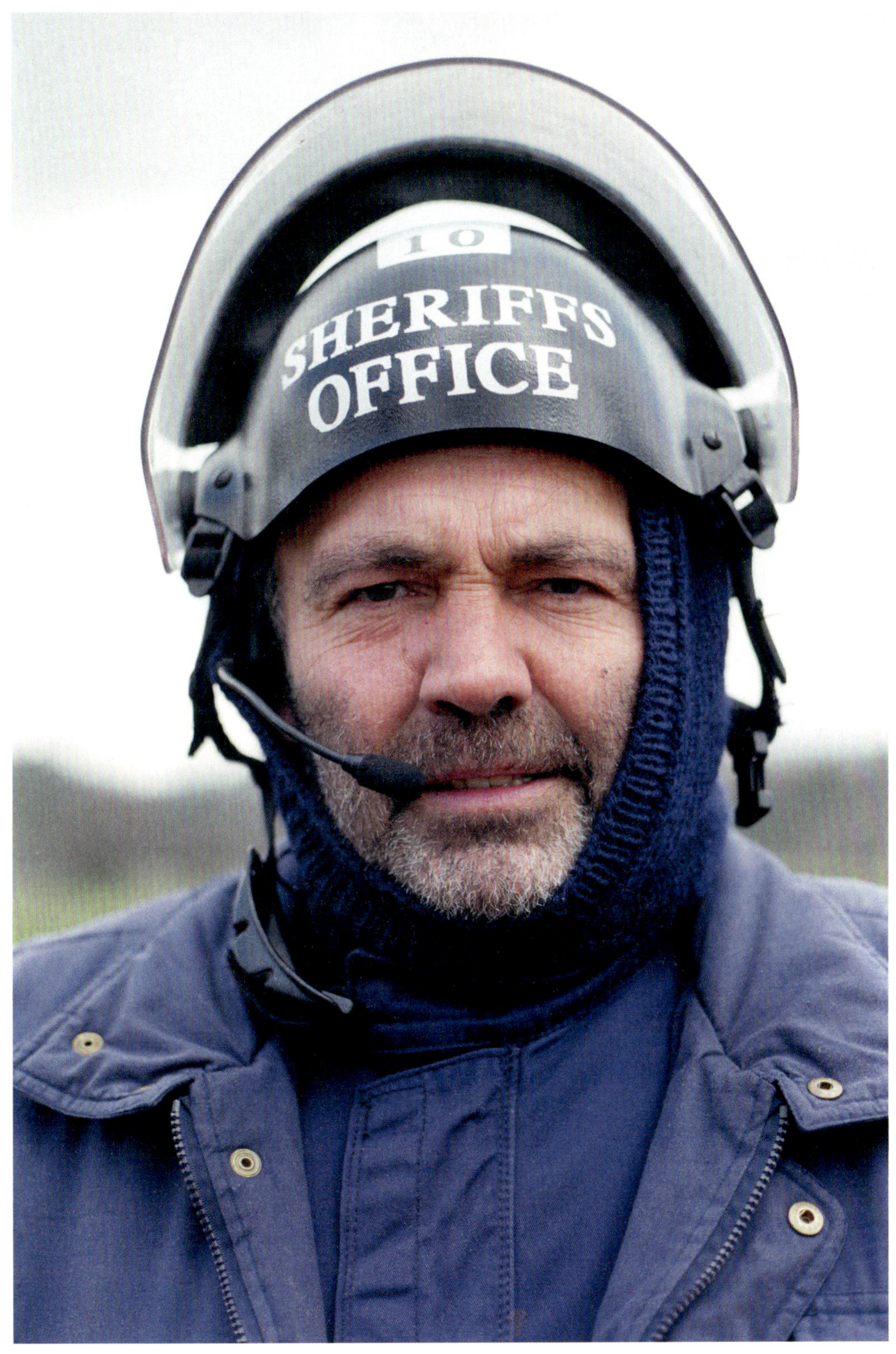
10
SHERIFFS
OFFICE

There was only one Corsican pine on the route. This mighty tree was an extraordinary 165 feet high when including the ladder perched on top which was designed so an activist could D-Lock their neck to the top rung during eviction. I can't even begin to think how terrifying that must have been. Getting into the pine involved a vertigo-inducing 30 minutes of prusiking up a single 75 foot rope. Once in you were greeted by a double story treehouse that could accommodate 20 with a cosy wood burner, another tree house was some 40 foot higher. How many years of growth it took for this tree to reach its splendour. How many minutes for it to be destroyed.

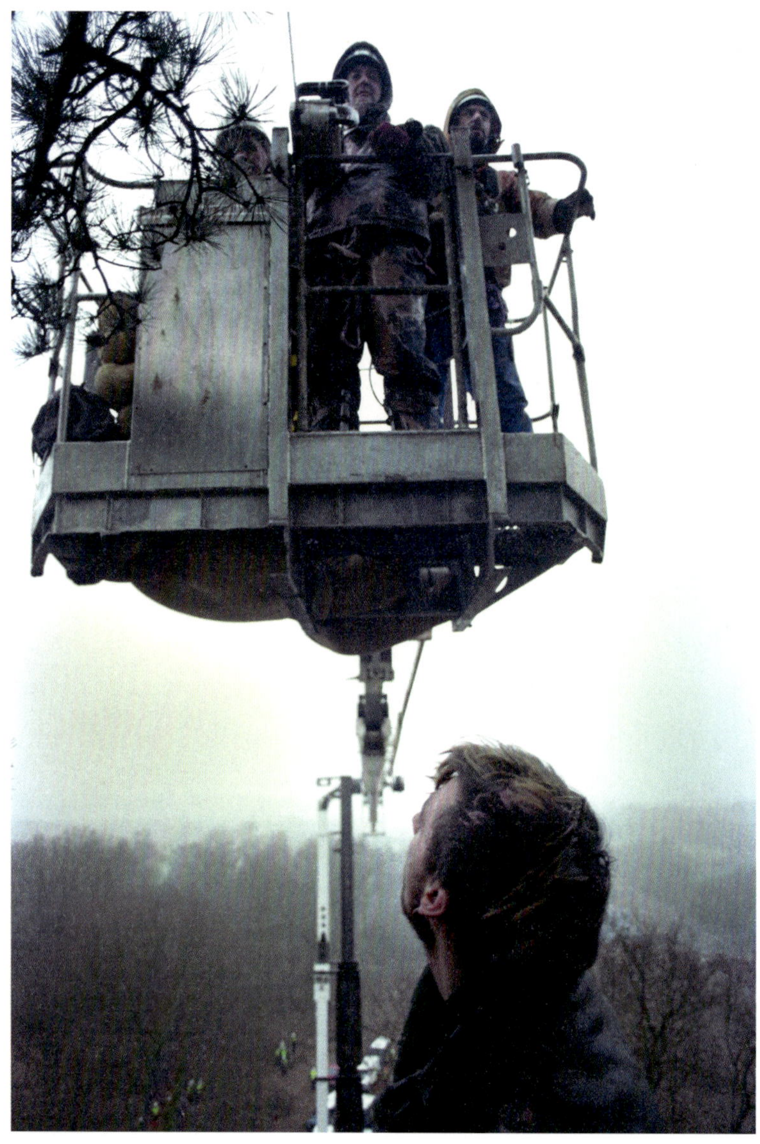

Newbury Bypass

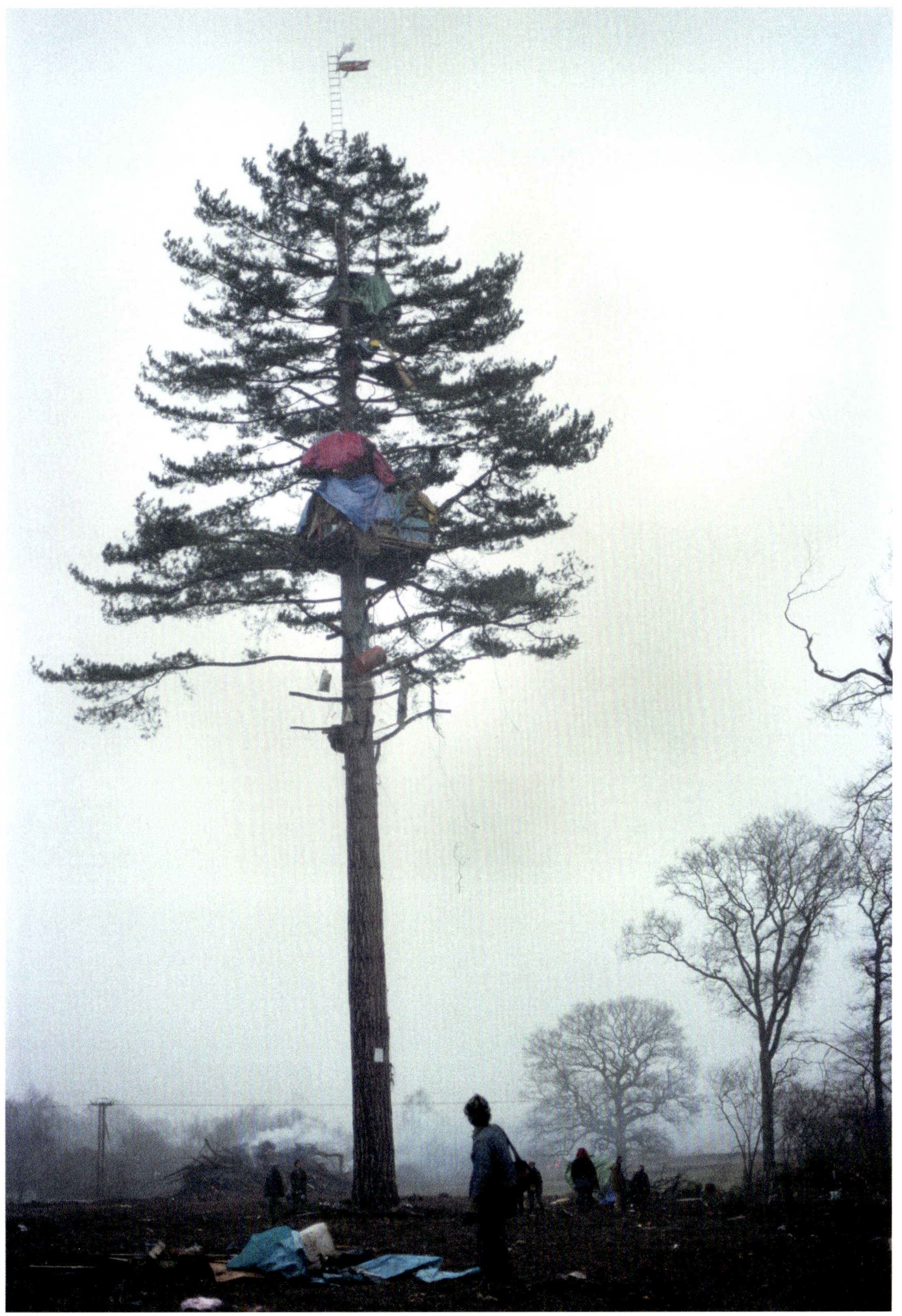

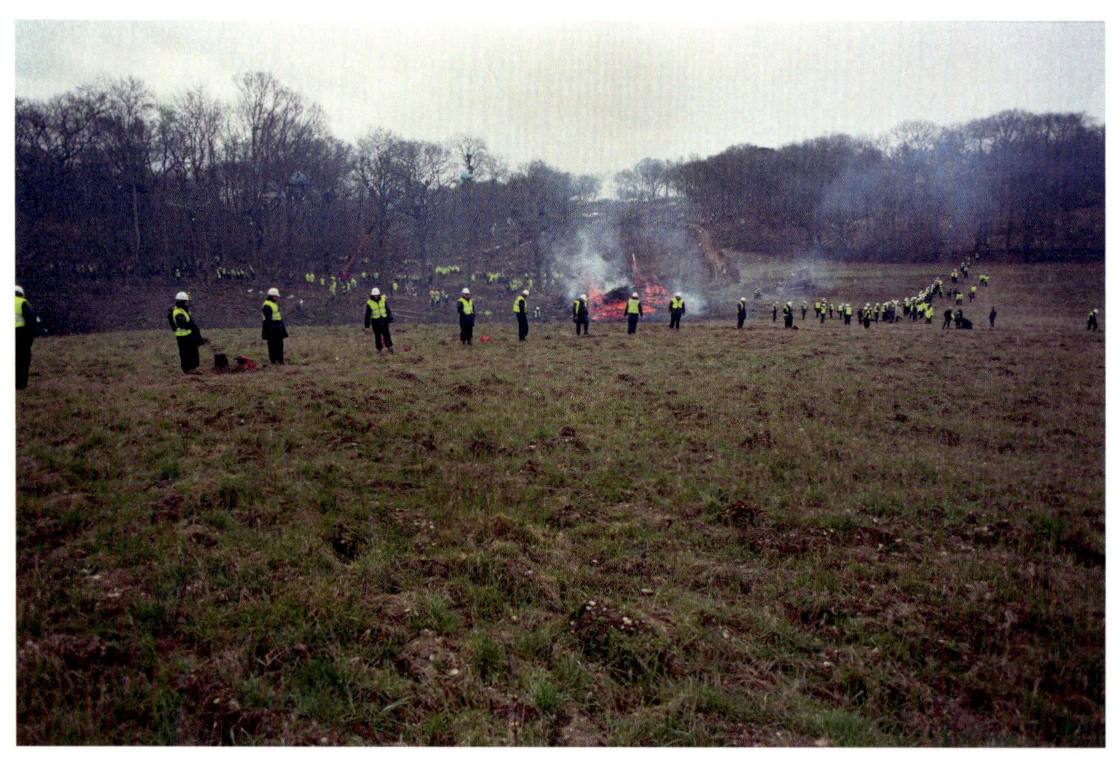

Newbury Bypass

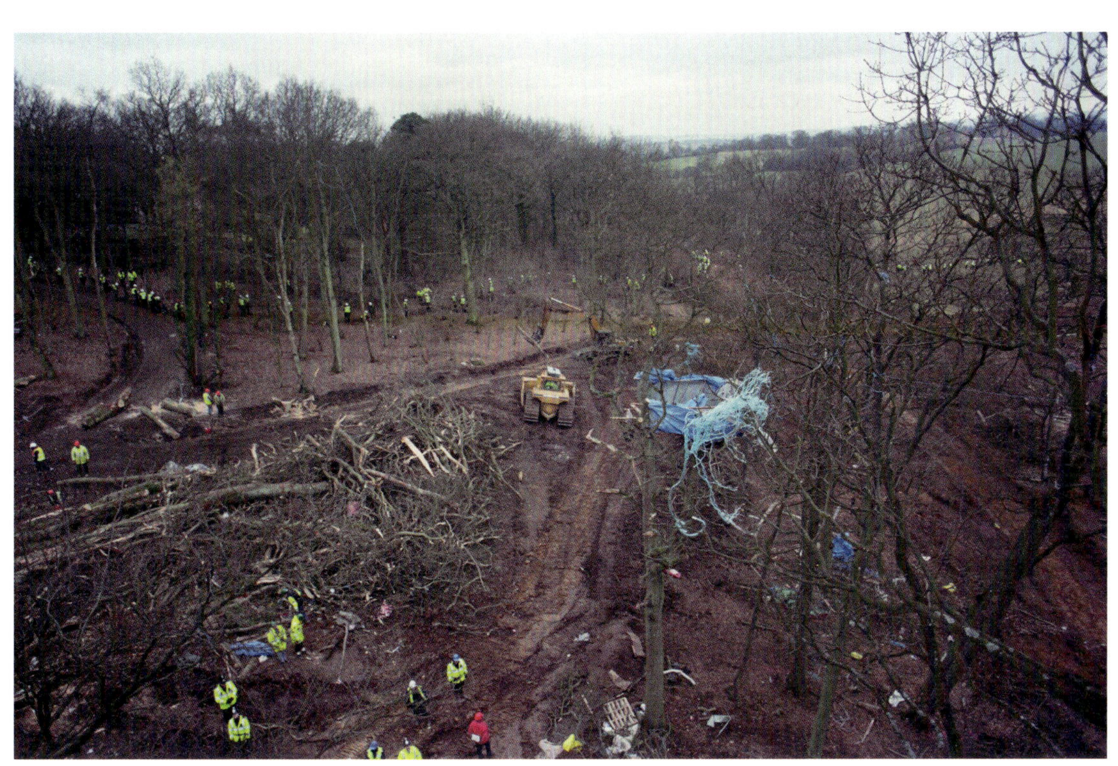

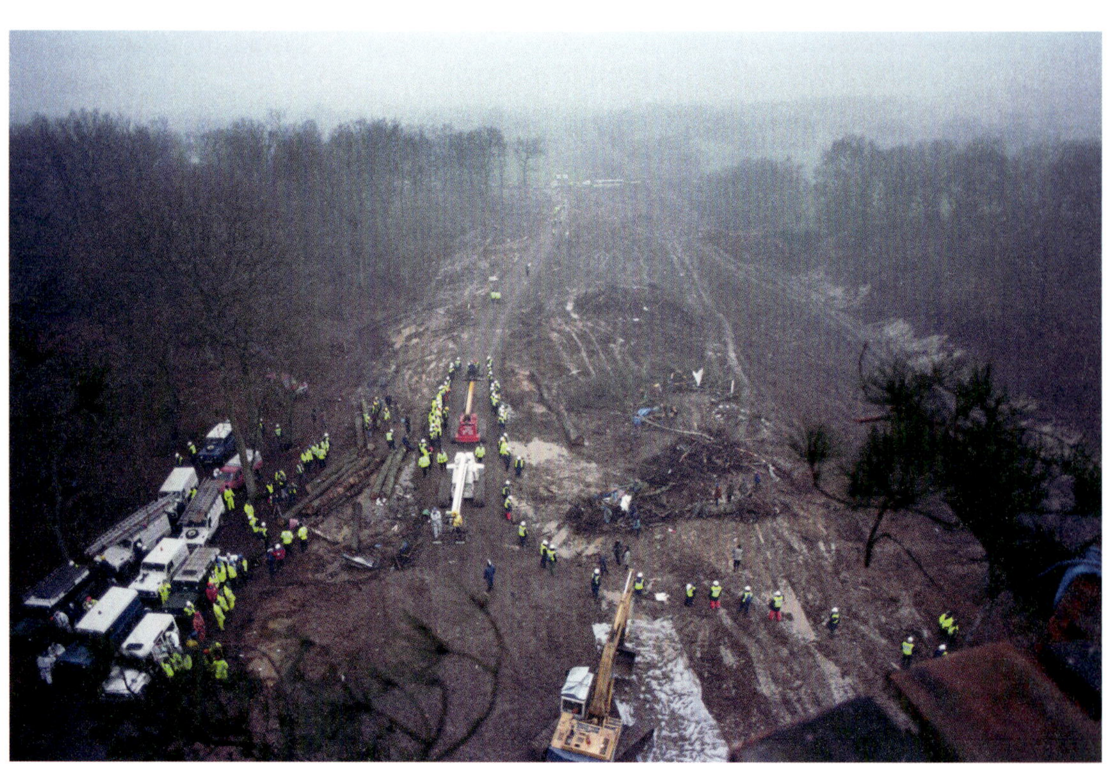

Newbury Bypass

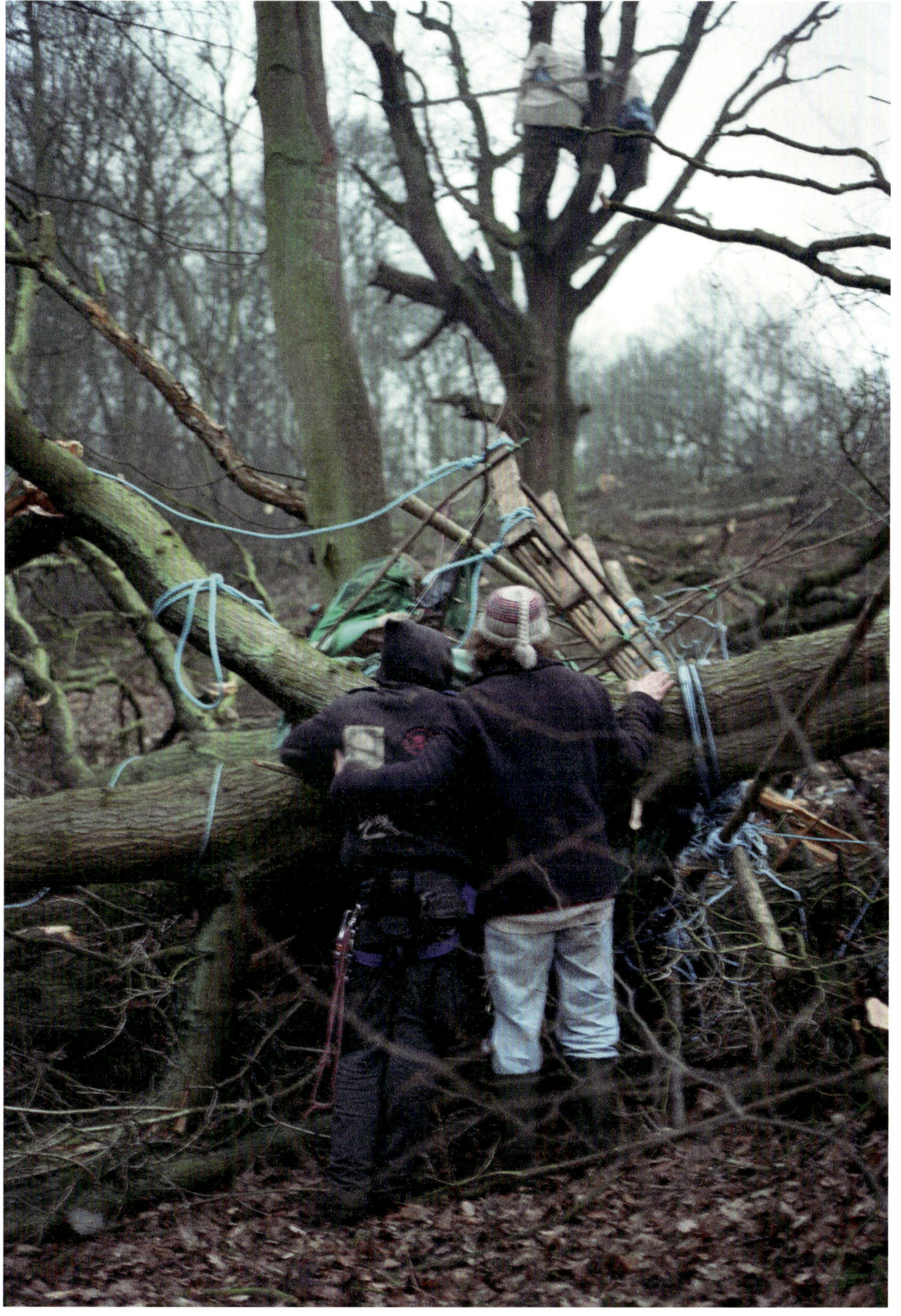

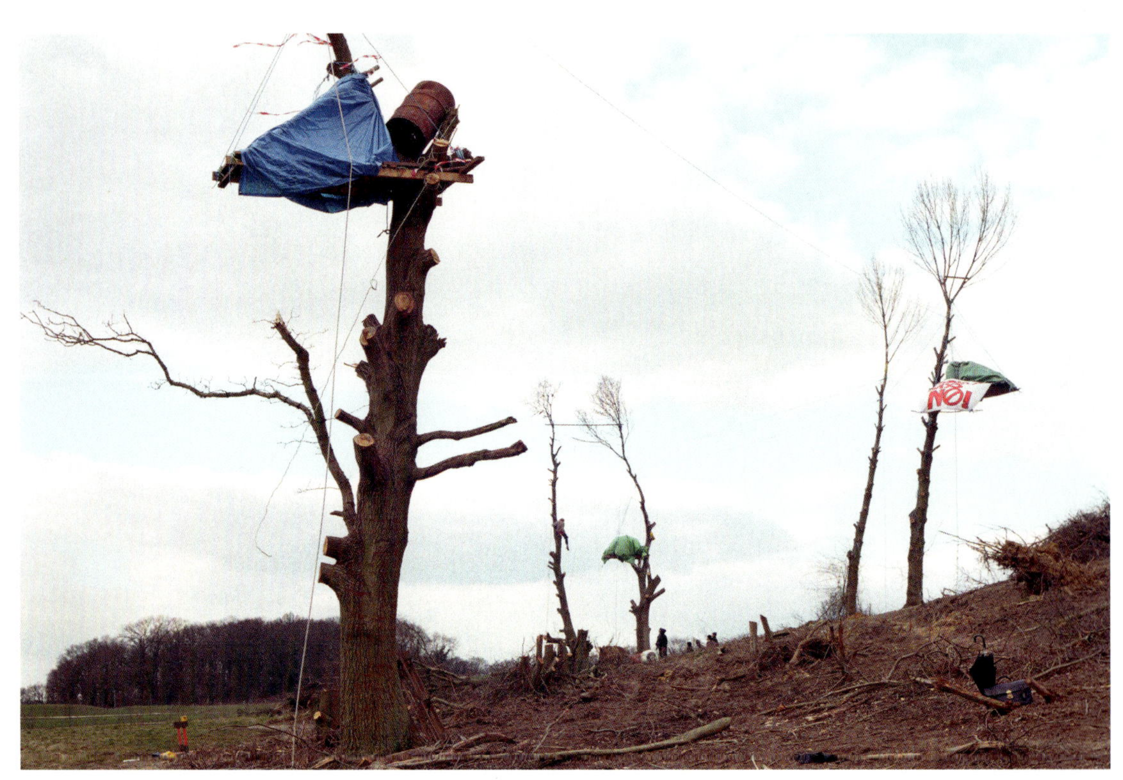

Reminiscent of a scene from a first world war battlefield some of the last few remaining trees stood before also meeting their untimely death. A briefcase and umbrella make an unlikely appearance, perhaps from a visiting government official to ensure the state had been thorough through the whole nine mile bypass route in its annihilation of hedge, tree, bush and flower.

Newbury Bypass

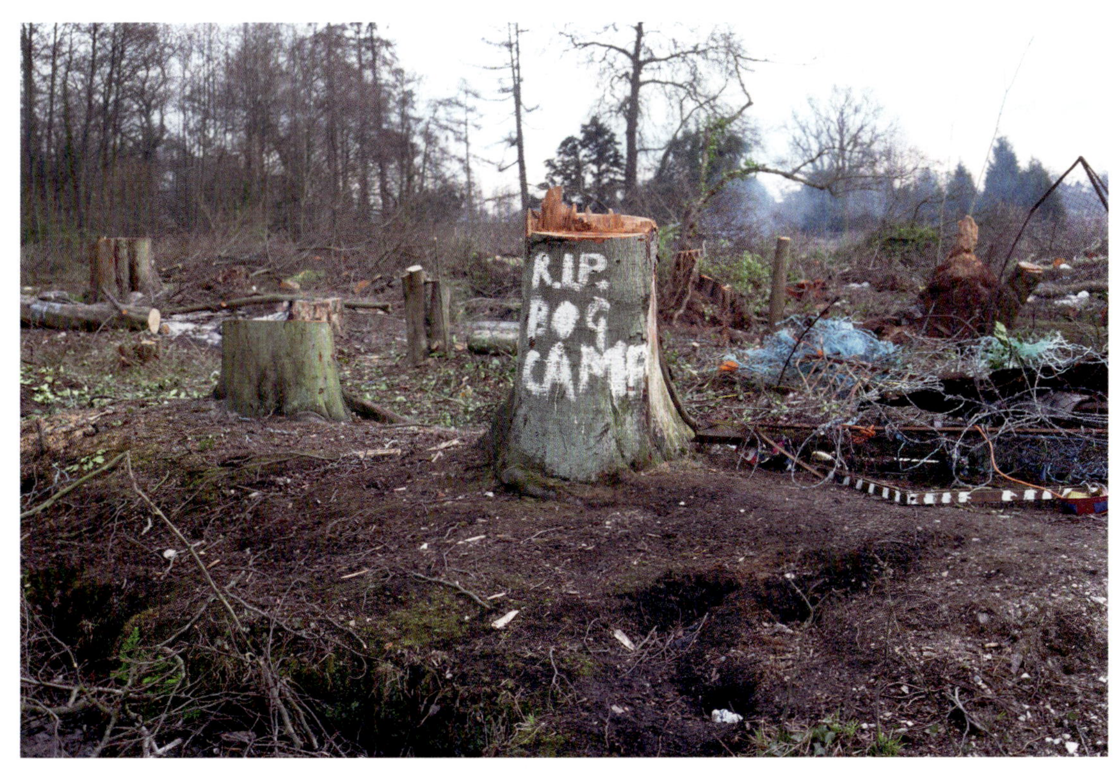
R.I.P.
BOG
CAMP

Critical Mass
1995–1996

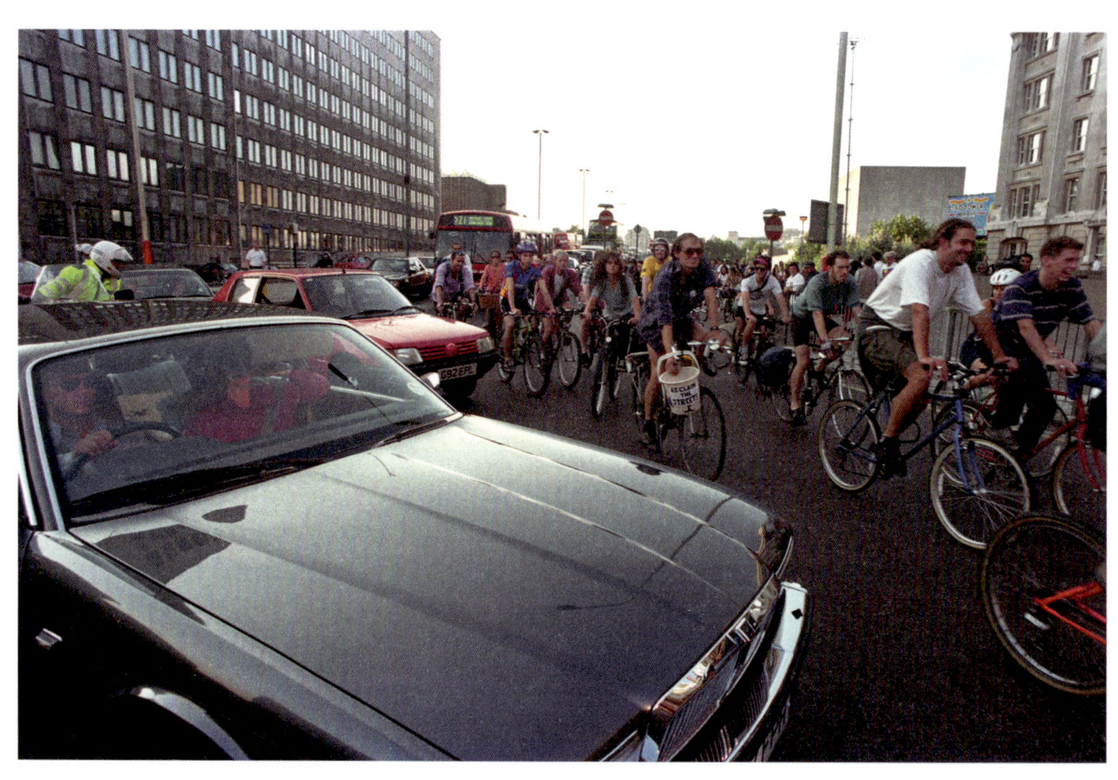

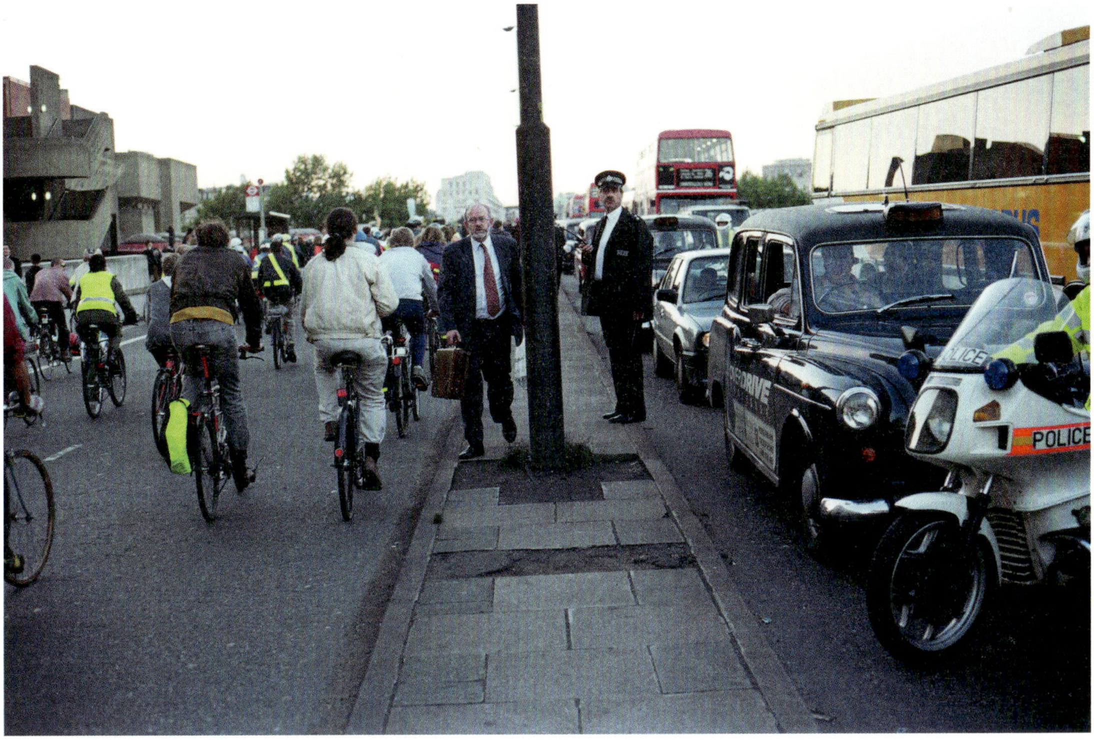

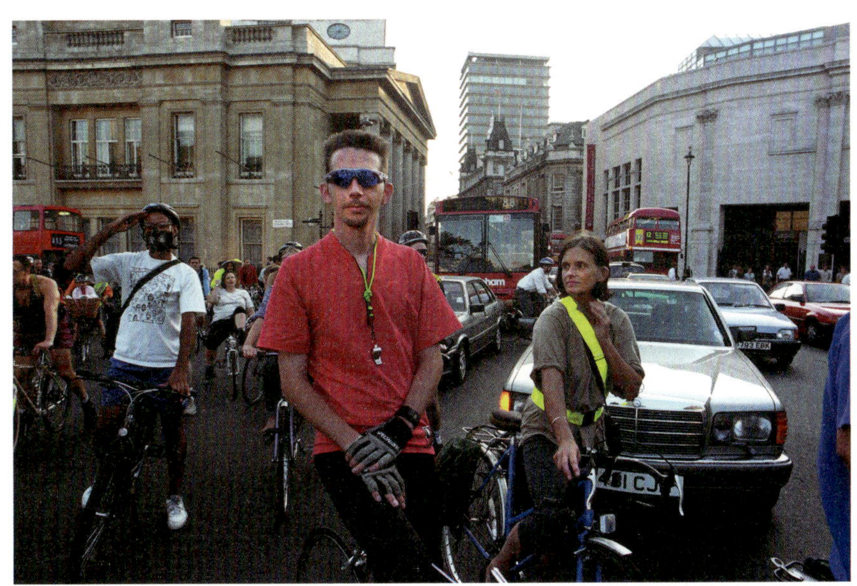

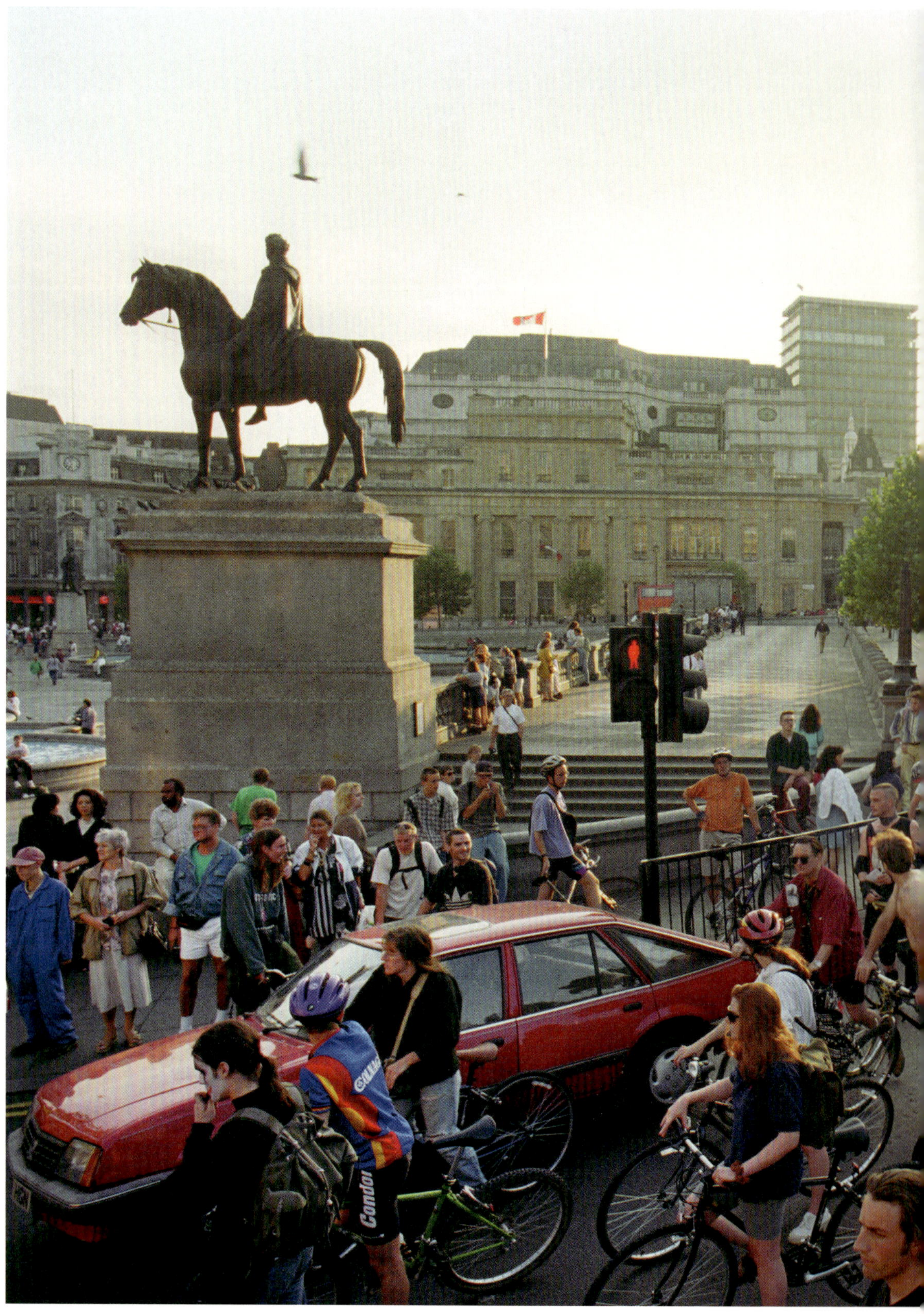

Critical Mass

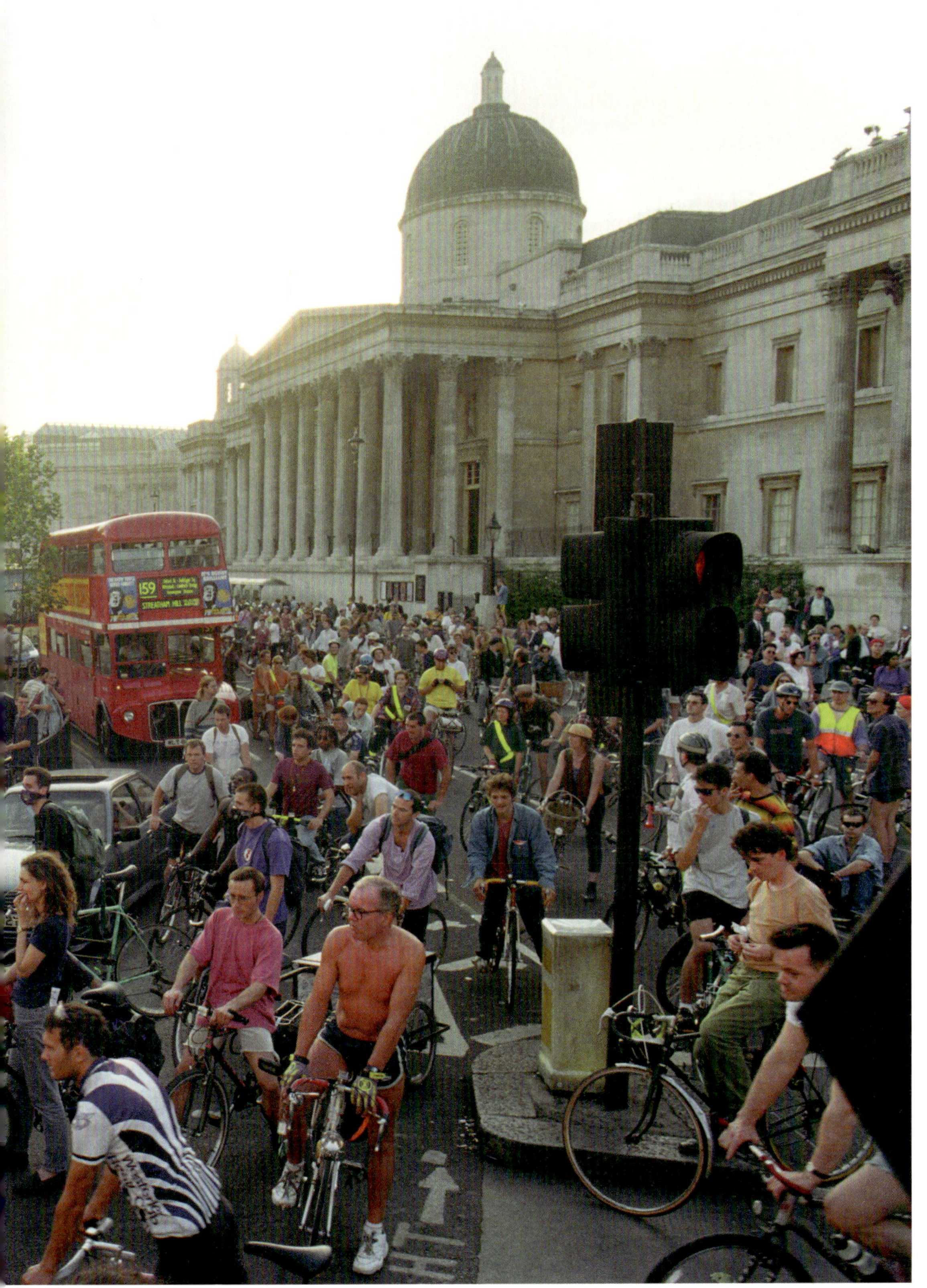
159
STREATHAM HILL

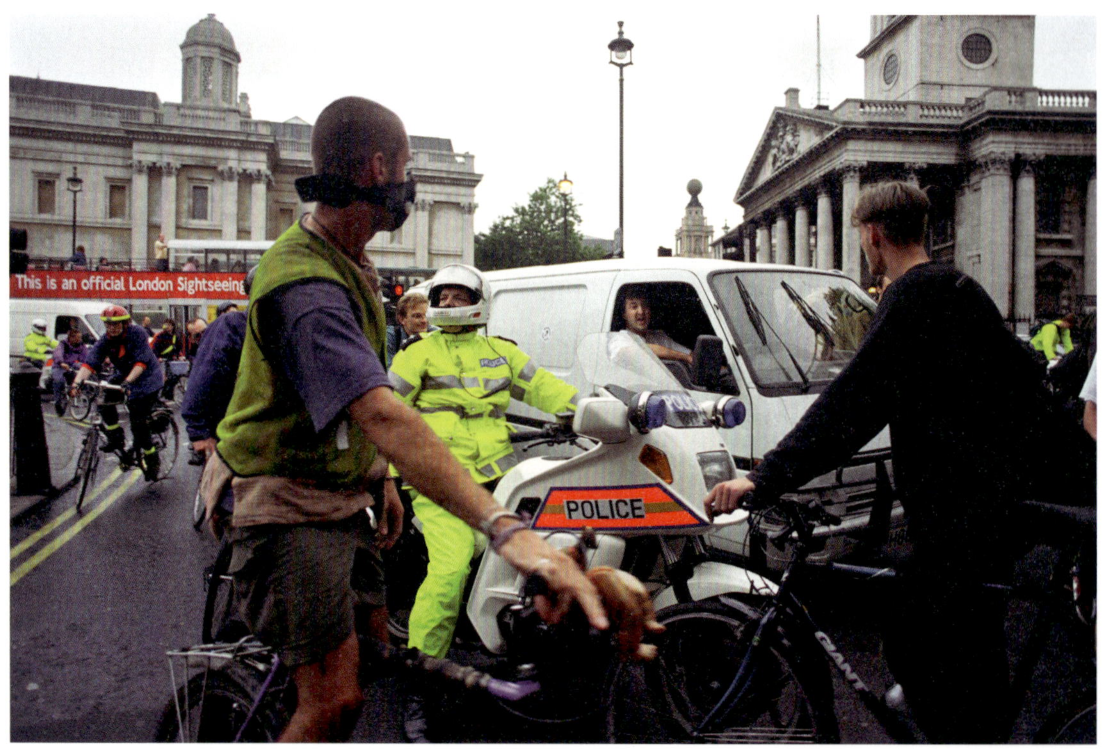

Critical Mass

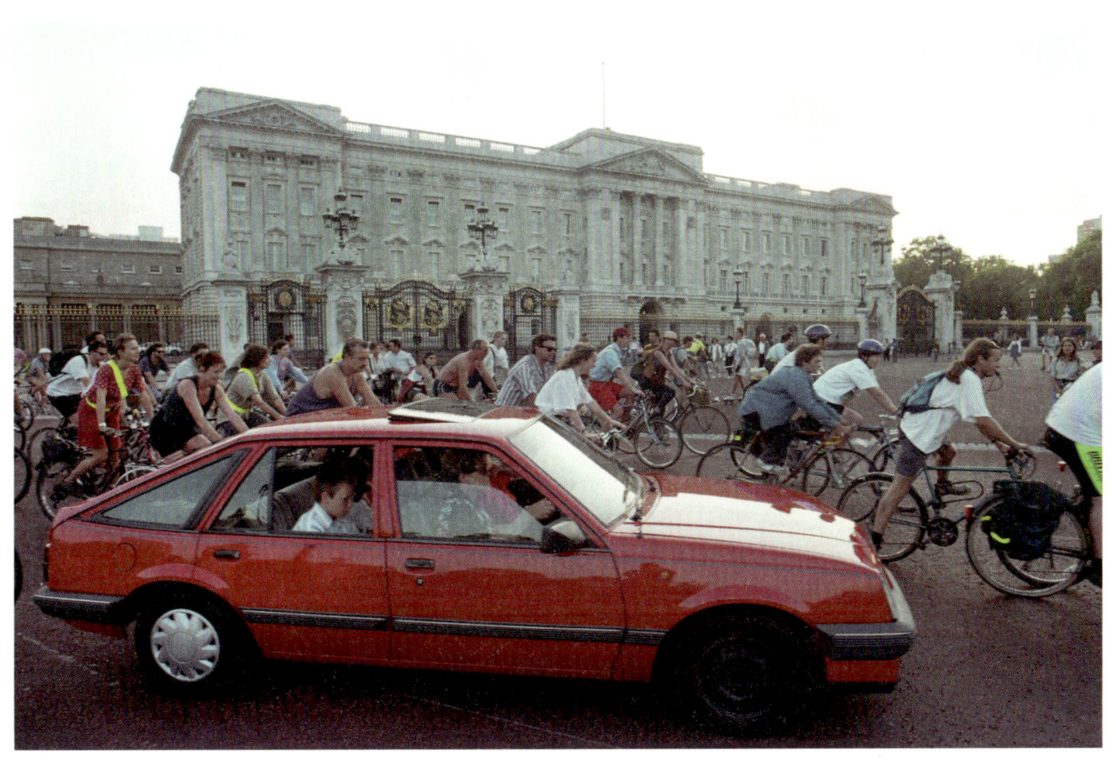

The Motor Show at Earls Court London was an annual celebration of everything the environmental movement felt revulsion for. These steel carriages were contributing so much to global warming and the plan was to invade the show and let our feelings be known. Critical Mass, the monthly get-together of cyclists taking over London's streets, were all set for the action. At the last minute the plan was foiled by the police and in a moment of frustration, unity and belief in a better world to come everyone lifted their bikes above their heads and shouted in simultaneous rage and celebration of life.

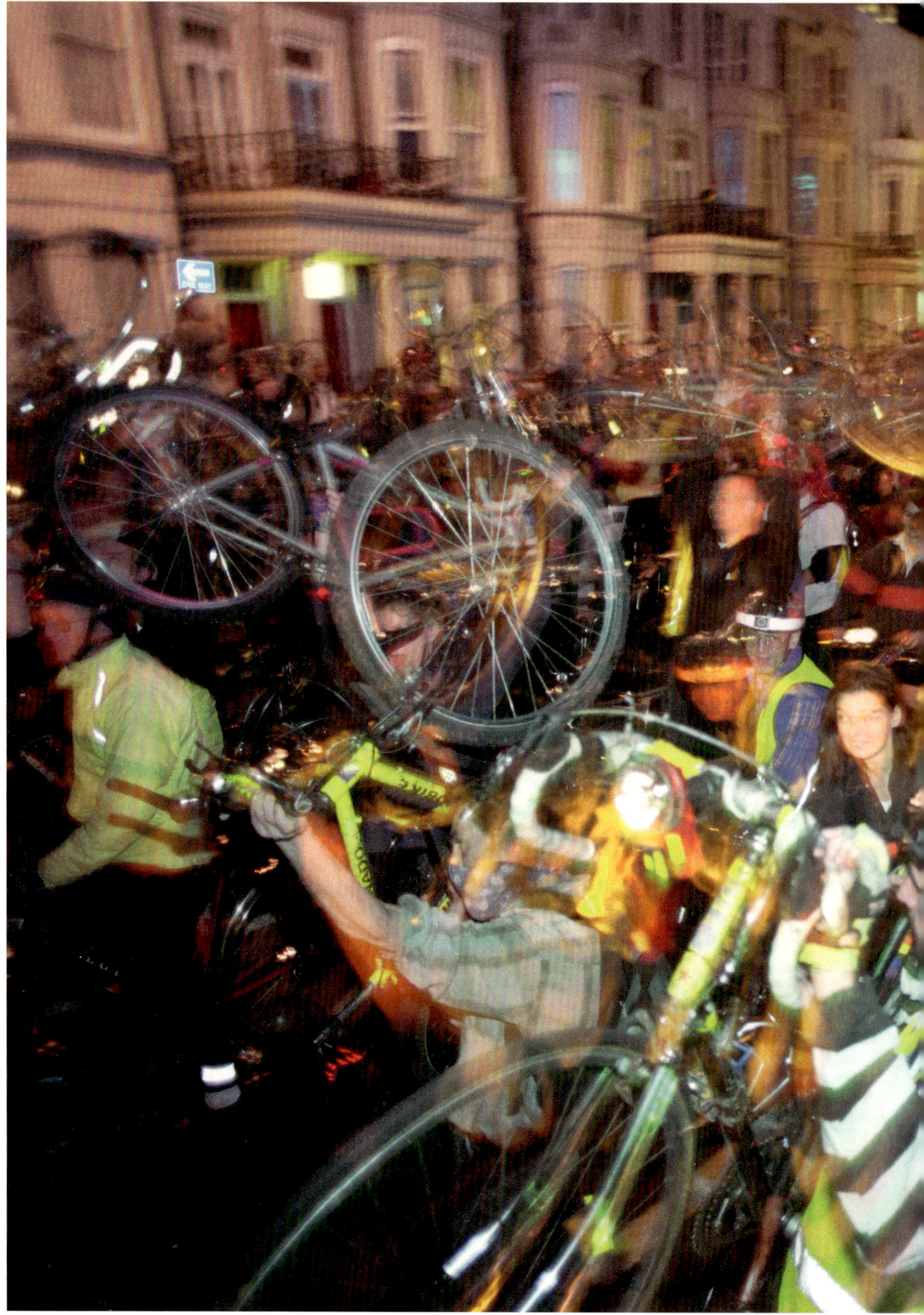

Critical Mass

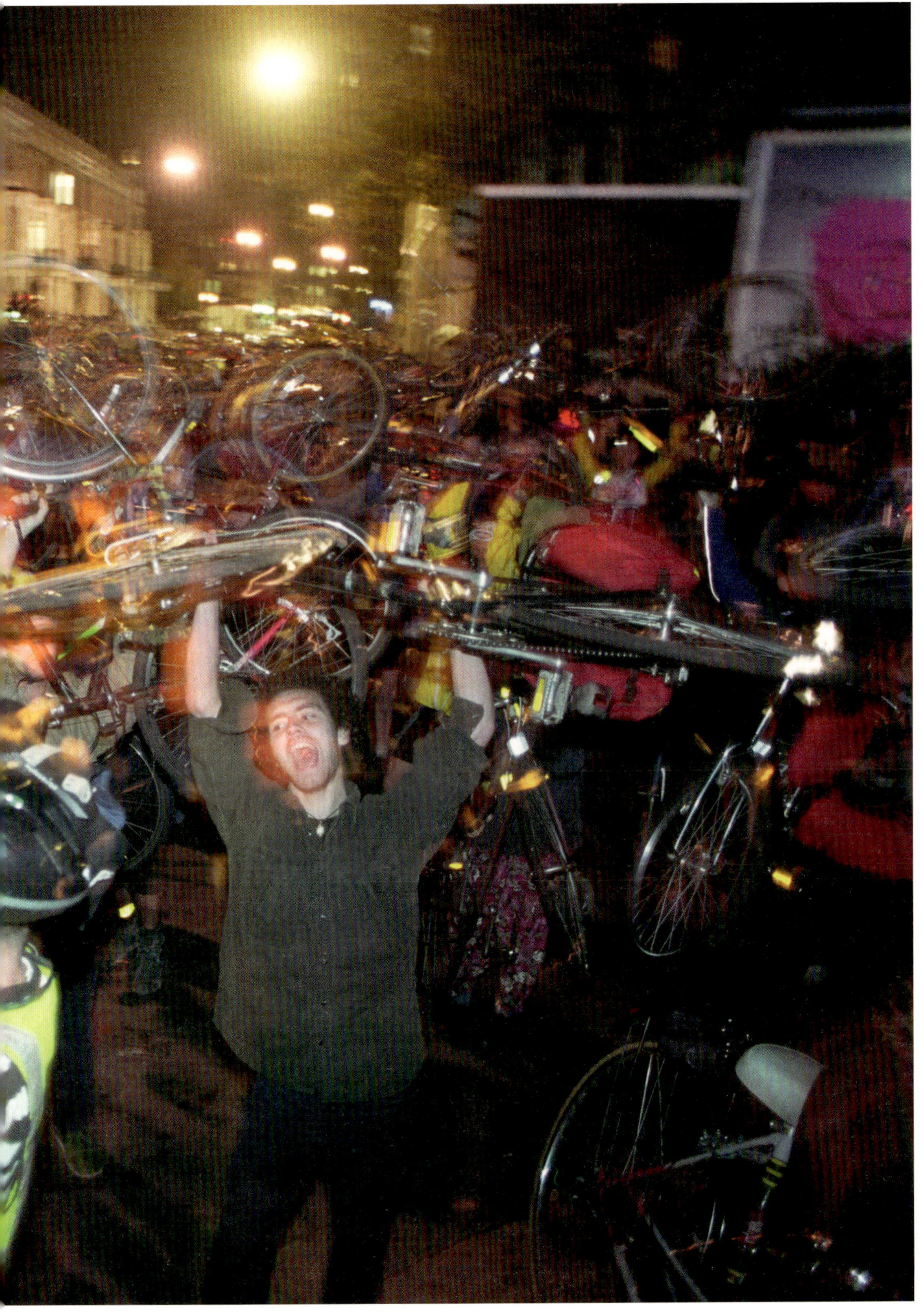

Reclaim the Streets: Shepherd's Bush, M41 July 1996

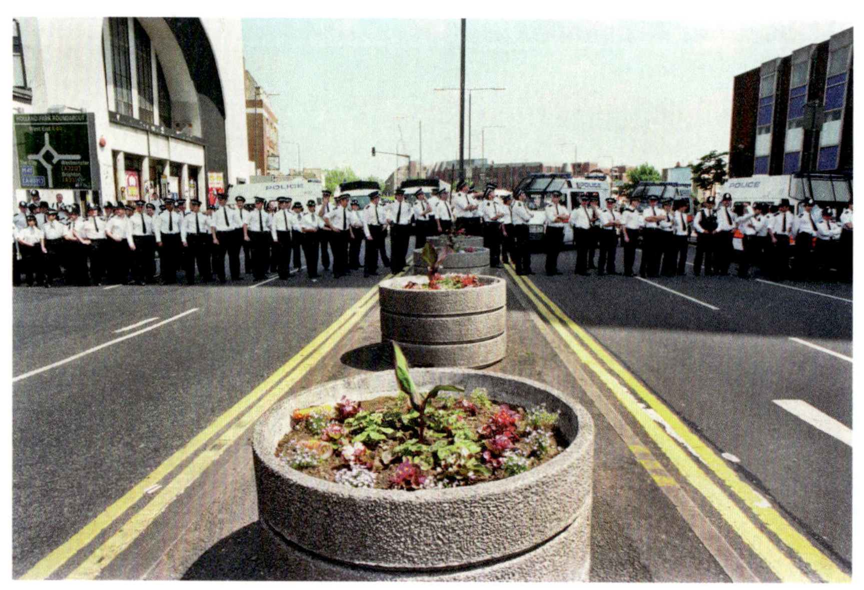

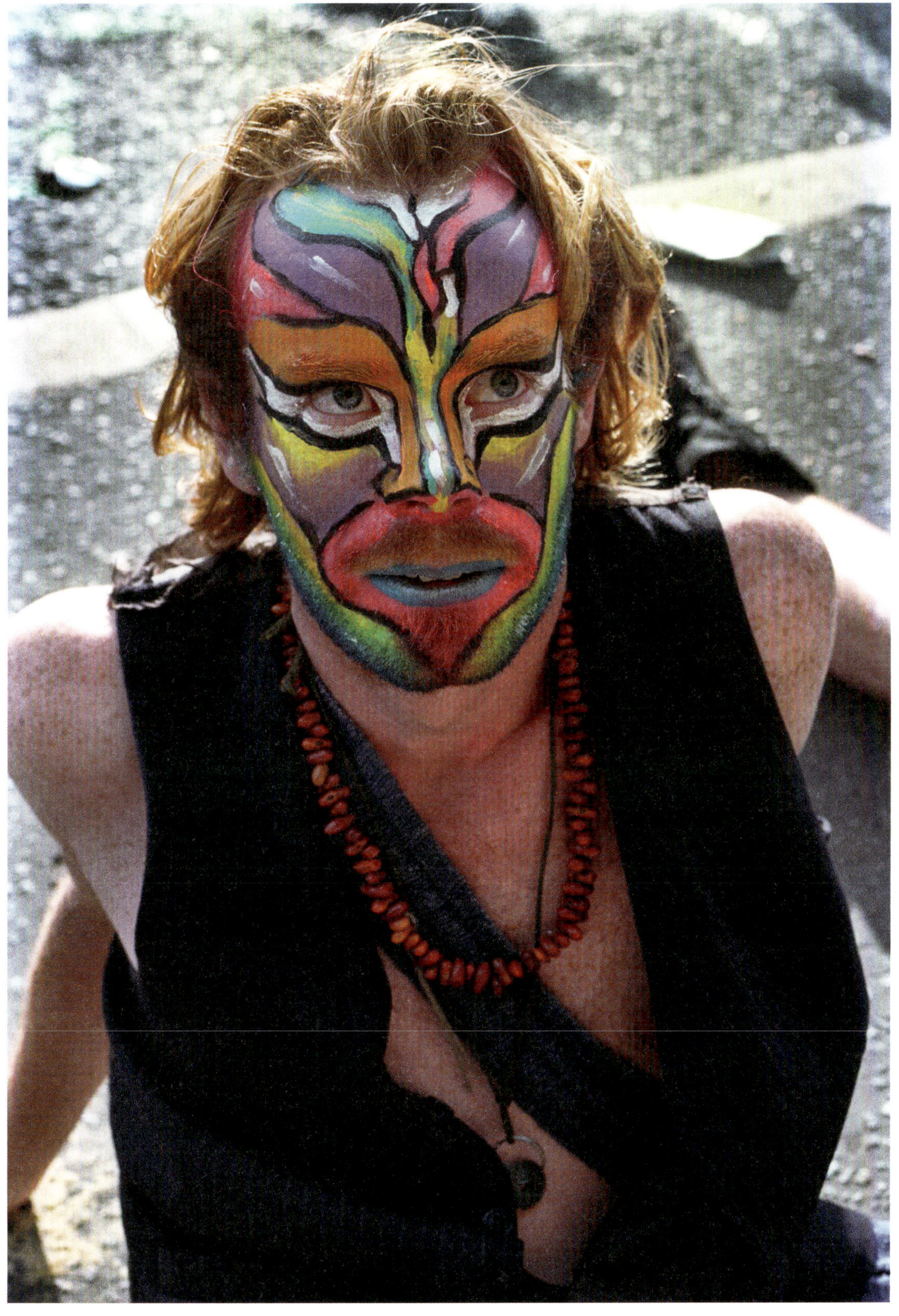

Exiting Shepherds Bush tube station we were greeted by a formidable number of policemen blocking our route to the M41. Was it going to be a riot or a rave? At that point it looked like the former. However the police underestimated the tenacity of those who had come to express their frustrations with the dominance of cars in London. Finding a back tunnel, we realised it was possible to sneak around the cops. Quietly moving through the dark concrete structure and then suddenly out into the beaming light and running towards the lorry with hidden sound system. In no time at all the police had lost control of the situation and the day was ours.

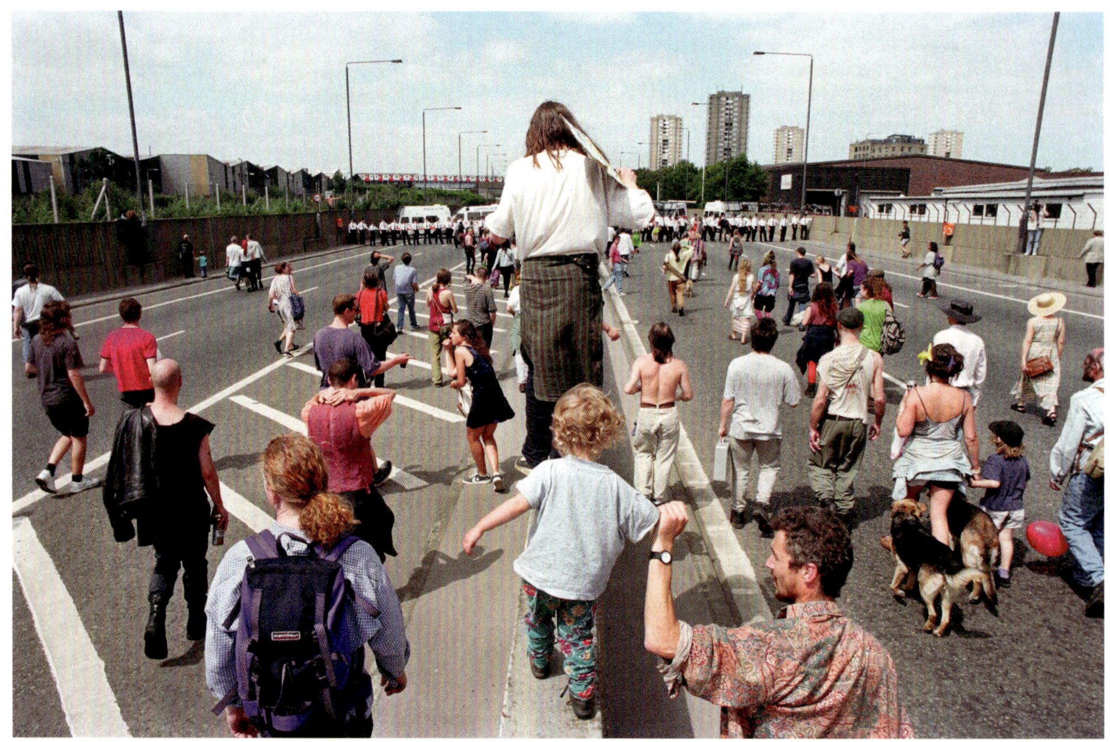

Reclaim the Streets: Shepherd's Bush, M41

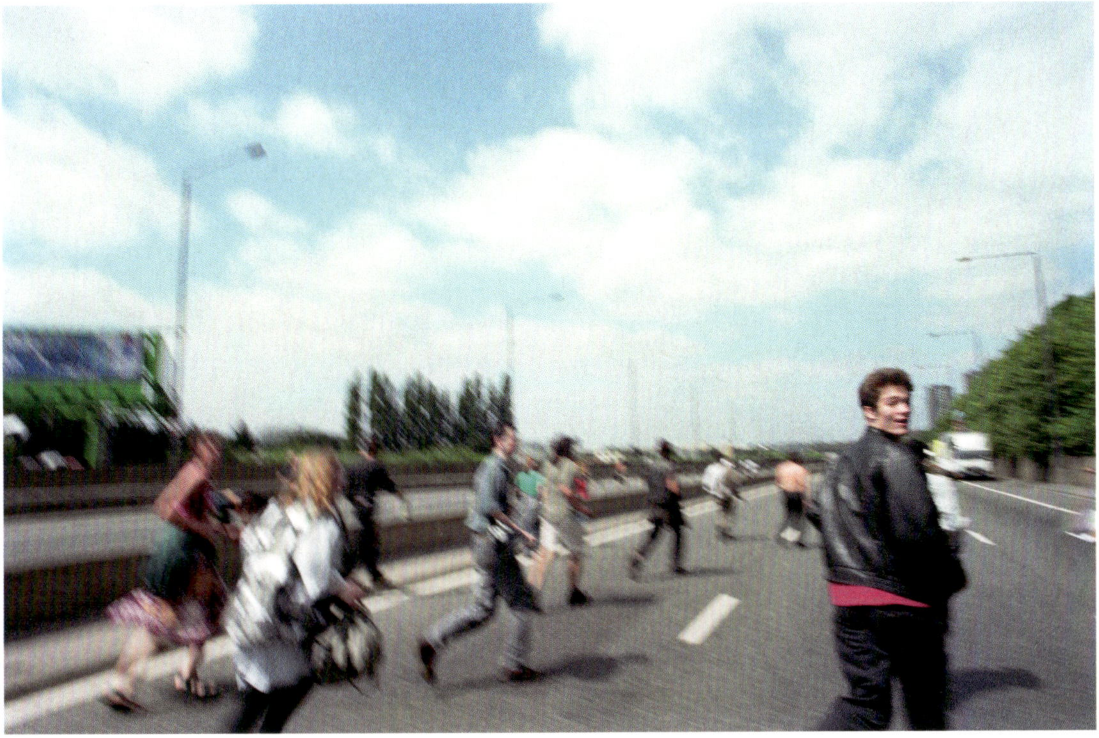

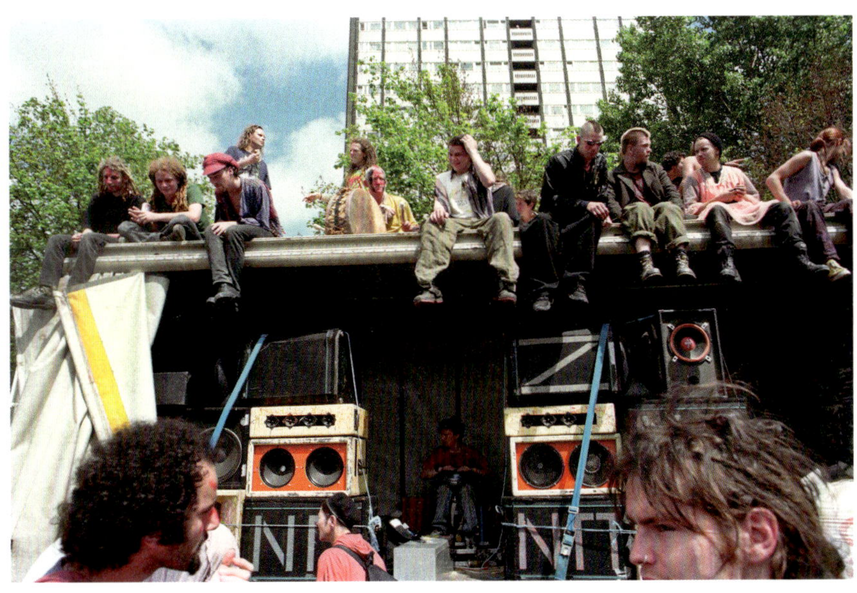

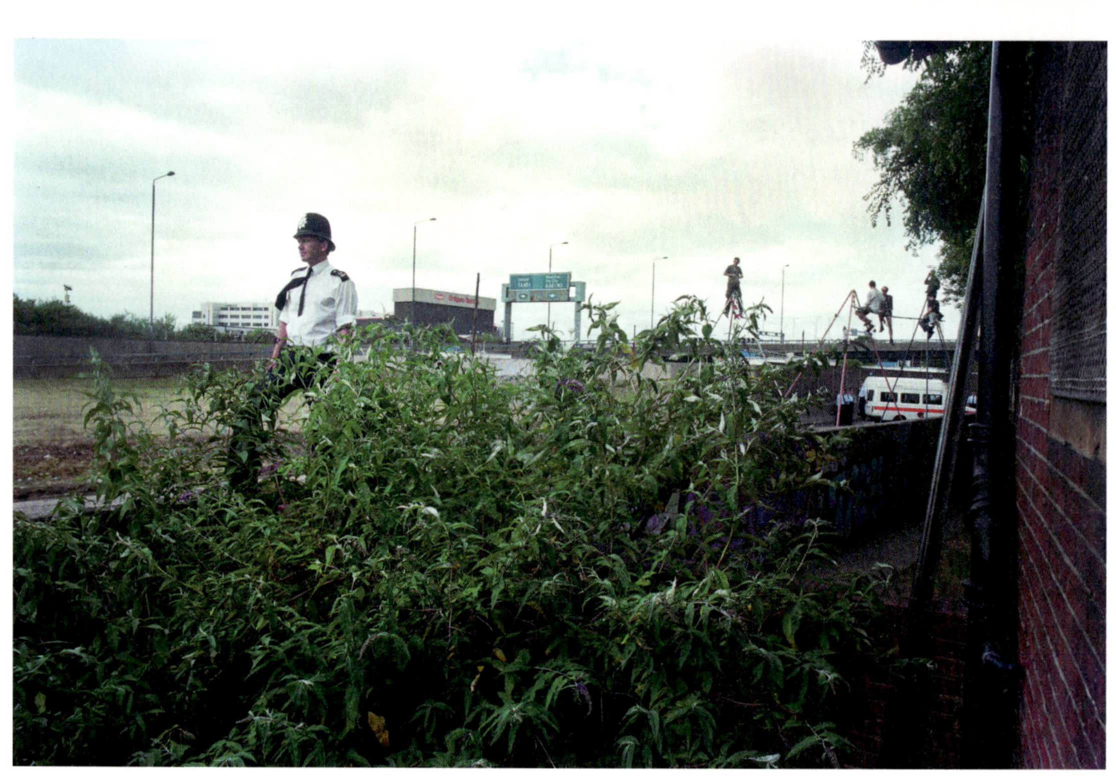

Reclaim the Streets: Shepherd's Bush, M41

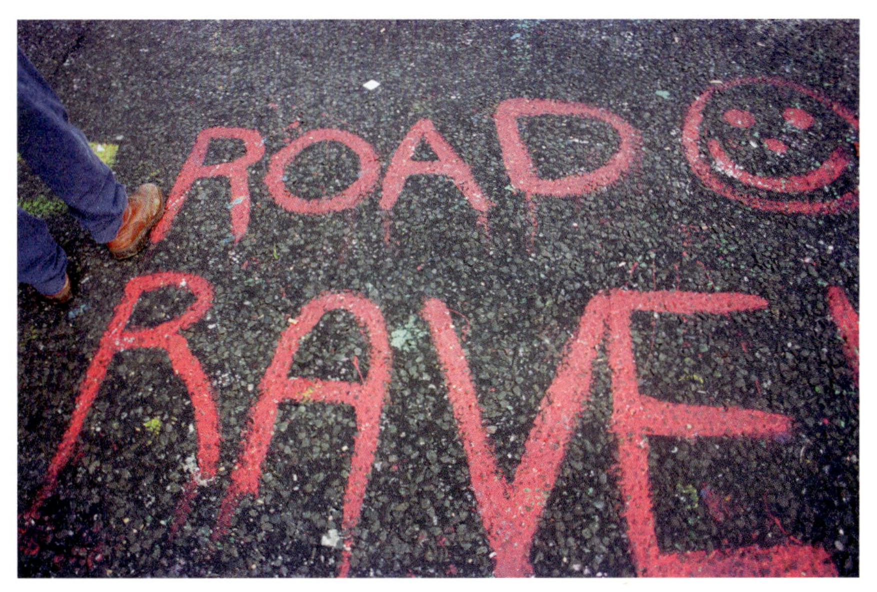
ROAD
RAVE

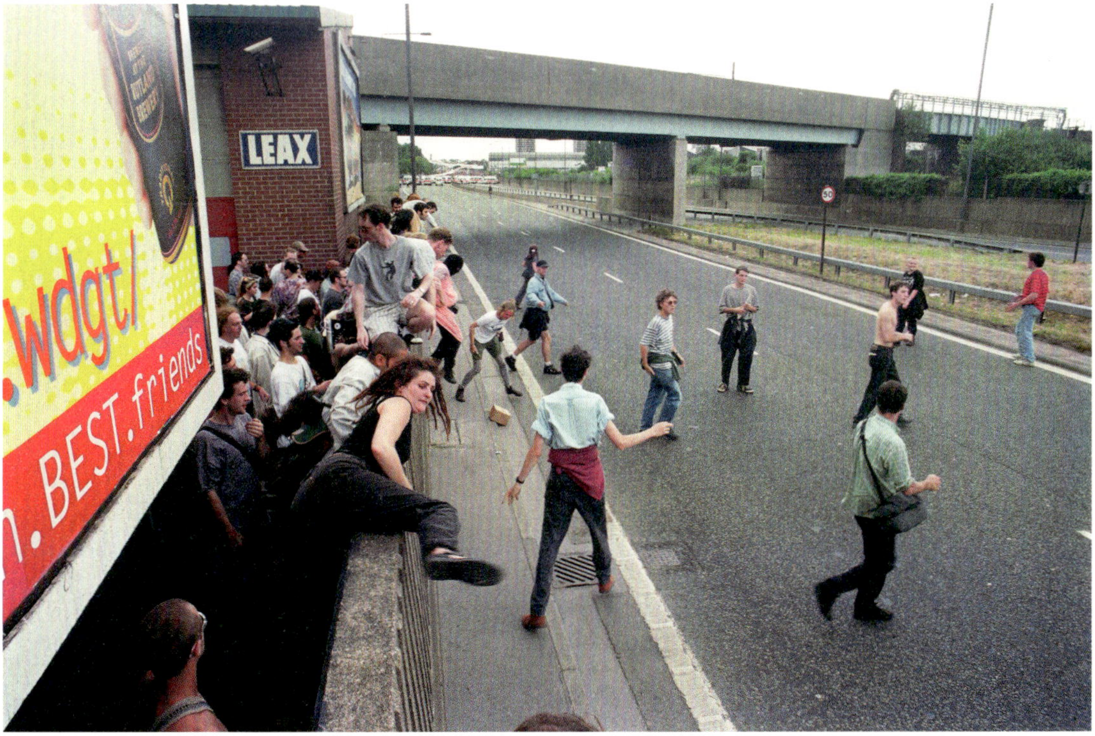

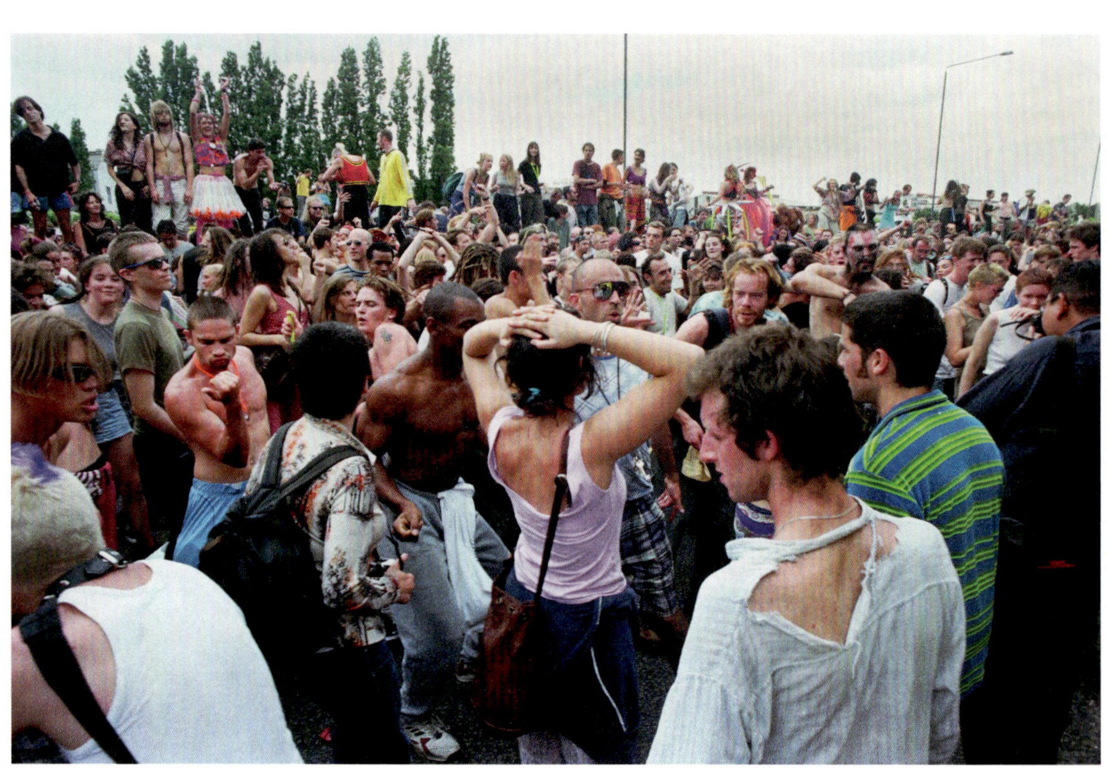

Reclaim the Streets: Shepherd’s Bush, M41

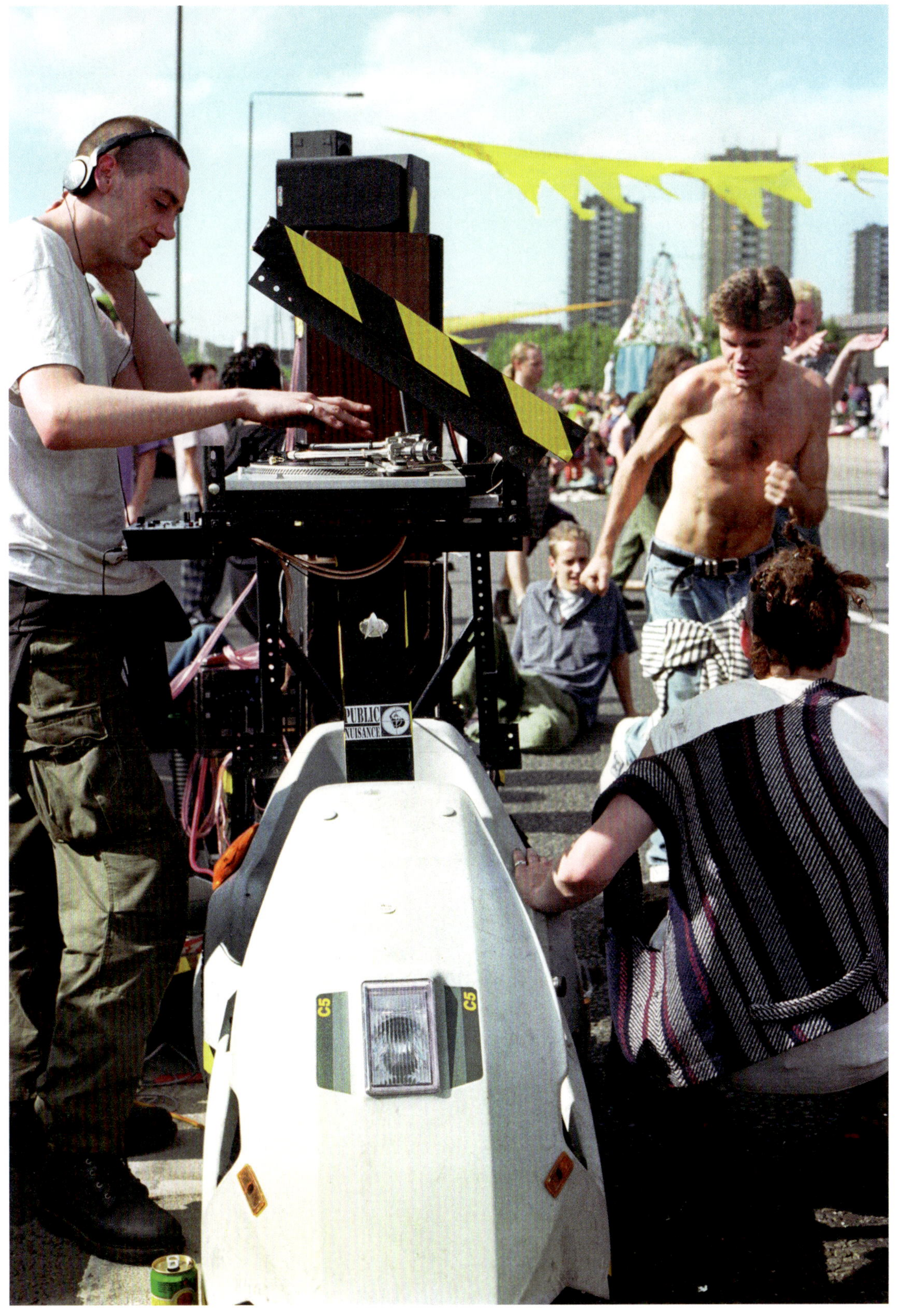
PUBLIC
NUISANCE
C5
C5

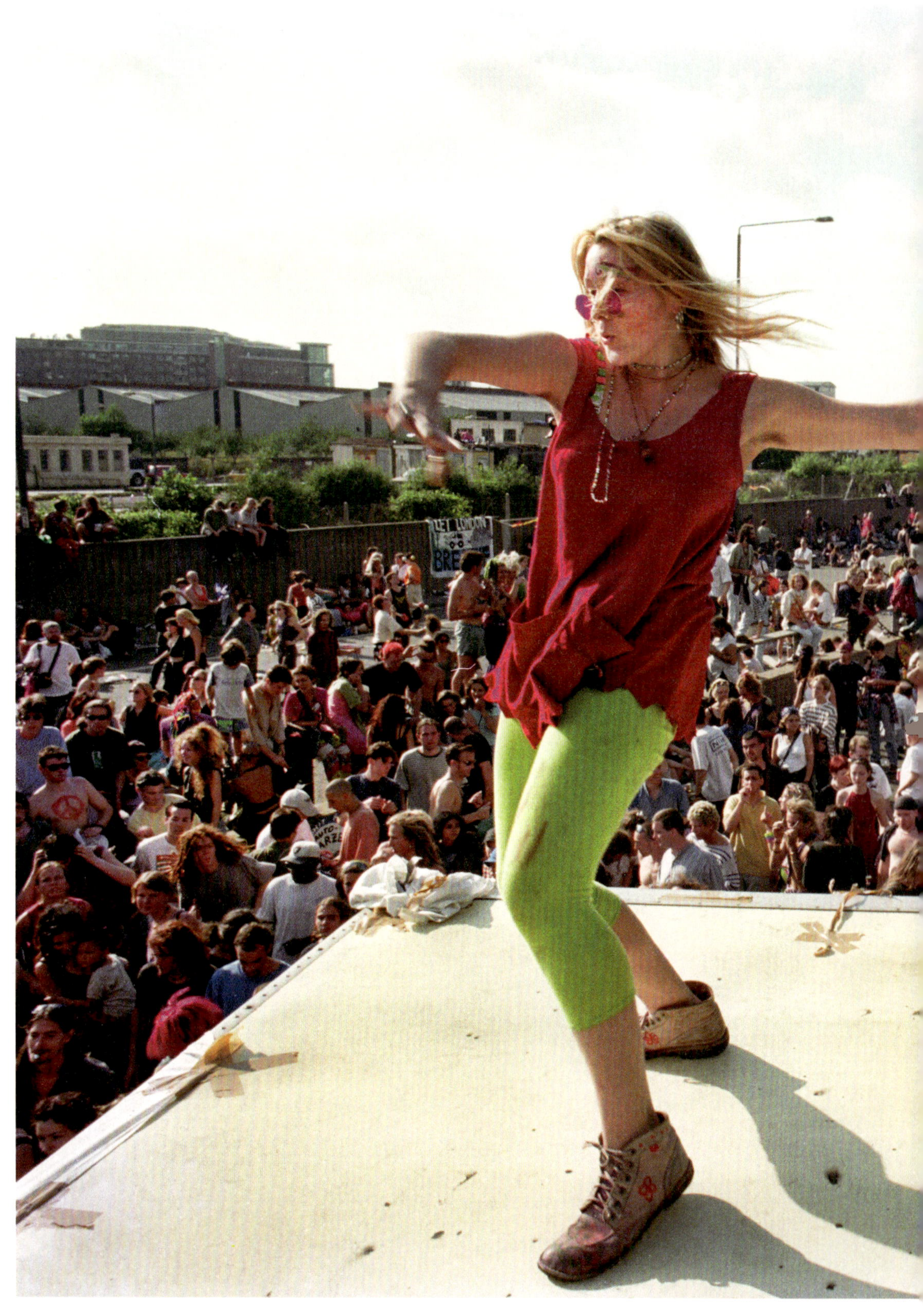

Reclaim the Streets: Shepherd's Bush, M41

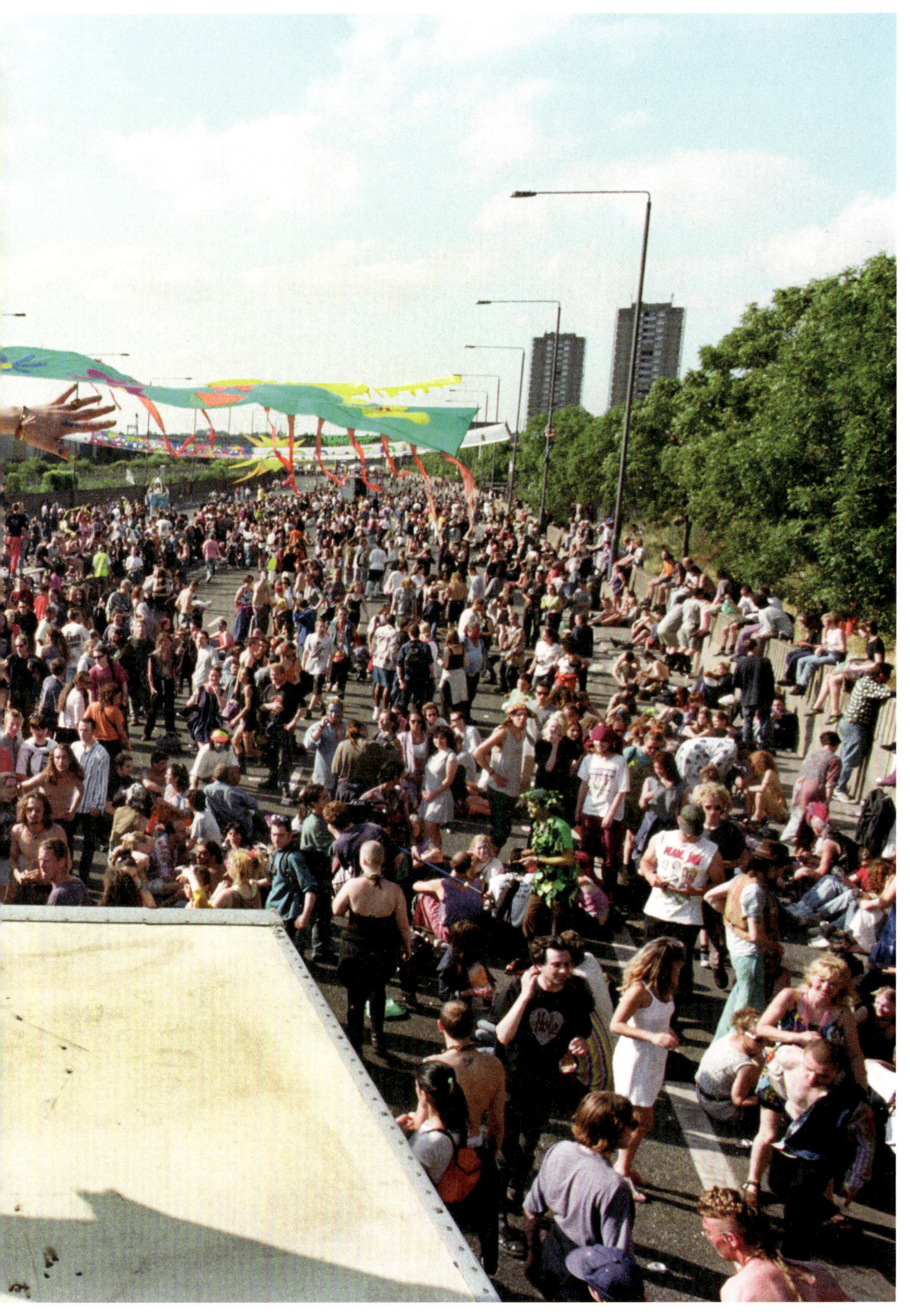

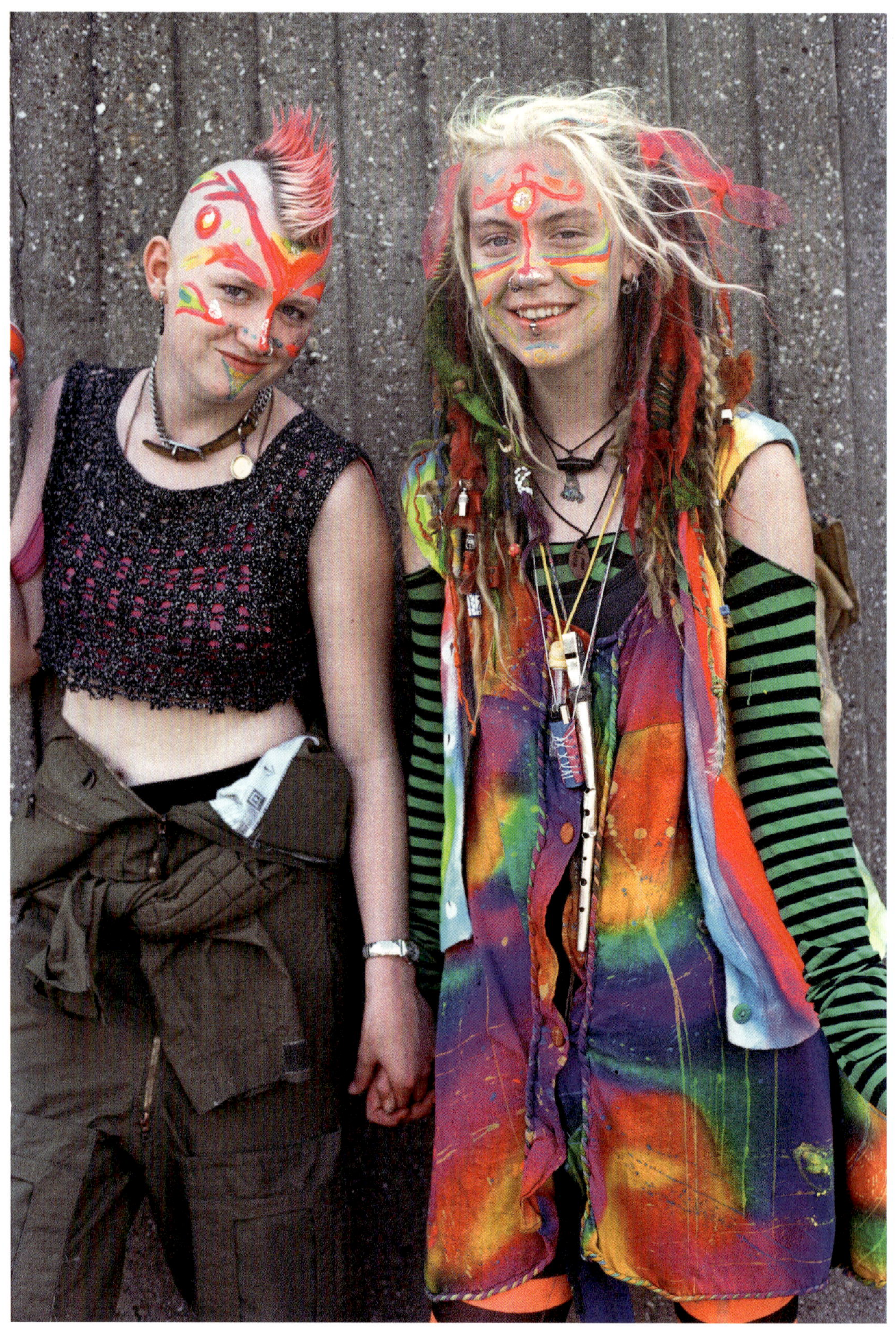

Reclaim the Streets: Shepherd's Bush, M41

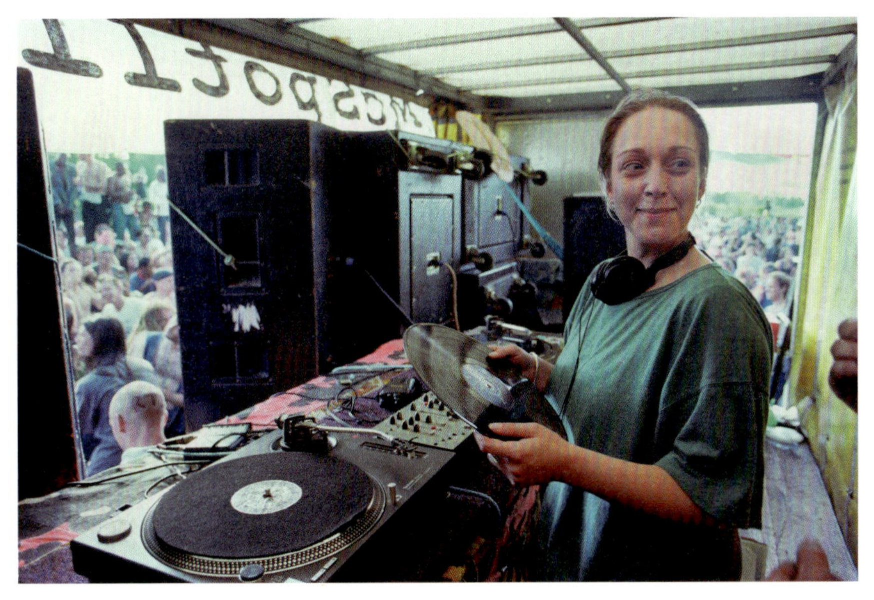

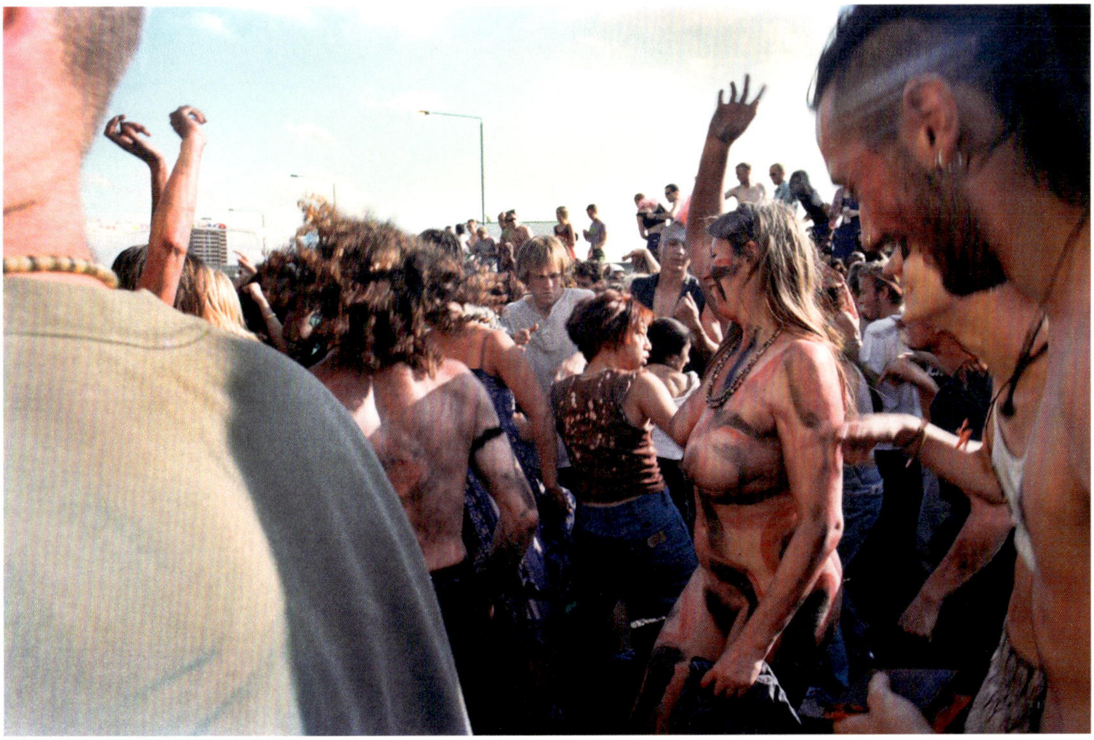

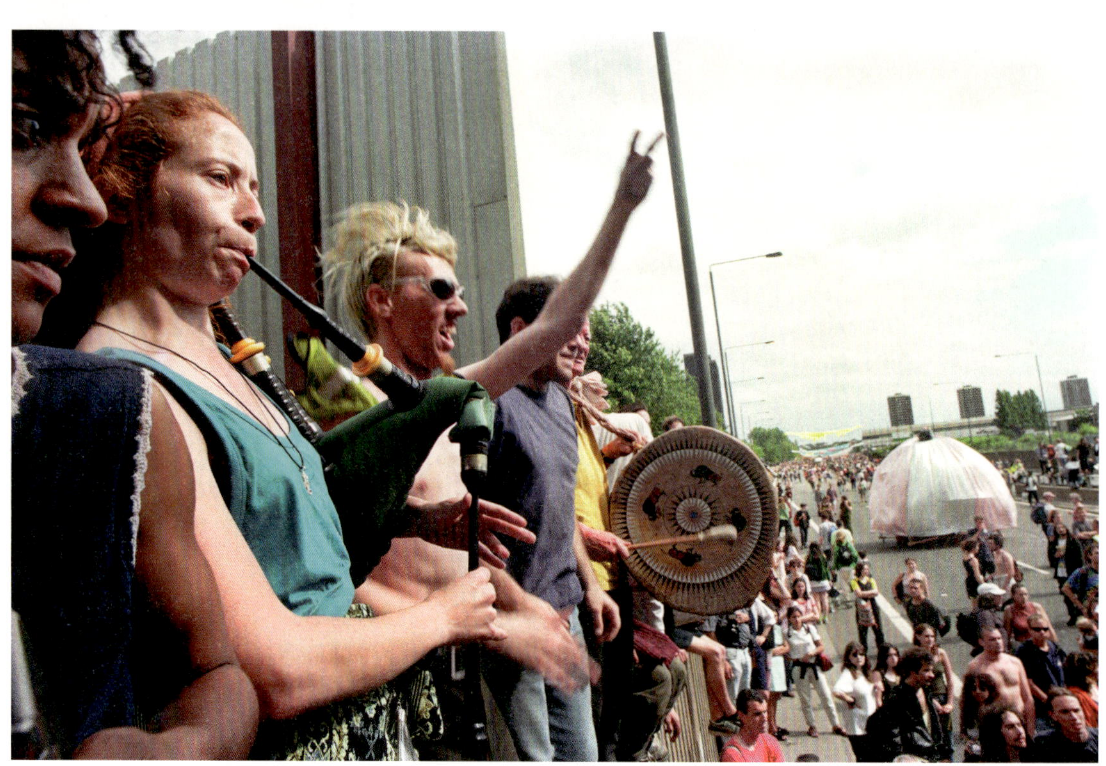

Reclaim the Streets: Shepherd's Bush, M41

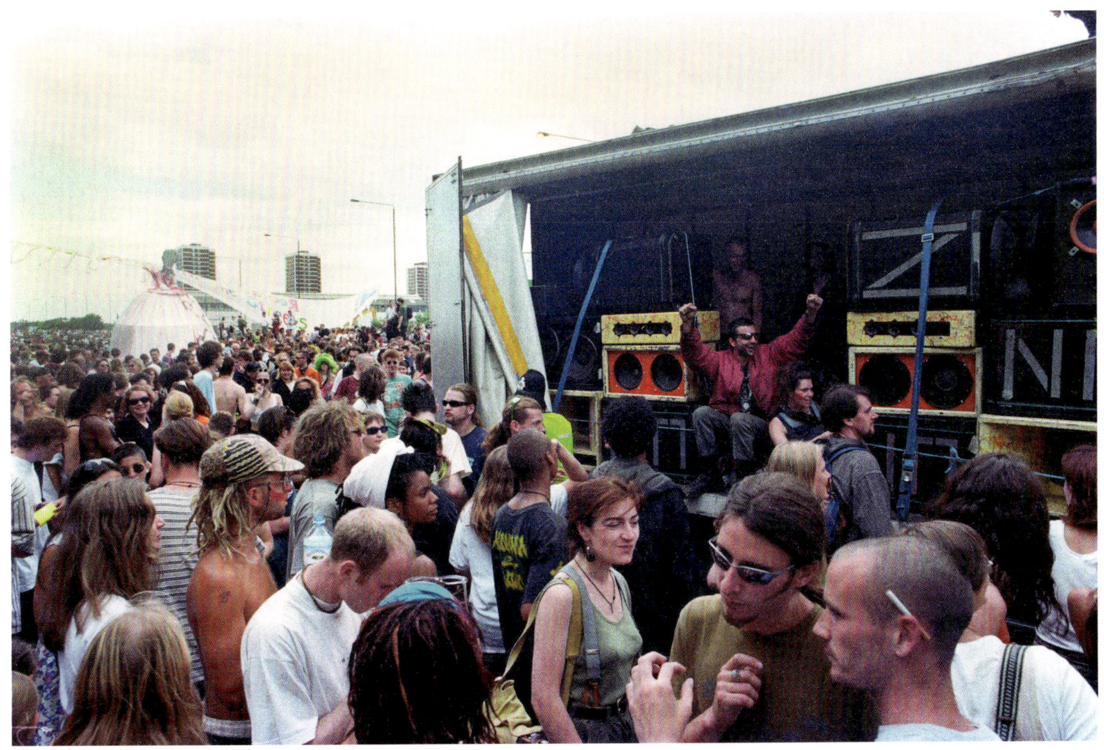

The woman with her huge ballroom gown served more purpose than entertaining everyone with her theatrical costume. Situating herself close to the pounding thump of the sound system meant a different kind of theatre could take place underneath her dress. Under there it was hot with an intense and exciting atmosphere. A shrill pounding revealed a pneumatic drill digging up the motorway. Later in an act of anarchic poetry a tree was planted where previously dark oil soaked Tarmac had lain.

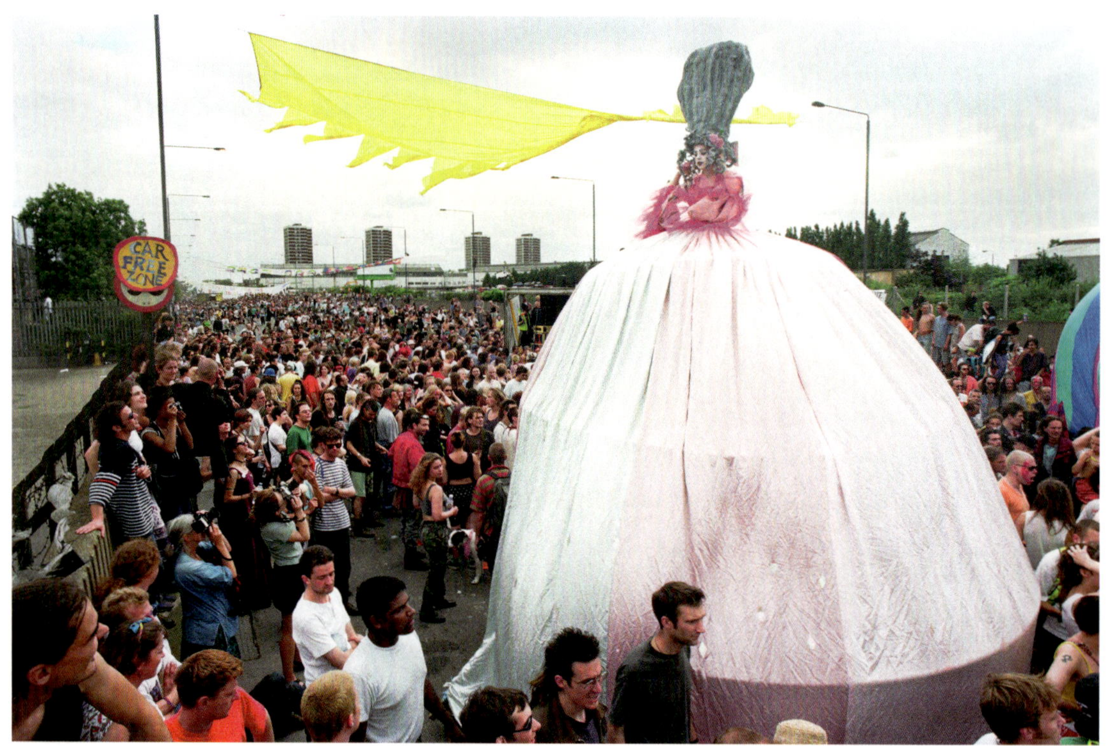

Reclaim the Streets: Shepherd's Bush, M41

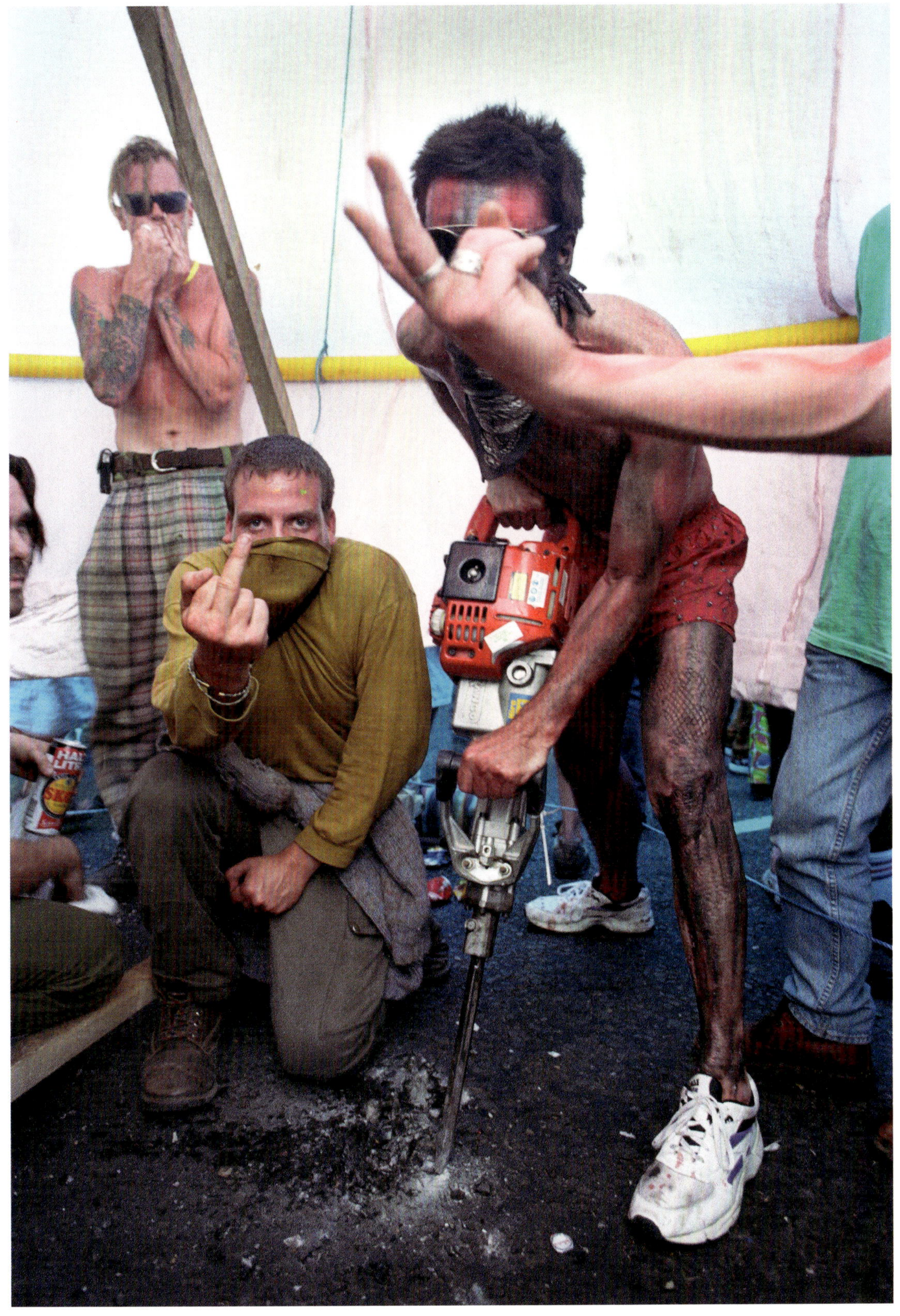

Reclaim the Streets: Trafalgar Square April 1997

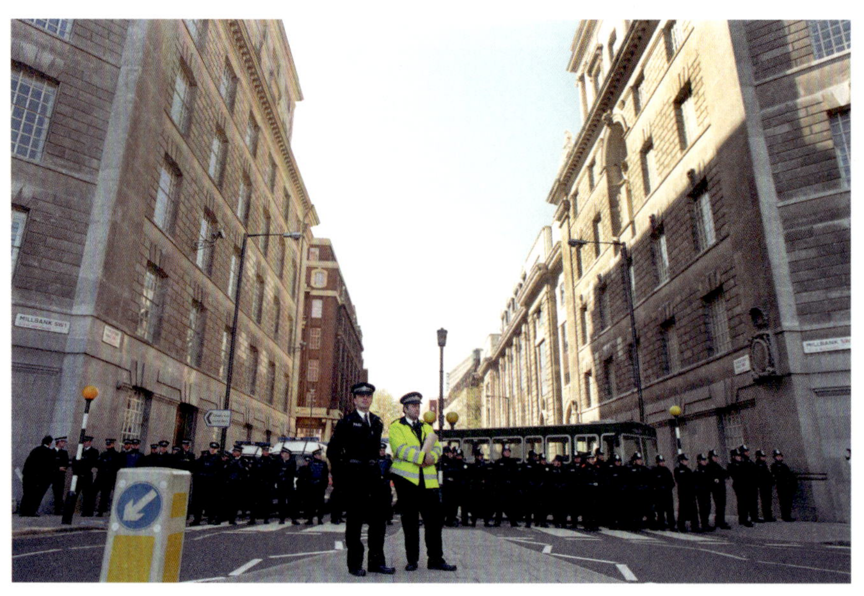

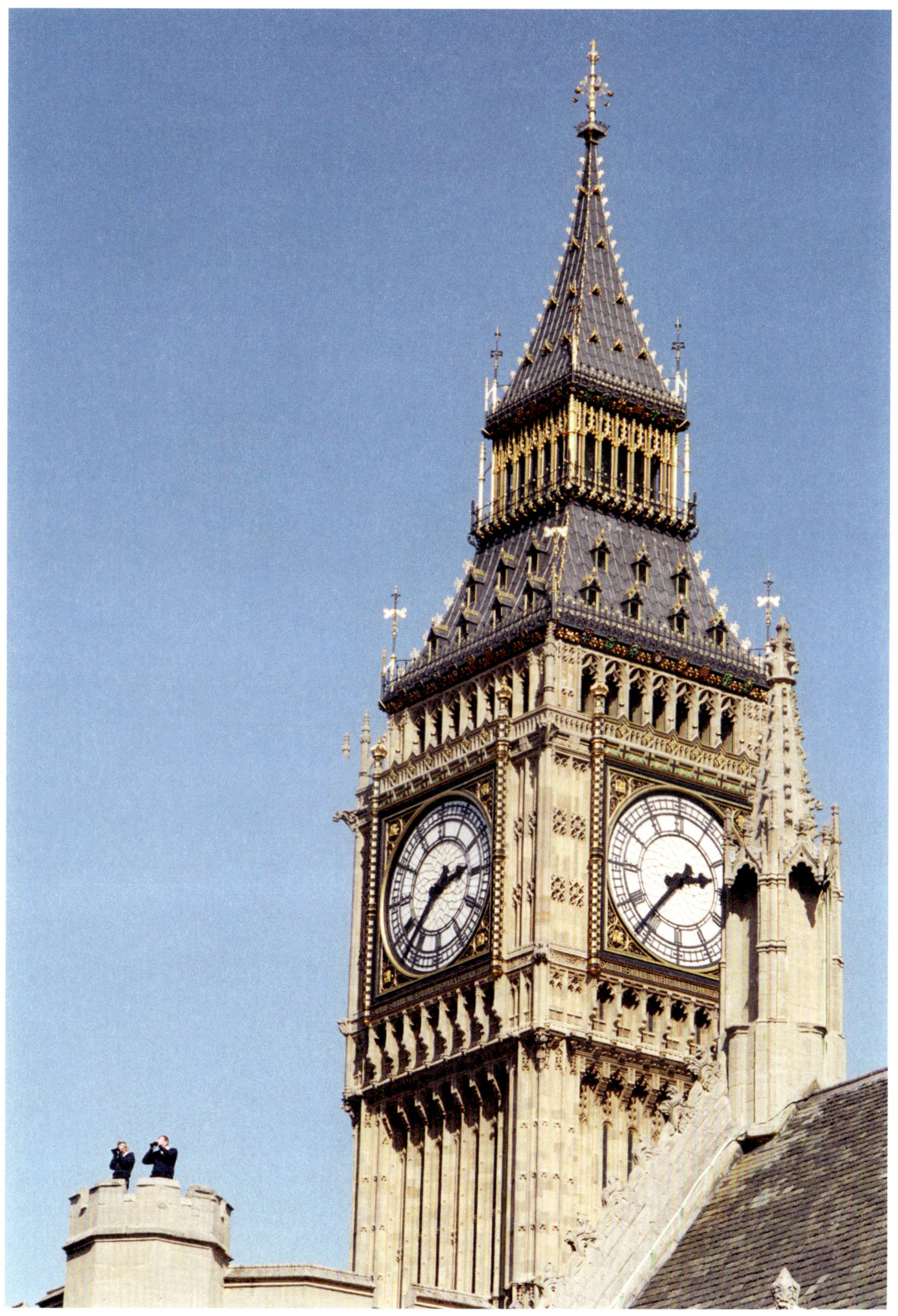

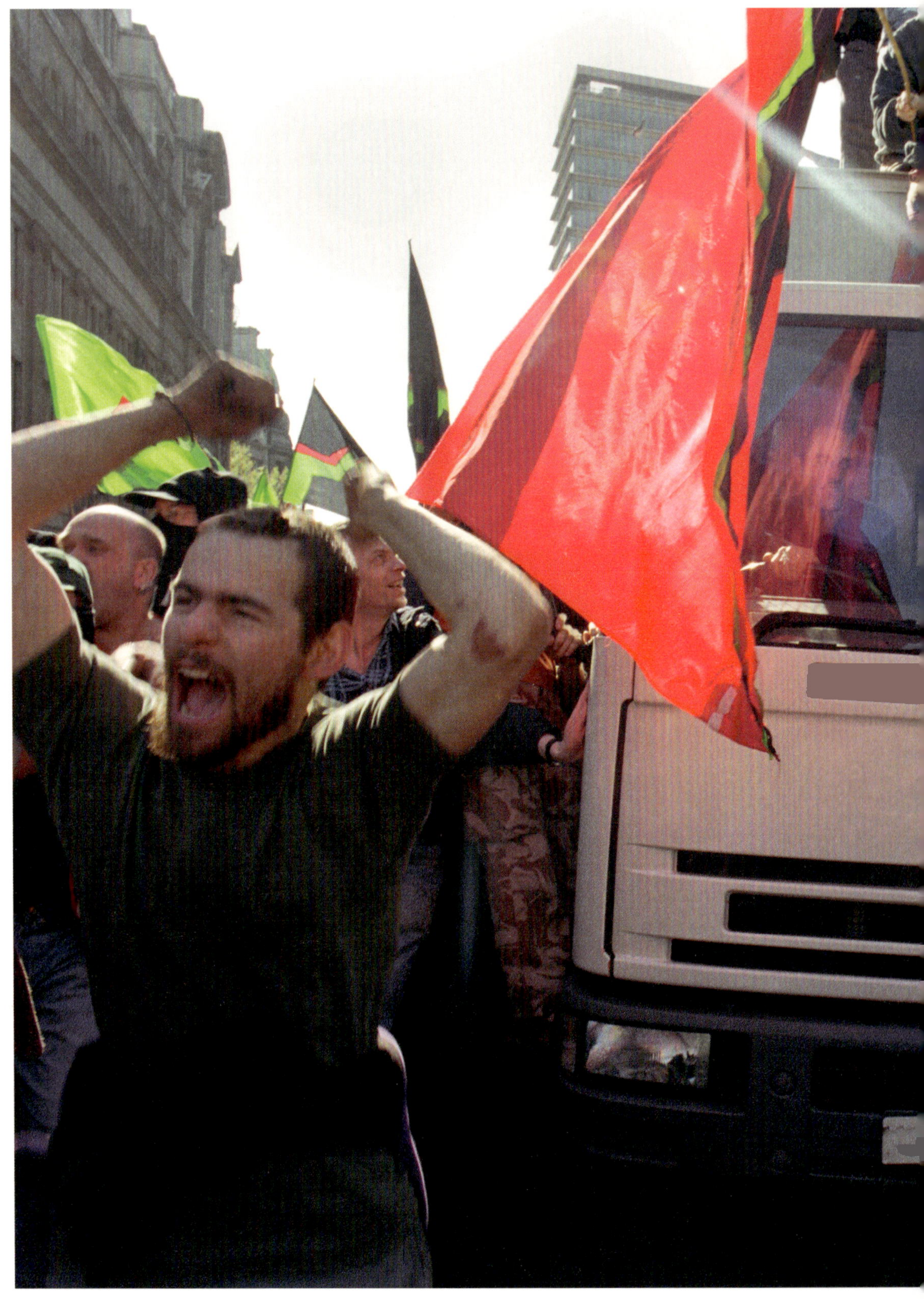

Reclaim the Streets: Trafalgar Square

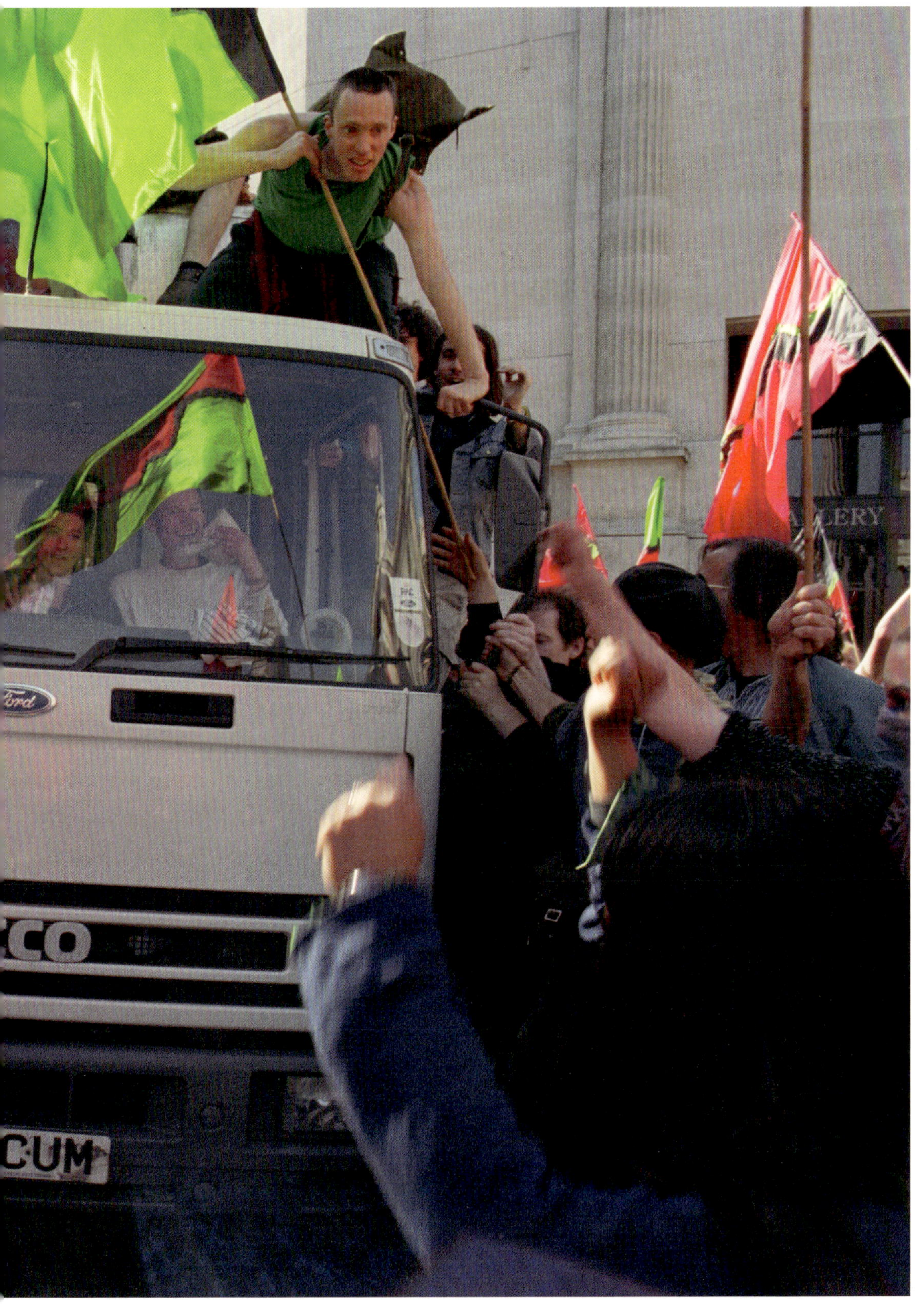
Ford

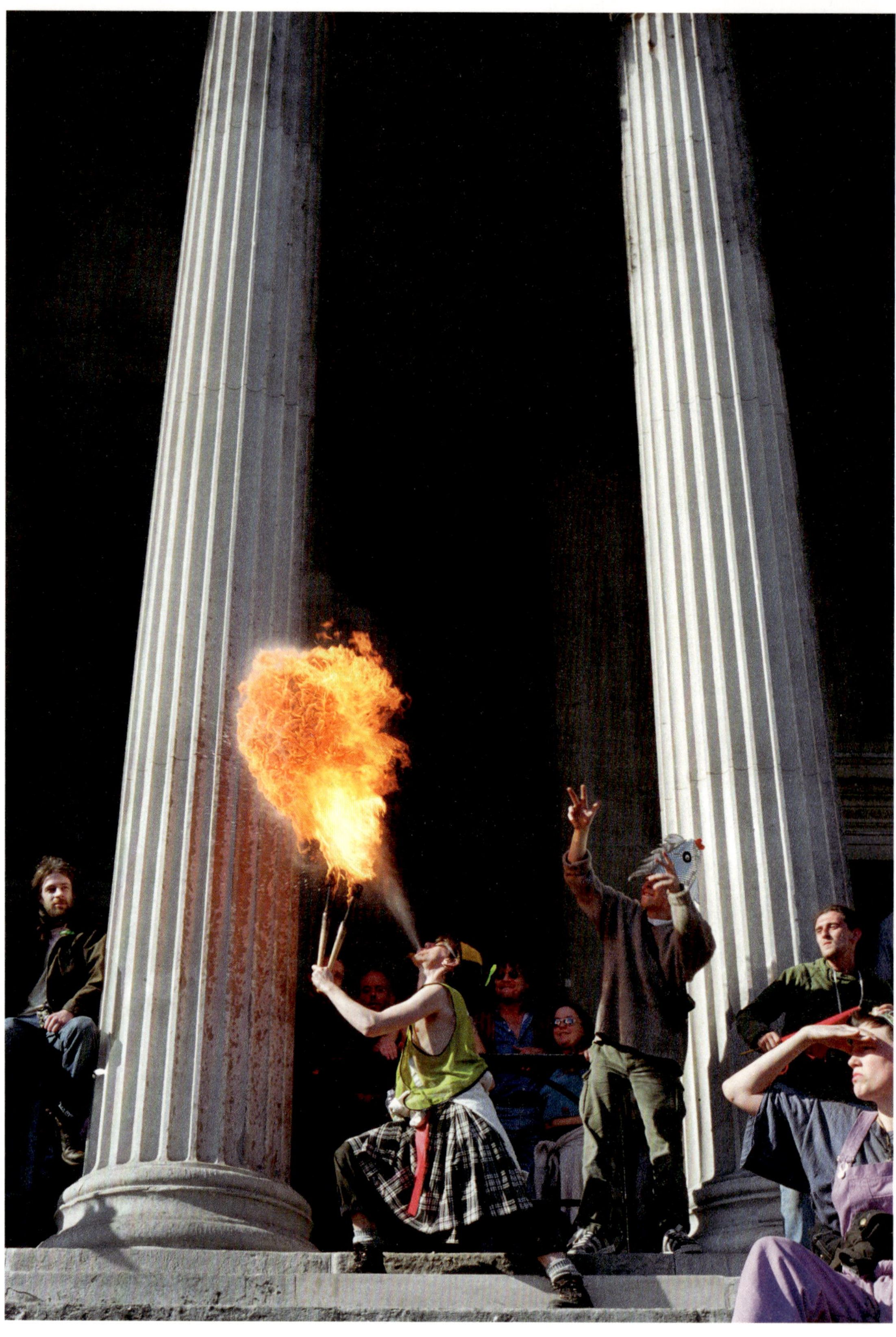

Reclaim the Streets: Trafalgar Square

Out of nowhere there was ecstatic cheering, as if someone had just scored a winning goal. I looked up to see a lorry had somehow broken through the ranks of police and made it into Trafalgar Square. A police baton had damaged the fuel filter meaning a swarm of bodies had to push the vehicle to its resting space in front of the National Gallery. That was the moment when thousands of environmental activists went nuts because suddenly we heard the hard squelchy beat of acid techno, for the lorry had a big sound system concealed. Later in the day the driver was arrested for attempted murder having knocked a police bike while driving into the square.

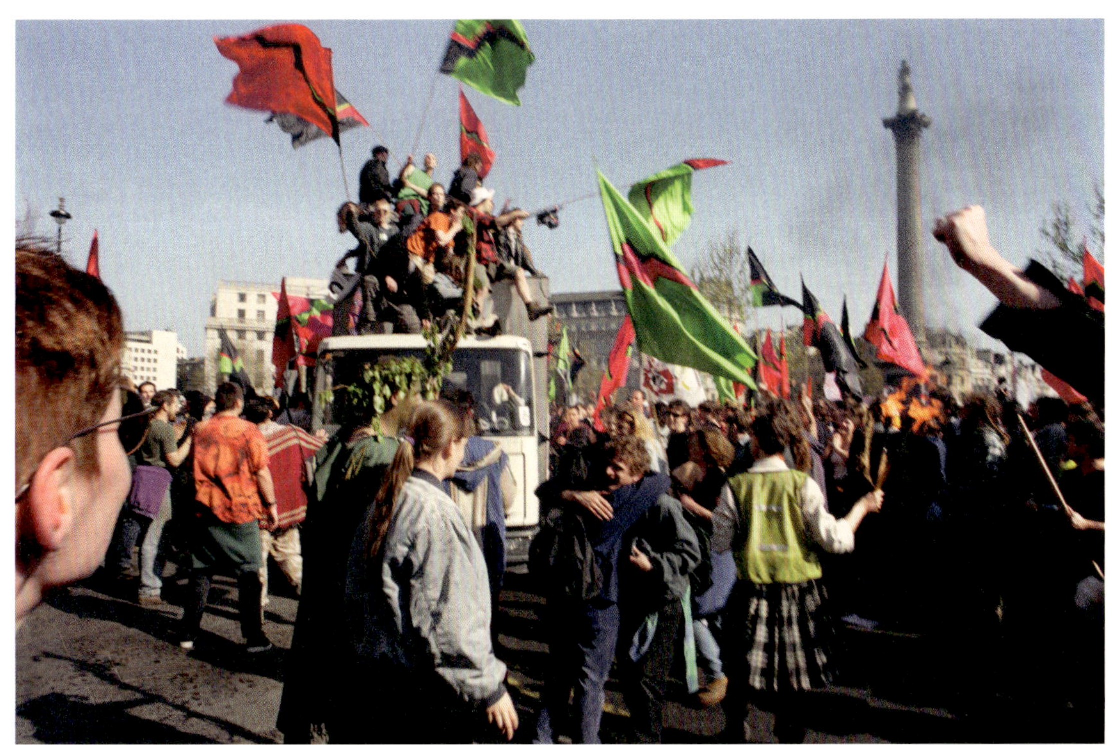

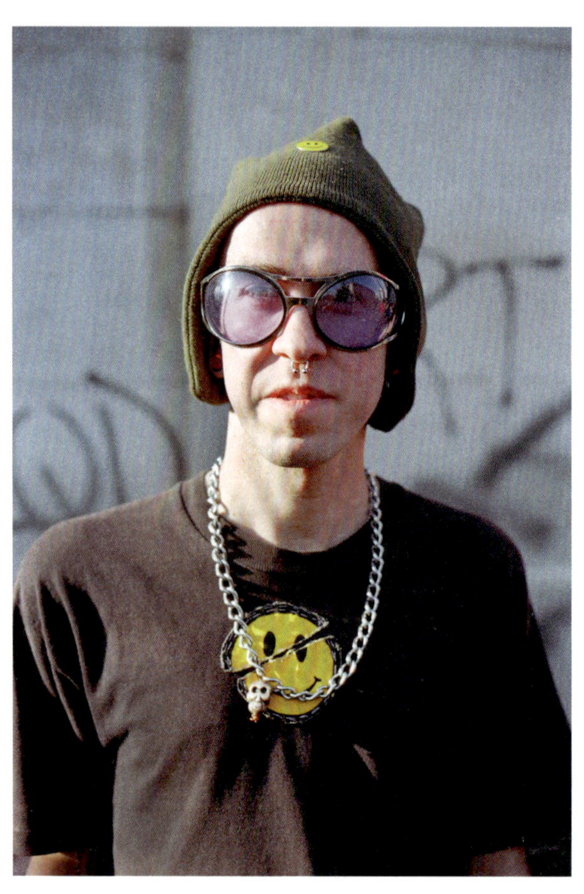

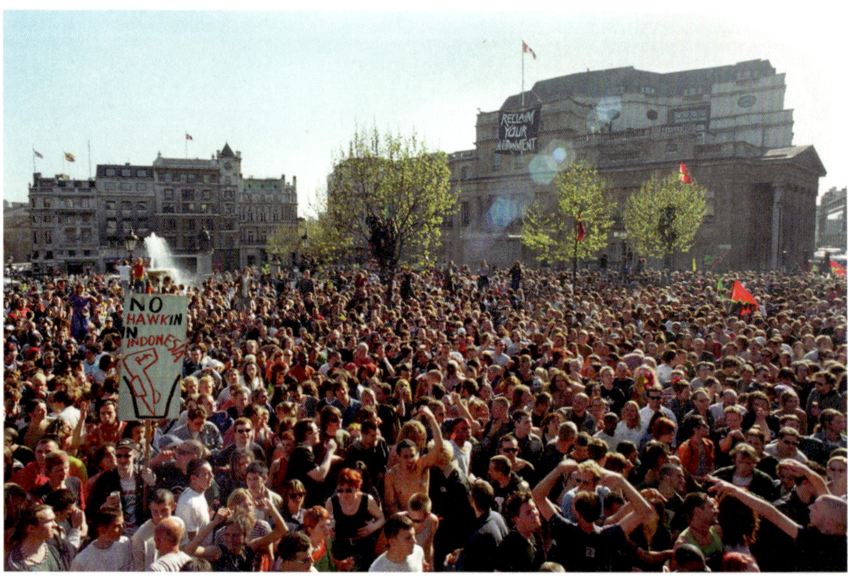

Reclaim the Streets: Trafalgar Square

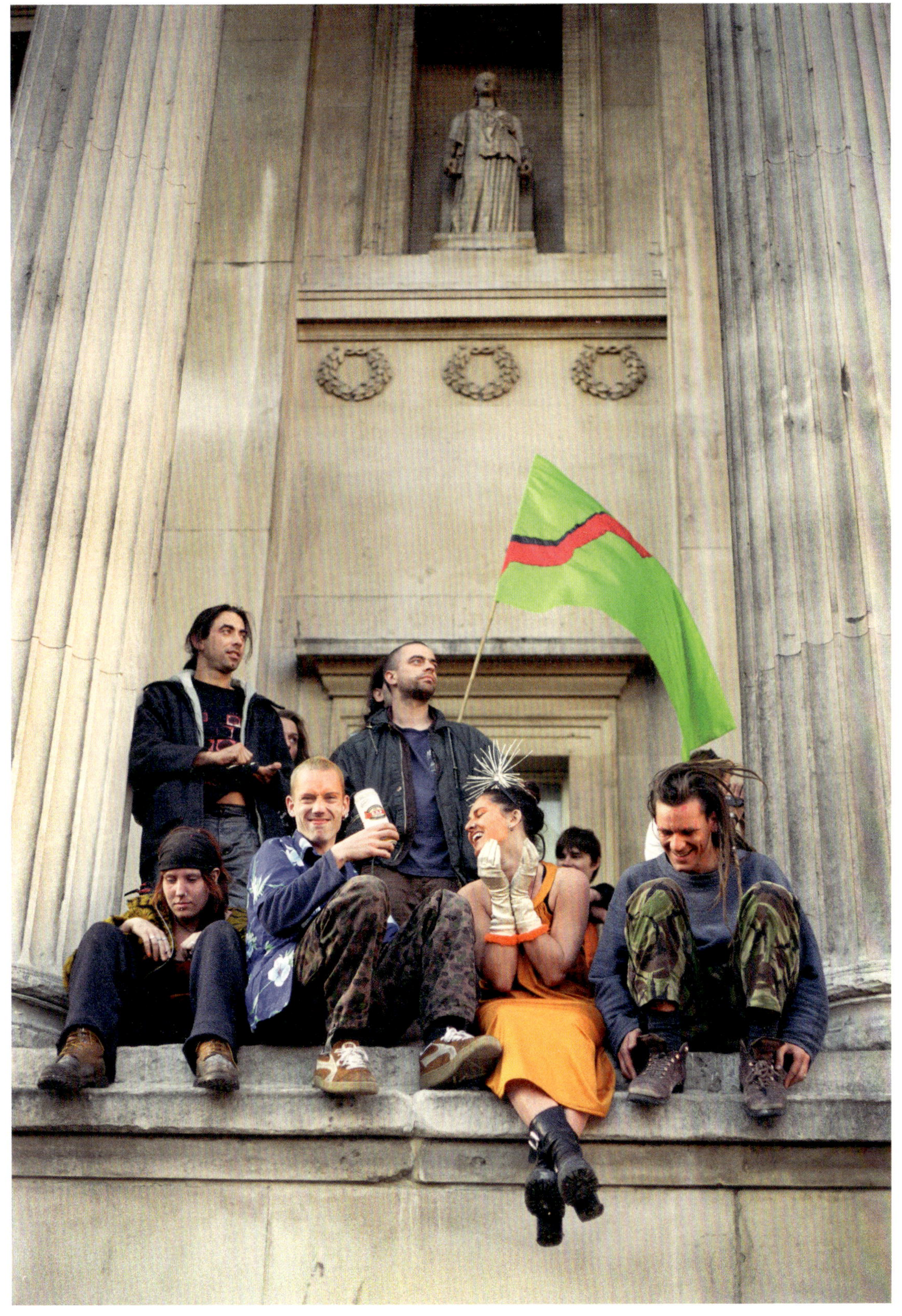

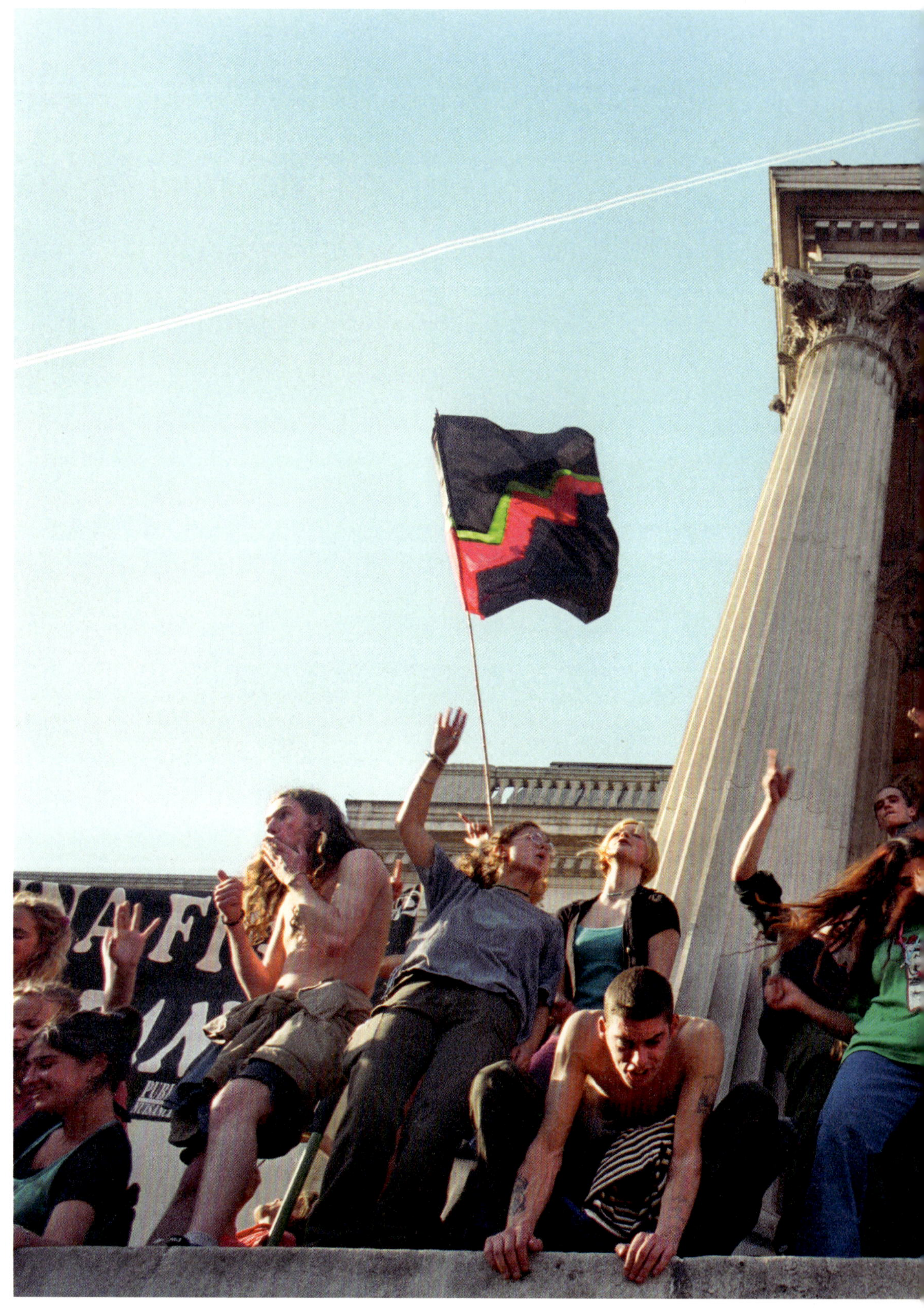

Reclaim the Streets: Trafalgar Square

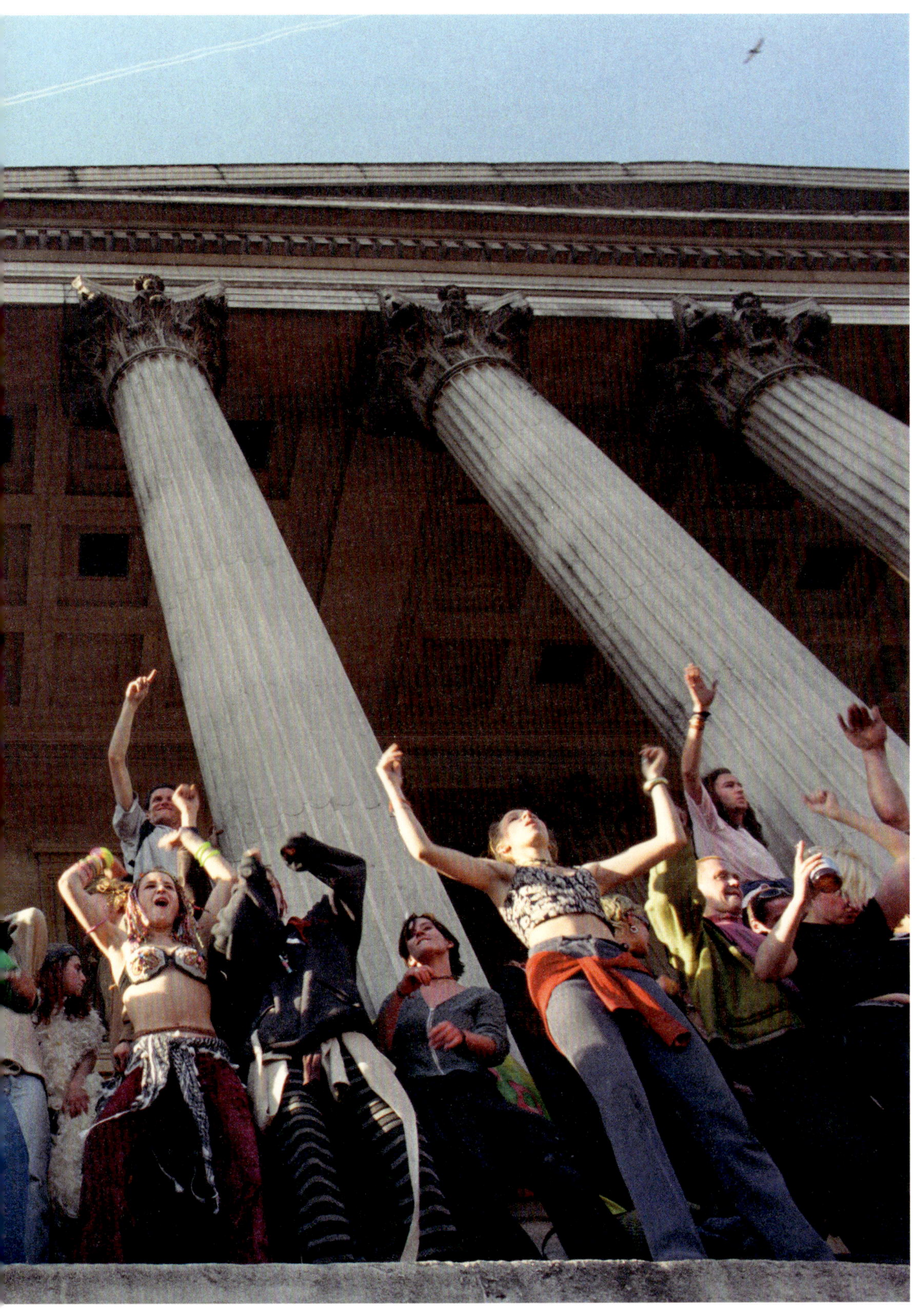

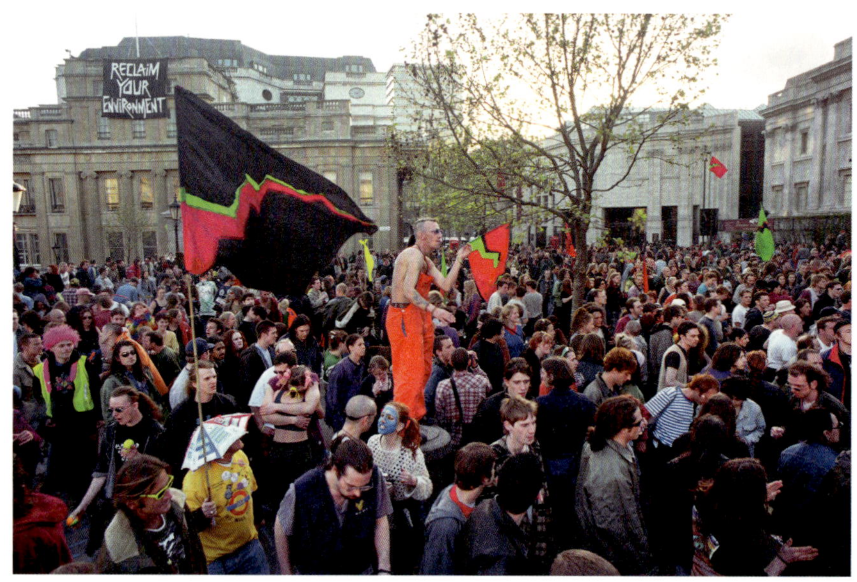

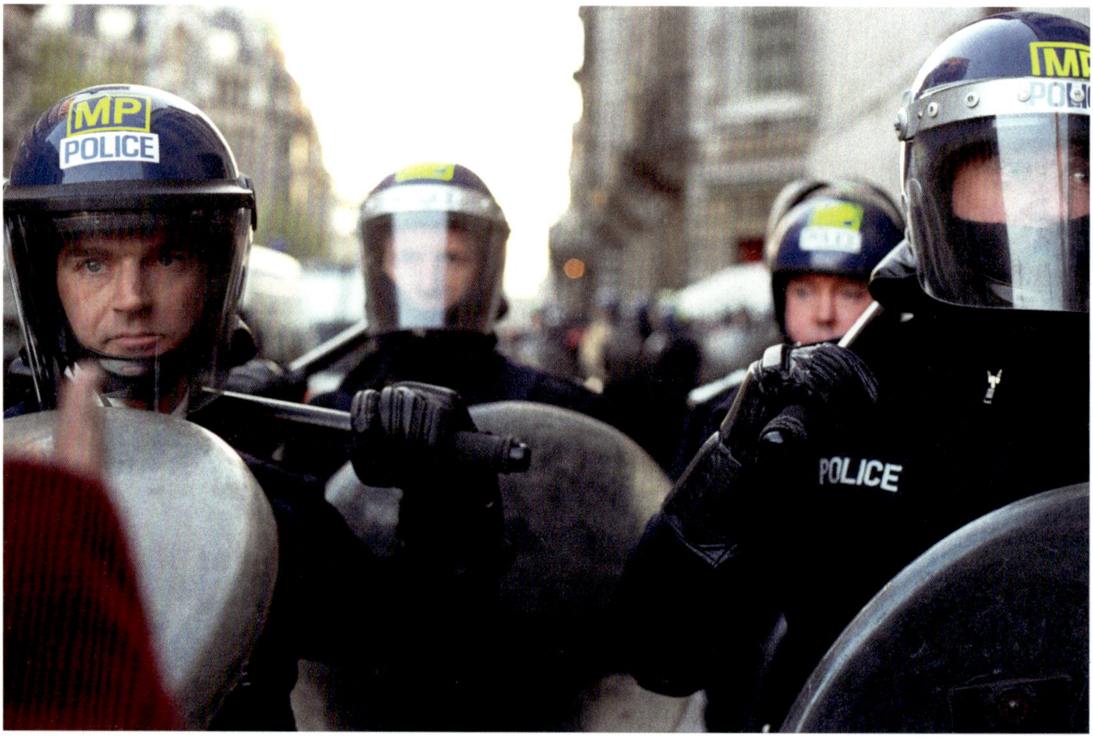

Reclaim the Streets: Trafalgar Square

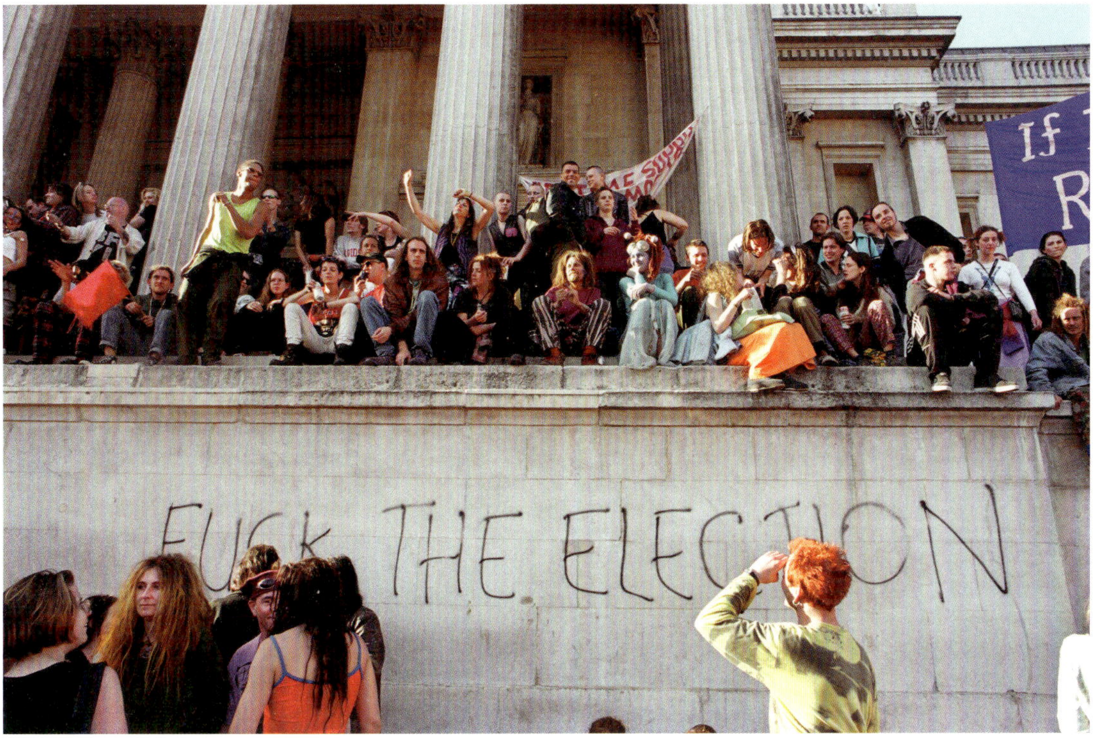

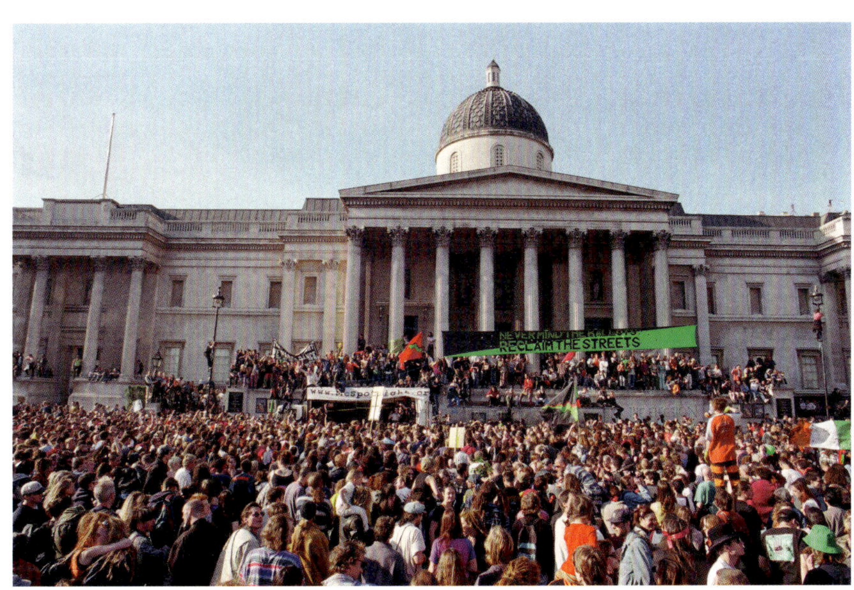
RECLAIM THE STREETS

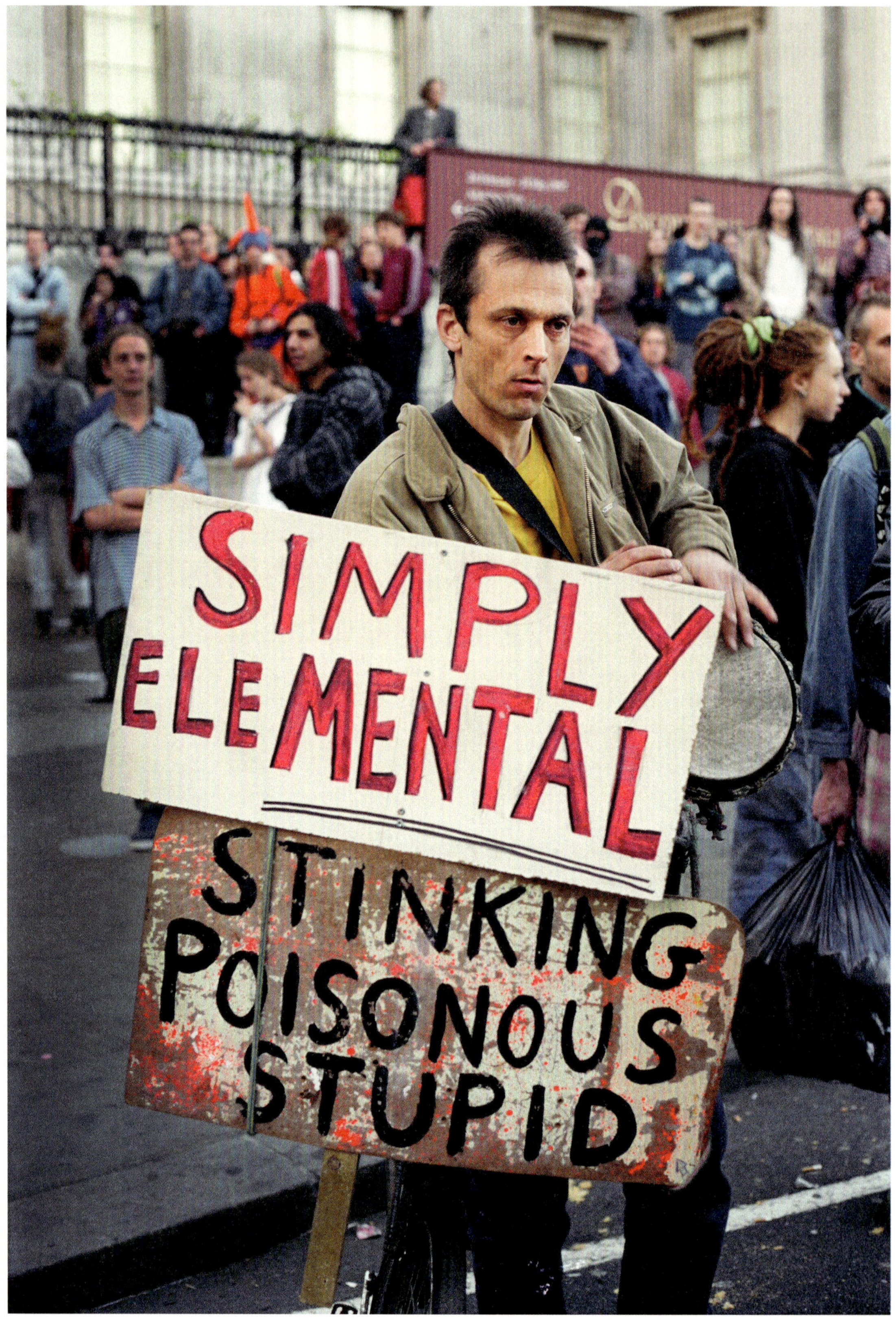

Reclaim the Streets: Trafalgar Square

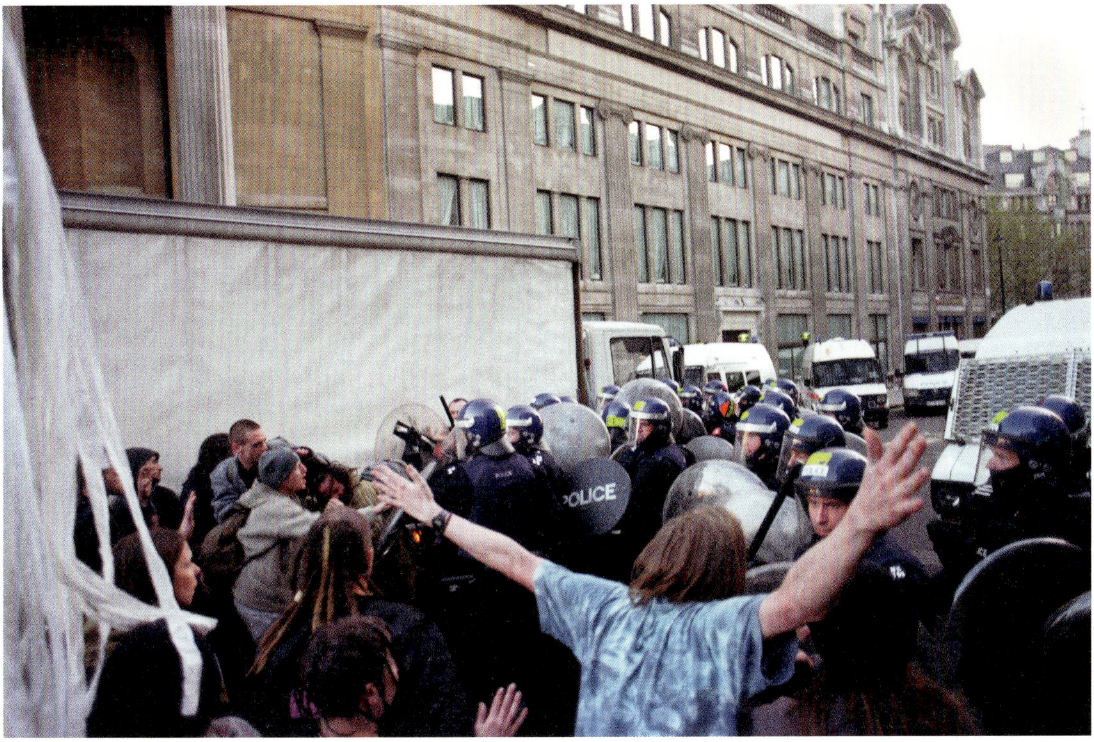

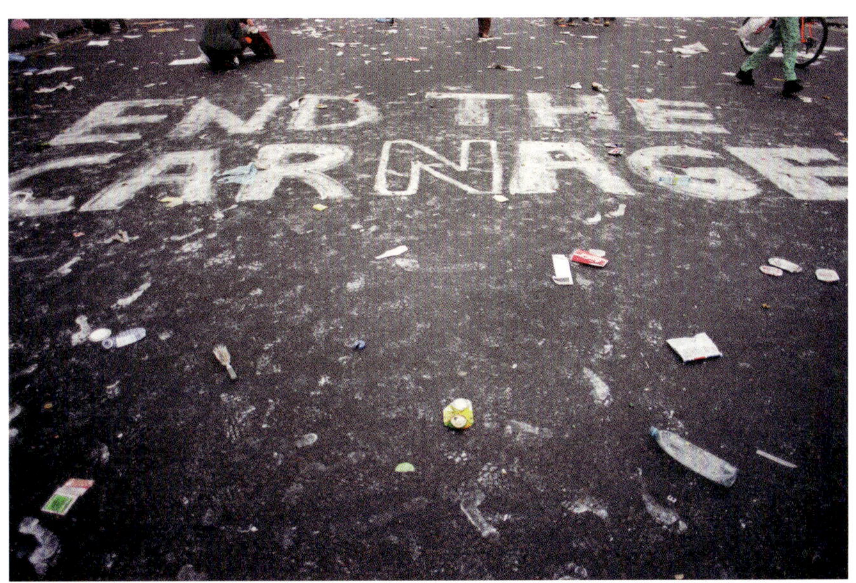
END THE
CARNAGE

Reclaim the Streets: Tottenham
June 1998

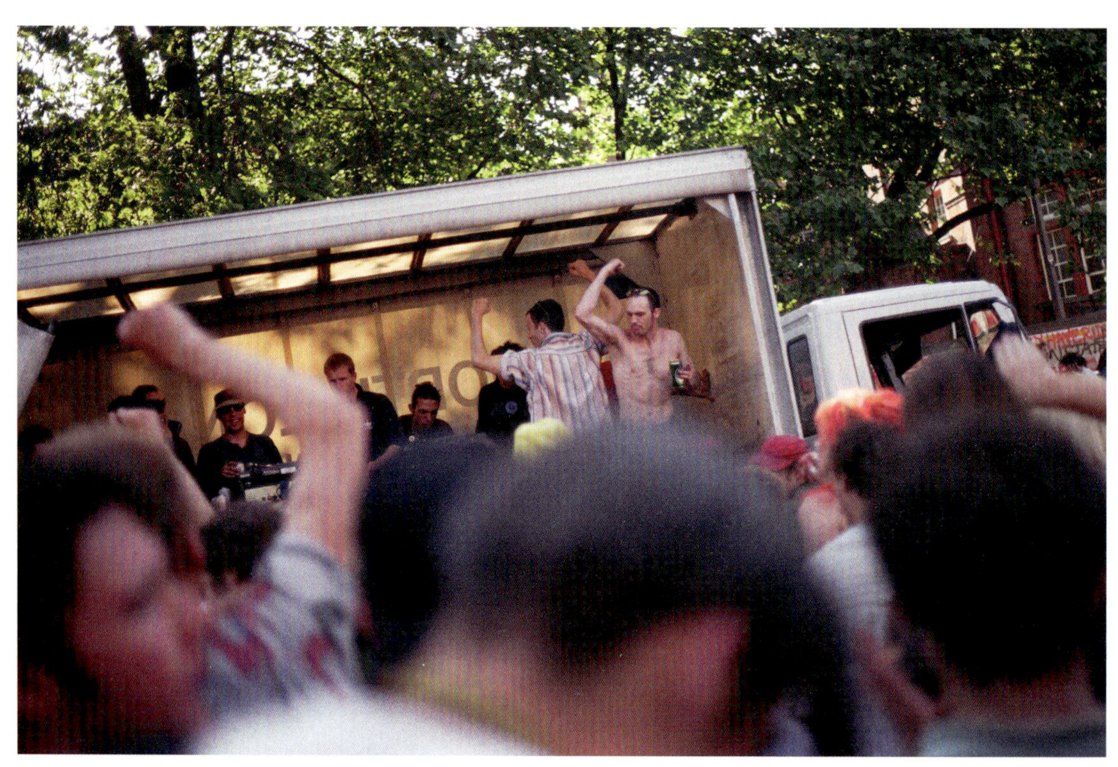

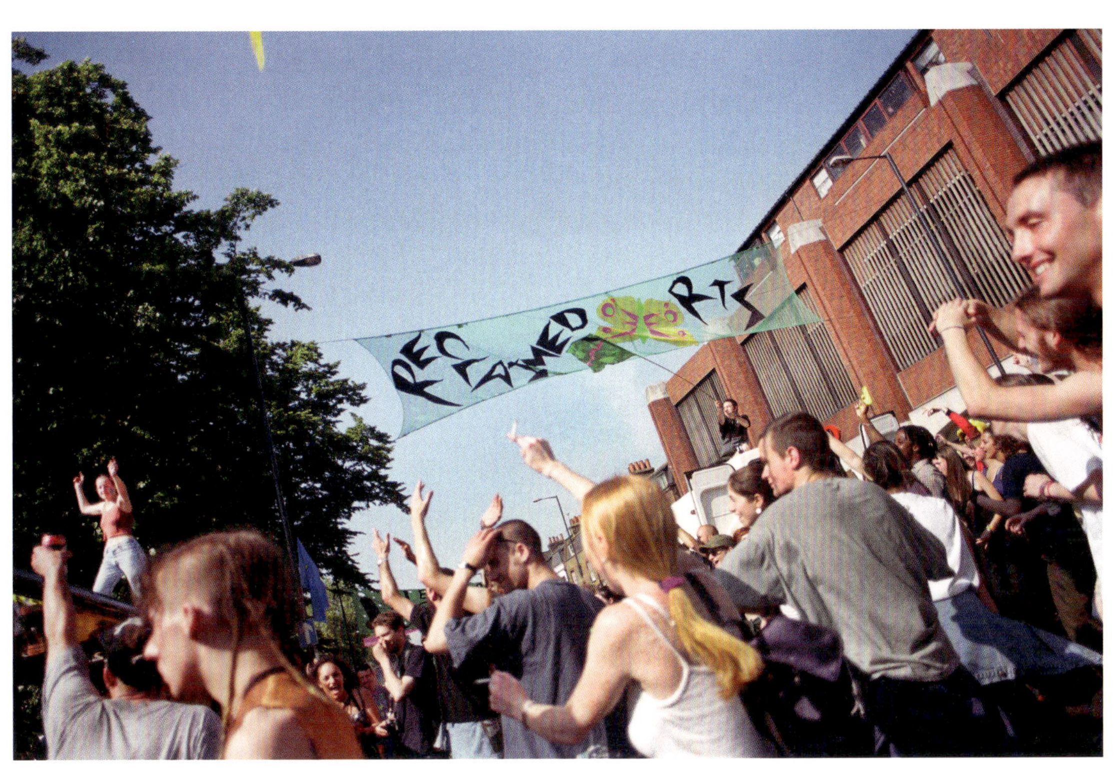

Emboldened by the success of previous protests an audacious day of two simultaneous actions was planned: one in Brixton and the other in Tottenham. At the latter people made their way up from Kings Cross and took over the road as a mass of concerned environmentalists. There's something liberating in being able to walk up a street that only moments before had been a treacherous environment of stinking cars pumping a steady stream of toxic CO_2 into London's atmosphere. What if the streets were dedicated to people rather than traffic? What if there was a radical overhaul of the cities' public transport system? What if people actually started to listen to us?

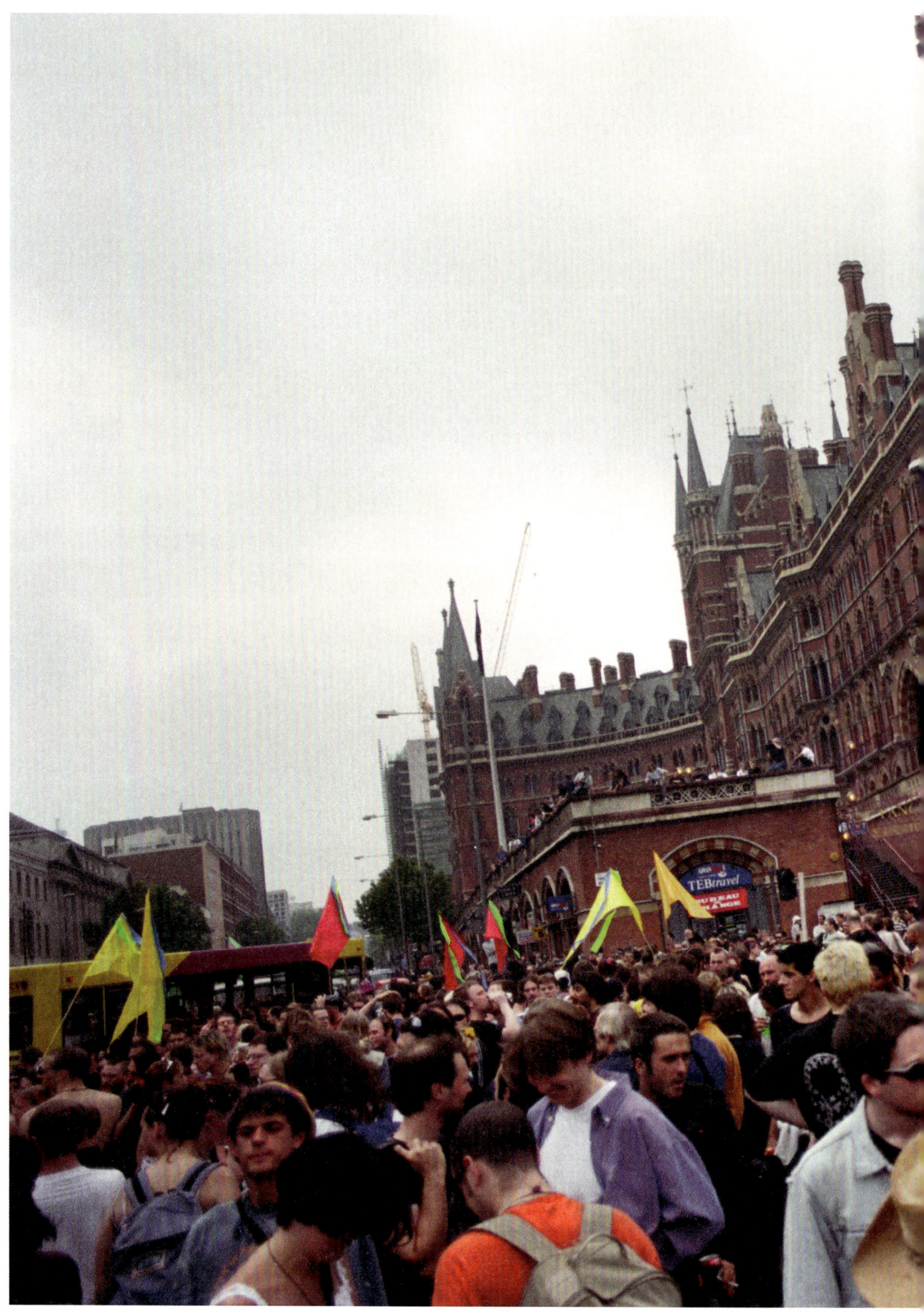

Reclaim the Streets: Tottenham

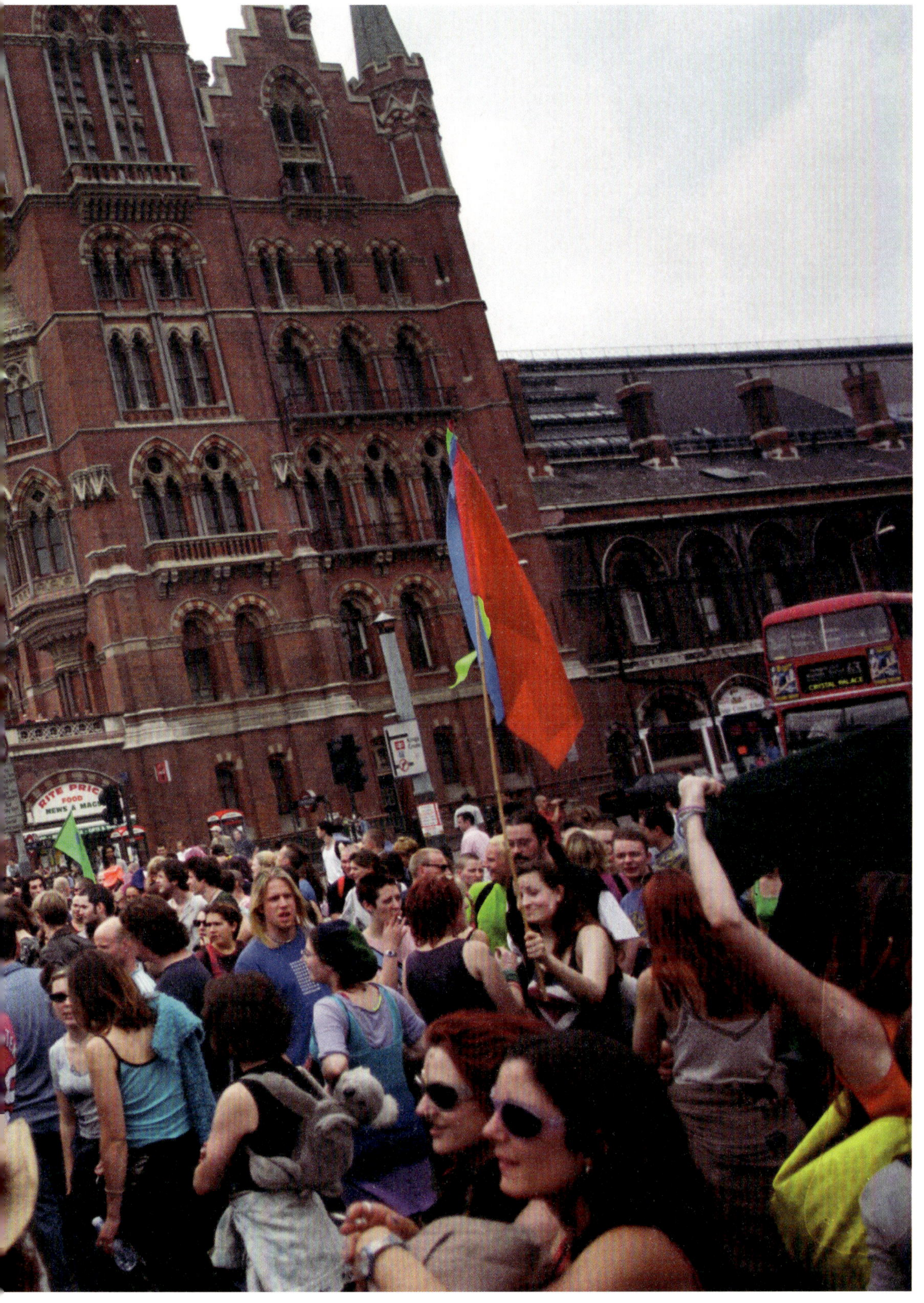
FOOD

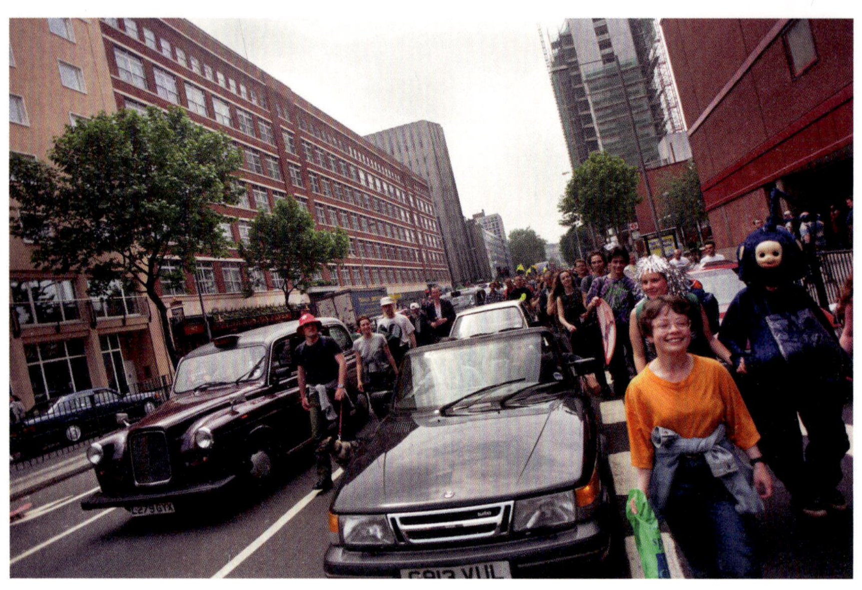

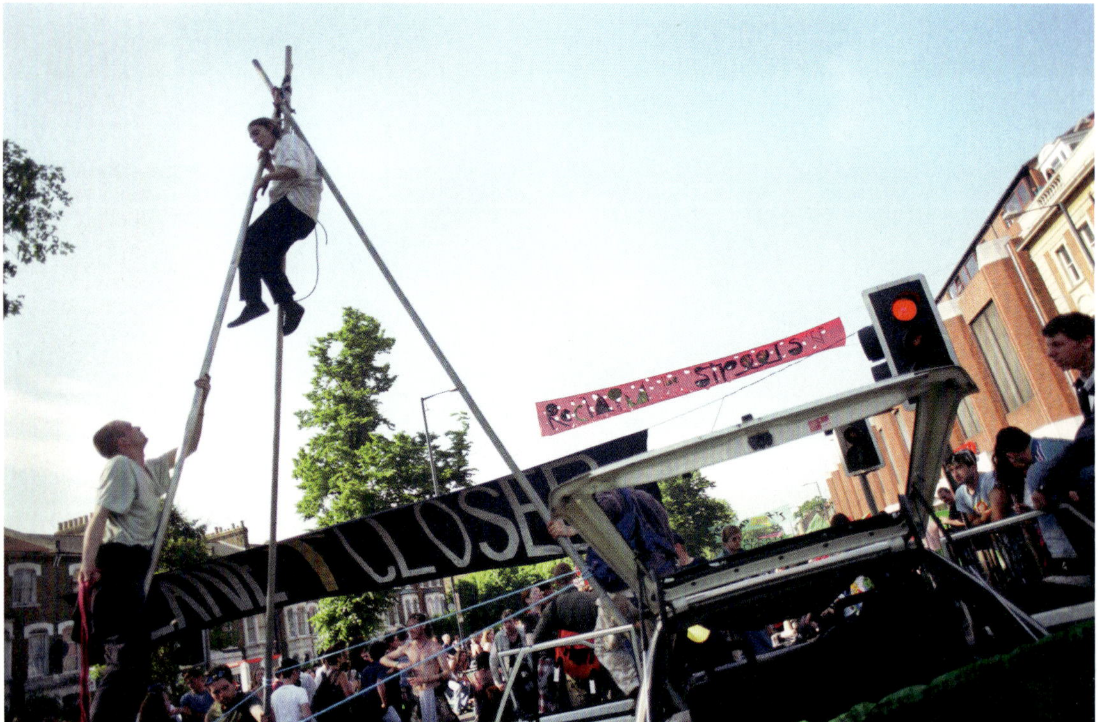

Reclaim the Streets: Tottenham

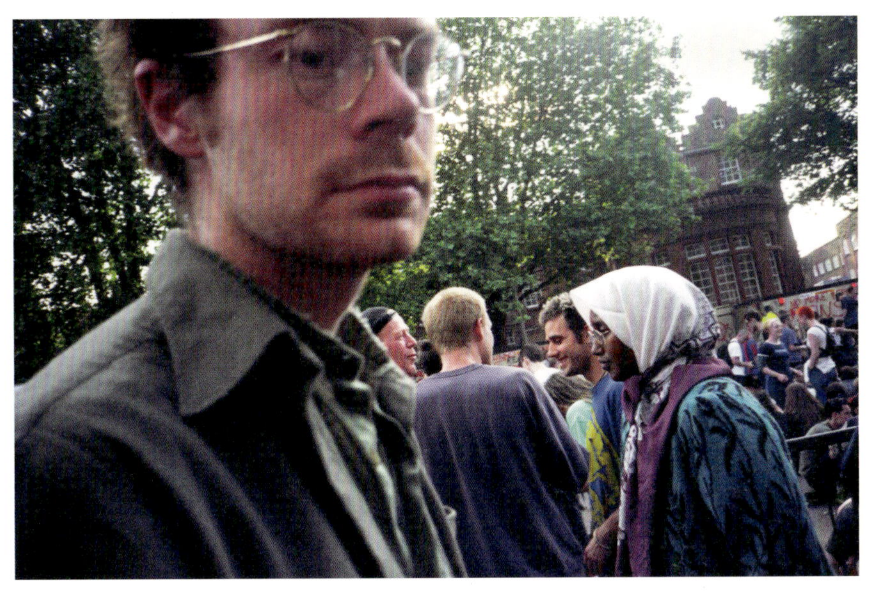

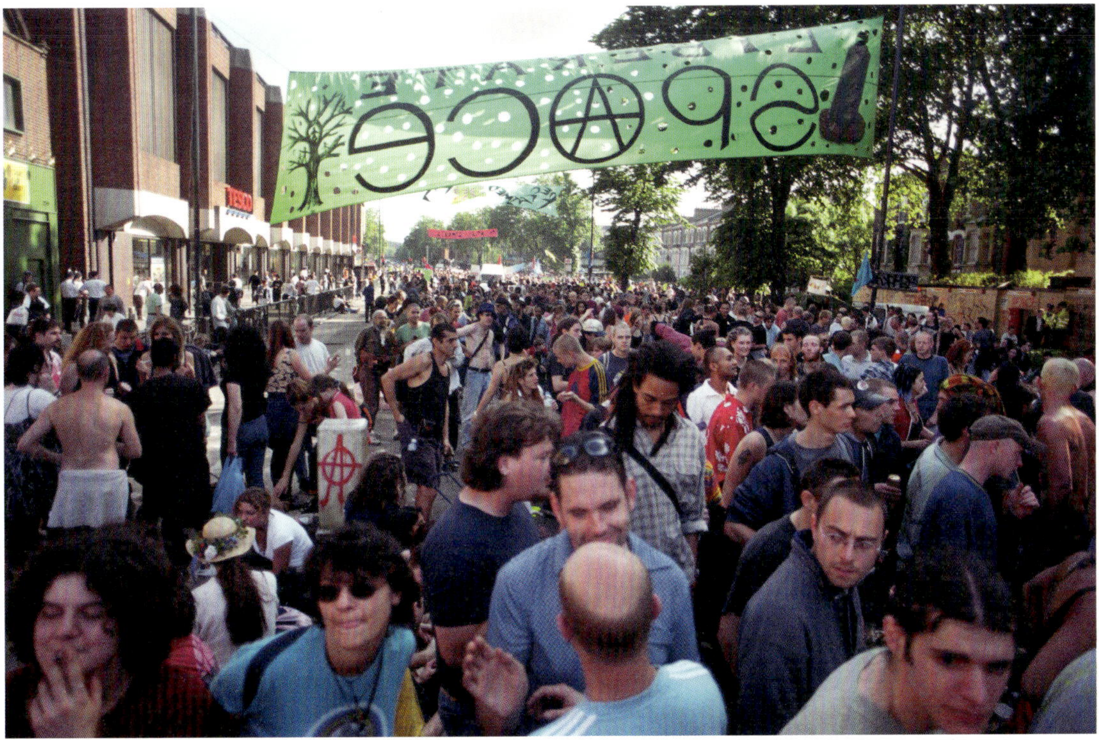

Reclaim the Streets: Carnival against Capital June 1999

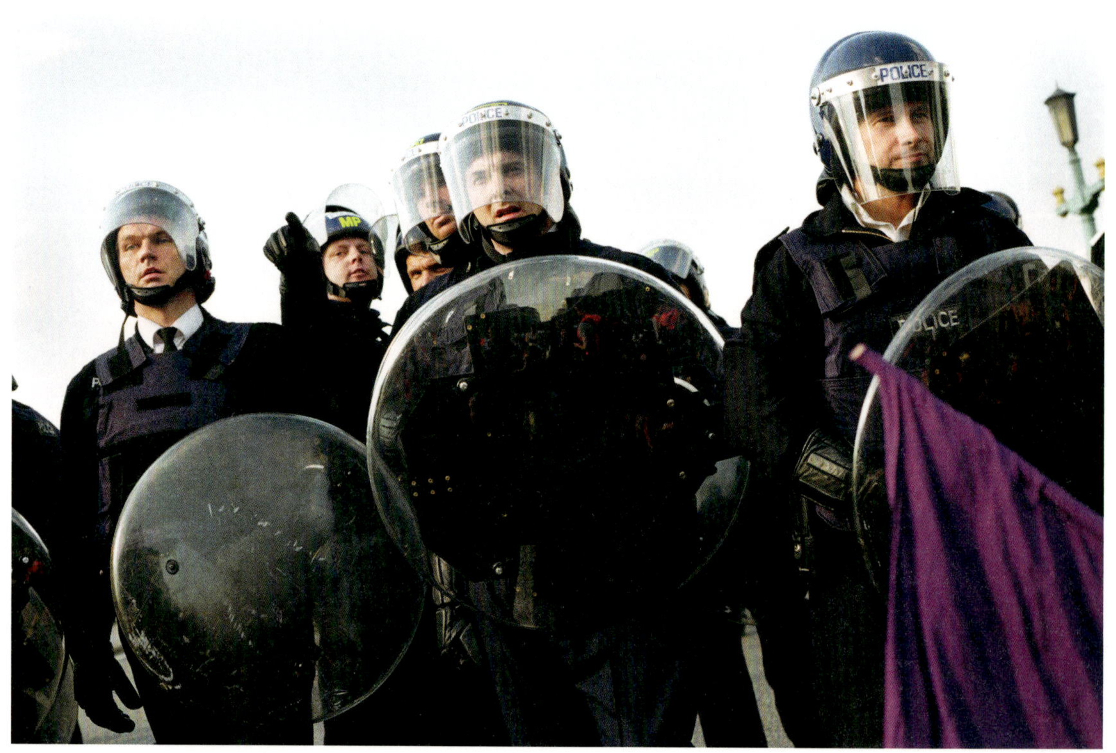

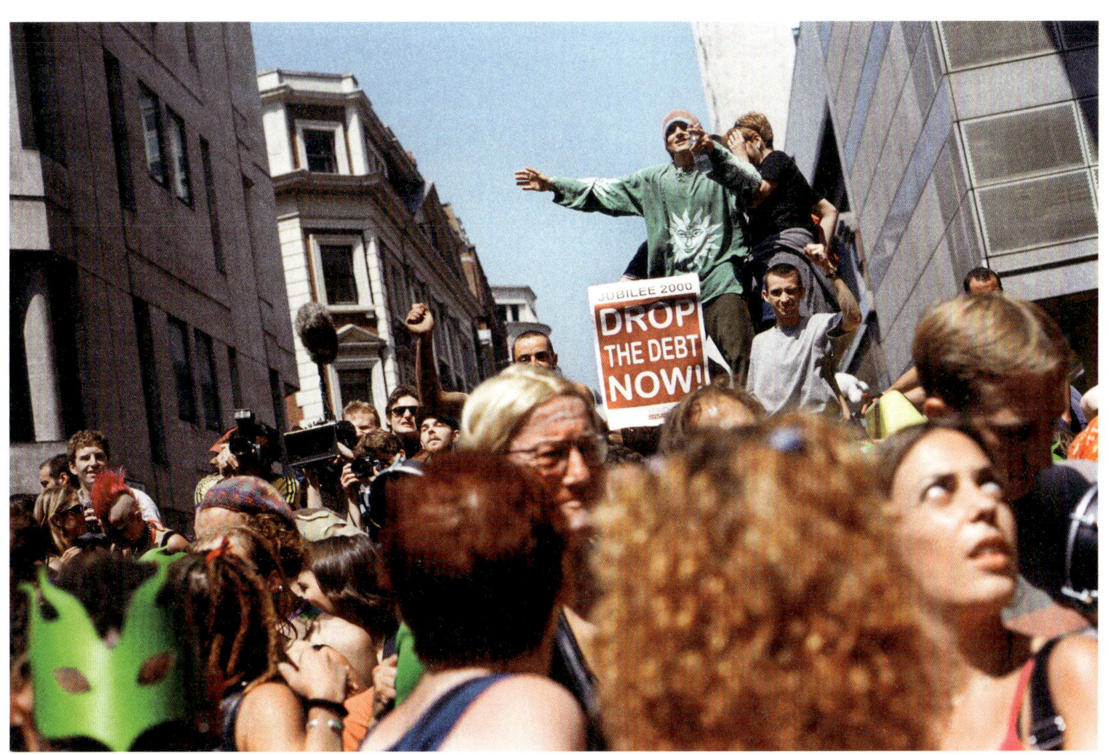
JUBILEE 2000
DROP
THE DEBT
NOW!

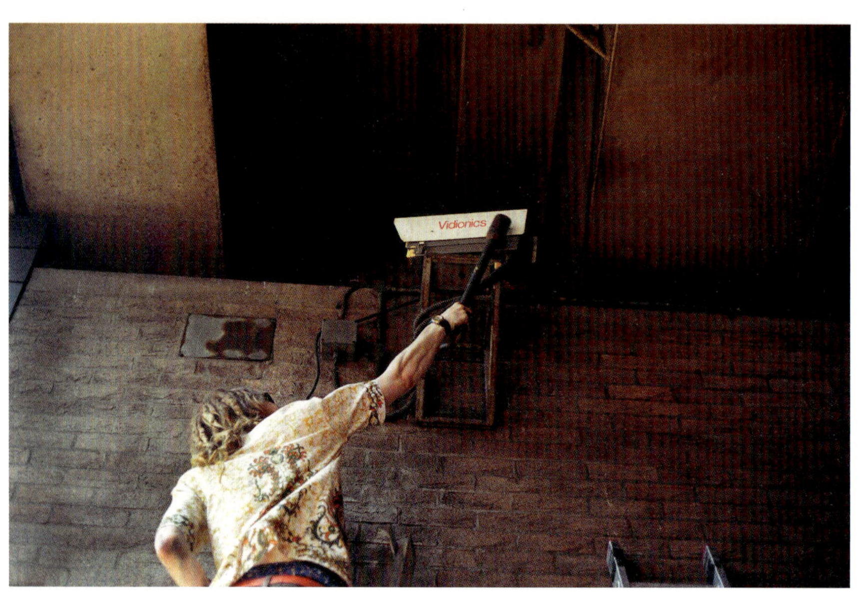

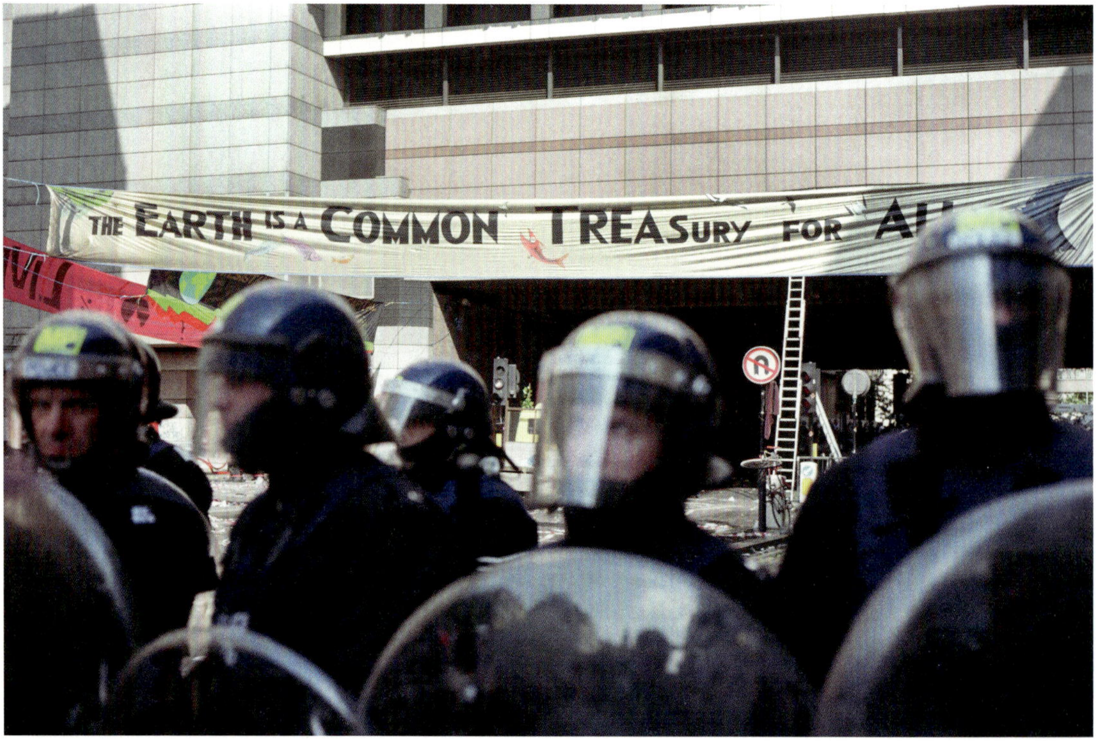

Reclaim the Streets: Carnival against Capital

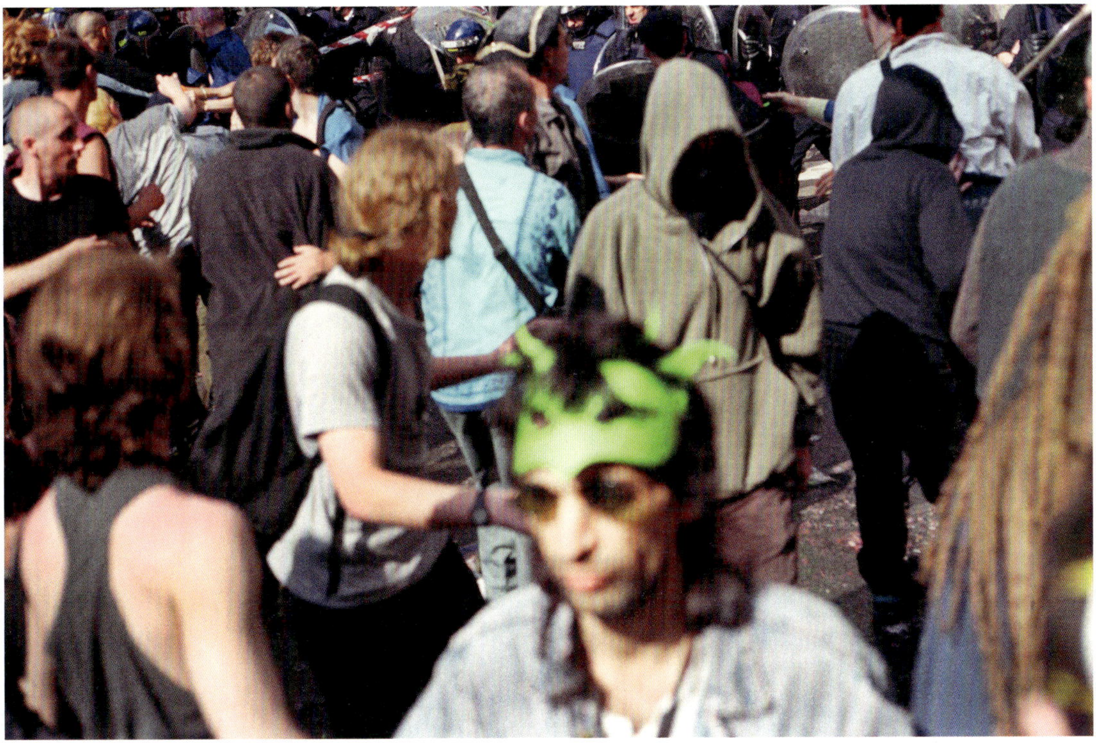

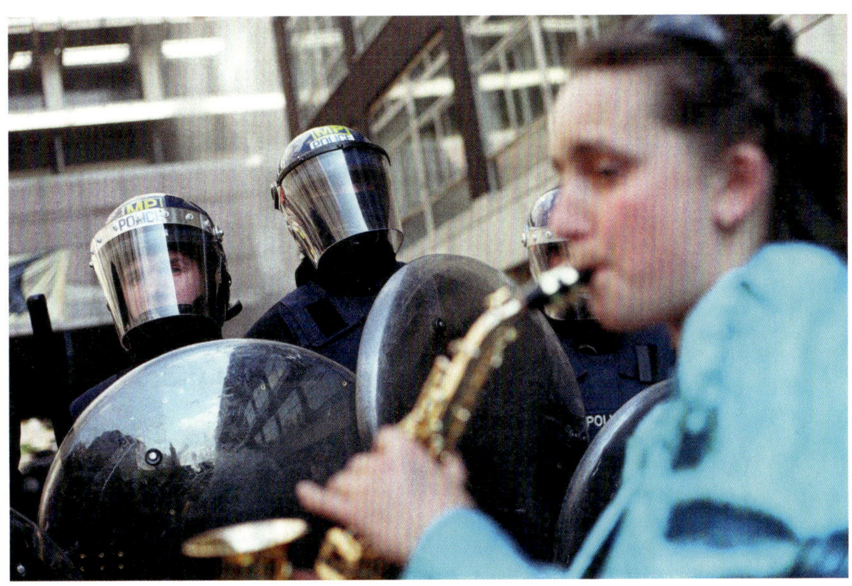
POLICE

The bankers and city workers appeared high on a large balcony to watch the theatre of the riot below. In celebration of the system that served them so well they photocopied £50 bank notes and threw them from their ivory tower to the environmental demonstrators below. They made no attempt to understand the fear and concerns of those who had marched through the city that day. They seemed unwilling or incapable of understanding the destruction the financial district of London was causing to climate and the natural world. In a quirky act of David and Goliath a lone protestor let his feelings be known through a simple flick of the V.

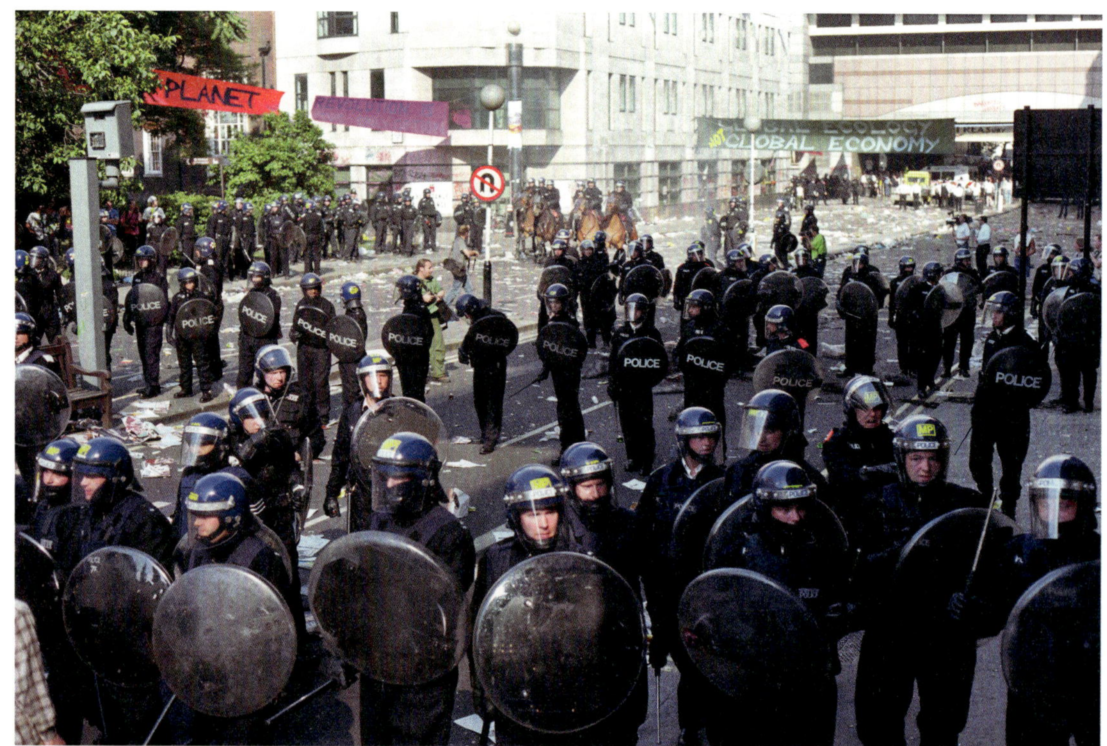

Reclaim the Streets: Carnival against Capital

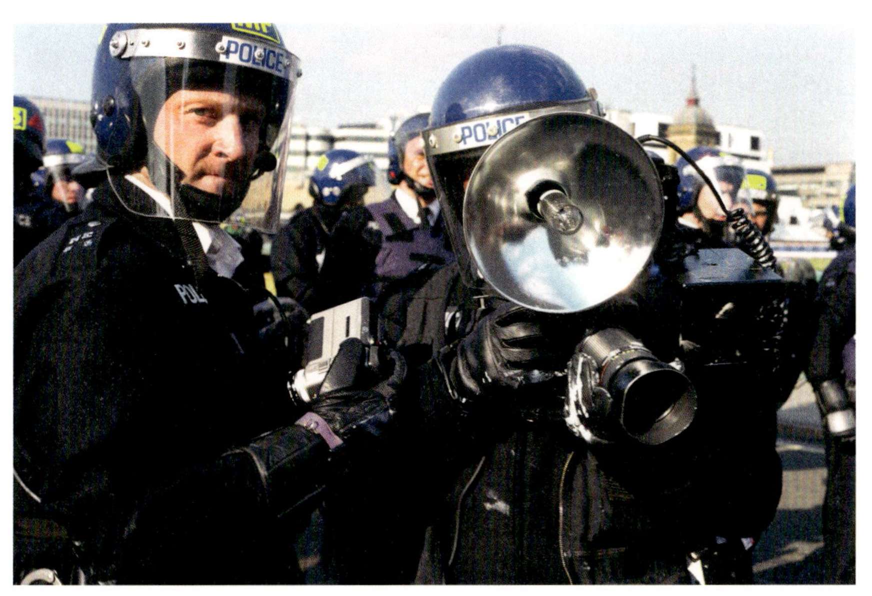
POLICE
POLICE

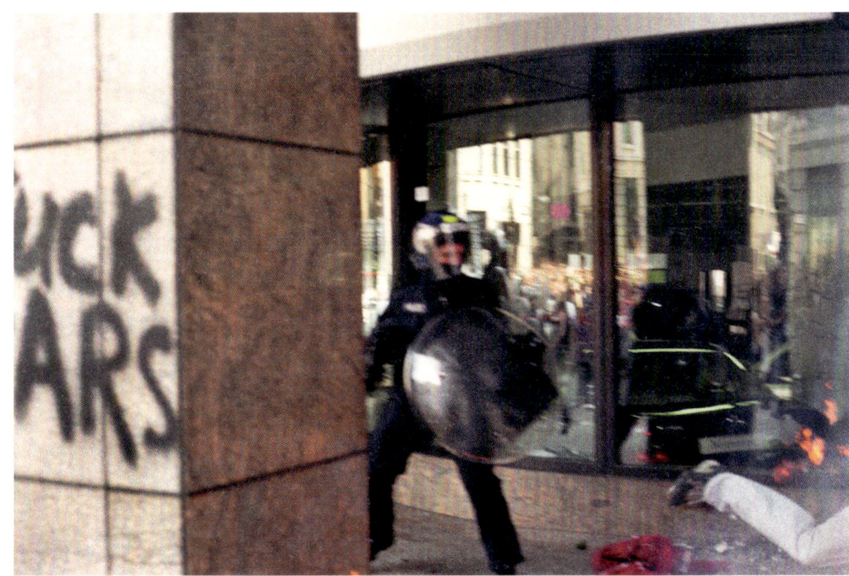
uck
ARS

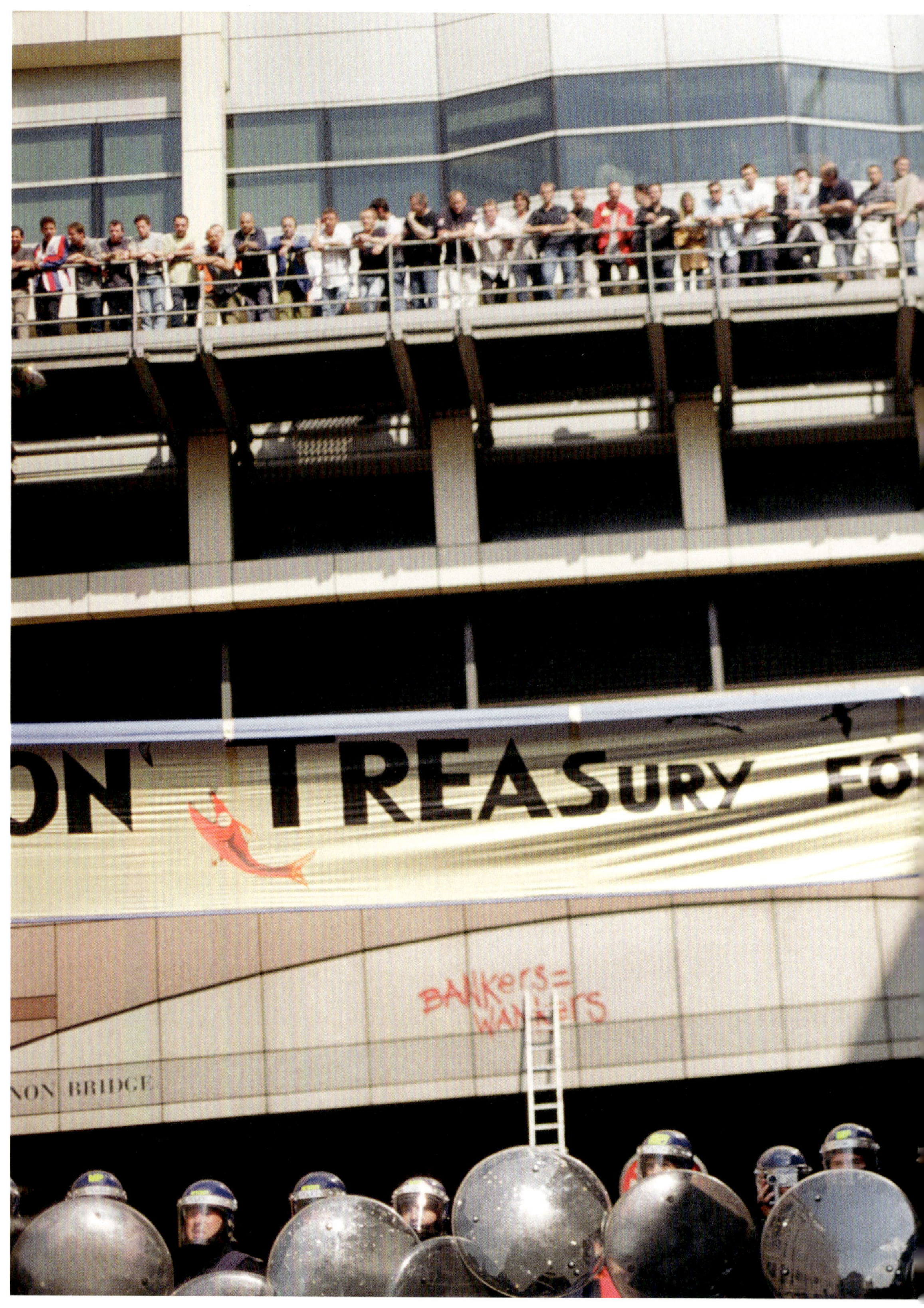

Reclaim the Streets: Carnival against Capital

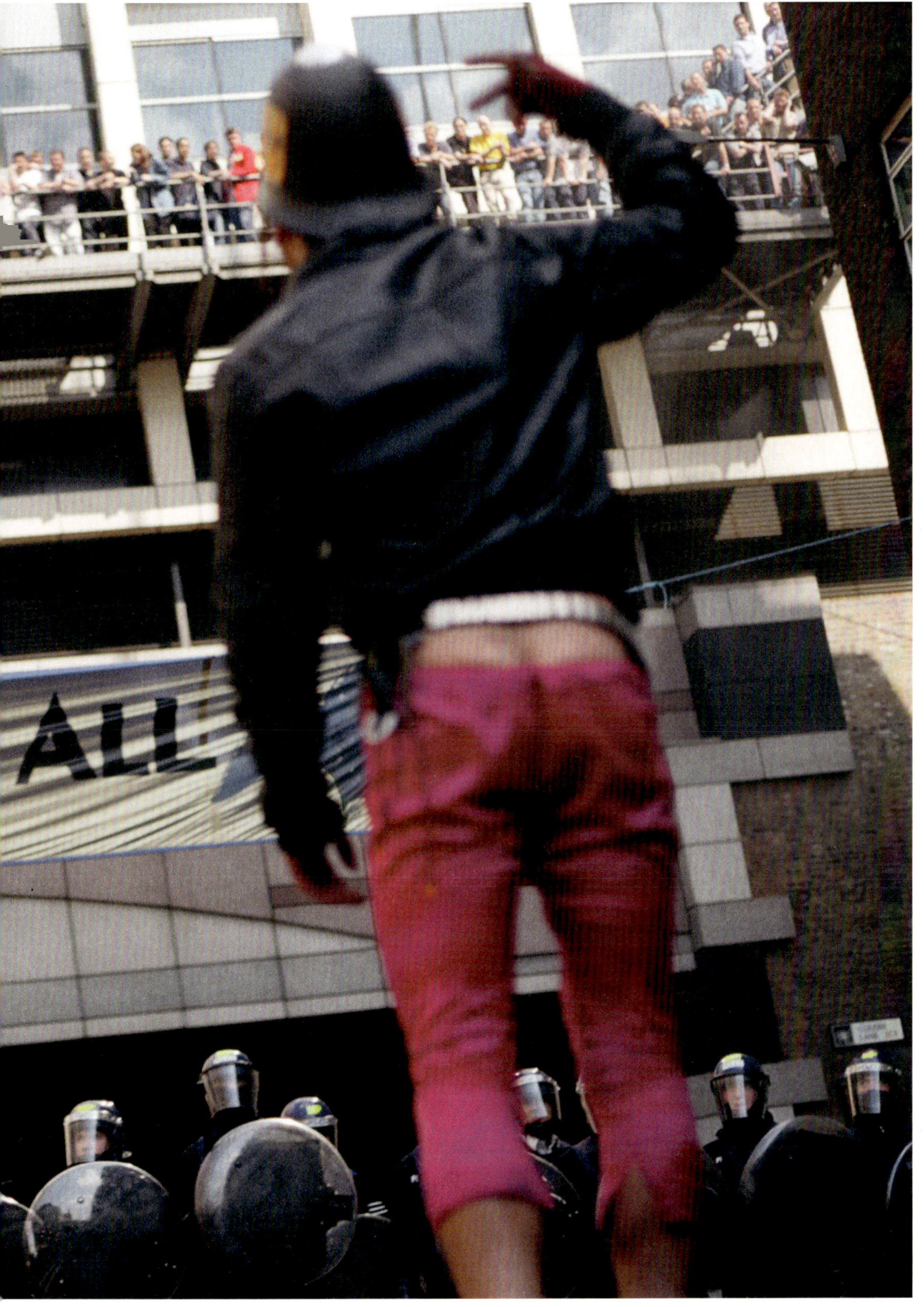
ALL

In London when it comes to demonstrations all hell breaks loose if you cross a certain line and that line sits around the City of London, or the Square Mile. The financial district has its own police force designed to protect the institutions, companies and elites that have used capitalism to eat away at the fabric of our society over centuries and now destroys the very planet that sustains us. The government response to Reclaim the Streets that day showed they would use any means necessary to ensure the old order remained in place. The government had no vision other than to protect The City and its profit margins and as far as the rest of the country was concerned, they could suffer the consequences of those decisions for centuries to come.

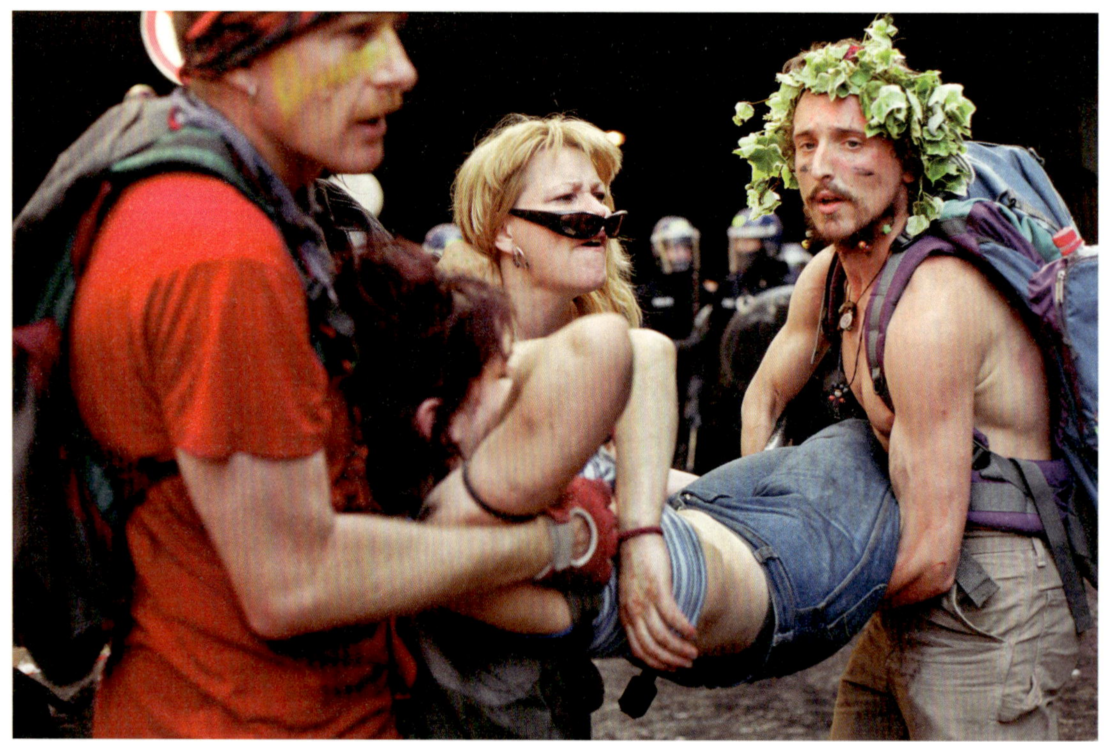

Reclaim the Streets: Carnival against Capital

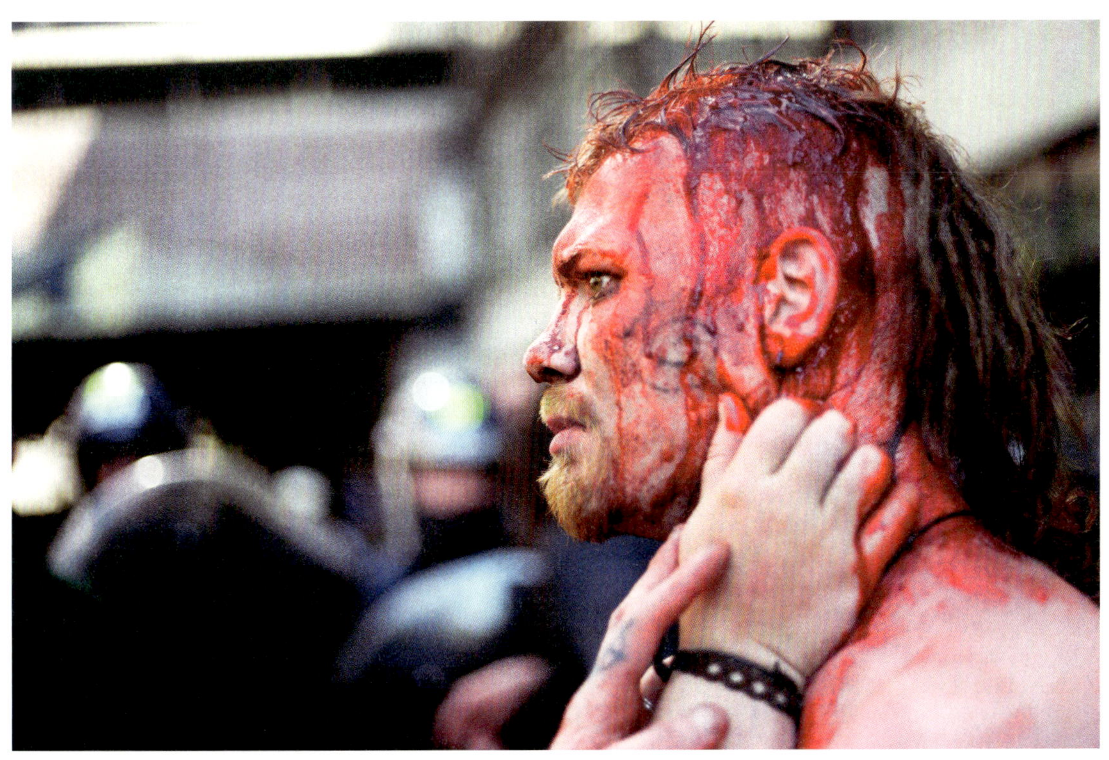

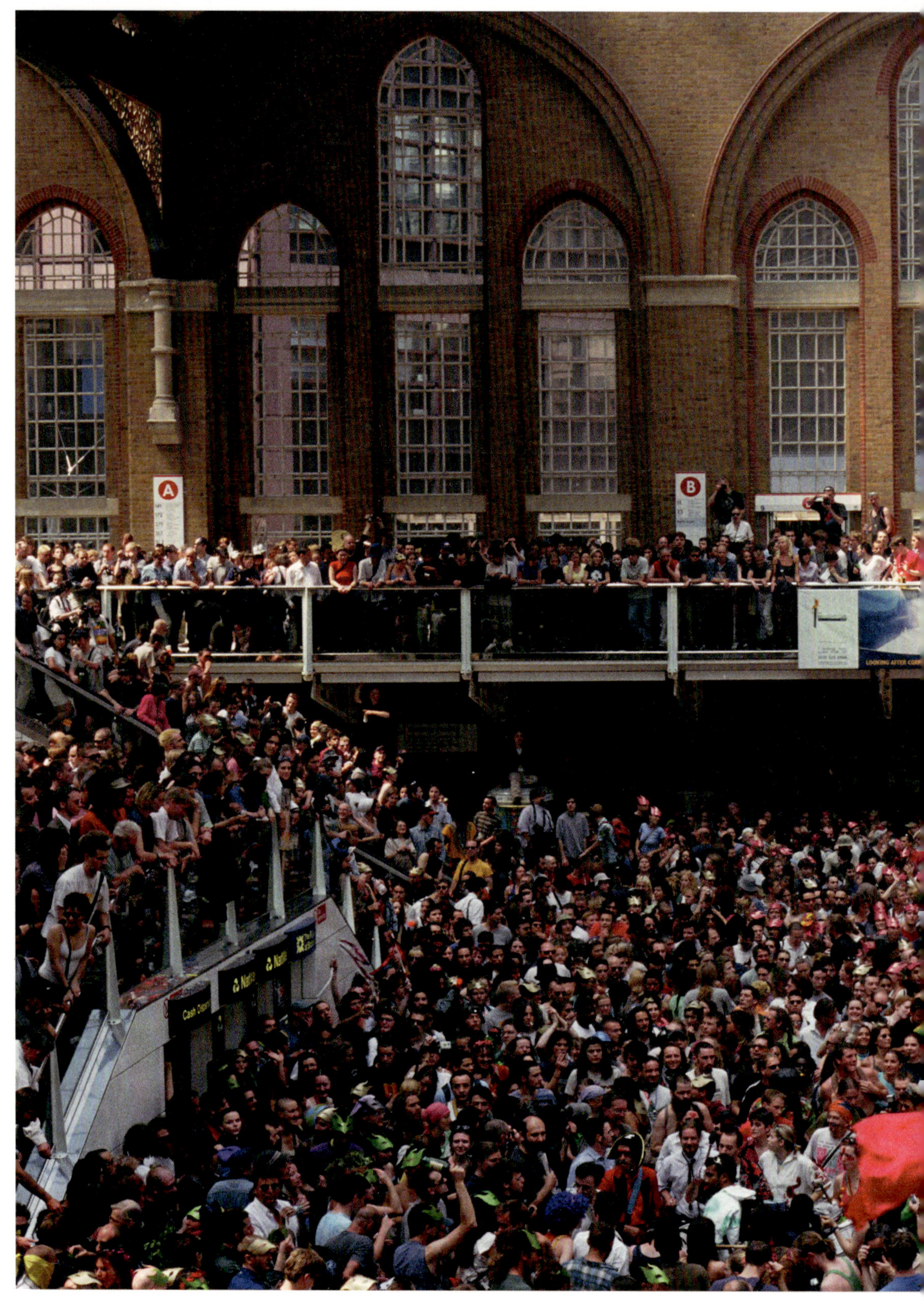

Reclaim the Streets: Carnival against Capital

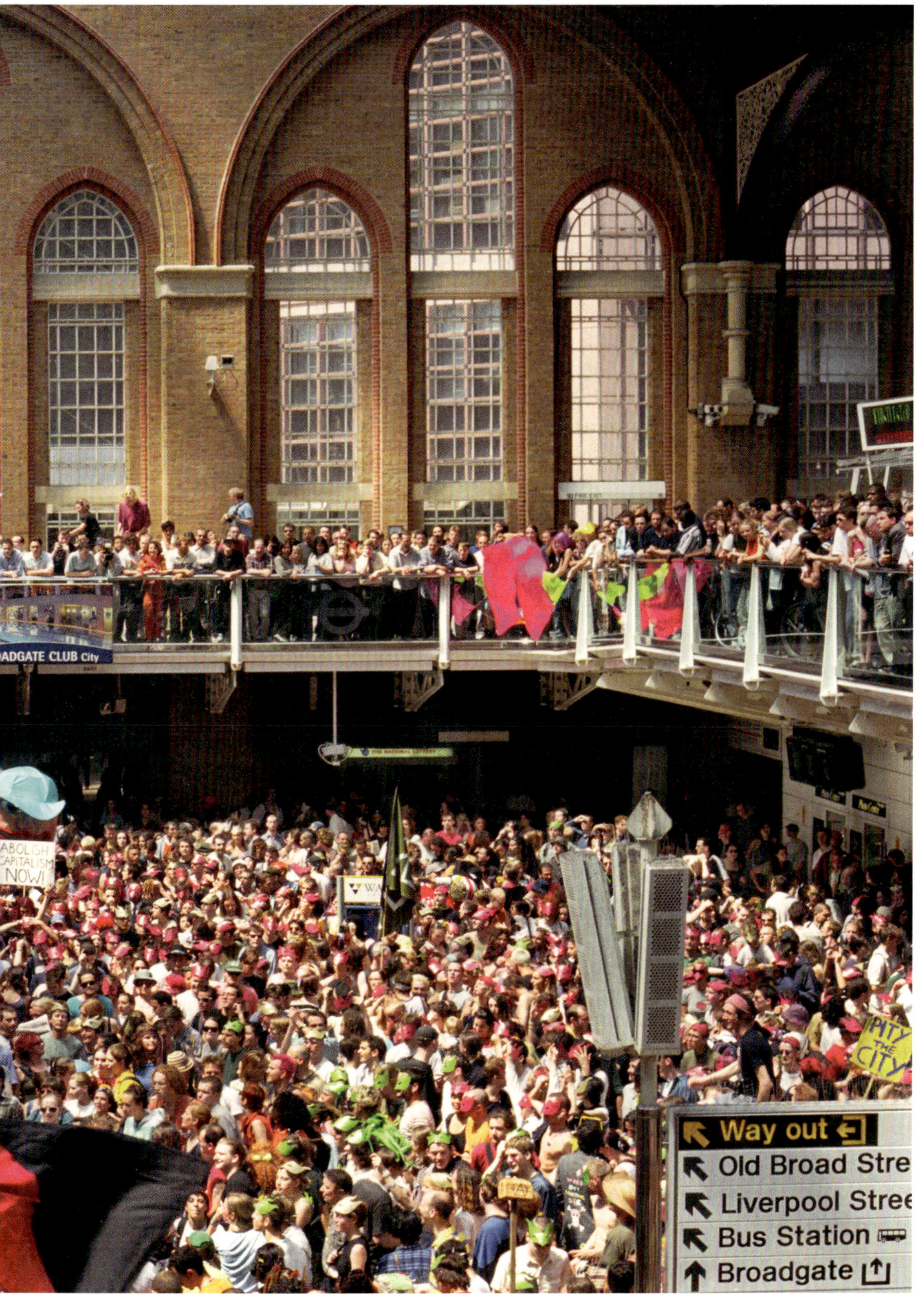
ADGATE CLUB City
ABOLISH CAPITALISM NOW!
PITY THE CITY
Way out
Old Broad Stre
Liverpool Stree
Bus Station
Broadgate

The generous supporters of this project, who believe we must do everything we can in order to preserve our precious planet:

Aaron Trinder
Accept & Proceed
Adam Mitchinson
Adele Green
Adrian Ashton
Alan Kelly
Alan Lee
Alastair Robinson
Alex Blackwell
Alexandra Winton
Alfie Allen
Algy
Alice Howes
Aline Figueiroa Costa
Allan Brown
Amanda Burrell
Amy Scaife
Andor Merks
Andrea Brock
Andrew Fawcett
Andrew Ferguson
Andy Godfrey
Andy Letcher
Angus Carlyle
Anika Nixdorf
Anita Dhillon
Annabel Allison
Annabel Kennedy
Annie Grove-White
Annie Thurgarland
Anthony Jarman
Anton C
Antony Price
Applied Works
Aris Papathéodorou
Aurora Solá
Barry Menmuir
Beki Moon
Ben Blossom
Ben Gross
Benedict Southworth
Bert
Beth Jordan
Beth Snyder
Bob Schwaller
Bobby Kool Van Kleef
Bobby Mardybum
Brett Kellett
Brette Howard
Bridge Murphy
Bridget McKenzie
Calum Pretsell
Carmen Hall
Caru Sanders
Catherine Kelly
Cez Barraclough
Charlie Bolderow
Cherry Wyld
Chloe Hulse
Chris Butcher
Chris Cooper
Christophe Moille
Claire Eichhorn
Claudia MacGregor
Coley Lehman
Conrad
Corine Wood-Donnelly
Craig Payne
Craig Spiby
Dan Fox
Dan Holdsworth
Daniel Holdsworth
Daryl
Dave Gibbons
Dave Simms
David Lloyd
David Luke
David Raymond
Demelza
Dennis Badger
Dhruv Boruah
Diego Ulrich
Donna Landry & Gerald MacLean
Dylan Cook
Ed Hurst
Eden Staples
Edwin James
Elanor Rose
Ella Saltmarshe
Elvis McPlonkington
Emily Scott
Emily Wood
Emma Diggle
Emma Iller
Felix Preston
Fiona Cunningham-Reid
Fiona Marie Miras
Fritz Catlin
Gary Bryan
Gemma Mahoney
George Phillips
Gitanjali Chaturvedi
Gleu Yew
Greg Muttitt
Hannah Watson
Harebell
Helen Abraham
Helen Beynon
Helen Steel
Hermann Jahrmann
Howard Johns
Hughes Melanie
Ian Bailey
Indra Donfrancesco
Isabella Kavanagh
Isola Press
Ivan Smaggheq
Jack Taylor
Jackie Gatenby
Jai Redman
James Kurén Weldon
James Samson
James Swindells
Jamie Brett
Jan Vozenilek
Jane D'Aulby
Jane Dunford
Jason Royce
Jeff Middleton
Jess Rickenback
Jez Tucker
Jo Baines
Jo Renshaw
Jo White
John Taylor
Johnny Dufort
Jon, Tom & Mini Johnston
Jonathan Swinstead
Josephine Holt
Josh Allen
Josh Zatz
Joshua Dugdale
Joth Shakerley
Julia Saxby
Julia Woollams
Julie Hotchkiss
June Holmes
Justin Shanley
Kai Shai Suraya
Kane Maskell
Kate Christie
Kate Hewett
Katy Niker
Kennet Simon
Kevin Doye
Kevin Hooper
Kråster Jack
Laura Smith
Lee Evans
Leo Simon Smith
Likklewicked Lora
Lisa
Lizzie Hall
Lou Hudson
Lucie Puttipap
Lucy Cade-Stewart
Lucy Chalmers
Lucy Medhurst
Lynne Fearnley
Lynne McCabe
Maggie Westhead
Mags Gainsborough
Mani Singh
Marc Pou
Marina Pepper
Mark Bobbitt
Mark Ford
Mark Gladstone Robertson
Mark Harris
Mark Howard
Mark Kerrison
Mark Ruddell
Markogov
Martin Porter
Mary Cade
Mary Ferguson
Mat Stephens
Matt Barnes
Matt Mellen
Matt Stuart
Matthew Boyd
Matthew Collin
Matthew Ryan
Max Saber
Maya
McWilliams Colette
Mhairi Logan
Micheal Haran
Mike Davey
Moshe Halperin
Mouse Green
Nathalia Westmacott-Brown
Nathan Griffiths
Neil Medlicott
Neil Perch
Nick Daniel
Nick Woolley
Nicky Scott
Nicola Chester
Nikki Little
Noel Cass
Olivia
Olivia Stephenson
Owen Espley
Pamela Woods
Pat Armstrong
Patricia Auchterlonie
Paul Minett
Pete Bateman
Pete Burch
Pete M E Fisk
Peter Merry
Phil Pritchard
Phil Shankland
Polly Kathleen Burton
Polly Pereira
Quentin Johns
Rachel Jones
Richard Holland
Richard Smith
Rina Golan
Rob Blakemore
Rob Simmons
Rob Smith
Robin Friend
Rory Stevens
Rosalind Watts
Rosamonde Birch
Rose Gridneff
Rufus Thurston
Ruth Alderman
Ruth Bennett
Sam Worrall
Sara Barnard
Saras Chowgule
Saya Robinson
Scott Grant
Shane Collins
Shengnan Knudson
Sheryl Garratt
Simon Bannister
Simon Denyer
Simon Parfett
SL
Sophie Hill
Sophie Rochester
Steffen Rault
Stephanie Reeves
Steve
Steve & Bek Compton
Steve Fenn
Susan Millar
Suzi Crockford
Tabitha Chambers
Tanja Schomann
Tansy Baigent
Tanya & Tom
Tara Beynon
Tara Donovan
Tenzing
Terri Hassan
Terri Windling
Tessa Stewart
The Friends of Nancy Fouts
The Roblarkys
Theo Miller
Thomas Chadwick
Tilia
Tim A
Tim Bennett
Tim Myatt
Tim Webster
Toby Blume
Tom Bramble
Tom Dennison
Tom Morley
Tom Sewell
Tree Kelly
University Arts London
Uri Fruchtmann
Vanessa Sloan
Verity Owers
Vicente Contreras
Vishal Reddy
Wendy Shrubsall
Wesley
William Todd-Jones
Zoe Lyne

A very special thank you to:

Janet Bomback
Kate Auchterlonie
John & Remi
Suril Desai
Pritam
Ronnie Rich

1

SCAFF TRIPODS

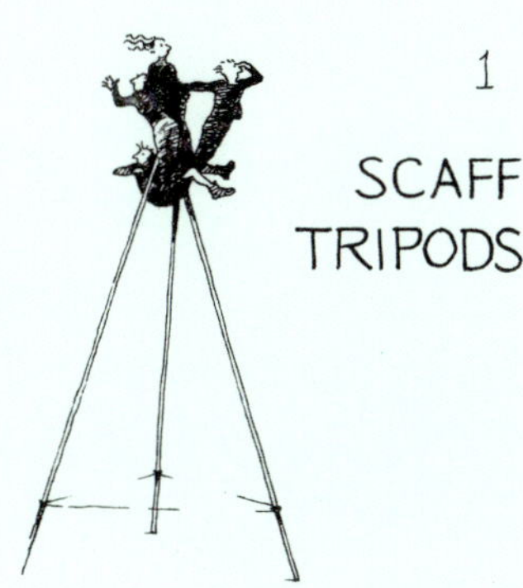

For your basic tripod, acquire:
3 scaff-poles, about 25 feet long;
2 swivelling scaff-clips;
and some rope — cheap, blue polyprop is fine. And a spanner for the nuts on the clips.
You also need a fairly large (high if indoors) space for fixing them, experimenting + practising.

It is tricky to get the clips fitted on so that the poles can lie parallel as well as erect into tripods.

See the assembly as 2 main poles in an 'A' shape, plus a 3rd pole to prop them up.

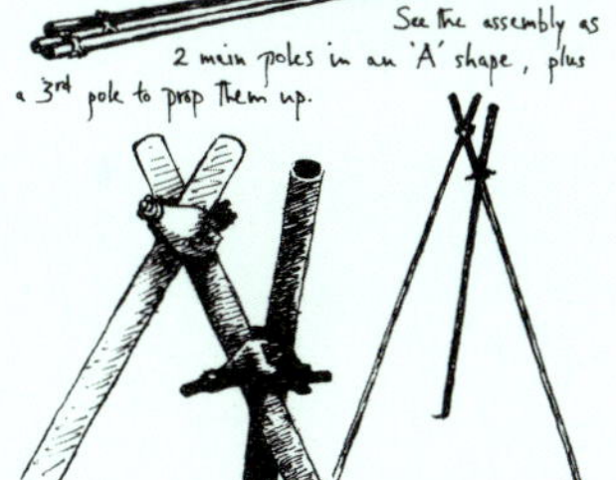

2

The clip for the 3rd pole has to be about a foot below the main poles' clip, to allow the main poles to close over it, and the central swivel of the clip should be at roughly 120° round the pole from that of the main clip. Experiment until you get the clips placed so that the poles can lie parallel + open into a tripod.

With iron poles you will probably need at least 5 people to erect it:

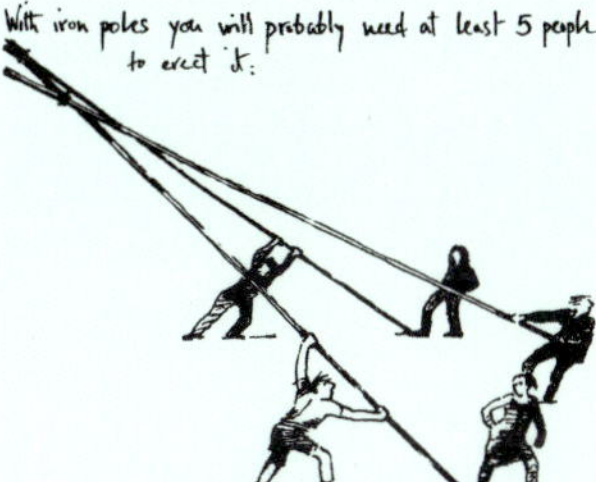

At least one strong person to lift each of the 2 main legs by walking down beneath it from apex to base; one person to do the same with the 3rd leg and, at a crucial moment, to swing this leg out to prop up the 'A'; and one person with their foot braced against the base of each main pole to stop it skidding forward. With lighter aluminium poles you might manage with 3 people.

ONCE IT'S ERECTED, at least one person must shin up a pole at the speed of light, to be out of reach at the top.

A simple circumference rope tying the 3 poles together about 3 feet from the top can be fixed in advance and then stood on by up to 3 people.

A hammock sling is more comfortable and rather stylish. Make it out of a length of strong, light material, such as rip-stop nylon, knotted at either

3

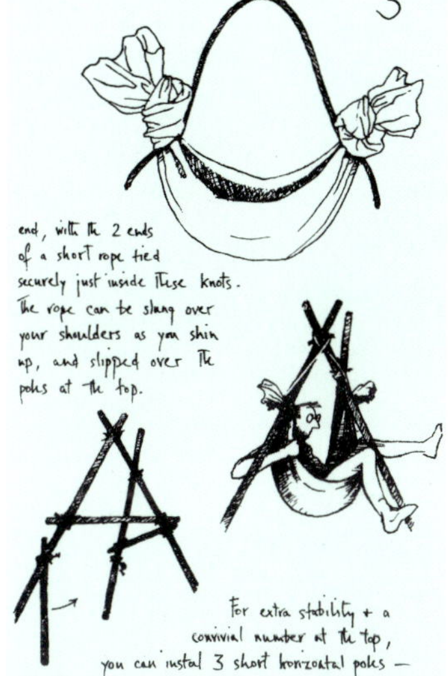

end, with the 2 ends of a short rope tied securely just inside these knots. The rope can be slung over your shoulders as you shin up, and slipped over the poles at the top.

For extra stability + a convivial number at the top, you can instal 3 short horizontal poles — with clips. Leave each short pole dangling from one clip until the tripod is up, then do up the 2nd clip. Don't forget the spanner. A climbing harness and slings make this job easier. The augmented tripod will be heavier. You may need more people to lift it.

A tripod lacking these extra bars can be stabilised against accidental slippage, though not against attack, with a circumference rope linking the legs a couple of feet above the ground. Exhaust-clips are useful to stop this rope riding up.

PRACTISE putting it up. Shambles develops into lightening expertise.

— B. Dahl.

First Edition
Published in Great Britain in 2022

A catalogue record for this book is available from the British Library

ISBN 978-1-7397502-0-6

Designed by Zoë Bather & Linda Byrne
Typeset in Nurture Display & Real Text Pro
Printed in the UK by Impress Print
Printed on GardaPat 13 by Fenner Paper
with Wibalin Natural cover by Winter & Company

The paper in this book is FSC© certified and produced in accordance with ISO 14001 systems using selected ECF pulps. All printing is vegan approved. The cover and spine are made using biodegradable and compostable materials. The interior is printed on a fully recyclable matt paper that is FSC© accredited and carbon balanced through the World Land Trust.

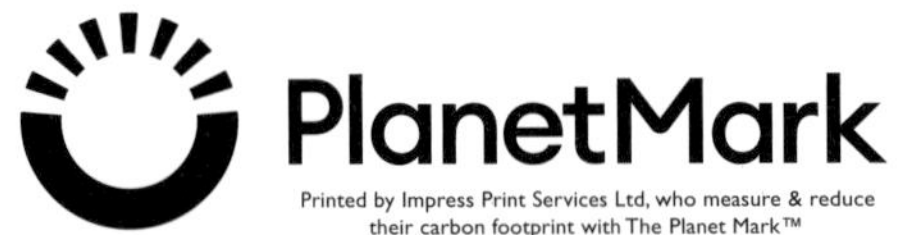

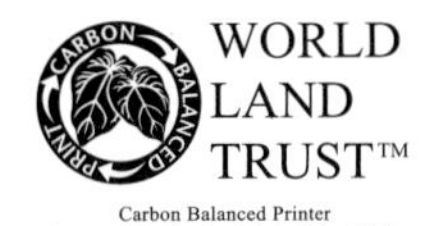

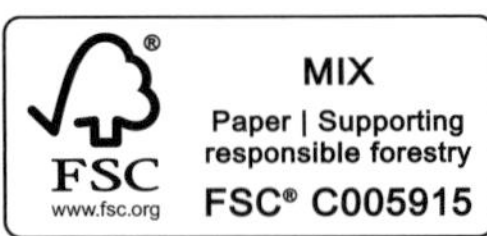